What Am I Still Doing Here?

Previous Orchidaceae

Rewards and Fairies – an edition of Kipling

Stage People – a pre-remaindered harlequinade

The Memoirs and Confessions of a Justified Sinner –
an introduction to James Hogg

The Life and Death of Peter Sellers – a masterful elegy

Charles Hawtrey: The Man Who Was Private Widdle – a dirge

Anthony Burgess – a non-bestselling portrait

Seasonal Suicide Notes – a popular chronicle

Forthcoming

My Hairy Aunt and Other Misprints – a toilet book

A Childhood Under the Nazis – growing up in Wales

The Wonderful World of the Dignitas Clinic – an illustrated
testimony

Give Up Literary Criticism! –
the Oxford University Chair of Poetry Lectures 2040

Roger Lewis

What Am I Still Doing Here?

*

My Years as Me

CORONET

First published in Great Britain in 2011 by Coronet
An imprint of Hodder & Stoughton
An Hachette UK company

1

A CIP catalogue record for this title is available from the British Library

Hardback ISBN 978 1 444 70868 4
Ebook ISBN 9781444708707

Typeset by Hewer Text UK Ltd, Edinburgh
Printed and bound by Clays Ltd, St Ives plc

Hodder & Stoughton policy is to use papers that are natural, renewable and recyclable
products and made from wood grown in sustainable forests. The logging and manufacturing
processes are expected to conform to the environmental regulations of the country of origin.

For
Quentin
and
I. M.
Dame Beryl Bainbridge
'a lass unparalleled'

'They do not heed, do not see, do not listen to me. What have I done to them? Why do they torment me? What do they want from poor me? What can I give them? I have nothing. It is beyond my strength, I cannot endure all their torments, my head is burning, and everything is whirling before me.'

Nikolai Gogol, *The Diary of a Madman*

'To remark the folly of the fiction, the absurdity of the conduct, the confusion of the names and manners of different times, and the impossibility of the events in any system of life, were to waste criticism upon unresisting imbecility, upon faults too evident for detection, and too gross for aggravation.'

Doctor Samuel Johnson, on Shakespeare's *Cymbeline*

Prefatory Matter and Acknowledgements

by Professor Johann Lampenschirm, M.D., D.Psych.

What is he still doing here? Well, he's only got himself to blame. Believing himself born to the purple, destined for the House of Lords and the Nobel Prize – in fact, delusional South Wales butcher's son Roger Lewis, despite his considerable academic achievements and scholarly exertions, would have been better off, happier even (and so would his handful of readers), if he'd chosen as his career path something less provoking than writing, like selling dead people's spectacle frames in a hospice charity shop.

There is always something intensely pathetic about a person whose ambition and abilities exceed their reach (or is it that their reach exceeds their ambition and abilities: I must apologise – English is not my first language); always something off-putting about non-public-school people who think that the world is theirs for the taking. Because why should it be? By what right?

Roger Lewis is an object lesson in thwarted aspirations, missed targets – perhaps even an object lesson in how the lower orders should not be exposed to too much higher education, as it creates only dissatisfaction and self-pity. Indeed, the results of Roger Lewis's dissatisfaction and what amounts to persecution mania are all too evident in this book – as they also were in its ridiculous and immature precursor, *Seasonal Suicide Notes*, which thankfully made him no money – as money would only have made him more intolerable, if such a thing is possible. Roger Lewis has nevertheless told me that he is a 'cult', which when I looked it up in the English/German dictionary appeared to mean 'vagina' [vulg.] – so you can see why he is now in my professional care, undergoing treatment.

One of the most laughable moments in this book is when Roger Lewis complains about his continual rejection by the Royal Society of Literature. As if this Monmouthshire upstart could ever stand comparison with such luminaries and Men of Letters as Piers Paul Reid, Philip Hensher or Anthony Thwaite. As when Roger Lewis attempted to strike up a conversation with Sir Howard Jacobson in the Groucho Club* in 2002, the Fellowship Committee, like the Booker Prize-winning novelist, was quite right to turn away in disgust. Really, Roger Lewis should not be allowed to leave the Herefordshire Balkans. He should be electronically tagged. Also, his Groucho Club subscription is always in arrears.

Though he claims that Bette Davis, the late Hollywood actress, was his auntie, and though this indeed may account for the way he walks upstairs backwards wearing an eye patch, Roger Lewis is, in fact, the reverse of extraordinary, if truth be told. What he thinks of as his unique personal disappointments and rejections, his abhorrence of deadly conventionality, his plights when having to look at the dim and mediocre characters who seem to be succeeding and leaving him behind – these are very ordinary experiences indeed, shared by millions.

Roger Lewis is, one might say, a fantastical Everyman figure. He has more in common with you – or you have more in common with him – than you (or he) may care to realise.

The only difference that I can see between Roger Lewis and what you English call 'the man in the street' is that the modern world has passed Roger Lewis by – to an extent that is farcical. He cannot use his mobile phone, for example, because the Keypad Unlock function has never unlocked. He believes that Rafa Nadal is a dress designer.

Good people invite this buffoon to lunch, they put themselves

* An outpatient clinic in Dean Street, London, for mental defectives. Notable for its private dinner parties.

out (and put themselves to considerable expense – he is quite a greedy guts; nor will he die of being parched) – and is it any wonder that they don't wish to see Roger Lewis or hear from him ever again? In person he is an appalling and morbid sight, a grease spot. His work, too, is nothing more than an attempt to make his secret sufferings public, which is bad form to be sure.

Some generous commentators find his writing funny – I regret I cannot see a scintilla of humour in it myself. In any event, a comic gift is the sure sign of a lightweight, a flibbertigibbet, a third-rate mind. You don't find 'jokes' cluttering up the pages of, say, Dame Antonia Fraser or Lord Julian Fellowes, which is what got those august personages where they are today. Nor did Rosemary ('Rosie') Boycott get to be a member of BBC Radio 4's *Test Match Special* commentary team by wearing a cheerleader kilt at the Hay-on-Wye Literary Festival, waving a pom-pom and shouting, 'Go, Sir Vidia! ra-ra-ra!' Boris Johnson, who has composed books in Latin, only became your esteemed *Burgermeister* when he put away childish things like comedy, stopped all this silly laughing, and bought our Mercedes-Benz bendy buses instead.

I write these notes from Melk. Roger Lewis is currently my personal patient at the Hospital for *Very* Nervous Diseases, having been sent here in an unmarked van from the Dignitas Clinic, where he outraged the directors by asking for a Loyalty Discount Card. That is probably an example of his 'humour'. By glancing at my notes I can tell you that he is suffering from thrombosis, dizziness, tachycardia, bouts of melancholy, diabetes and the piles. The medical word in German is *nervenanspannung*. The nearest English equivalent is 'fucking nuts', if you'll pardon my French.

Because he is under sedation – the reason I am speaking in a whisper is I don't wish to wake him up – it is now incumbent upon me to acknowledge the team of people who, despite what he says, always help Roger Lewis get from A to B and back again. These selfless men and women are like the Knights Templars of old, propping up the author's ego during those rare moments when it falters: Geoff Atkinson; Paul Bailey *FRSL*; Graham Ball; Lynn Barber; Chris Beetles; Terence Blacker; Mark Booth; Gyles Brandreth; Craig Brown; Jane Bussmann; the late Ken Campbell; Barry Cryer OBE; the late Willie Donaldson; Duncan Fallowell; Stephen Fry; Kieran Grant; David H. Harries; Michael Herbert; Graham Holderness; David Howard; Rachel Johnson; naughty Jonathan King; Herbert Kretzmer OBE; Quentin Letts; Jeremy Lewis *FRSL*, the author's cousin; Steve Masty; John McEntee; Jan Morris CBE, *FRSL*; Mavis Nicholson; Tony Palmer; Sandra Parsons; Claire Van Kampen (Mrs Mark Rylance); Frances Welch (Mrs Craig Brown); Francis Wheen (Mrs Shufflewick); Kevin Whelan; Michael Whitehall; Dame Barbara Windsor; Michael Winner; and Clair Woodward.

Furthermore, the Features Editors of the *Daily Mail*, the *Daily Telegraph*, the *Mail on Sunday*, the *Sunday Express* and *The Times* need to be fulsomely thanked – though such are Roger Lewis's puerile and regrettable rants, commissions have mercifully been drying up.

As for the good citizens of the Bromyard township in the Herefordshire Balkans – their way is clear. They should burn Roger Lewis in effigy.

The only reason I can come up with to explain how the great Ronald Searle was prevailed upon to design the front cover of this book – or this *raving* – is that Roger Lewis must have pointed a gun at the poor man's head until he got going with his paints. The result is a mixed blessing, as how can Roger Lewis's prose possibly live up to the brilliant jacket design that Mr Searle has provided? About the only sensible thing Roger Lewis has said to me during our many hours of consultation is that it should be *Sir* Ronald Searle. Amen to that.

In a life that even I, as a leading Austrian clinician,* can see has

* With a powerful yet popular bleach-based stain remover named after me – *Der Lampenschirm Beliebten Patentiertden Schleuze* – most often to be whiffed in the wealthier care homes. See me afterwards for a discount.

been pretty much a glorified dead end with lots of cloudy days, Roger Lewis was smiled upon by the gods once – his wife of thirty years, Anna (née Dickens), has supported him, financially, morally, practically and metaphysically. He is nothing without her – or without his three sons, whom he complains about endlessly but loves dearly. He says it is 'a Welsh thing', being vehement and derisive when what you mean is to be affectionate. Here in Melk, we don't really know about Wales, so I can't possibly comment. (Do they have Christmas in Wales?)

Exceptionally thin-skinned and ultra-sensitive to criticism, though ruthless and obsessive when it suits him, who or what is Roger Lewis? An artist, a genius or a madman? That is what we are trying to ascertain here at the hospital – so far without success. He is already fast becoming a ghost. He is getting used to the silence, though to Roger Lewis the real world always seemed remote. He has been here months, reading both Dante's *Inferno* and old copies of *Bunty* with equal fervour. He claims that his life's ambition is to compile the definitive English/Welsh dictionary*, though thus far this is as far as he's got:

Wanker: Winkog
Cunt: Cnusty
Prat: Pratssy
Gobshite: Gobshittynog
Bullshit: Bullynogshat
Fucking idiot: Fucnogydidyot
Bollocks: Bollylockytig

What is he still doing here? Well, he has nowhere else to go. Literally and figuratively, he has nowhere to go but *on*. We

* *The Lewis Lexicon*, in collaboration with Kevin Whelan.

have been experimenting by withdrawing everything that ever over-stimulated him. All that he has been left to play with are words.*

Spezielle Krankenhaus fur *Sehr* Nervos Krankheiten,
c/o Medizinische Universitat, Melk
May 2011

---

* With a creosote brush stolen from the gardener's boy, he has daubed these words on the wall of his private room:

> Mine was not an enlightened mind, I was now aware: it was a gothic mind, medieval in its temper and structure. I did not love cold harmony and perfect regularity of organisation; what I sought was variety, mystery, tradition, the venerable, the awful. I despised sophisters and calculators; I was groping for faith, honour, and prescriptive loyalties. I would have given any number of neo-classical pediments for one poor battered gargoyle.

The author of this quotation is Russell Kirk (1918–94), an obscure American philosopher, known to us in Melk, however, for his book *Die Konservative Geist*.

January

What am I still doing here? By rights I should be speaking to you as a ghost from the grave. My liver went bang on Boxing Day. I'd had these pains and cramps in my legs. I had the gout, which afflicted every extremity including my ear lobes, and was as testy as a colonel in the *Beano*. I had drenching night sweats, yet also shivered with cold. My capillaries were in an uproar. Then my mottled fetlocks started swelling up – and Dr Twelvetrees explained that my liver was demanding satisfaction under the code, fighting a duel to the very death with the Lagavulin, my favourite single malt. I pictured Holmes and Moriarty grappling on the brink of the Reichenbach Falls. Prayers were said for me at church – I still don't know what comedian is responsible for that.

As I attempted to hoist my elephant legs on the weighing scales, Dr Twelvetrees said, 'All these years, you haven't listened to a damn thing I've said, have you?' – a rhetorical question if ever there was one. For the record, I've also consumed a bottle of claret every day for thirty years. So that's 10,950 bottles of red wine or approximately 65,700 glasses. Tally it up and put like that, it doesn't sound so very much.

I was despatched for a scan in the county hospital. What appeared on the screen was like Jacques Cousteau's extraordinary under-the-sea world. There were translucent blobs and fronds. There were shoals of minnows. An electric eel darted past, rolling its eyes. There were shadows of sharks and whales, and plenty of jellyfish. I'm convinced I saw a sailor in peril.

The radiographer said my liver was 'fatty' (to which I was tempted to reply – 'and you're an ugly twat') and that she'd 'seen worse' ('up the bum and no babies to you'). Anyway, I was told to give the grog-tray the cold shoulder for a few months. So for a few months I duly bolted my food, barred myself from spirituous liquors, and slunk away from the table, feeling left out of convivial luncheons and dinners. I became a spectre of my former self, nowhere near what was the top of my form. It was as if I was hanging upside down. In a ditch.

As self-dramatising as Mr Toad, I took to my bed and drafted the following, with instructions that it should be printed in due course in those newspapers of note, the *Western Mail*, the *Brecknock and Radnorshire Express* and the indispensable *Bromyard Record*:

LEWIS, Doctor Roger Clifford.
Unfathomably Neglected Writer & Kentucky Colonel.
Rotund, Dark & Difficult & Withal Dearly Beloved
Husband & Devoted Father
Whose Ashes Have Been Scattered in the Salzkammergut.
By the Express Wishes of the Deceased No Welsh Persons
Were Present at His Obsequies.
Ubi Saeva Indignatio Ulterius Cor Lacerare Nequit.
[He has gone where fierce indignation can
lacerate his heart no more.]

On top of this, the central heating broke down, so to quote a medieval poet on the subject: plumber was icumen in. Bloody big to-do.

A funny thing happened at Elsie's funeral this morning. The old chap in front of me sighed loudly, sat down with a thud, and fell sideways – stone dead. Words can't describe the colour of his face:

ashen, stark white, veal grey, yellowish, shocking pink, magenta, mauve, royal blue; or greenish ginger ivory; or the pallor of dirty snow. 'Will he get a discount as you're here already?' I asked Mr Gaunt, the undertaker. Isn't that what one is meant to do at dark moments, crack a joke? The corpse lay there across two pews, his glasses wonky and stuck up his nose.

It doesn't end there. Anna told me later that the man hadn't died. He'd only fainted. It has happened often before and he's been laid out twice. The undertakers see him coming. Half an hour after Elsie's funeral he rose up – 'in the sure and certain hope of the Resurrection to eternal life' (nobody picked up this reference when I made it – a sign of the times) – and tottered home. What an anticlimax.

❧

As a result of the difficulties I always face, the spirals of debt and the claims of illness, and as I try to finish *this* book or *that* book and have to interrupt my concentration with hack journalism, because there are urgent bills to pay; and as I am always anxious for what I write to be good – *great* if possible – and because of this professional stress and the domestic stress of the children and family responsibilities, and the guilt that comes with those: well, I do dream of getting away from it all, taking leave of the world. Fiji, Eastbourne, Cromer, the Dignitas Clinic – such paradise gardens, blue lagoons and treasure islands call out to me. 'To chuck up everything and just clear off,' as Larkin put it. I can't say 'Stuff your pension!' as I don't have one to speak of.

❧

The trusty old firemen of Herefordshire went to the rescue of 'thirsty pigs' after pipes froze at a farm in Goodrich. 'We sent along an appliance and a crew of six,' said the station manager. So now we know where to find Pugh, Pugh, Barney McGrew, Cuthbert, Dibble and Grub.

❧

One of the things that get on my tits – on my big floppy squelchy wobbly man boobs or moobs – are all these people who say how happy they are to be fifty. 'I still wear a bikini and I still wear a miniskirt too,' bragged Christa D'Souza – and, yes, you look like Morticia Addams, love. 'Being fifty is a great boost to clarity, spirit and drive,' claimed Greta Scacchi – actresses are always a bit dim, don't you find? 'I'll have fifty parties for my fifty years!' announced Carol Vorderman. 'I've never stopped. I'm a driven person' – I'm really glad I don't know Carol. 'I used to be obsessed with how I presented myself. I'm more relaxed now,' said Annie Lennox – sorry, never heard of her.

I've been getting letters from insurance companies, offering me a policy to pay for my funeral costs. The telegraphic code for the Queen Mother's State Funeral was 'Tay Bridge' – so mine is 'Rhymney Bridge'. Upon receiving this message, insurance companies can start shitting themselves – because I want a gun carriage, Morris Men, the Kentucky Colonels with swords drawn, and representatives from Islay's single malt distilleries looking morose. No expense to be spared. When Spike Milligan heard that Harry Secombe was ill he told him, 'I always hoped you'd die first, because at least then you won't sing at my funeral.'*

The GP has told me that I am in the 'at risk' category and must have a flu jab. I walked into the waiting room and wanted to walk right out. These old people – I can't possibly be in the same 'at risk' category as that lot? They all must have turned up on the wrong day. The lame, the loopy, the recently retired – fat and ghastly and dilapidated and looking as if they are covered with livid brick dust.

* Though Sir Secombe *did* die first, a recording of him enthusiastically belting out 'Bread of Heaven' was nevertheless played at Milligan's funeral, in March 2002. So he didn't quite escape the blast of Welsh *hwyl* after all.

I've had another official letter warning me about strokes and aneurysms.

❧

I've been to buy inner-soles for my shoes. Only an old person buys inner-soles for their shoes. I'll be after tartan zip-up bootees next. And I need thicker lenses from Mr 'Mint' Jelley, the splendidly named Bromyard optician.

❧

I find myself interested in getting an unheated greenhouse.

❧

I have a fondness for piers – but they always burst into flames, don't they? They must be made of cardboard. I'd be afraid to move to Cromer or Eastbourne in case I'm a jinx.

❧

Another horror of hell. My knackers dangle so low and loose – like a pair of marbles in an old pigskin purse – and have become generally so scrawny, a week last Wednesday, when I was minding my own business, waddling to Legge's for a nice bit of fish, they flew backwards, looped-the-loop, as it were, in my XXXL thong, and got stuck up my arse. You'll be thanking me for telling you that. I was reminded of Scrotum, Sir Henry Rawlinson's 'wrinkled retainer.'

❧

The circus bit he loved, the fourteen or so performances every week, but Tristan also had to help put up and dismantle the tent in all weathers, drive a World War II lorry to the next venue, and he was demoralised to discover that he was being paid considerably less than the Romanian backstage crew, who only did the manual stuff and didn't have to act in the show. In previous seasons he never noticed the mud and the rain – he was having such a great time. But this season Tristan didn't even get on with the other clowns, who pulled rank if he won a bigger laugh, or a different laugh, or if he invented new business. So he also felt crushed

5

artistically. So — time to move on. Where he's moved his caravan is to the bottom of our garden. He's like Rooster Byron in that play of Mark Rylance's — and Mark is his godfather.

~

One of the things he had to endure last year — though it was only broadcast recently — was to appear in the background of *Masterchef*. Don't those two wallies on *Masterchef* get on your nerves? I hate all cookery programmes since *Two Fat Ladies*. I loved *Two Fat Ladies* because they had an air of camp — Jennifer and Clarissa could have been pantomime dames, and in Japan they were dubbed by men.

I've hated cookery shows since they stopped being poofy and started being an army boot camp — not the same thing as *camp camp* at all. Did they think they had to be like this so that 'men' would go in the kitchen? I'm old enough to remember Galloping Gourmet Graham Kerr. Robert Carrier in a cravat. Even Keith Floyd wore a bowtie and flapped his arms about.

Which reminds me of the old joke: woman from Wales is in Spain on a self-catering holiday and wants some eggs. Doesn't speak a word of the Spanish so makes a clucking noise and does an elbow-and-arm flapping mime for the shopkeeper, who hands over toilet rolls.

Anyway, *Masterchef*. It was the fakery of the *X-Factor* pauses and the lingering close-ups of neurotic, boring cross-eyed contestants chewing their fingernails as they waited to know if they were through to the next round, the whizzing about editing and the electronic menacing music that bugged me. Oh I *hated* it. I hated Piggy Greg filling his Specsavers face and being Sarf Lunnon-ish and that chum of his (whoever he is) with the sarcastic eyes . . . They don't even have the grace or wit to be like a pair of poofs. *This is cookery, guys, not the initiation rites for the Royal Marines*, I kept shouting.

The contestants cooked this disgusting vegetarian goo and had to feed it to the Zippos' artistes, ages back when they were in

Peckham. There were brief – subliminal – shots of Tristan in a top hat and stripy waistcoat. Everyone looked very self-conscious and sheepish, and I know these people – for David Konyot to look self-conscious and sheepish you'd normally need to pump him full of strychnine. I think they were there hours doing the retakes. The whole thing about 'You've only got ten minutes left, nine, eight . . . Go, go, go, *now*!' is totally staged. As if you'd not have guessed. I know for a fact that when it was over, the clowns and Norman the ringmaster went back to their caravans for a proper meal, e.g. meat and jelly. The embarrassing thing is, we got every member of the family to watch it and record it. No one has phoned up to congratulate or offer their views.

૭

Isn't *Masterchef* the show that years ago had silly goose Loyd [sic] Grossman on? I liked it then – as Loyd [sic] had a touch of the Kenneth Williams about him, particularly with that absurd voice. But can you imagine if they brought back *Face the Music*? Vernon Dobtcheff! They'd have Joyce Grenfell and Robin Ray abseiling off cliffs, Bernard Levin in commando gear telling us about Wagner as he poses next to the grave of Colonel 'H', and Joseph Cooper playing the dummy keyboard on the bridge of HMS *Ark Royal* in a Force Ten gale. Because anything gentler and quieter and more civilised would alienate the youth audience and the alleged immigrants who need a deafening jungle beat.

૭

Alan Bennett told me that the only thing he can stomach watching on television is *Come Dine With Me*, 'for the voice-overs.' What I notice, whenever we go with the camera into real people's ordinary homes – not a picture on the walls, not a book, let alone a bookcase. Not even a Danielle Steele or a Maeve Binchy strewn about. Not tasteless exactly, these dwellings, but no taste – nil, null, nothing, *nada*. Also, the contestants can't converse; all they do is fall out, bicker. It is as if everyone is atrophied, dead already.

7

There is no evidence of any imaginative faculty. And don't get me started on the ways they try and hold their cutlery. You feel they'd be more comfortable squatting on their haunches and using their hands. They *weren't brought up properly*, is my judgement.

Tristan did some gigs for a company called Area 51. They send magicians, jugglers, dancers and so forth to corporate events. They also represent dwarves. Tristan said that in the warehouse there are all these dwarf Darth Vader costumes, which were worn recently at a *Star Wars* convention. I'd be keen to hire a dozen or so Oompa-Loompas to mingle at a book launch party. I've said it before and I'll say it again – you can't go wrong with dwarves.

❧

One of Tristan's new colleagues is Pip The Mighty Squeak, who according to reports* built his own miniature shower, as the water pressure from a normal shower caused concussion.

'I saw her on New Year's Eve and she seemed agitated,' said Margaret Bubb. 'She wasn't her usual bubbly self.' Nor was she. Ex-nun Christina Withyman from the Poor Clares at Much Birch drowned herself in the Wye. A sad business – but like a poem by Gerard Manley Hopkins.

❧

John Bratby – all that paint! I've been leafing through a book about him. But the way he applied his paint to the canvas straight from the tube was wasteful rather than generous. He was slapdash – too vivid. When he puts black lines around everything, his people or plants or fruit (or whatever) look like drawings. This had the effect, in his portraiture, of making faces into hollow masks. But I'm sucked in somehow – the volcanoes of colour can't be ignored, even if they are stormy and queasy. Yet there was

* See *The Heart Felt Letters* by Liz Reed (Edinburgh, 1998), where Pip is said to have participated in an unbroadcast pilot called *Disabled Gladiators*.

something (fatally) ungenerous about Bratby – a *smallness*. He was egocentric and aggressive (in real life he was a drunkard), without being interestingly powerful. You can tell he's not very taken by his subjects, only by their celebrity, by their ability to meet his fee – he solicited work by writing to the entrants in *Who's Who*. If he'd got to me before he croaked, would I have gone along to his studio in Hastings? Of course. (The pier in Hastings has just burned down.)

Bratby's grumpy flamboyance appealed to Alec Guinness, who wrote and starred in *The Horse's Mouth*, the film about a scruffy bohemian living on a houseboat. For all his avowed blurred anonymity, Guinness liked to portray loud eccentrics (Fagin, Professor Marcus, everybody in *Kind Hearts and Coronets*) – but the scrofulous Gully Jimson, with paint rags in his pockets, is tiresome. Too much of a 'character' altogether.

Guinness had a sympathetic imagination – he inhabited completely the minds of other people when he played them – so if Jimson/Bratby comes across as self-aggrandising and second-rate, this is paradoxically only too authentic. Guiness is doing his job all too well – so the more Jimson growls that he is a genius, the more we realise he is a buffoon. My sympathies are entirely with the collectors and patrons whose homes Jimson invades and desecrates. Robert Coote, who has to feign apoplexy when he sees the mess, was Roderigo in Welles's *Othello*. You hope someone will boot Jimson up the arse.

For the film, Bratby painted all the pictures that Guinness pretends to paint. What would have been much more fascinating – it would have transformed everything – is if the film-makers had approached Francis Bacon, who may have been glad of the work and the attention in 1958. He was still making his way then. He wasn't the silly camp dowager he later became, spilling champagne on the carpet at The Colony Club and saying 'So you're the old lace-maker's *niece*, are you?' to the nephew of Jackson Pollock. There is something in Bacon's sadomasochistic

quasi-religious imagery that would have transfixed Guinness –
and inspired him, I think, in disturbing ways.

ços

In a book I've got somewhere about a woman called Florence
Farr's correspondence with William Butler Shaw and George
Bernard Yeats, there's a remark that goes to the heart – the nub
– of why I'm so interested in actors and acting. Florence Farr,
said Clifford Bax, though who the fuck he was escapes me for the
moment,* 'had too much personality to become a good actress'.

Hence, the blankness of Peter Sellers or Alec Guinness; or why
the real life of Laurence Olivier was when he was on stage acting –
performances filling them out. But what made them great artists is
also to describe a kind of psychopathology – a nothingness that can
be quite dangerous, like those murderers who, when arrested and
upon investigation, turn out to be sad little fellows living a nothing
life, friendless, lonely, with zero charisma – zero personality – who
kill to give themselves colour; or like confidence tricksters, with
their pretend names and aliases, their desperate attempts to make
themselves appear interesting and impressive.

Thus – the third career option for the would-be actor or
criminal is to join the Security Services. John le Carré's novels
are about the theatricality of espionage.

ços

Peremptory posh bird Hortense Van Ping Pong (not her real name
– but close) tells me that, 'Oh you're so lucky you don't work
in an office. It's so dreary here, day after day. It's absolute hell.'
So what I told her was this: 'You must escape! Join Zippo's and
acquire circus skills! Then write a book about it, which I'd review

---

* Balham-born Clifford Bax was the brother of Arnold Bax, the composer,
if that is any help. Clifford edited an artistic and literary magazine called *The
Golden Hind*, promoted the works of Aleister Crowley, published a biography
of W. G. Grace, and wrote and produced radio plays about Shakespeare,
Rasputin and Buddha. He died in 1962, aged seventy-six. His papers are held
in McMaster University Library, Ontario, Canada.

10

glowingly. Then Natalie Portman can play you in the movie.' Or Kathy Burke. 'You are an exotic jungle plant stuck in a dentist's waiting room – you can't bloom there, woman!'

I've always claimed to be the sort of person who loathes routine. The thought of being a commuter, going to an office, having to have meetings, and so forth – Christ! Imagine having to have *colleagues* and *bosses*. I'd become a serial killer out of sheer bottled-up rage. I'd be like Bodkin Adams or Crippen or one of those. John George Haigh, played in a television film by Martin Clunes, had a harmonium in the bedroom and played 'Abide With Me' and 'Nearer My God To Thee' as the corpses bubbled in the acid bath.

Yet I have my routines. I wear the same clothes – I have dozens of XXXL black T-shirts. Even though I piss and moan non-stop, I quite like looking after people, the shopping routines, the cooking routines. I like going on holiday to the same places, staying in the same room in the same hotels. I go to the same restaurants (Sheekey's and Rules), where I sit at the same table.

So not only do I have my routines, I actually loathe surprises, loathe change. Yet in my work the main thing I do is provide space for surprise, as I chase ideas about, climbing above the material, not being held down by anything. My routines – the same pen (Waterman's), the same quality of light (I keep the curtains closed), the same sort of paper (A4 narrow feint with margin) – give me the freedom for concentration. Though saying that, I write this in the kitchen with about a thousand people running around making a disgusting mess and I'm in a murder mood, shouting and swearing like the editor of a mass-market tabloid.

Hereford and Worcester Fire and Rescue Service has 'blamed squirrels for blaze' – when a fire broke out at a farm in Bircher. Not content with nicking hazelnuts and chasing up and down trees, squirrels are now arsonists. I hope that the Station Commander has been warning shopkeepers not to sell matches to the little demons.

Inside I am a great clot of anxiety. If I possessed a capsule of potassium cyanide, as distributed to the Nazi high-command in Hitler's bunker, I would gobble one down without hesitation. I'd gobble two or three. It would be lovely to be free permanently of my worries, my self-disgust. In his diaries Michael Palin mentions listening to Max Wall list his ailments, including a 'dropped arsehole' – I think I may have one of those. My teeth have become brittle, like sharp maize stumps. My pallid skin is covered with the red blotches of *Mycosis Fungoides*, though now they call it Cutaneous T-cell Lymphoma. Thirteen years ago I was given ten years to live. Imagine what it is like carrying that knowledge around in your head – it's like Captain Hook being pursued by the crocodile, and the crocodile, you will remember, had swallowed a ticking clock. I am morbidly obese, and broke the bed, which is propped up by books. I smell. I fester. I lack comeliness. I am gross. No matter how often I bathe and cover myself with Woods of Windsor lavender talcum powder the aroma of death and decomposition cannot be masked. Everything has taken on the damp odour of exhaustion. Is it my liver liquefying? Is it that the soap I use is reverting to its original constituents of animal parboiled gristle and yellow horn? I am reminded of childhood slaughterhouse smells, congealing blood and fat, shit and hunting fear. Coffee and tea taste bitter, metallic. My light is low. Nothing is sweet to me. Nothing has brightness. No birds sing.

ᏽ

When I read the above to my loved ones, they started chuckling round about *I am morbidly obese* and were wiping tears of mirth from their eyes by *my light is low*. Bastards.

But I have nailed it. The X-rays and abdominal scans; gout; diabetes; cardiovascular stuff – all the things relating to being fat may be disregarded. Even being on the water-wagon isn't going to help. Well, yes, there is a bit of a question mark over the liver – but the thing is, what I am suffering from is: Cancer of Freelance Journalism.

The swellings and chills and fevers have been induced by years and years of financial insecurity, disappointment, rejection, and pervasive humiliation. I hope the condition, now it has been so neatly specified, may be named after me, too. Like Parkinson's is named after Michael Parkinson. 'I've got Lewis's Disease and he's got mine.' Little Michael Parkinson and I could say that when we meet each other.

Up in the night always with the insomnia, these past few weeks I've watched the entire boxed set of the David Suchet *Poirot* series. How many episodes is that? A hundred? A hundred thousand? He has an Art Deco personality, does Hercule Poirot, with his fondness for geometry and sharp neatness, as revealed by the fold of his napkin or the decor in his ultra-modern flat. I'm told that the flat in Clerkenwell used by the film-makers for their location is a popular venue for swingers' parties – where that apparition always appears: the hairy nude fat bloke on the stairs forking down a ham salad. Poirot himself would be mortified. He is so fastidious and repressed, he never quite wakes up to the fact that he's an old nancy. The walk Suchet gives him – he is a martyr to the piles.

The later films, especially, are stylishly done – particularly *The Halloween Party*, with its pumpkin colours and tilted camera angles. The producers clearly enjoyed cooking up misty graveyards and weed-choked ponds. The puzzle-solving element aside, the clue to the success of the classic detective story is here I think: the pervasive cosiness, the country house or vicarage setting with the nicely tended rose gardens, and the puffing steam trains; and then the violence and viciousness that lurk underneath the nice formal manners and teatime social rituals, like serpents in Eden.

Poirot is a bit tiresome, I find. Vain, puffed up, self-important. There's no depth. You can see Suchet working hard not to be cartoonish, not to be camp (as Ustinov was). I prefer Joan

Hickson as Miss Marple. She was marvellous as the frail little old lady, sitting there knitting, yet she goes after psychopaths! 'I am your *nemesis*,' she says to one malefactor – and she's a bit chilling. She comes from another dimension, like Alastair Sim's Inspector Poole in *An Inspector Calls*. Joan Hickson compares favourably with Ethel Barrymore in *The Spiral Staircase*, when Ethel as chronic invalid Mrs Warren struggles out of bed, totters to the landing and confronts the villain head-on by delivering just that one word, '*Murderer!*' You need to have been a star before the turn of the last century to carry off a scene like that – you needed to be part of the grand theatrical tradition, which has gone for ever.

ৎ৯

Up every night, I've also watched the full fifty-two hours of *Oz*, the HBO prison drama. Lots of swearing and stabbing. It's like the planet of the apes in that penitentiary. And it is very badly run – the guards are (of course) sadistic and the shambling governor is incompetent. He condones gang anal rape as 'levelling'. We see a lot of anal gang rape. Killings are cursorily investigated – people are dispatched in gruesome ways and it is never mentioned again. Luke Perry is burned and buried half-alive behind a wall in the cafeteria *twice*. There are no consequences. Nobody even mentions that Luke has gone missing.

It is already dated – there are no CCTVs, mobile phones or computers. It is pre-9/11 so the Muslim inmates are sanctimonious rather than fanatical. I watched the boxed set from start to finish, finding it difficult to know quite who the nastiest character is. The winner of the coconut is Rita Moreno's Sister Peter Marie. Her little psychotherapeutic self-help groups would make a man doing three weeks for failing to pay his council tax run amok with the Yorkshire Ripper's screwdrivers.

ৎ৯

I want ideally to clear a few weeks to work on a book – my long-delayed *Growing Up With Comedians* – but without the journalistic

14

assignments coming in regularly I feel very cold and panicky. Not simply because of economic bleakness but because one suddenly feels unloved and forgotten.

✌

I am a literary festival leper. Not only am I never invited to Hay-on-Wye, which is practically on my doorstep, or to the one the *Sunday Times* organise in Oxford, but I have never been invited to Buxton or Aldeburgh. It is always little Melvyn Bragg, P. D. James, A. S. Byatt, Sebastian Faulks or Debo Devonshire. Gyles Brandreth appears at several *simultaneously*. I am doomed to be an outsider, left to struggle in lonely limbo. No wonder I am glum and disillusioned. But anyway – Sylvia at The Falcon said in that case she'd inaugurate the Bromyard Literary Festival, at which there'd be only one speaker: me. I nearly didn't make it. Anna had been away and I was changing the beds and I got stuck inside a double duvet cover. Sylvia said, 'Who shall we have next year?' I said 'Quentin Letts.' 'Too famous,' said Sylvia. 'We'll have you again.' I sold one copy of a book called *Seasonal Suicide Notes*, which the purchaser's husband took to Oxfam in Hereford the next day 'by mistake'.

✌

I do hope I get invited to Hay one day, so that I can turn them down. Up the bum and no babies to literary festivals! I am *very against* them, actually. Writers are writers, not performers, unless you are Gyles Brandreth. Hence I suppose all these television comedians and celebrities who throng The Rosie Boycott Memorial Marquee, selling their ghosted memoirs.

I went to Hay once to see a great hero of mine (no relation), Norman Lewis. He was terrible. Mumbled, fell silent, awkward, boring. And it made it hard for me to read him again with pleasure. Though one is great on the page, it doesn't follow that one can scintillate in public – though that's not the prevailing view, where style and presentation are confused with substance.

15

Indeed, people are getting to be unaware that there *is* a difference between style and presentation and substance.

Everything that's shitty in the entire universe follows from this inability to discriminate.

&

Terence Blacker was *slightly piqued* when I said somewhere or other that the only way you get invited to Hay-on-Wye and suchlike literary festivals is if you play the guitar and have a singalong. 'We authors have to make a living and sell copies any way we can, you know.' He thought it was a reference to himself. Which it was.

I am to take up the euphonium, like 'Professor' Jimmy Edwards. So, put that in your pipe and smoke it, Sir Salman Rushdie! Does Sir Rushdie play what my mother would call a scimitar, I wonder? Debo Devonshire's boogie-woogie piano sessions are famous at Chatsworth, I hear. Or is that Jools Holland? All these people named after places. Eileen Derbyshire. Sarah Lancashire. Stuart Hampshire. Arthur Machen. Jack London. David Cornwell, aka John le Carré. The Earl of Hereford once said to Patrick Garland, 'My name is Hereford, I live in Hereford and I breed Herefords.'

&

Terence Blacker, the newspaperman, novelist and biographer of our mutual friend Willie Donaldson, is the son of the late General Sir Cecil Hugh Blacker GCB, OBE, MC (though not FRSL – thank God), known to his friends as Monkey Blacker, and Felicity Mary Rew, known to her friends as Zulu Blacker.

In a typical month, Monkey Blacker would box for the Inniskillings, have a picture he'd painted hung in the Royal Academy, write a column for the *Spectator*, win the Military Gold Cup at Sandown, and during the working week he'd discharge his duties as Vice-Chief of the General Staff at the War Office in Whitehall.

A great man, with a touch of the John Buchans. When I said to Terence that I should liked to have met the General (who died in 2002), because he sounds like a figure from a better, earlier age,

16

Terence said, 'He would have hated you.' That put me in my place. Seeing my face fall, Terence added, 'But I don't know, though. He was a very curious man.' But the point had been made. I am not someone who stacks up in a crisis.

Saucy England, Merry England: where has it gone? It's a long time since 1838, when a fourteen-year-old Welsh boy infiltrated Buckingham Palace and 'was caught making off with a pair of Queen Victoria's undergarments stuffed down his trousers'. He was transported to Australia. I wonder if this was Dame Barry Humphries's great-grandfather?

Eastbourne, Cromer or Buxton: what is it that such places arouse? One's boyhood. Safe. People speaking in the English language. One can feel relaxed and at home. I think a need for this is implanted in us, yet when the producer of *Midsomer Murders* pointed out that olde worlde Englishness was the appeal of his long-running series, he was accused of racism and worse. Most of Britain is like the Wild West, filled with nomads. Soon it'll be mosques in Bromyard. Multiculturals long since bought up Knightsbridge, with money from oil that is extracted with Western technology. They even have Muslims now in *Norway*.

When Laurence Olivier first went to Hollywood – this would have been in the early Thirties when he played impetuous and slightly annoying young men in wholly forgotten films with Zasu Pitts, Gertrude Lawrence and Gloria Swanson – what he most remembered, what he'd still chuckle about forty years later, was wandering among the studio back lots and coming across 'little English cottages overlooked by Arabian mosques', i.e. he was tickled by the architectural, historical anomalies. Yet the hyper-reality of RKO or MGM is no longer fantasy.

I could never stand *Midsomer Murders*, if the truth be told. John Nettles was so muffled and dim he could be encased in a Valium shroud. The programme was preposterous but without zest, without style. Those brightly lit Oxfordshire and Buckingham leafy villages got on my wick. Possibly if Hercule Poirot walked around in the present day I'd be bored, too – but I am nuts about Art Deco. The Ocean Terminal at Southampton. Gone for ever. Ditto the gaslight and fog of Sherlock Holmes.

I'm convinced these popular mysteries only exist to give work to old character actors. There can't be anyone left in Equity who hasn't been a murderee. At least *Inspector Morse* had John Thaw being crabby and full of self-disgust – he was another of those snarling actors from Up North who were filled with chippiness and self-loathing because what they do for a living (costumes, make-up) is a bit whoops-ducky.

My own personal idea/ideal of an actor is Lord Jonathan Cecil in a purple fedora. I *want* actors to be foppish. John Nettles did a documentary about my beloved John Betjeman that sent you to sleep. If you want to see how shite *Mogadon Murders* is, think of what Charles Dance – who has a mad dangerous glint – could have done with the role of Detective Chief Inspector Barnaby. He'd be perfect for Willie Donaldson in a film adaptation of *Both the Ladies and the Gentlemen*.

Although slow and boring, at least *Mogadon Murders* concealed within its present-day setting a fantasy of a Fifties England, which is a draw to so many of us. But of course nostalgia is not permitted today. Nothing much is permitted today – in that they don't show Westerns much any more (because of the treatment of Red Indians), or old films where people smoke all the time; soon it will be taboo, racist somehow, not to have our coloured brethren all over the shop, though contrariwise no white person is allowed to play Othello. I suppose they can CGI them in, as when they updated the special effects on *Star Wars*.

You'll have Dame Margaret Rutherford's Miss Prism in Anthony Asquith's film of *The Importance of Being Earnest* changed into Hattie McDaniel from *Gone with the Wind*. Lord Olivier's Henry V will become Eddie Murphy, and in Errol Flynn's *The Adventures of Robin Hood*, the outlaws will become a jolly black and white minstrel troupe. Easily done.

What I hate – the way we are meant to feel guilty about being white and middle class and European. Incidentally, in Gogol's *Diary of a Madman*, one of his hallucinations, and why he gets locked in the bin, is that in France they've all become devotees of Mohammedanism. When the refugees start floating across the Mediterranean from Benghazi, this will soon be all too true. Mark my words.

Furthermore, the theme of *Othello* is not that Othello is black (which is irrelevant), but that he is an outsider. I'm getting to be more like Othello every day.

∽

Though the world I love is vanishing – everything is being flattened to build disabled-access mosques – here and there I do notice glimmerings of an England that world wars were once fought to preserve. For example, the Reverend Andrew Proud, Area Bishop of Ethiopia and the Horn of Africa (Egypt with North Africa and the Horn of Africa, the Episcopal Church in Jerusalem and the Middle East) has been appointed the Bishop of Reading. And on the same day, in Torquay, the funeral was held of ninety-year-old Joya Roberts, the widow of General Sir Ouvry Lindfield Roberts and beloved mother of Ouvrielle, Pelham, Hugh, Dennis, Jean, Martin and John. Not only that, but the Life Barony conferred upon Sir Gulam Kanderbhoy Noon MBE was gazetted by the name, style and title of Baron Noon of St John's Wood in the London Borough of Camden.

∽

Anna went with the children to Hereford to see The Circus of Horrors. There was a profane dwarf in a kilt who attached a Hoover nozzle to his dick and swung the hose around the stage. He then stuck a firework up his arse and for an encore suspended a five-pound weight from his knackers. He also flashed his arse gratuitously. Though Anna said she pined for Norman Barrett's budgies, I've said it before and I'll say it again, you can't go far wrong with dwarves.

∾

A favourite dwarf story. A dwarf goes to the doctor for some free contraceptives. The doctor says, 'Yes, of course, by all means. But I'm bound to ask – how have you managed up until now?' – 'Well,' says the dwarf, 'it's like this. I stand on a biscuit tin and when I go red in the face my wife kicks it away.'

∾

I had a letter informing me that I have been elected a member of the Welsh Academy, though because they insist on spelling it 'academi' I resigned immediately. *Ambwlans, snwcr, pwddin, ffon, ffacs, tacsi**– all this annoys the hell out of me, as does Max Boyce with his humorous giant leek, and Welsh women who make a point of wearing full make-up and jewels to go to rugby matches.

Founded as long ago as 1998, 'to provide the national literature support service for Wales', the Welsh Academy/Yr Academi Gymraig, an outfit hitherto unknown to me, seems to be devoted to inflicting poets on prisoners and schoolchildren. Which reminds me of something I overheard in the hospice shop. 'Is your daughter still on probation?' – 'She's doing her baccalaureate.'

Surely any notion of a 'literature support service' sounds a bit crap, even though *I'm not sure what it even means.* Support as in *truss*? Service as in *bus* or *train*? In any case, I do not believe in the idea that literature can be used for social change. Literature with a political message is propaganda. It's junk. I also don't like

---

* Wouldn't you know it, but those words mean ambulance, snooker, pudding, phone, fax and taxi respectively. It is not a difficult language, though, as Kingsley Amis spotted, there must be one or two Welsh people who've not come across the letter 'x' very often – hence *bocsio* is boxing, for instance.

the notion that, given the opportunity, anyone can do it – or has a right to do it – which seems to be the message in the big pack of bilingual bumf I got sent. I have enough people sending me the freshly printed-off manuscripts of their novels, plays, poems, epithalamiums, villanelles, rondos and eclogues to know whereof I speak – that hardly anyone can do it. There is in any event plenty of verse and there are ample short stories already, thank you very much. Though everyone can (and should) acquire fundamental grammatical skills, spelling, and so forth, as I did as a Mixed Infant in Mrs Harrington's class, the rest is a lifelong slog, a vocation – literally *a calling*. In my case, a *howling*.

Perhaps basic literacy is considered elitist and taboo these days, because the paragraph about me on the 'academi's' website was illiterate beyond. According to them I was born in Bedwas (it was Caerphilly), educated at Wolfson College, Oxford (where I was a Fellow), my two doctorates are from the University of Herefordshire (which doesn't exist), I was a Visiting Professor at Birmingham University (they must mean Birmingham City University) . . . and so on and so forth.

Perhaps English is no longer allowed to be anyone's first language the other side of the Severn Bridge? There's probably a move to stamp English out. I can just picture these index-linked functionaries in Cardiff (Caerdydd) or Newport (Casnewydd) muttering and gibbering, with the black spittle pouring from the corners of their mouths, as they say or fulminate *Who does this fancy-pants Doctor Lewis with his over-the-border ways think he is, believing that English is the superior language?*[*]

❧

How old was Betjeman when he wrote *Summoned by Bells*, his account of 'the sheltered life of a middle-class youth'?[†] Odd

[*] 'Pwy ddiawl mae Doctor Lewis yn meddwl yw e, yn credu fod Saesneg yn well iaith?'
[†] Published in 1960, when Sir John was fifty-four – so I win. Just.

that I should feel the urge so strongly to do roughly this same sort of thing now, to go on what shithouse publisher's blurbs or television commissioning editors would call a *journey*. Why now? The answer: not hard – because when I look ahead my tombstone is already on view. And when I look back, there's Wales, and me a delicate, highly strung boy in it. The photographs of me as a child – I am so *serious*, so deeply *apprehensive*. What was it I'd already suspected was heading my way?

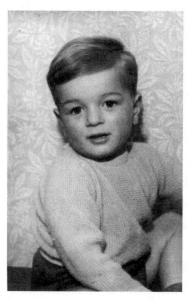

I remember that wallpaper. Ostensibly shells or flowers – though all I could make out were mean goblin grimaces; burning eyes, snarling mouths with protruding tongues. I was always upset by ugly devil faces in the grain of a piece of polished furniture – by an imp's portrait in a nest of tables. To my imagination, furniture and decor were quite capable of changing shape, right before your eyes. My mother had to slap emulsion on that wallpaper – a greenish egg-white – to cover it up. Yet still the indentations of teeth and lolling tongues protruded. As a child, nothing lulled me. Except music, books, films, puppets.

Memories return to me, like birds flying in from the sea. It started with my dreams after my father died and now I do it deliberately, when I'm trying to drop off – pacing in my imagination the streets of my childhood town, Bedwas, a watering place on the shores of the upper Rhymney. Church Street, St Mary Street, Tydfil Road, Pandy Road, The Cwm, where there was a stream. The dripping trees and hedges pulled up; the fields and pallid flowers built over. The struggle with the ugliness and meanness. Nothing could be done about the tips – nothing grows on them. The disfiguring brown lumps, like melanomas. The coal dust that settled on everything, which we breathed in and out.

Bedwas Square wasn't a square at all, but a twist in the road. On the corner in the house that became The Ingle-Nook Restaurant, and when that failed The Bedwas Balti, there lived, during my childhood, a crone called Rowlanda Hurst. Rowlanda Hurst had briefly been a governess in a Scottish castle, but she was sacked when she wrote home on the noble family's crested notepaper. That was mean of them. She never recovered from this humiliation.

Everywhere in Wales there are people with comical nicknames. In Bedwas there was Tommy Seven Suits, Billy Bang Bang and Tommy Two Loos. At the age of eighty-five, Dollar King's husband still boasted about his morning erection. He'd apparently always come out with this (oo-err) when the butcher's shop was full of female customers. When he was at the pit-head baths, the apprentices used to be shown his enormous incumbency. Allegedly, when he went home covered in coal dust after his shift, Dollar would cover him in newspaper so that they could have a couple of quick ones, with a hole chopped in the newspaper for his cock to poke through. He'd also not notice if she was eating an apple.

Because my family were butchers, W. G. Lewis & Son, my Wales is that of the slaughterhouse yard, with the huge old boiler, the rusty pipes, gauges and flues. The flagged floor, with big brass rings set into it. The open drains, hoists, pulleys and rivers of blood. The spoil heaps. The hides and piles of sawdust. The grime.

Living in a slaughterhouse, I got used to dung-hill smells; the smells of rot and death. The sharp cold tang of fresh meat from the walk-in fridge; the dull fatty sourness after meat has been hanging about – my father had something of this. The warm sickliness of freshly killed meat – as I walked among them, the red and yellow sides of beef would always take me by surprise by twitching, the nerves here and there literally defying death. For a day or so, bits of sinew and muscle were continuing to live. Frankenstein would have been entranced.

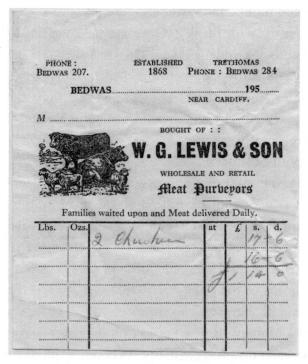

Wales, though. You'd think the dry-ice machine was working full pelt once you cross the Severn Bridge, the way people go on about mystical Wales, bardic Wales, folkloristic Wales. Perhaps one day it will be a separate little state, like the Duchy of Grand

Fenwick in *The Mouse That Roared*. Wales could issue its own stamps. Maybe it already does that.

My friend Jan Morris holds these romantic views. Her hero is Owen Glendower, or Owain Glyndwr as she inevitably spells it. He was something of a magician, who made his palace sink into a lake and become invisible, according to Jan. Surely the more likely story is that he built it on a bog and there was subsidence. He was probably not much of a mechanical engineer. And it is easy to vanish in Wales – into the fog and the warm black rain.

I know it is a country of castles and forts and earthworks; of pit-gears and huge iron spinning wheels; of stone circles – some as old as sixty or seventy years and erected for an eisteddfod; of wizards and monks and religious ecstasy and madness. But it is also a country with fucking awful poems and songs about oak leaves, ponds at midnight, the bread of heaven and making sure you bring your little saucepan back.

My Wales (such as it is – I mean the one that goes through me like a watermark) remains Bedwas, Machen and Trethomas. Can there be a drearier spot than Trethomas? Specifically that intersection of Llanfabon Drive and Bryn Dolwen, where the Spar shop is? The cheap construction of those poxy brown pebbledash houses – so stark and cold. Put up by Wimpey in the Fifties for Coal Board employees. Messy streets with old cars on the muddy grass – you can't call them lawns or gardens. Nothing of beauty on view. Woeful. *Fucking* woeful. The houses are built up against the slag heaps of the colliery. What could be more dreary? The black stone of the claustrophobic terraces – I knew somebody who had a Mongol sister who was kept upstairs in one of those addresses and never seen, whose existence was never mentioned.

Artistically, however, my imagination – that bit of you that escapes circumstance – owes much to Graham Sutherland's thorny, insectile Pembrokeshire, to John Piper's orange and black skies, and the mansions he drew that are settings for Jacobean masques. I like the Camelot Wales of the Butes at Cardiff Castle. The *Casino Royale* Sixties Wales of the Investiture, which was designed by Snowdon and Carl Toms.

We had a concert in Bedwas for that. Rehearsed for months. I was dolled up as a guardsman and wore a red dressing gown with plastic ladybird-shaped buttons and a bearskin made from purple crepe paper. I banged out the beat of 'Men of Harlech' and 'God Bless the Prince of Wales' on a snare drum. Annette Maslen (Annette Filer before she married a man who restored drop-leaf tables), a woman who went in for having a swooping actressy voice, like Maggie Smith's, and who took the vamp roles when *Offenbach* was put on by the Craig Amateur Operatic Society, conducted the band. It was her big night.

❧

Glory did shine upon the place once – on Wednesday 6 November 1946, wearing her favourite dress of Chinese green silk, Kathleen Ferrier, no less, gave a recital in Bedwas Workmen's Hall. Seven years later, she died.

❧

Caerphilly Castle: I was born in its shadow (well, in the Miners' Hospital nearby) – I'm always surprised how bleak it is: the smooth blackish-green walls and the brown lakes, with their dangerous sluices. There is no decor or ornament of any kind. It is something of a fist – like Mussolini's restoration of Rhodes Old Town or the over-restored city of Carcassonne. It is a building – the second-biggest castle in Europe after Windsor – that, as it were, *stares one down*. Of course the Marquess of Bute restored Caerphilly Castle in the Thirties and it has the austere planes, curves and lines of that era. What we might call a Dictator's Art Deco. Leni Riefenstahl could have mounted pageant in Caerphilly Castle. It has none of the fairy whimsy of Castell Coch or Cardiff Castle, the other nearby Bute properties. I think I'd have preferred it in its ruined state. It had elegance and mystery when shrouded with brambles – I have seen old daguerreotypes showing this. Picturesque debris.

No wonder Polanski filmed *Macbeth* in Wales, at Castell Coch, even if his masterpiece turns into an instant laughing stock when Keith Chegwin comes on as Fleance. Wrapped in drizzle and rainclouds, the place is full of witches. Another film filmed at Castell Coch/The Red Castle was *Barry Mackenzie Holds His Own*, where South Wales (easily) stands in for Transylvania. In that little photoplay, Dame Edna Everage, the biggest witch ever created, is kidnapped by Donald Pleasance.

Long before Llandaff's Roald Dahl came up with the conceit, I used to think Bedwas NSPCC was a secret coven of witches. Perhaps they were simply plain freaky hags. Nevertheless, they'd turn up for their meetings in cars with purple curtains and tassels, which spat fire from the exhaust. My mother did her stint as the honorary treasurer, until it was pointed out that the columns of figures would never quite tot up accurately if she kept adding in the date.

↬

During my childhood, the Victorian world was still to be found, though dying. All the old people about the place were from the previous century. They had been through two world wars and an uncle in Abertridwr had served in the Boer War. The furniture and books in dark panelled rooms were old and dusty. There was a stone barn in the Arch Field containing abandoned agricultural machinery from the days of slow shire horses – the ploughs, hay-tossing devices, threshers, saddles and horse-brasses. Bedwas was a mining village, with slag heaps on the hill and a pit-head wheel, but rural life went on – blacksmiths, gravediggers digging in the warm damp earth, the district nurse on her bicycle. My father could identity grasses and country flowers and winter flowers. The hedges were full of berries. There were hayricks and dark red cattle. What all this gave me was a preference for things that are out of date.

↬

Every Saturday, until I went to university, and again during the vacations, when Anna drove the van, I used to earn my keep delivering meat around Caerphilly and along Pandy Road. I could follow those routes now, and still do in my head when I can't sleep. What I remember is that the customers were very clean. They were often still damp after their weekly bath, and would be sitting there in their vests. I'd collect the money in a leather satchel and write down in a stout red book what they wanted delivered mid-week or next week – the joints and chops, the scrag-end and brisket. I enjoyed going into people's houses – like any Welsh person, I am a nosy and inquisitive bastard and that is why I am or was a biographer. I am also deeply secretive and evasive when it comes to my own self – again: Welsh.

❧

I have a few envelopes stuffed with miscellaneous papers. That's all that's left of any of them, my ancestors in Wales. Invoices for boots, collars and gloves. Funeral announcements. Unfilled-in pocket diaries. There's also a bundle of muzzy unannotated photographs, so at this distance these people will never again be identified. But they'd have all known each other once upon a time, these women in the cloche hats, these men in collars and ties, smoking their cigarettes. On the beach at Ilfracombe. A charabanc trip to Cheddar Gorge. Dog shows. Agricultural shows.

I have a group photograph of my great-grandfather and great-grandmother with all their grown-up children. They are assembled in what looks like a Garden Centre or the play area of a Happy Eater. The actual location was the patio next to Dolly the wet nurse's grace and favour lean-to. They are attired for a wedding – whose I wonder? It is exactly like Larkin's sardonic lines: the 'fools in old-style hats and coats,/Who half the time were soppy stern/And half at one another's throats.'

Those tailcoats the men are wearing weren't hired, incidentally. They were bespoke and hung in the wardrobes at Troedyrhiw House,* eventually making their way to the attics – and into my home-movies. I salvaged one of them and wore it at my own wedding, at various graduation ceremonies and to the Encaenia at Oxford. Harold Macmillan saw me in it, when we doffed mortar boards at each other and spoke Latin. It wouldn't fit me now. I'd have to lose five stone. A century on from its creation, the garment currently resides in Oscar's room in Bromyard. It is in perfect condition still. Magnificent tailoring. I also accumulated top hats and bowler hats, which I gave to Tristan for the circus.

* Briefly wealthy in the Edwardian era, my family built a nine-bedroom red-brick villa up the road from the shop, at the foot of the hill: hence (in Welsh) Troedyrhiw. That's where my grandparents were to be found. When my grandfather died in 1973, my parents, who until then had lived above the butcher's shop, went there to live themselves. Troedyrhiw was later sold and became an old folks' home. The first thing the new owners did was to rip out the marble fireplaces and box in the carved solid walnut staircase.

In the middle at the front there – dominating in every sense – is my great-grandfather, Wyndham Gardner Lewis. He looks a humorous, wise old thing, like the town marshal in a Western. I bet he was very proud of that moustache. He drank a bottle of whisky every day and used to eat raw bacon fat, which he'd slice from the slabs of cured meat suspended from the ceiling. On his left is my great-grandmother, Mary Blanche Rowland, who came from a village north of Caerphilly called Abertridwr. Her cousin was the Bishop of St David's, William Havard.

A splendid-sounding fellow, the Right Reverend William Thomas Havard (1889–1956) was a chaplain during the Kaiser War, when he was Mentioned in Dispatches and awarded the Military Cross. In the Twenties he was the Dean of Divinity at Jesus College, Oxford, where he gained his rugger blue. He later played for Wales against New Zealand. He was capable of preaching in both the Welsh and English languages, was a Visiting Lecturer at St Andrews, and became Chairman of the Education Council of the Church in Wales. He did very well for a man with a Third in History.

Such was his illustriousness, it was a connection that made my own family think they were minor gentry – or, because this was industrial South Wales, gentry. But Wyndham Gardner Lewis was never more than the Bedwas butcher, even if his brother, Edgar, was High Sheriff of Monmouthshire – and in due course the grandfather of my cousin-several-times-removed Jeremy Lewis, who has had a much more successful career as an author than me. Jeremy has been drawn by David Hockney. David Hockney hasn't even offered to cover me from head to foot in whitewash. Jeremy is a Fellow of the Royal Society of Literature, a body that has repeatedly slammed the door in my face *again* and *again* and *again* and *again* for decades.

Wyndham Gardner Lewis and Mary Blanche Rowland were married in 1895 at Eglwysilan Parish Church. *Eglwys* is Welsh for church, like the French *eglise*. Welsh is perhaps French with added lisps and coughs and splutterings. St Ilan was, or is, one of the least-known Welsh saints, and that's saying something.

The year 1895: the *fin-de-siècle* was at its most rampant! *The Yellow Book* was being published by Elkin Matthews and John Lane. Victoria was on the throne, Lord Salisbury was in Downing Street, and a week before my great-grandparents' wedding, Oscar Wilde had been arrested at the Cadogan Hotel. Elsewhere in that seminal year, Lifebuoy soap went on sale for the first time, and Hardy wrote *Jude the Obscure*. Robert Graves and Prince Albert (later George VI) were born – and one way and another I am already hidden in the future.

Mary Blanche née Rowland had thirteen babies in total – the ones in the sepia group photograph, plus Elizabeth Jennett (b. April 1897), Enid Mary (b. June 1899) and Blanche (b. September 1900) who croaked in earliest infancy, poor dabs. These names are inscribed on the family tomb. I've often wondered this – back in the Victorian days when everyone had big families so that at least by the law of averages some would survive to maturity, was the grief as searing as the grief about dead babies is today? How can we ever tell? These things cannot be measured. Yet it must have been. It must have been so.

That poor woman: *thirteen* babies! It was said my great-grandfather only had to throw his trousers on the bed and she was pregnant. Her minge tunnel must have been like a wizard's sleeve, though you wouldn't think that to look at her here. She looks like Virginia Woolf's Mrs Dalloway.

❦

It was the year of the Mexico Olympics when I was sent away to live with my other grandparents, my mother's lot, in Upper Machen – to a Georgian farmhouse called The Gelli, pronounced Gethley, which smelt of meat and vegetables and half the time was filled with my coarse uncles, my mother's brothers, grinning, chuckling and ruddy-faced, looming over me like ventriloquist's dolls. Hard glassy eyes, they seemed to have, and though there was a mood of constant levity, there was no lightness of heart, only incessant ridicule, or so it seemed to me. The grinning and the glaring and hyena laughs were forced and derisive, related, I always felt, to an animal's habits of spitting and biting and snarling. It was all nips and pinches, insults and condescension – an absolute avoidance of tenderness. Farting and swearing were much prized.

Scene of the Author's Banishment

How different the men's voices were in the morning, until they'd cut the phlegm with cigarettes. The blue pall of smoke hovered across the room – like the ghosts of dead babies as depicted in the *Casper* cartoon. My uncles would cough until their puce faces went black. Their spittle was black.

I am always sensitive to anger or disapproval, to malevolence, somewhere in a room. This started when I was at The Gelli. One of my uncles, a feckless sponging alcoholic called Eric, used to extort money from his parents – my Grandpa and Grandma George. He'd get nasty if he couldn't get his way – frightening them into signing cheques for his business ventures that never came off and always went bust: a yacht accessory shop in the Gower, a pub at Nottage, a community magazine for Caerphilly. He had a sickly charm, I suppose – and there were various bastards that had to be provided for (not by Eric). He used to beat up his wife, throw her down the stairs, and she'd appear occasionally, bruised and helpless, seeking sanctuary. Eric was a monster – after disappearing for a while as a steward on a liner, he ended up claiming a 'Carer's Allowance' for neglecting Grandma George, whose furniture he sold off. She sat there in an empty house in a deckchair. News only reached us last year that Eric had died in a nursing home for retired Royal Air Force officers. He'd been pretending to be an ex-squadron leader.

✷

I loved wandering off on my own, poking around in cupboards or the backs of drawers, where I'd find sets of Great War medals or postcards from Mr and Mrs Charles, richer farming neighbours who'd visited California. I was once given Jack Charles's hand-me-down bespoke two-tone tan brogues. I still have them in fact, though I can't bend down to do up the laces. I got them re-soled in The Turl, when I was at Magdalen.

✷

Crime Wave Corner. 'Thieves' (who else?) have been stealing salt and grit from the salt and grit bins in Glewstone. A spokesman from the council said, 'Herefordshire takes such thefts seriously and would ask the public to report any suspicious activity.' It'll be the damn squirrels again – check their burrows. Frisk squirrels on sight, say I.

✷

I've just had to sit through luncheon with an ex-curate. With religious people – why are we meant to assume that these vows

33

of poverty are admirable? I had to listen to this ex-curate crap on about how marvellous the Bishop of Tanzania was because he, the Bishop of Tanzania, only possessed one pair of underpants. I prefer to believe that poverty – as the butler says in *Sullivan's Travels* – is not the lack of anything, but a 'positive plague, virulent in itself, contagious as cholera. It is to be stayed away from, even for the purposes of study. It is to be shunned.'

It would seem to me that the less people have materially (like all those sods in desert countries), the more religious they are – therefore, the more sophisticated and advanced a culture is (e.g. Western Europe), the less it needs to rely on such supernatural tenets as looking forward to the afterlife, worshipping a deity who is in charge of our destinies. We have evolved – we have Ikea and the John Lewis Partnership; we have Tesco's Online Shopping – and don't require religion, in its traditional forms. You'd have thought all this would be admirable. What is the point of pretending to admire and accord respect to a Stone Age or primitive society; or in wanting to re-establish such a society (e.g. through totalitarian means, such as radical Islam)? I love my *things*, my *clutter*. I appreciate adornment.

❧

Where I'm happiest (not that I trust being happy) is in Austria: the elaborately carved altars and church tableaux, e.g. The Adoration of the Magi in Gmunden; the high altar in St Wolfgang. The figurines, the angels and saints, glow with gold and black – and the poised heads and hands, the gestures, are very theatrical. I'm reminded of the Salzburg Marionette Theatre. Perhaps there are links? A local wood-carving tradition and skill, the pine and the spruce? The stylised presentation of the wooden figures – the effigies – and the way the puppets seem to be springing to life: this is scary. I am put in mind of wood-demons and trolls; or of the three ethereal boys in *The Magic Flute*: 'the power that lifts them into the air is greater than that which ties them to earth' (Kleist).

I remember as a child being lifted into the air by my father, to look at a carved mahogany cherub on my grandmother's Welsh dresser. He was trying to show me that it was not frightening – but face to face suddenly with this scowling fat brown polished goblin I was screaming.

∽

There are angels all over Austria.

∽

The Austrian baroque statuary is light and fluffy, like the pastry. White and pale blue. Spanish and Italian churches leer down at the worshipper, dark and sinister – demonic, threatening, haunted.

∽

Traditional English hymns – often adapted from German poems and tunes. But look at the imagery: the many references to pools, rivers, water. It is an English landscape, pacific and tranquil. Yet the underthump is martial, imperial, and about conquest and mightiness. Quite right. I'm all for that.

∽

I've been watching Jacques Tati. I love Tati even if I don't find him particularly funny. I love looking at his images of provincial France, particularly the oddly shaped timber-framed boarding house and the hotel on the sands in *Les Vacances de Monsieur Hulot*, or the hay fields and galloping horses in *Jour de Fête*. It's like the Normandy I recall from having lived there.

That's a great opening gag, too, in *Les Vacances de Monsieur Hulot*, with the crowds of noisy panic-stricken people, clutching their heavy luggage and trying to find the correct platform – up and down the steps they go, as the steam trains glide in and out and the tannoy barks sharp instructions. Though the film was made thirteen years after the end of the war, to what extent I wonder is this an allusion to France's round-up of its Jewish population? I can never see those little cardboard suitcases on a foreign station without being reminded of such deportations.

How busy everyone keeps themselves – the rituals of recreation. Excursions, meals, fancy dress parties, card games, keep-fit exercise on the beach. There's a running joke about a businessman in white shorts always needing to be near the phone, and he is finally called to the phone when he is in the sea.

సౌ

It's a bit chilly, now and again, too, the mood, with the funeral sequence and that long convoy of cars, detouring across a field – towards nowhere. The soundtrack is composed of echoes.

సౌ

Tati's face: he doesn't have Keaton's battered, weathered clown's face, or Chaplin's conniving face. He almost doesn't register things. He never expresses surprise. Fellini wanted him for Don Quixote. If he reminds me of anyone it is Fernando Rey.

సౌ

When Tati spent some time in England, he played rugby in Sydenham – also in the team was Johnnie Cradock, Fanny's future husband. This is one of the three strangest facts I know.

సౌ

His films have the precision and lightness of a line drawing. *Playtime*, set in a city of glass and steel that is beautiful, is like abstract art, with its greys and pale blues. The street lamps are in the shape of flowers.

సౌ

The thing about *Les Vacances de Monsieur Hulot* – i.e. *Monsieur Hulot's Holiday* – is that M. Hulot is always on holiday. He never does a stroke of work or has any cares or responsibilities. In *Mon Oncle*, his sister attempts to get him a job in a factory. This predictably does not succeed. He's more at home with the wild children or the wild packs of dogs, among whom is Dackie.

సౌ

I love Dackie, the dog in *Mon Oncle* – he's the star of the show. His master wears a matching tartan smoking jacket. Is there a funnier scene in movies than the one where Dackie's wagging tail activates the electronic beam for the garage door, which slams shut on the Arpels?

✎

The principal colour of Tati's *Trafic* (only one *eff*) is yellow. Egg yolks, custard, Van Gogh's sunflowers, the sun itself. It was filmed in Holland.

✎

What I'd liked to have seen – Jacques Tati as Don Quixote and Tommy Cooper as Sancho Panza. Instead of a nag and a donkey, a motorcycle and side-car. The hotel at night. Long, loud fart. Quixote enters the bedroom and lights a candle. Huge explosion. We cut to the pair of them on the road the next day, their faces blackened by smoke. Sancho produces and hands over to his master, as they are driving along, a cup of tea.

✎

What I have noticed about Tommy Cooper (born like me in Caerphilly) – he is in this magic fog; a strange mist envelops him and all he does – a spell is cast and we are invited in. Sir Ralph Richardson, W. C. Fields, Tati, Sellers (as Clouseau) – they all had this quality; they managed to make us believe that the normal laws of the universe are suspended. Seemingly clumsy or accident prone, they are of course immensely elegant – as elegant as dancers.

Compare them with the comedians I don't find funny (Billy Connolly say) – who are sharp and pointed; sharp and *pointy*. Too fond of themselves rather than being a mystery to themselves.

✎

Though I think of myself as generally friendless (solitary, moody, a pain), there's nobody I laugh with more than with Craig Brown. A literary masterpiece beloved by us both is *The Crossroads Cookbook*, with its helpful translations from the French: 'Chasseur is the French for "huntsman", and the theory is that the hungry hunter

37

(not you, David!) collected some mushrooms on his way home through the wild autumnal woods'; its tips on how the nervous young housewife can avoid lumps in her sauces; its glorification – its deification – of the pineapple chunk.

Craig lives in a *maison de maitre* in Aldeburgh that gets pelted by pebbles during storms. I visited once. No, twice. There's a huge marble fireplace upstairs, with firelighters from the Co-op that won't light. A grand piano, upon which Chopin is strummed by Regimental Sergeant-Major Welch, Craig's studious wife. A dog called Beetle – though to get this chronicle up to date, Beetle now (2011) resides in a Tupperware box in the pantry next to the Weetabix. The new Beetle is Pip, a West Highland terrier, 'who is a lot easier' – though surely not as easy as a pile of ashes?

I kept thinking it was 4.14 in the afternoon all day, but that was the temperature in the fridge. When it is British Summer Time, the temperature in the fridge goes on an hour – to 5.15.

Given the chance, Craig and I like to dine on *Crossroads* specialities, such as Honey Glazed Gammon ('Here is a dish Meg Richardson particularly enjoyed') and Pavlova ('I bet that must have slowed up her Dying Swan quite a bit' – a classic quip of Sandy's).

This all on my mind today because I've been eating Grapefruit with Prawns, Crown Roast of Lamb and Chocolate Mousse. If I can't live in the past, I can at least eat its meals.

❧

How young the old people in books are. Mr Knightley is thirty-eight. Perks in *The Railway Children* is thirty-two. Casaubon? It has to be plausible, his marriage to Dorothea. So he'll be forty, I reckon. Craig said King Lear is seventeen.

❧

One of my favourite hotels is the Europa in Prague. They spell it Evropa. Gloomy, dusty, sepulchral, with a miserable porter creeping from floor to floor, turning off the lights. The night porter wears a heavy three-piece suit and drags his lame club foot behind him, Karloff fashion. Cut glass, etched glass, smoked glass; Art Nouveau mirrors, cornices and tiles; vertiginous light wells. It would make my ideal *pomme de terre*, as it would also for Count Dracula. But the Europa/Evropa may be rivalled in my affections by the Hotel de Paris, on the Norfolk coast. I've been giving it a Google. Paradise.

✴

One of the little games I play to help pass the time – which will pass anyway, I do know that much – is to try and anticipate the subject of Libby Purves's next column: attend to the wisdom of the old; good manners ought to be encouraged; demoralised teachers should be given a boost; even non-celebrities are important in their own circles locally. It's incredible how often I am correct. Libby used to scare the living daylights out of London's literary crowd by breastfeeding openly at parties – openly breastfeeding her babies, I mean, not breastfeeding Salman Rushdie or Auberon Waugh.

✴

One of my favourite scenes – Danny Kaye doing 'the vessel with the pestle has the pellet with the poison; the flagon with the dragon is the brew that is true', from *The Court Jester*. The gag originated with Eddie Cantor in *Roman Scandals*: he's Nero's food-taster and there's a line about the poison being in the partridge with the parsley. Then there is Bob Hope in *Never Say Die*: 'There's a notch on the muzzle of the pistol with the bullet and a nick on the handle of the gun with the blank.' My friend George in New York can recite all these beautifully.

✴

'Free Chlamydia Testing Here' – Can you possibly imagine a more thoroughly off-putting sign? Nevertheless, there it was prominently, in the window of a chemists in Malvern Link. What in the name of Satan's Portion are you meant to do? Go in and flash your poorly fanny (your front bottom, your Wookey Hole)

39

at the pharmacist? Actually, I didn't know that Chlamydia was a sexually transmitted infection, until Anna explained. I thought it was a posh bird's name, like Candida.

❧

It is already twenty-nine years since Pat Phoenix, who played Elsie Tanner in *Coronation Street*, visited Moreton-on-Lugg to promote Pye radiograms and present the keys of an Austin Mini to the winner of a raffle.

February

What am I still doing here? I've been awake hours. I'm like that Princess with her pea. The slightest thing on my mind, I can't sleep. A letter that needs posting off – I can't sleep. I toss and turn anxiously. It's the same when I'm staying at hotels – the dread of the maid coming in and catching me unawares, on the bog or in the buff (which one of us would be the most terrified or traumatised?); or the demented hours they have for breakfast – I can't sleep because I know I have to get up. I've never slept on an aeroplane or on holiday, unless unconscious (blotto) from drink.

'Wales is so little different from England, that it offers nothing to the speculation of the traveller' – Doctor Johnson to Boswell in 1774. Try saying that to Doctor Lewis in 2011 you twat-shaped twat and I'll knock your wig off.

In Mrs Harrington's class we spent a year doing a project on Australia. It put me off ever wanting to go there – because I have fully imagined it. Upside-down and inside-out, with night and day reversed and the seasons topsy-turvy. I have a book that explains everything. *The Children of Down-Under*, badly printed in overlapping colours, it pictures the place as a red planet, like Mars, populated by roos, abbos standing on one leg, and merino sheep. The only adult in that vast rich land was Chips Rafferty. Dame Barry Humphries told me he couldn't wait to leave Australia for Europe – 'I hankered for a damper climate.' He should have pitched up in Wales, then.

❧

My mother's kitchen – upgraded several dozen times since, I am sure (rumours have reached me of a conservatory extension), but I'm talking about my childhood, when it was something of a death-trap. Everything was broken. Chipped cups and mismatched plates too wretched to put under plant pots. Bone-handled knives eroded by the dishwasher. The cutlery drawer a tangle of tarnished prongs. The powder-dispenser didn't work on the dishwasher so the powder was ladled in with a trowel from the garden. You had to hold the washing-machine door shut for ten minutes to activate the switch. There was no actual drain outside, so everything from the sinks and the appliances poured through a spout in the wall and created scummy lakes. Inevitably a tyre floated in the scummy lake. On the cooker, the OFF/LOW switch actually meant ON/HIGH. My mother didn't go in for popular cleaning fluids like Jif (now re-named Cif – why?) or J-cloths, only thick brown towels from the butcher's shop. The Hoover pipes and hoses were repaired with bandages. And now I'm exactly the same. I kicked up a hell of a fuss when Anna wanted to replace the broken fridge and oven. The toilet only got mended because even I got fed up with plunging my hand into the cistern to activate the flush mechanism.

❧

In the 24 February edition of the *Hereford Times*, a Mr Eric Morris was incorrectly referred to as Derek Morris. What a cloth-eared reporter. Worse still, John Saunders of Upton Bishop died on 9 December from asbestos exposure, not on 12 December. These earth-shattering inaccuracies.

❧

I have a Frank Auerbach etching. Black and silver squiggles, which I thought depicted a crumpled bed, because Auerbach is fond of drawing his subjects asleep. Splinters of line, nervous broken-off strokes: a nightmare of tangled sheets and heavy blankets. Looking again, however, and rotating the thing, I'm now pretty certain that, on the contrary, it is a close-up drawing of a woman's head. Nose, forehead, hairline, chin, ears can just about be made out – but it is by no means clear or clear-cut. So the scribbles must be wrinkles and strands of hair – and the face is rather ghostly, as if it is on its way to disappearing. (People asleep in paintings and photographs usually look dead.) All the erasures and crossings out, the fierce rubbing out and, in his paintings, the scraping away of pigment, then piling it on: Auerbach is a very unconfident artist, never certain whether he has finished or not – labouring at something that looks sketchy, provisional, unformed, panic-stricken. He must be a genius to produce work that resembles the efforts of a backward child.

✥

Verdi's *Falstaff* was my father's favourite opera, as it is mine. Bryn Terfel (real name: Doris Klunt) has the virility of voice, which suits the virility of the character. Falstaff isn't an old disgusting lecher, though that is how he is always portrayed – always the same costume, too, the vast belly, an equator-size belt, medieval sleeves and tights; the curly grey beard and bald pate. But inside – which is what music represents – he is still lusty and forthright. The music is full of trillings and gambollings. He should be admired for his seductiveness – for his persistence, as he chases the merry wives and tries to ignore the chimes at midnight, i.e. death. But winter is closing in fast.

Why, by the way, is *mezzanotte* far more thrilling than 'midnight'? In the opera we actually do hear the chimes at midnight, and it's one of my favourite scenes, that final act in Windsor Great Park. I wonder if anyone has done the opera in modern dress. There's Italian sunshine in Verdi's music. It's not Windsor, it's Roma! Marcello Mastroianni was Verdi's Falstaff. What a film Fellini could have made.

I suddenly realised what *Falstaff* is like – the trilling, tripping, flighty music: the opera is full of birds, birdsong; a parliament of fowls. Full-throated calls, chirrups, peckings – the fussy, beady-eyed, waddling women; hawks, barnyard birds, songbirds, crows. The parroting of Mistress Quickly; the trilling of Alice Ford; Falstaff the preening, massive turkey-cock. Like pheasants or partridges – the russet gleam of the plumage, and the whir of wings; autumnal – or winter. A shooting party. Reds, browns, golds. The hunting season, stalking, camouflage. The musical beat is of birds hopping, looking for worms and grain. Nanetta and Fenton: the billing and cooing of love birds, of two pigeons. Chickens in the barn, gossiping together, flare-ups, clucking – hens enjoying their own malice and panic. A production could be mounted to express this – feathers, fluttering; to be set in a farmyard, with rusty farm equipment, old tractors, split fertilizer bags. Woodcocks and ortolans; woods and bracken; scented wood fires; goose livers, garlic, mushrooms, juniper berries. Poultry.

❧

After three weeks away, I had a job shaking out imperial Austria from my system and settling again in feudal Bromyard. It's no good going into Laming's the bakers and saying, 'Show me your torte!' On the other hand, Konditorei Zauner's doesn't run to Eccles cakes, iced slices and ham baps.

❧

The world I was raised to be in no longer exists. Is being wilfully destroyed in fact. Even Austria worries me on this score. The new buildings that are going up everywhere are ugly and spiky beyond. It is as if they deliberately don't want anything that looks a bit Habsburg. Salzburg railway station is being re-developed. Yet I used to appreciate the offices there, the marble stairways and ironwork, the mahogany booking hall. All being torn out. There's a hotel in Bad Ischl called the Hubertushof. They have just had a new extension built, fronting the road next to the Kaiservilla gates. It is like a nasty Sixties golf club. They tore down a lovely glassed-in veranda.

It is ignorance, really – and the fact that architects these days are qualified in physics and engineering and whatnot and have zero artistic sense or cultural knowledge. All part of everyone wanting to shake off the past. One has *vague sympathy* with this in Austria, I suppose, given how the Second World War kicked off. Though the past is the only place I want to be.

Ֆ

All these impressions – travelling by train from Austria to Venice on the 10.12 a.m. from Salzburg, which got me to the Serenissima in time for tea. What a terrible tea it was – the worst sandwich in the world (for the price) at the Gritti: white sliced plastic bread and a bit of red gristle. Thirty-five Euros. They do it better in the Bromyard Co-op. I haven't stopped moaning to Michael Winner about it.

Apart from sitting on a Japanese lady whom I mistook for a bench on Gleis 5 of the Salzburg Hauptbahnhof, nothing much went wrong, though over the fact that I fell asleep in the Dining Car and woke up as the train pulled into Zagreb we shall draw a discreet veil. It's quite nice, Zagreb.

The onion-domed churches vanished, and campaniles replaced them. The steep roofs of mountain buildings gradually became gentler, flatter. Wood gave way to stone in the construction, then brick. An ornamental, Mediterranean (or Adriatic) style started to become apparent. There is also a self-conscious flamboyance about the Italians themselves – they all wear sunglasses indoors. Have you noticed? They think they are movie stars at Cinecitta. This annoys me.

There's a scruffiness, too, in Italy. Litter in the gutters. Unemptied bins. Broken umbrellas outside cafés. In Austria, shop windows are polished twice a day. Still, better they use their surplus energy up doing that than in invading Poland. In Bromyard I never wash the windows, as otherwise the glass would fall out. You'd think the panes had been put in with Vaseline.

Having checked and double-checked that the Venice Carnival was not on, because I'd wanted at all costs to avoid it, the Venice Carnival was on. Lots of people in eighteenth-century-style cloaks and tricorne hats and masks, as if they were performing in an outdoor production of *Don Giovanni*. There's something quite erotic about a mask – you don't know if what's behind it is lovely or gross. If I were to put one on and take it off, however, everyone would make me put it back on again. Bastards.

Most churches were closed. Well, it was Sunday, wasn't it? I noticed that the bridges have ramps – ugly planks and scaffolding – for the cripples. They are allowed to get everywhere now.

At night the drains gurgled and large puddles emerged between the stones. St Mark's Square had quite a number of deep pools. Not sewage water – sea water. Nature is reclaiming the city. Nothing can be done about this, which doesn't displease me.

❧

How dilapidated it is; very little seems thoroughly restored. It is still Ruskin's city of collapsing doorframes and broken windows, eroded brickwork and leaking roofs. It is a city that attracts the bereaved – the couple in *Don't Look Now*; or poor old disintegrating Aschenbach. Wagner too died in Venice. Ezra Pound. Diaghilev. I also have any number of books with moody photographs of the mists and fogs. There's even a film with Klaus Kinski called *Nosferatu in Venice*. I'd like to see that.

It is a place for those mastering the art of losing – and I kept feeling my father's presence (or absence) very strongly; the city he never visited but would have loved. He was never here – but I got a sense of him, causing me to stop with a quick intake of breath. There are lots of old boys around who look like him – prosperous gents in expensive coats and hats and polished shoes. I keep seeing his ghost, as if it were waiting for me in the wet dusk. And it is a city of apparitions, of disappearances – the alleys and bridges and black shadows. This wonderful town.

St Mark's Basilica — more of a fortress than a holy place. Ramparts and turrets. The greenish gold — and the extraordinary rolling, undulating floor, as if it is under the sea; the aqueous light; the gold and red thrones for the doges, like Bacon's electric chairs. The horses — apocalyptic beasts; winged lions; flying monsters. Green, verdigris, warlike, supernatural.

❧

From one of those shops selling handmade paper, I bought a little drawing book, a glass pen blown on Murano, and a bottle of ink — and sent it to Ronald Searle. At ninety-one, he may need his supplies replenished.

❧

Gyles Brandreth has had a hard year. His mother died. His brother died. During his one-man show in Redditch a man died in the second act. They are clearly tough and unyielding critics in Redditch (pop. 77,128 — though better make that 77,127).

Redditch was the birthplace of Charles Dance, but as I did not read any press reports of his unusual death, or even his death, I wonder was it Robert Harris dropping dead to make a point?

Not that I committed this to memory or anything, but in the *Sunday Times* on 1 November 2009, Robert Harris really did write of poor old millionaire National Treasure candidate Gyles Brandreth: 'Limitless energy and a desire to show off can take a man only so far . . . There is a weird failure to develop, either professionally or emotionally.' I wonder what this means exactly? Limitless energy is a good thing to possess, and only mediocrities develop. Yet Harris was poking his tongue out and clearly intending to be derogatory. Added to which, this is also a perfect description of me.

❧

Crime Wave Corner. A tractor and a water pump have been stolen by 'thieves' (again) from a farm in Dilwyn.

My birthday weekend. I decreed that I wanted no presents, no fuss. I was taken at my word. I was given a shoe horn, a towel rack for the bathroom, and a salt and pepper set in the shape of Laurel and Hardy, with Laurel missing. Two cards.

Last year for my birthday we went to London for the weekend and at one point piled into Mark Rylance's dressing room. Mackenzie Crook was cowering in a corner and I said I wanted him to play my Charles Hawtrey in a Charles Hawtrey biopic. I've also already offered this role to John Hurt and little Tony Robinson, him off *Blackadder*, who took offence. If they all decide to accept, I'll be devising a surprising script about identical triplets.

Mark, so massive and imposing as Rooster Byron on stage in *Jerusalem*, had shrunk back to his normal size after the show. I've known him since he played Peter Pan for the Royal Shakespeare Company, getting on for thirty years ago. He has a fascinating, ethereal dimension – as if Shakespeare had Mark in mind when he created Ariel, Puck, Oberon, Hamlet.

Mark Rylance and the unfeasibly slender Author stroke their pussies, c. 1985

Anyway, this time it was cocktails at the Groucho. *Frankenstein* at the National. Drinks at the Savoy. Dinner at Rules. That was the plan, as well organised as Churchill's funeral. Oscar missed his train. The cast of *Frankenstein* had the shits and the understudies went on – indeed, they ran out of understudies and for the role of Victor Frankenstein's father they'd seemingly roped in Mr Patel from the corner shop down the Waterloo Road. And parenthetically what would Sir Laurence Olivier have thought had he seen on the Olivier stage that bears his illustrious name, Jonny Lee Miller, red and raw and in the buff with a half-hard, squirming about and grunting as he learns to be alive?*

* The understudies – and the understudies' understudies – went on: except Jonny Lee Miller, who was truly powerful and athletic as The Creature. We did indeed have twenty minutes at the start to fully admire what in *Young Frankenstein* is called his 'enormous schwanzstucker'. The Creature was also warmly intelligent – as well as being a mass murderer, though we forgave him that as he was only copying the ways of mankind. That was rubbed in by the script.

He was sexy somehow – you sense why Elizabeth, the doc's neglected fiancée, is attracted to him, though he mars the good opinion she is beginning to form of him by twisting her head off. You can see how Mary Shelley based the character on Lord Byron. Years ago I saw a version of *Frankenstein* written by Christopher Isherwood – the monster was beautiful to begin with and grew physically repulsive as he acquired more and more human experience. James Mason was Doctor Polidori, Frankenstein's mad mentor. I think Ralph Richardson was the blind hermit. What a cast.

A rather Spartan staging, here at the National, except for the massive bank of pulsing lights overhead – fierce, scorching electromagnetism. It was *Monsieur* Frankenstein, too, I noticed – he's even lost his barony now.

No traditional creation scene (no shrill 'It's alive!'), no hunchbacks (no 'Igor, throw the third switch!'), no tension or fear about what the monster will be like once unveiled, no spooky castles on hilltops. (We were in the Orkneys for some reason.) Castle Frankenstein was a few window frames and a tilted floor.

I liked the bell, which was suspended above the stalls. I wouldn't half have minded giving that a ding. But they could have done such a memorable creation scene in the Olivier, using their state-of-the-art stage machinery.

At the Savoy, the American Bar was full, so we had a glass of champagne in the cupboard where they keep the coats, served by an obliging though sinister dwarf who looked like something out of *The Shining*. I'd requested the table with a banquette under the painted skylight in Rules for 10.15. It was approaching midnight when we were shown to a table in the Gents.

I suppose Danny Boyle, the director, was going in mortal dread of James Whale campery or Mel Brooks spoofery. But it was like having a musical without a big dance number. When the Bride of Frankenstein appeared, she popped from behind a hessian shower curtain.

Too many themes, perhaps: master/slave, love/duty, beauty/ugliness, loneliness/companionship, father/child, innocence/experience, love/death. The best lines were quotations from Milton. *Paradise Lost* Milton, not Milton Berle – not that there's anything wrong with Milton Berle, whom legend has it possessed 'an enormous schwanzstucker' too. Possibly the biggest in Hollywood.

I much regret not seeing Benedict Cumberland Sausage as Doctor Frankenstein – though I can perfectly envisage him doing the doc as Sherlock Holmes, i.e. as the haughty genius not good with girls, the intellectual without (overt) feeling. I much admired The Sausage as Sherlock Holmes – he played the role as a very modern gay: acerbic and non-effeminate. Not like the shut-that-door stereotypes we always have. I must admit, though, I used to love Jeremy Brett: so exquisitely agonised.

Really, they should have cut the whole *Frankenstein* thing right back and made it purely a Frankenstein/Creature duologue and put it on in the Cottesloe. Because Jonny Lee Schwanzstucker and Cumberland Sausage alternated the roles of Frankenstein and The Creature, but unless we all saw the show twice, back to back, with the alternate casting, this doubling really went for nothing. Ian Richardson and Richard Pascoe once alternated the roles of Bolingbroke and King Richard II – a similar gimmick.

When Richard Burton and John Neville alternated the roles of Othello and Iago at the Old Vic, they one night had a few drinks and both came on blacked-up as the Noble Moor, though neither noticed. How I'd have loved it if Jonny and The Sausage had got their diaries in a muddle and met on stage and had come face-to-face, both of them twitching and growling in full Creature make-up. If I was a billionaire I'd try and bribe them to do just that.

The way the names are arranged on the posters, *Blithe Spirit* is being performed by Alison Hermione, Robert Ruthie, Steadman Norris and Bathurst Henshall. Weren't Steadman Norris and Bathurt Henshall the cricket-mad old boys in various Hitchcock films? I've always wondered if there is a village somewhere in England called Thorley Walters, with the nearby beauty spots of Peggy Mount and Benny Hill, from the summits of which on a sunny day several counties can be seen. Clamber up Geoffrey Hill and you'd see fuck all. Dense green fogs for miles around.

The Groucho crowd: Steve Pemberton, smaller than you'd expect; Stephen Campbell Moore, taller than you'd expect; Dominic Cooper . . . what was this? *The History Boys* Class Reunion? Leigh Francis was dressed as Keith Lemon, and remained in character. Mine was the only name I didn't recognize.

The fire alarm woke us at 6.30. This was followed by builders and plumbers hammering their hammers and drilling their drills. Hoses and pulsating cables made the stairs a death-trap. The bedrooms, by the way, had been recently refurbished by a comedian – glass doors on the bathroom: Mrs Lewis and I may have been married for nearly thirty years and love each other dearly, but we still don't want to watch each other taking a shit. The window blinds were cleverly designed to let in the light. Also, someone had decided to get rid of all the carpets. They've done that at Mahis, too, in Bromyard. Why this sudden vogue for bare boards – the forest floor effect? I'm not one for the outside. It's something I decided many years ago – that if I have to walk anywhere, at least let it be on a carpet.

Isla Martin was 'left devastated' after losing her rabbit on the bus to Belmont. Anyone who finds 'her grey floppy bunny' is to call PC Stacey at Crimestoppers. If I found a bunny on a bus I'd be screaming and leaping on the seat – resembling a cross between the black maid in *Tom and Jerry*, hoisting up her skirts, and James Stewart in the film *Harvey*.

That's my Great Uncle Ron, the family poof. Wyndham Ronald Lewis, born in 1910. He went up to Jesus College, Oxford, and took Holy Orders. He was the Vicar of Holy Trinity, Ardington, and Rector of All Saints, Lockinge, Berkshire,* where he got to know Princess Margaret. A pernickety, fussy, unlovable man, he had the off-putting habit of doling out stern, unsolicited advice. When I was eighteen and had just got my A Level results, he said, 'Don't take your parents' care and concern for you all for granted. One day, perhaps soon, you'll have to bear that kind of responsibility and you'll see what I mean' – this from an acidulous queen who never had a partner, never had children. And I was *eighteen*.

I made the mistake of showing him a university essay once, and it came back covered with schoolmasterish ticks, crosses and corrections, which I thought bloody uncalled for. I wasn't the only one who came in for his strictures. Great Uncle Ron admonished T. S. Eliot for errors he'd made in *The Confidential Clerk*, regarding the constitution of the Parish Council and the procedures for the appointment of an organist. T. S. Eliot wrote back saying he really was quite aware of the correct constitution

* After the boundary changes of 1974, the parish moved lock-stock to the Vale of the White Horse in Oxfordshire.

of a Parish Council and how organists are appointed, 'being a Church Warden myself'. I inherited the letter, until forced to sell it to Maggs in Berkeley Square for £200 when I was broke – quite recently in fact.

Great Uncle Ron wasn't in the slightest bit religious – it was more that he thought the Church a posh profession for younger sons. With luck he'd emulate man-of-substance Bill Havard, the warrior-priest. He was a RAF padre during the Hitler War, where he was known as Binder Lewis, because everything was a bind. The pinnacle of his achievement was when he won an ankle competition at the church fete in Ardington, for as St Paul put it in his Epistle to the Romans, 'How beautiful are the feet of them that preach.'*

He retired to Kidlington, but died before I got to Oxford – thank goodness, because we'd never have shaken him off. He was very lonely. My father went to visit him once, said goodbye, popped back because he'd forgotten his car keys – and found Great Uncle Ron already in floods of tears. During his last few years he moved to Usk, so that my grandmother and her friend Floss Cadogan could cook and clean for him for free. A miser, who walked on grass verges to save shoe leather, who re-used envelopes (decades before compulsory recycling came in), who never switched the heating on or fed himself properly, and who refused to own a record player because 'I would get tired of repeated playing of my own records', what he did do was play the stock market. He left about £1 million, which was divided up among his many nieces and nephews as he was apparently intestate. My dad's slice kept him going in treats for years. I always thought, however, it was very odd that a man so careful about his money should not leave a properly

* That dreary little parsonical witticism about St Paul and the ankles was considered well worthy of publication in *The Letcombe Regis Gazette* on 4 May 1962.

executed Last Will and Testament. This has the makings of an Agatha Christie plot.

✑

I was brought up in houses that had not been decorated or cleared since before the war. The Zulu War. Hooks in the fireplace. Ancient hobs and stoves. Black saucepans. Gas brackets on the walls. Bakelite switches. Electricity that fizzled and bustled irritably along brittle wires. It's no wonder I do not belong in the modern world.

✑

Horses and cattle loomed in my childhood – manger scenes, familiar to Our Lord. Such darkness of the slaughterhouse animal pens, and the gates and barriers made from GWR railway sleepers, uprooted by Beeching. In the lofts – boxes of nails and wing-nuts, barbed wire rolled up like Persian carpets, pegs and poles. Abandoned bridles and leather straps from the days of horse-drawn carts.

✑

I'm trying to write a book about the essence of comedy – and the essence of comedy is fear. Even with Groucho: you'd not want to be the victim of one of his put-downs. Dame Edna hauling people on stage – it is ritual humiliation, as all or most humiliations are. The aggression of Brucie, who has a cruel face, who is cold and sarcastic. Eric Morecambe slapping Ernie Wise's face. 'I'm the comedian around here,' hissed Dick Emery to Ken Campbell, when Ken Campbell got a bigger laugh. Everyone finds a clown's face scarier than werewolves or Frankenstein's monster. Kenneth Williams's face might have been painted by Francis Bacon – it is a piercing scream of cynicism and doom.

✑

Another one I should like to write is a biography of Jesus. Elia Kazan said that Marlon Brando could 'project the inner struggle of conscience' – and though I'm not sure what this means exactly

54

with regards to Marlon Brando, I think with Jesus one would need to show precisely this self-doubt and pain; the vulnerability and the yearning.

෨

Crime Wave Corner. A car hit a gatepost near the junction of Sheridan Road and Cliveden Grove. No one was hurt and the driver drove off. Nevertheless, Crimestoppers say that this will be treated as 'a criminal offence' because the motorist failed to report the collision.

෨

The way he's flaring his nostrils and twisting his head about, Michael Sheen OBE, who recently played Our Lord on the beach at Port Talbot, must have looked at a few Francis Bacons in the Tate before starring in *Fantabulosa*. The agony – no ecstasy. Actually, you watch all these biopics about comedians (there have been *tons*) and you get no real sense that these people *were* comedians – only that they were sad and lonely failures. It is my fault of course. I invented the genre, with *The Life and Death of Peter Sellers*.

Anyway, here we were again with poor old Kenny Williams, being fired by Hancock (there's another one), being typecast in the *Carry Ons*, and ending up doing voice-overs for Jeyes lavatory detergent. He was a chat show buffoon, with a handful of sneering or grand voices, over-enunciating for caricatured effect. He was fearful of relationships, had a horror of sexual contact – which would have meant both physical and moral contamination; he was insanely fastidious; and he was simultaneously vain and insecure. A self-loathing narcissist, his thwarted sensibility sums him up.

As with Sellers – another smothering relationship with his mother (Cheryl Campbell – my, she's piled on the weight), and a weak father. Like Kenny himself, Charlie also committed suicide. Peter Wight gave a most affecting performance of an affectless

55

man, who tried to love and understand his unique son, but who was repulsed, who was ganged up on.*

Big Cheryl played Louie as Miriam Margolyes's Peg Sellers. Peter Wight did Charlie as Peter Vaughan's Bill. Though the make-up people did their best to make him grotesque – his quivering nostrils were painted black; he was presented to us as tired, strained and pale – Michael Sheen was too good-looking (too chunky) for Kenneth Williams, who was morbidly uncomfortable with what he believed was his vile body.

ஒ

Williams's punishing austerity – the empty flat; the celibacy; the studiousness: it has a religious (monkish) dimension. He never felt anything except pain.

If he was a parody Christ, Joe Orton was the carefree Devil – that Orton was killed by Halliwell seems almost a primal, religious act of retribution. It was an execution.

ஒ

Tragedy lurks nearer to comedy than anyone has realised. The smiler with a knife. The ruffian on the stair. Laughter is not attractive to watch – it is a howl or a snarl; a convulsion, reminiscent of the bestial nature of sex or sneezing – grappling, biting, penetrating, and hostile to any nonsense about romance.

ஒ

With Kenneth Williams – the buoyancy and high-spirited face-pulling of the performances, and then the unresolved anxieties and oppression he felt when back at home. He hated his audiences for being taken in by him, so he set out to be spiky, prickly, like a thistle. Particularly so in his diaries – where fear eats his soul.

He lived in dowdy, grim, prim, cheap surroundings; basic fixtures and fittings – no style of personality in evidence in his flat. A dismantled life. Yet if he'd gone in for fine china and a

* Peter Wight was a baffled, heavyweight Claudius to Mark Rylance's RSC Hamlet, which I saw about six times.

villa in Provence he'd have been Dirk Bogarde. Another creature fearful of contact, of friendship, of involvement. The excruciating despair – they *exult* in it.

❧

Biography – apart from my own unappreciated and remaindered efforts, can't they ever be a work of literature, operating on a variety of sensory levels? I tried to find the prose equivalent of Orson Welles's deep-focus photography. A mix of colour, monochrome, freeze-frame techniques, posed stills, overlapping scenes, superimposed dialogue; the conversations and taped interviews; the mechanisms of magic – there are all these different ways of telling a story, of using the raw material, but nobody bothers with an imaginative structure. It is always ancestry – birth – schooldays – apprenticeship and struggle – maturity – old age and death – the memorial service. This isn't writing, it is carpeting.

Placidity, tameness, squeamishness make me see red. I fractured the genre, went in for formal experimentation, to try and depict – *evoke* – the inner fantasies of my characters. This was additionally fascinating (and complex) when my subjects were actors, who kept walking out of their own lives to adopt new identities.

❧

Dame Margaret Price obit. Welsh girl, lived in Munich. I was taken as a child to see Dame Margaret Price in Welsh National Opera's *The Magic Flute*, at the New Theatre, Cardiff. It was one of those dreadful trendy productions, with an Age of Aquarius set, bits of which kept whizzing about in unpredictable ways.

During the duet with Tamino, when he and Pamina have successfully undergone the trials of fire and water, Dame Margaret was required to sing while perched on this perspex pedestal, which was meant to weave among the flames and fountains, taking the soprano with it. Of course Dame Margaret fell off.

As one, the audience gave a gasp of horror, rose up and peered into the orchestra pit. The next day, as I remember it, there was a photograph in *The Western Mail* of Dame Margaret with her leg in plaster, cheerfully raising a glass.

❧

Overheard by me in New York: 'That's Jessica Tandy' – 'No, it's Angela Lansbury' – 'Oh yes, Charles Laughton's wife'. Sometimes you stumble across things that are too complex, too full of compounded misunderstandings, to disentangle and rectify.

❧

It is already four years since Les Dennis was last seen in Great Malvern.

March

What am I still doing here? 'My fiftieth year had come and gone,/I sat, a solitary man,/In a crowded London shop,/An open book and empty cup/On the marble table-top.' Except I am not in London – or for that matter in Manhattan or Rio de Janeiro or *anywhere interesting* – but in The Thorn, disobeying Dr Twelvetrees by having a civilised just-the-one (bottle) with Chirpy, Strawberry Blonde Karl and Moist Jane. Moist Jane's mobile rang. I answered for some reason. 'Ck. Uc. Ome. Bstds. Uck. Fff.' It was like Buzz Aldrin speaking from *Apollo 11*. I ignored it completely and popped Moist Jane's mobile in Ginger Shane's Peroni. Minutes later, though in fact it was three hours later, but in The Thorn time plays tricks, Zany Antony appeared at the threshold. 'Fuck off home, you bastards. *Fuck off*!'

Zany Antony had been in the Dorchester with an ICU nurse, had phoned up to see if everything was fine at the pub, I'd told him (allegedly) that we'd managed to put the fire out and that Dani had bought the police's silence with what was left of the float, so he'd hopped in a taxi and had driven back to Bromyard. After shouting at us he returned to the Dorchester, where he later said he saw Nicole Kidman in the lift. It was one of those evenings that have the quality of a dream.

❧

You never hear about anyone suffering from a rupture any more. There's an affliction that's gone, along with scrofula, neuralgia, flat feet, tonsillectomies and adenoids. (When's the last time you had dropsy let alone a quinsy?) The word 'truss' doesn't cause immediate merriment and chortling – people assume you mean that *Eats, Shoots and Leaves* woman, Lynne Truss. Spike Milligan's many jokes about hernias are one of the things that date him. Yet upon investigation I discover that there is such a body as the Hernia Forum, which sounds to me like a select housing estate near Sevenoaks. 'Oh we've got a lovely semi with up-and-over garage doors in Hernia Forum' – 'Fancy!'

There's also The Cluthe Rupture Institute, though perhaps they have closed down by now. The Cluthe Rupture Institute patented The Cluthe Automatic Massaging Truss – which was advertised with the faultless slogan: 'So Much More Than Just A *Truss!*' Their italics. I wouldn't mind having a go with one of those, eh girls, eh boys?

Lynne Truss is actually a chum of mine, though she failed to get me elected to the Royal Society of Literature *even though she is on the committee* (my italics). She's indubitably so much more than just a *Truss*. She ought to put that on her books. I'll suggest it.

My publisher asked me for what in the trade they call a 'strapline' for one of my own books – a slogan or some snappy rubric that can help sales. I thought for a moment and came up with:

Buy This Book Or God Will Give You Cancer

Or what about:

Free Fucks With This Book

Imagine those on stickers in Waterstones.

Next to Great Uncle Ron, Great Uncle Gardner – George Gardner Lewis, born in 1907. He always seemed a bit simple to me. The (untranslatable) Welsh word is *twp*, which is perhaps cognate with the French *taupe*, meaning 'mole'. He talked in a slow sing-song Welsh accent and told me – and you've got to forgive me for telling you this – that the word 'wog' meant workers on government sites. I believed him – and still believe him. He also said he'd seen The Marx Brothers in *The Cocoanuts*,* which was released in 1929. I don't think he got out much, though he was in Palestine during the war. He wrote every week for two years to ask if the chickens were laying well.

Great Uncle Gardner worked in a bank in some lowly capacity, and was once attacked on a train when it went into a tunnel. The gossip was that Great Uncle Gardner was also 'interfered with' by Great Uncle Ron, hence his dazed look. He looked in point of absolute fact like Benny Hill's Fred Scuttle. He had a nice house in Lisvane – indeed, all these brothers and sisters were very well set up by my great-grandfather, who'd educated them privately and bought everyone homes or farms and got their businesses going. When Gardner died he couldn't be buried for ages because the ground was frozen solid. His daughter (my godmother – I met her once a thousand years ago) married a man she met at AA. And I don't mean the Automobile Association.

⋙

Community Safety Manager Laura Walker of the Hereford and Worcester Fire and Rescue Service this week held useful courses on 'Smoke Alarm Advice For The Deaf'.

⋙

Alexander Graham Bell worked on a machine through which we could talk to the dead – to reach another world, converse with phantoms. Dame Barry Humphries told me he possessed Oscar

* So spelt in the Marxist literature. I prefer *coconut* to *cocoanut* myself. An American thing, like *tomato* and *tomato*?

Wilde's telephone book. I asked him if he'd been tempted to call some of the numbers. What if (say) Lord Alfred Douglas or Walter Sickert or Charles Conder *answered*? I think Barry puts on a quilted smoking jacket, gives them a tinkle, and chats away with these people most evenings. God knows, I would.

ॐ

Laurence Olivier appeared to Ken Campbell at a séance and told him the world's greatest actor is Jackie Chan.

ॐ

I've been watching *Closer*, as written by out-in-front Patrick Marber. The problem is Julia Roberts. She is so dazed and bland – as if bewildered by the burden of her own beauty. People in the film keep telling her how beautiful she is. This must be similar to how I feel when people keep telling me how fat and ugly I am – *as if I didn't already fucking know*. As if this is *new information* I'm pleased to be receiving. Anyway – I couldn't believe that Julia was this famous photographer, because simply as a person she is incapable of snapping into focus.

And is she attractive, come to that? She has large lumpy features and is almost cross-eyed. The doe-eyed look – so pained. Why? What about? What about, *prithee*? Clive Owen has real power – he's wonderfully wide-awake and smart; Jude Law is devious; Natalie Portman – also devious.

These are not nice people, the people in *Closer*. It is like the *A Midsummer Night's Dream* quartet, without the supernatural intervention. Tiresome and self-seeking. Despite the title, nobody is close to anyone else; nobody is emotionally intimate. Cruel, selfish, squirming, hurtful people. The only characters who do connect (after a fashion) are Clive and Jude, the two boys, when they exchange anonymous pornographic emails.

It is about people who react only with the fantasies they have of each other; the fictional ideal. They think that their moment-to-moment feelings are significant, so they switch partners without compunction. They are disloyal. They cannot stick with anyone for long. The Clive Owen character is a dermatologist, and emotions here are skin-deep.

⋐

I always bridle (something churns and snaps inside) when I am introduced at ill-attended Rotary Dinners, provincial Poetry Recitals, English-Speaking Union events in Llanrhaeadr-Ym-Mochnant (these are my level I'm afraid) as a *biographer*. It is limiting, and anyway I have scant admiration for the genre.

⋐

If I'm not listening to Schubert, I'm listening to Oscar Peterson. I had the good fortune to be present at Oscar Peterson's very last concert – though I suppose Oscar Peterson wouldn't have felt fortunate had he known it was his very last concert. He'd had a stroke, poor devil, and one arm was effectively out of action, but I personally didn't notice any gaps in the music, any silences or interpolated humming. What I did notice was his incredible – exceptional – responsiveness to the music and to the other musicians scattered about the stage. He was continuously nodding and smiling, bringing them in, being appreciative. It was as if his emotions – his musical instincts – were very near the surface, his consciousness hyper-alert.

And he was also alert, moreover, to every shift in the audience's reactions, to our levels of attentiveness, to how spellbound we were. Like a wily old stag he was sensitive to the slightest mood and nuance, as if noticing the smallest change in air pressure, wafting to him across as it might be the purple moors.

When he was playing rapturously, he looked enraptured. For a number called 'Requiem', dedicated to his dead jazz friends, he looked desolate. Here was a man – an artist – who seemed to be living a spontaneous life.

The dignity and majesty of the man – yet he only played with his right hand. The left side of his body slumped. Apart from Tristan,

63

my Oscar and Sébastien, there were no young people present in Birmingham City Hall. It was mainly dozens and dozens of old chaps who looked like my late father.

Was this the equivalent of seeing the croaking Sinatra at the end, or Callas – you were there for the legend rather than the actual performance itself? I am convinced Oscar Peterson caught my eye several times. The children said they'd felt he'd been looking at them, too, now and again.

๛

From the sublime – to the sublime. I saw *Confessions of a Window Cleaner* the other night. One is not always in the mood for a Jean-Luc Godard or an Antonioni, I find, despite having two doctorates. Sometimes one is in the mood for *Lesbians in Wellies*. However. Though.

I first saw *Confessions of a Window Cleaner* in 1974, when, underage, I sneaked into the since-demolished cinema in Caerphilly. I was no doubt proudly dressed in my black rubber mackintosh from Peacocks, pretending I was Peter Sellers. I gave the game away somewhat by asking the cashier for a child's half-price ticket. When I sat down at the back of the stalls, there suddenly everyone else also was – Fatty Prescott, Pansy Banfield, Ian Gough, Ronnie Pudding, Friskin, the whole lot of them. Sticko Richards, who was to have an asthma attack while swimming and drowned in Germany.

Confessions of a Window Cleaner is not a continuation of the *Carry On* series, as is usually thought, but a contradiction of them – because people here are cheerfully having it off, chief among whom is our former Prime Minister's father-in-law, Tony Booth, as Sidney Noggett. How vain he is about his hair – he still is: that baking powder white mop. The original Sidney Noggett bucket, which bore the legend 'We Rub It Better For You', was sold on eBay the other day for £200.72.

Nevertheless, to look back at Britain's saucy cinema is to be

64

amazed at the sheer innocence of what was on offer — slap-and-tickle romps, with the girls in skimpy G-Strings and yards of chiffon, and the men sporting crushed velvet flares. It's no worse than *The Two Ronnies* or *The Benny Hill Show*. Mary Whitehouse, however, said that X-rated movies endangered marriage, led to adultery, and 'encouraged promiscuity amongst teenagers'. She said she'd personally met adolescents who had dark patches under their eyes, who suffered weight loss and lack of concentration and, worst of all, they had 'illegible handwriting'.

The plots of the *Confessions* series and of saucy Seventies cinema generally were always the same — bored and ditzy housewives opening the front door in their negligees to admit milkmen, plumbers, doctors, taxi drivers, private-eyes and handymen. The girls were wholesome and full of smiles and often played by Diana Rigg's ex-stunt doubles. The absent and cuckolded husbands were usually played by Bob Todd or Windsor Davies. Parenthetically, it was never explained how these unlikely marriages had come about in the first place.

The randy interloper was Robin Askwith. The French had Belmondo and Alain Delon. The Italians had Marcello Mastroianni. We had Robin Askwith, grinning gormlessly and tripping over his bucket. After nearly forty years, Robin Askwith still retains a slim sexiness in these films, with lots of shots of his bobbing arse. He has a huge boyish grin, which almost cuts his head in two, like a sliced watermelon. Whatever happened to laddish Robin Askwith (b. 1950)? Does he still make the blood throb? I bet he looks like shit. Didn't he take early retirement and move to Gozo? He was in a Pasolini film, I recall, and I can see how he'd have been *exactly* Pier Paolo's type.* Somebody who was a lot like him, Barry Evans, who

* Indeed, Pasolini said of him, 'Che io penso che lui usa troppo il suo cazzo' — in effect, you look like you use your cock a lot. Not that we ever saw it. The censor found the penis problematic.

likewise traded on the boyishness, ended up driving a minicab in Leicester, and was then murdered.

The Seventies fashions suddenly don't look too abominable on the screen – platform shoes, ruffled shirts and long hair being back. (It's the cars in the background that date things.) What a waste, as ever, of John Le Mesurier and Dandy Nichols in supporting roles. Indeed, it was in Britain's saucy cinema, to which I was devotee in my rubber coat in Caerphilly, that legendary British character actors could still all be found, making their final appearances and glad to be paid cash-in-hand. Dennis Price was in *Vampyros Lesbos*. James Robertson Justice and Charles Hawtrey had cameos in *Zeta One*. Terry-Thomas gazed at the crumpet in *Spanish Fly* and said 'Absolutely splendid!' with his inimitable leer. In *Percy*, the one about the todger transplant, Denholm Elliott was the pioneering surgeon, and in the sequel, *Percy's Progress*, Vincent Price was on view, as was a youngish Dame Barry Humphries.

An overqualified cast always reported for duty: Hugh Griffith, Alfie Bass, David Niven, Michael Hordern, Harry H. Corbett and Irene Handl, who was particularly unabashed. 'If I was a bit younger I'd get my tits out with them!' Irene told reporters. In *Rosie Dixon: Night Nurse*, Arthur Askey had a whale of a time, whizzing around in a motorised wheelchair, pinching nurses' arses.

'My Timmy would never lose his nerve,' says Dandy as Robin Askwith's mother. 'He'd go up anything' – meaning ladders.* There are lots of young girls – crumpet again! Bring back that word! – with their boobs out and Robin is in his element, bouncing and bounding into their boudoirs, a wingéd phallus. Nevertheless, his personal copy of the *Confessions of a Window Cleaner* script, listed on eBay last week at the Buy It Now price of £76.61, unaccountably failed to sell.

* In *Confessions of a Pop Performer*, Rita Webb prods Robin Askwith with her brolly and demands, ''Ere, have you seen my Fanny?' – meaning her vagina.

It is not possible to find edible food in Herefordshire. Today Anna's fillet steak was sliced off an old disabled person's shoe. I think the disabled person was still wearing it. My venison was school dinners diced beef. The waitress came up to me, very shyly and sweetly, and said, 'You're a writer?' – 'Well . . .' – 'I've written a book.' – 'Oh that's good. A *whole* book? Most people give up after a few pages.' Anna piped up, 'What's it about?' – 'Smugglers.' God strike me pink, sometimes I don't know how I ever regain consciousness.

❧

A New York chum called Patrick Tull has died. Actually he died in 2006, but it's only now I've got your attention. He did the Patrick O'Brian Talking Books, now and again would be in a Stoppard revival in Philadelphia, and in the long-ago was a Welsh chef on *Crossroads*. What was his real accent? He was educated at King's Canterbury, so there were English origins. He did a season with John Neville and Judi Dench in Nottingham. His uncle was Desmond Llewelyn of Q fame. But it is true that his accent wandered all over the place – not because he was versatile at voices (his Welsh was woeful, and made you wonder about all the others), but because he was such a nervous person – and his insecurities were half hidden behind a blustering, bullying façade. He'd have made a good Baron Ochs, in *Der Rosenkavalier*, if he could sing.

There was a lot of anxious showing off. The crotchety little fat man, with his random indignations. He'd pretend to be a growling Brooklyn cabbie, public school English, sour New Yorker, Birmingham – you'd get the lot. All delivered fortissimo, too. And tears were never far off, either. He'd get emotional and maudlin, and embarrassing. I didn't like being told that he'd meet couples on the internet who'd put him in nappies and shackle him to a hook in the ceiling, and then they'd . . . Let's leave that there.

Patrick reminded me a little of playwright/novelist/screenwriter Wolf Mankowitz – the bitter self-hatred (and aggression) of a man who felt he'd not quite received his due homage from the world, but who also knew (secretly) that he was not really up to it. John Wain, who was the Oxford Professor of Poetry, was like this, even though he got the CBE. Failure creeps up on a person, slowly, little by little. Like Alec Guinness said of baldness, it doesn't happen overnight – it's not a sudden thing. Patrick (and Wolf – and John Wain for that matter) alternately sneered at me and embraced me as the greatest of friends, as a protégé. Both stances and views were contrived, and ill-mannered. Let alone unwelcome, because if I get like that it's Dignitas time.

෨

Elizabeth Taylor has died at long last – she had every illness known to mankind, including probably prostate cancer. She bored me slightly. Not much of an actress. Spoilt child star. After *Lassie* it was downhill, and watching *Cleopatra* you long for the asp. I can't think what else she did. *National Velvet? The Flintstones?* She made more of herself with heaps of marriages, her Roman Empress lavishness, her range of perfumes, her weight gain and weight loss, than with anything else. She had horrible eyes.

The two times she divorced Richard Burton she absolutely took him to the cleaners financially. All the jewels they'd bought as joint investments she kept. Plus lavish settlements and alimony. Grasping and spiteful. She didn't give a toss about what she was doing to Debbie Reynolds when she captured Eddie Fisher, and I believe Sybil Burton was similarly devastated. Anyway:

Ten Notes on Richard Burton

ONE. He did the usual Welsh thing – getting away because of the urge to be somebody, and then being nostalgic, dreaming and declining. His home in Switzerland where he died and is buried was called 'Pays de Galles'. His Wales was the Wales of chapels and pubs, sex and obstinacy.

TWO. It was a very queer parental set-up – when he was 'adopted' by that creepy teacher Philip Burton. Queer in the sense of bloody odd *and* up the bum. His real father was hardly there. Philip Burton was a homosexual – he was like that chap who 'adopts' Dorian Gray and teaches him social graces. Don't tell me no one in Pontrhydyfen spotted this. I've always been amused by certain members of that Jenkins family in Wales, who try to be low-key and local and all that, but they were a bit grasping too, wanting houses and holidays paid for and what-not. Ugly little gnomes, in the Welsh way – and then there was Richard Burton (Jenkins) himself, who was glorious-looking, 'a man who made hearts beat faster', according to Marlene Dietrich – surely a changeling?

THREE. He was in Laurence Olivier's shadow (though he lacked Olivier's true audacity) – and though Burton did play Shakespeare's Henry V on stage he is best known for playing King Arthur in *Camelot*. He husbanded his genius unthriftily.

FOUR. He and Elizabeth Taylor were vulgar versions of Olivier and Vivien Leigh, who seem primly Victorian by comparison: the ostentation, the luxury-loving, the sleaze; the lack of satisfaction despite being voluptuaries. Instead of Shakespeare's *Antony and Cleopatra*, or Shaw's *Caesar and Cleopatra*, they made that epic film, *Cleopatra*.

FIVE. Stars are people that live beyond us – so what do we expect from them? Burton never knew. Because he was from Wales, where women wash the pavements, where there are narrow streets and terraced houses you can't tell apart, he remained provincial. The colour and glitter of the gala-world, its pleasures and delusions, threw him off-balance. To leave Wales is always a catastrophe – you can never quite go back

69

to it, not if you are a hit, that is.* Dylan Thomas, Rachael Roberts, Dorothy Squires, others: the outcome is Celtic self-destruction and burn-out. The inability to cope with fame and success. A fatal restlessness. A mingled glory and shame. A split in consciousness.

SIX. He always shone and glowered in his roles – a strong personality comes through. But how could he be expected to survive Elizabeth Taylor? She got the better of him. Despite the braggadocio and excessive masculinity (all that boozing, all that tedious rugby talk, all that laughing at danger), he was something of a mummy's boy, requiring protection. He didn't mind masterful women.

SEVEN. Elizabeth Taylor, theatrical to the hilt, became an honorary Welshwoman in his company – dumpy, arch, embarrassing, chopsy. She was his rival – and accomplice. They found each other exotic. You could always tell that Richard Burton, grand and romantic, was *impressed* that he'd married her.

EIGHT. What happened with Burton – which he brought to *The Spy Who Came In From The Cold* or *Look Back In Anger*, among many others: because he couldn't help but convey his intelligence –

---

* I'd better watch it not to be too out-of-date here, as there's a new generation of Welshpersons (among whom technically I should take my place) – Rhys Ifans (Rees Evans), Ioan Gruffudd (Joan Griffiths), Bryn Terfel (Doris Klunt), Michael Sheen OBE, and so on, who are decidedly *cwl* (hot).

'When you become comfortable, when you start to take the piss, that's when you are actually advancing,' said Russell T. Davies perceptively. Russell is responsible for the revamped *Doctor Who*, which is filmed in Cardiff – as is the Mark Gatiss/Cumberland Sausage revamped *Sherlock*.

This is indeed all *a very big advance* on the damp personalities of the past. Perhaps Burton was the last of them? The Manic Street Preachers and the Stereophonics are vastly to be preferred to close harmony male-voice choirs. And who'd you rather do, Katherine 'Face like a Ballistic Missile Early Warning Satellite Dish' Jenkins or Glenys Kinnock?

he couldn't prevent himself from implying his disdain. Once he failed to take delight in himself, he has this permanent scoffing expression. You see him fidgeting, growing drowsy. He is brooding – about what? He is on the run – from what? To where? Burton played tragic heroes; then became one, a wounded king.

NINE. Yet there was a frankness about him, a desire to be rebellious, that is his allure. As for his alleged virility as an actor, however – I never sensed any athletic outpouring. There was always something sickly, ailing about Burton. His skin, his joints, his back, his shoulder. The chronic alcoholism. He was at the end of his rope. When I see him in interviews smoking, he gulps at the smoke, he traps the smoke in his chest, like a dragon. Then the fatal brain haemorrhage when he was only fifty-eight. *Fifty-eight.*

TEN. His sinister melancholia. The groundswell of his voice – the voice of the damned.

Typical Welsh Beauty

For some people the greatest beauty since Time Began will be Cleopatra (i.e. Elizabeth Taylor) or Helen of Troy; or it might be Vivien Leigh; or Grace Kelly; or if you are King Kong – it's Fay Wray. But I from an early age have only ever had one Platonic Ideal – Venus on that cockleshell in the Botticelli painting: namely Judi Bowker.

Judi Bowker, eh? She still has a place in my imagination. It's horses again – there she was when I was eleven, in her velvet ribbons and Laura Ashley shrouds, in *The Adventures of Black Beauty*. I used to subscribe to *Look-In* in the hope there'd be a Judi Bowker feature. Do you all remember *Look-In*? Instructions on how to make the *Magpie* studio out of a Weetabix box. Acrylic paintings (quite good) instead of photographs. An *On The Buses* comic strip. *Tomorrow People* T-shirt offers. Lena Zavaroni's cookery-cum-celebrity gossip column ('Bruce Forsyth was lovely and I really enjoyed working with Leslie Crowther'). Crap prizes – badges or £1 postal orders.

Simply mentioning all these cultural highlights takes me back to an era that seems more remote than the Roman Empire. As regards *The Adventures of Black Beauty*, which first aired in September 1972 and was shot in Rickmansworth, anyone who has heard that fruity theme tune, 'Galloping Home', composed by Denis King and performed by the London String Chorale, not only will never have forgotten it, but surgery will be required to make them forget it. Da-*daaaa*, da-da-da-da-da-da-da, da-*daaaa* . . .

Judi was (is) my dream girl even more than the one in *The White Horses*, who was a bit moody and tomboyish. Nice though. Gorgeous. What was her name? Julia, I think, played with *attitude* by Helga Anders. Or Julka, in the original Yugoslavian. There Julia or Julka was, week after week, cantering in a carefree way through a dappled meadow near Ljubljana. I could tell then and I'm more than certain now, looking back, that you weren't going to knock *her* from the saddle and win *her* trust with a sugar lump. You'd need something bigger and more interesting than that.

The White Horses, or *Snowy White Horses* as I thought it was called, a co-production from 1965 between Radiotelevizija Slovenija and Sudwestfunk of Baden-Baden,* also had a theme tune that stuck in the brain. It was a black and white programme, filmed on location on a real Lipizzaner stud-farm, and it looked like a beautiful old woodcut on our ancient Baird.

The dialogue, however, was badly dubbed from the Serbo-Croatian. Until I first went to Lake Bled in what is now Slovenia in 1988, I thought the locals thereabouts really did talk in that off-register way, opening and shutting their mouths a lot to produce a small grunt or not moving their lips at all and yet being able to come out with yards of expositionary dialogue, like a race of hiccupping ventriloquists.†

Helga Anders, I am sad to report, she of the snowy white jodhpurs and snowy white thighs, of the budding snowy white bosoms under a gently heaving snowy white blouse, died in 1986 at the age of thirty-eight. The drugs and the drink got her.

What a contrast altogether with Judi Bowker – Odette to Helga's Odile, so to speak. Judi's character in *The Adventures of Black Beauty* was called Vicky. Vicky was one of those lovely serious English girls with flowing silky hair who cared for others, who cared for her pets and her parents and uncles, even if they cop a feel. Unlike Julia/Julka, who you can just bloody well tell will soon be switching her passionate allegiance from ponies to the head groom, Vicky was pure and innocent.

Too innocent to *live* – she was replaced in the second series by

---

* The dubbed version was first broadcast in Britain in 1968, and much repeated. *The White Horses*, *Robinson Crusoe* and *The Singing-Ringing Tree* were the only programmes that ever seemed to be on for youngsters.
† The strangest thing I heard a ventriloquist say, though not in Ljubljana: 'Who put wet fruitbat poo into dead mummy's bed? Was it you, Verity?'

Stacy Dorning as Jenny. Up the bum and no babies to Series Two with Stacey Dorning as Jenny. Meanwhile, Judi Bowker, aged eighteen, was now in the Abbey of Sant'Antimo, Montalcino, Tuscany, playing Clare of Assisi in the lavish Paramount movie, *Brother Sun, Sister Moon*. That's to say – she went from being around horses to being a nun.

I can see how this happened. Her calm and her infinite blonde beauty; the way she seems capable of suffering, like a Madonna in a Renaissance painting – she was ideal for Zeffirelli, whose inspiration is always Italian art. Also meant to be in *Brother Sun, Sister Moon* was Robin Askwith – ideal for Zeffirelli in a quite different, less spiritual though no less important way, of course, but there's no need to dwell on any of that. Alas the schedules clashed and instead Robin (and his A-grade arse) went off to Pinewood to shoot *Confessions of a Driving Instructor's Window Cleaner in a Holiday Camp*.

Judi played a nun again, Sister Joanna, in the adaptation of Rumer Godden's novel *In This House of Brede*, with Dame Rigg. Yet there was never anything bland about her; though serene, she was not pious. When I watch her – as I still do: go and insert the DVD of *The Shooting Party* – she doesn't exploit her mysteriousness. She's never pert. Indeed, she's sensuous, with a dancer's prolonged economy of movement – a dancer's stillness. Also – she's not modern. I have never once seen her in modern dress.

The next phase was going to be obvious: she's the beauty whom the beasts want to get their claws on, because they sense that inside that's what this woman wants. They want to make her swoon. A marvellous word. I'll say it again. *Swoon*. From the Old English *geswogan*: to be overcome. Judi was the victim of Louis Jordan's Dracula. She was in a version of *The Picture of Dorian Gray*, as the girl the aesthete wants to corrupt. Wearing an identical white negligee to Laurence Olivier's Zeus, she's Princess Andromeda, chained up as bait for the Kraken, in *Clash of the Titans*. And she was in an adaptation of *Doctor Jekyll and Mr Hyde* that starred Kirk Douglas. 'Which one is he now?' must have been the question asked by every single visitor to the set.

Judi Bowker was the sort of woman to drive men sane. Like Robin Askwith and his prize-winning arse, Judi (b. 1954 – but I wish it was 1854 and that she'd been a model for Lord Leighton) must be very old by now; older than me. Getting on for sixty winters will have besieged her brow. I can hardly face the thought of it. Like Garbo, she has long-since retired from view. She used always to be in sunshine.*

---

* The male equivalent of Judi Bowker was Peter Duncan, also born in 1954, and who also when in his twenties was always cast as a teen. He became a (slightly silly) *Blue Peter* presenter and, later in life, when we'd all forgotten about him, the Chief Scout.

Peter Duncan was lovely-looking originally, with a huge friendly well-flossed smile. There was no darkness or moodiness about him whatsoever. He was loose and casual. I remember him best from *King Cinder*, where he was a speedway bike rider, and *The Flockton Flyer*, a series about a family who ran a steam train – it was filmed on the West Somerset Railway at Minehead. Peter Duncan was also briefly in *Flash Gordon*, where during an Initiation Test he had to plunge his arm into a tree trunk and get bitten by a snake.

I was always surprised that Peter Duncan never had followers – but perhaps girls were put off by his sheer unstoppable playfulness. He always behaved as if he were eight years old, and was never sexily curious, never mysterious. (The females he associated with on-screen were generally his *sisters*.) In programmes such as *Duncan Dares*, he became rather too boisterously fearless for anybody. He grinned non-stop.

In brief close-ups in *King Cinder* and *The Flockton Flyer*, however, you'd have been excused for thinking that here's an actor capable (possibly – if anyone could keep him still) of openness, freshness. He had such pale-blue eyes. But it never happened. The dare-devilry took over, the stuntman antics became his forte, and as a television presenter Peter Duncan became the new Roy Castle.

A better candidate, therefore, for the male Judi Bowker – brother sun to her sister moon – would be Gerry Sundquist. I bet there'll not be more than half-a-dozen people in the world who'll remember that name today. Gerry

Shoppers were treated to a 'parade of mobility scooter users' in Hereford on Friday morning. Should they have been tempted, citizens and ratepayers were also able to 'test drive a scooter or powerchair' — a *powerchair*? What's one of those? Ordinary wheelchairs are enough of a nuisance. I wish I'd pitched up as Boadicea in a Boadicea chariot or in full Peter Sellers-as-Doctor Strangelove rig and run amok.

๑

I thought the thing to do as a parent was provide a stimulating environment for them all to grow up in — books, pictures, theatre, foreign travel. Wrong. My children are affectless. They'd perhaps have made more of themselves if they'd suffered in a council flat with a Mongol upstairs. Tristan comes and goes from the circus, Oscar is a lovable dopey duck who drinks too much — and that's *me* saying a person drinks too much — and Sébastien is full of fizz and temper and stacks the shelves at the Co-op. His Royal Highness does one shift a week and we are

---

was born in 1955. Again, his stock-in-trade was being fresh-faced. He played Pip in *Great Expectations*, appeared in *Crown Court* and *Space 1999*, and was the hero in a Catherine Cookson saga, *The Mallens*.

Gerry, I'm sure, *was* pinned up on the wall of many teenage girls. Like Judi, he was a firm *Look-In* favourite. He had immediate erotic alertness.

So what happened to him? He appeared in a film in Germany with Nastassja Kinski, made a mini-series with Brian Blessed, *The Last Days of Pompeii*, in which he got to wear a toga, and his final role was in a low-budget horror film called *Don't Open Till Christmas*, released in 1984. Heroin addiction got the better of him and he disappeared to the Cotswolds. On 1 August 1993, having not worked for nine years, he committed suicide by leaping under a Waterloo-bound train at Norbiton station, near Kingston-upon-Thames.

Norbiton, by the way, was used as the filming location for *The Fall and Rise of Reginald Perrin*. Leonard Rossiter is seen approaching the station each morning in a state of intensifying depression. His character eventually pretends to commit suicide and assumes a new identity.

meant to be impressed by this. His plans to be a Royal Marines officer seem to have lapsed.

They – not just them: their generation – expect a festival feeling to be permanent. Yet in every instance, making whoopee is underwritten by the poor parents, who run these free hotels, hand over bundles of cash, who cook, clean and generally slave for children who don't intend being adults – who see the challenges of adulthood as not for them.

Perhaps it is because they had everything done for them from the beginning and were indulged – they literally had their arses wiped for them for years; the child safety locks remain on in Anna's Volvo – they have no zeal to be independent? In other words: *everything is my fucking fault*. As Anna often reminds me when we are having a row.

❧

I don't know for certain whether it is because I slept awkwardly – because I'd rotated the mattress and I'm now lying on springs and bits of wood; or whether I'm so fat my hips are caving in – but whatever the cause (obesity mainly) I've been in pain all day along my right flank. I took lots of tablets and sprayed myself with Deep Heat. My skin has so many red patches from the *Mycosis Fungoides* I look like a world map of our Empire in its prime. I am a disgusting spectacle. But at least I am not a Morris Man and at least I don't have a beard.

❧

There was an Open Day at Rowden Mill, near Bredenbury. The Herefordshire lanes were very pretty – and suddenly there was this little rural railway station, tucked away and lovingly restored. (Not that I have ever come across anything from a cathedral to a candlestick that was *unlovingly* restored.) A few carriages and trucks – the carriages with little bedrooms. But none of the carriages move. There are only a few yards of track. These old engines and stations belong to a lovelier England – the reassuring England that was vanishing even as Betjeman went round recording it, in those classic documentaries with Jonathan Stedhall.

What's off-putting (as at the Severn Valley Railway) are the creepy old train spotters with their expensive cameras and child-molester cardigans. They never dress themselves properly or spend money on haircuts, but they buy expensive cameras. One idiot marched about in a GWR station master uniform. He wasn't part of the Rowden Mill set-up; he was a visitor. I overheard him say he used to work at Kidderminster Station. He looked like the sort of steam enthusiast who'd entice children to play with his lever in the signal box.

My room at the Groucho (number 303) was a cabin above the air-conditioning duct, which did nothing but rattle and vibrate. Now I know what to expect if I get Parkinson's. The bed was on a shelf that I could barely reach. To open the bathroom door I had to stand in the corridor. It was hot and uncomfortable and in the mirror I looked such a sight Peter Cushing would have run a mile, and in the Hammer horror films he used to stand his ground.

The next morning I went mad and spent money I haven't got on: (a) a tiny bottle of perfume for Anna, in the Burlington Arcade, that looked like hemlock, which the lady packaged in a velvet pouch inside a white box with a wax oriental seal. (b) At the Royal Academy I bought a large ceramic platter by Terry Frost (signed and numbered 20/100) — a big white dish with blood-red gashes and black swipes of paint. I love Frost's work. It looks so simple, yet nobody else could do it. There's drama in his shapes and arrangements. (c) From Heywood Hill: three volumes of Kilvert and two volumes of Dougie Byng, with hand-tinted illustrations by Clarke Hudson. (d) To Trumper's, where I sniffed lots of cologne and bought a bottle of Wild Fern. I adore being in Trumper's, but after three or four sniffs I can't tell one posh pong from another.

A day of complete foolish extravagance, unseen in the West End since Bruce Chatwin ran amok buying Etruscan heads and Samurai suits of armour, which his long-suffering wife had to return the next day.

❧

Crime Wave Corner. A father of two in Ross-on-Wye, Shaun Evans, has been attacked 'by what he described as sticks' – though what the police found at the scene was a bat. What – a vampire bat, a cricket bat? There's a difference. His assailant, Mark Walker, said 'he only wanted to scare Mr Evans with the bat'.

I'd be shitting myself if somebody unleashed a killer bat in my direction. It's like Count Dracula. The judge has only confused the image that is half-forming in my mind. 'There was no immediate threat to yourself when you took the bat on a mission of revenge. The action was not justified,' he said, sending the vampire bat whisperer to jail for six months. Who is going to feed the bats now, is my worry?

But the concept of trained bats on 'a mission of revenge' is like a variation of the plot from *The Hound of the Baskervilles*, i.e. *The Bat of the Baskervilles*, with Mark Walker as Stapleton and Shaun Evans as Sir Henry.

❧

Doctor Lewis's Easter Homily. Here's a conjunction that will surprise you: Peter Sellers and Jesus Christ. There's the strange desire for self-obliteration; their sense of self-abolishing.

You get this with Wittgenstein also. He gave away his fortune, retreated to huts in Norway and Connemara, resigned from his Cambridge Chair to be a hospital porter, faced bullets in the trenches of the First World War – heroic or suicidal or both?

Sellers achieved his aims at the conclusion of *Being There*, where he totters off across the surface of a misty lake. He walks on water. In my biopic there were amplified plops of water. No other sound. Perfect.

Chance in *Being There* is the innocent man – innocent because empty; no knowledge or interest in sex; an aversion to the physical side of life. What Kierkegaard called 'this sweat-soaked, stifling cloak of mush that is the body and the body's fatigue'. (*Chwarae teg*, Soren! as we say in Wales: the *ch* is silent.) He comes out with horticultural gibberish that people mistake for Zen homilies.

Then there was the way Sellers reduced himself to nothing in his own life. He retreated to a snowbound hut in Switzerland. There was a rejection of his marriages and his children. He burned his possessions, his memorabilia – a self-divestment.

Religious conceptions played a big role in his life – his interest in the supernatural, ghosts, spiritualism, the playing out of destiny and fate. There was always a dread and a despair beneath his Age of Aquarius hedonism.

He was a singular being to be sure – yet he was a multitude: the welter of funny voices and physical shape-changing; the costumes and disguises. These were devilish gifts.

Yet though his was a whirling world, there was something gnomic – Christlike – about his statements about his own lack of character: 'If you ask me to play myself, I will not know what to do. I do not know who or what I am.'

❧

When John Paul I reigned briefly, even people in the Vatican joked, 'It's as if Peter Sellers has been elected Pope' – as there was indeed a marked physical resemblance. The late King of Nepal banned Sellers movies, because people also saw a facial likeness between the monarch and Inspector Clouseau.

❧

It is already a good four years since David Suchet was heard on BBC Hereford and Worcester, talking about how he'd set about playing Hercule Poirot.

April

What am I still doing here? Because I know what you'll all be thinking. You'll all be thinking, that Roger Lewis person, he's a blinking *one* he is. He is always off on jolly jaunts. He complains and creates about his terrible life – but he's never home. Look at the evidence. He's always out and about, filling his fat ugly face in a posh restaurant or knocking around backstage with Mark Rylance and having a good laugh with his high-profile mates such as Gyles Brandreth or Sharon Osbourne, who think the world of him. And there are children *starving* in Africa.

That Roger Lewis – what's the *matter* with the man? He exchanges Christmas cards with Tim Rice. Dame Barry Humphries waved at him in The Ivy in 2001 and definitely said 'See you later!' and only a churl would point out that ten years on he still hasn't. One of his masterful books (the one dedicated to Dame Barry Humphries as it happens – there's a coincidence . . . it's virtually *ironic*) was adapted by HBO, even if the producers said he couldn't attend the premiere in Cannes because he was 'only the author' . . . He's got two doctorates. He's a Kentucky Colonel and could start a war. He's been in *Who's Who* for years and is on first-name terms with Ronald Searle. Get a grip, Roger Lewis, you pretentious twazzock. Good God Alive, you make me *sick up carrots* on my shoes, the way you like to convey this impression that all you ever do is walk alone in graveyards, weeping.

෨

Undeniable. But also undeniable is the fact that for three hundred and forty days of the year I am stuck in the Herefordshire Balkans staring at my cactus, fending off calls from NatWest about an exceeded overdraft facility and wondering how I can best stage my suicide so that it looks like an accident (or murder). Another (related) rumination: can I come back as a ghost and spend the life insurance? I am worth vastly more dead than alive? Anna ought to get a good price selling me for medical science – I'll be a star turn on the slab at Barts. I am worth nothing alive. £23.02 a month from Aviva Life & Pensions doesn't keep me in Anusol, the popular and quaintly named haemorrhoids treatment cream. And I need bumper packs.*

So you'll be glad to hear I have just returned from an exotic adventure holiday sailing up and down the River Severn – or anyway up and down a canal that runs parallel to it – from Gloucester docks to Slimbridge, on board the *MV Gustav Holst*. To paint the picture: if you have seen the Dignitas advertisements you'll recognise the soft focus, the gently lapping waters, the nodding bullrushes, the gliding geese at sundown . . .

We left on Friday evening and got back here on Sunday, in time for me to bash out 1,200 words for the *Dacre on Sunday* about Marlene Dietrich, who according to this new biography wasn't a startling screen icon but a nice little haus-frau who baked cakes and put on a hairnet to scour the floor. Over the

---

* I'm so fat, I can't easily reach around to apply the damn stuff – so I have been in the shed adapting one of those prong-and-claw jobs the wheelchair fraternity use, when they want to grab books or objects off a high shelf. I am also utilising the springs off an old angle-poise lamp, a stair-rod gripper and the wing mirror from my mobility scooter. It's mainly a case of creating a few flanges and being able to manoeuvre and see around corners.

Though the prototype nearly had my knackers off, The Lewis Patented Pile Cream Applicator For The Stout may make my fortune yet. I shall advertise it in *The Oldie*, *The Lady* and *Saga Magazine*. Joanna Lumley can do the voice-over for the advertisements in her sultry way.

weekend I read some Anthony Powell. He wasn't very good, was he?

We had a tiny cabin, with two narrow single bunks. A shower/sink/bog behind a screen, with a squeegee mop to push the water down the drain. No ventilation and the window wouldn't open. They said this was because it was 'climate controlled' but the effect was claustrophobic and stuffy. It'll be ghastly in hot weather.

It was wonderful, though — not exactly white-water rafting up the Amazon with a hammock and a Bunsen burner, but it suited me. If you stay on board, the cruiser carries on to Worcester and Stourport-on-Severn. What could be better? A holiday that takes you right back to where you live.

The crew consisted of the skipper, a Gloucestershire 'character' who bored the arse off me with his tales of the riverbank coming over the tannoy; First Mate Malarkey, who ran the bar and the quoits and served at table; his beloved, Jo, who also served at table and did the chambermaid stuff; and lastly little Liam from Buxton, who blushed a lot if you saw him not in his galley, and who made mice out of grapes to go on the cheese board. The mice tails were made from a chive. If Liam went on *Masterchef* and produced his grape mice, there'd be an outbreak. Anna has already made dozens here at home, though with a sprig of rosemary instead of a chive for the tail. Circumcised mice.

But the great highlight: Oh Sweet Baby Jesus and All the Sainted Orphans how could this have been anticipated? Of the eighteen people on board — all of us *the* endangered species, *the* most loathed ethnic minority on the planet: the elderly or middle-aged white middle class — twelve were from Abercwmboi Rotary Club. They were so South Welsh you could have spent years and years trying to cast them if it had been a film. It was like a touring production of Kingsley Amis's Booker winner, *The Old Devils*.

They *screamed* South Welshness — the slightly pompous one (an optician or estate agent – anyway: 'letters after his name'), the little round one with a carefully trimmed beard, the drippy one, the ageing Lothario, the stone-deaf one, the clever dick, the one who said absolutely nothing ever, not even when his false teeth fell out during quoits.

We didn't have a small-town solicitor or lay magistrate with us, as is usual and I'd thought mandatory with Rotarians, but we did have a small-town solicitor's clerk, who when there was a road accident claim, it was his job to pop to the 'scene' with a measuring tape and camera. No doubt also a torch and a piece of chalk.

And everybody with a dash of ferret (*Putorius foetidus*) – the secret physical and behavioural characteristic of the South Welsh *genus*. Yellowish fur and pink eyes, with a tendency to explore remote corners.

Then the wives, every man jack of them named Beverley or Bev – like human poultry, talking non-stop for the sake of talking, chirping, pecking, beady-eyed. The way they dolled themselves up for the meals, though they all said they wouldn't. One woman, demure hitherto, came in with a black number covered with sequins – dressy even for Marlene Dietrich. We were onboard Fri/Sat/Sun. Not long. But these women changed their clobber six times a day.

And what was hysterical – the men were on one table, the women on another. They never mixed. Ever. It was like the Taleban. I said, 'Has there been a mass falling out or what?' South Welsh males are shy around women – I've noticed this before; or, to be more precise, shy around women in front of other men. I remember my father saying of a milkman in Machen, 'When he was at school he played with girls' – 'Commendable, surely?' – 'No, he played with the girls. He *preferred* them . . .'

After dinner, the men went out on deck to smoke cigars – we could have been in an episode of *Poirot* sailing up the Nile, not moored up next to a field in Frampton that had a shire horse in it.

The women swept to the bar for the gin-and-tonics, having first nipped to the cabin for another costume change.

Quoits may not often be considered an extreme sport, but one lady twisted her knee, and she wasn't even playing. She was watching her husband. First Mate Malarkey had to get her an ice pack, i.e. the entire complement of ice from the bar for the weekend. So no ice in drinks – and the usual palaver about looking for a slice of lemon.

As luck would have it, there was the *Daily Dacre*, with an article by me, and some other papers, with articles by me – and they all decided I was this incredible celebrity. Not too satirically, either, though they did give me a sailor's hat and I said 'I look like Matt Lucas with hair.' Though what I looked like to my inner-eye was Leslie Caron as Gigi.

Because I likes my celebrity tittle-tattle I does, I then told everyone the names of those monsters who have obtained super-injunctions – those snakes and worms who have used their wealth to purchase the British judicial system, using it to cover up their misdemeanours in the name of 'privacy'; but the joke was that the 'world famous actor' who dipped his wick in spud-faced Wayne Rooney's tart – and who cannot be named on pain of death, though the courts didn't have such scruples about the prostitute – is no more than a little television character actor. None of my new Welsh friends had heard of him – so that speech of mine went for nothing, even though we may all now be off to gaol for contempt of court. We may be fined and have our assets seized. Yet it is the judges who are colluding with this denial of free speech who are the ones contemptuous of the law.

❦

As luck would have it, back in 1998 I was in the Garrick Club on the very day the European Convention on Human Rights was incorporated into English law. The grisly old hanging judges and oily QCs up at the bar cackled with glee at the prospect of the big fees they'd now be earning. Because as any fool could see, the rights to privacy and the notions of freedom of expression were in immediate (and for the lawyers – lucrative) conflict.

I feel quite strongly about this. I applaud the Liberal Democrat MP John Hemming for making a mockery of these super-injunctions by naming Ryan Giggs in Parliament. I'm also glad Andrew Marr has been unmasked. Apparently there are over eighty other super-injunctions in place, whereby the wealthy and the famous are preventing any reporting of their leg-over situations. I hope we soon find out who they all are – because I love and cherish nothing more than my inalienable right to have a good laugh about attention-seekers, underwear models, dandies, creeps and other disabled pillars of the community.

But what strikes me as odd – the start of the legal year is marked with a religious service in Westminster Abbey. Each October, the Lord Chancellor, the judges and the QCs arrive in full regalia from the Royal Courts of Justice and the Garrick Club, to 'ask God to sustain us in our duties, to grant us humility, strength and guidance . . .' I wonder, does Almighty God really want this to include the official protection of adulterers and sexual libertines?

Mr Justice Tugendhat – who, along with his chum Mr Justice Eady, hands out most of these super-injunctions – says that where footballers, television personalities and disgraced bankers are concerned, 'there is a pressing need to prevent harassment and unjustified intrusion'. To which I say, the little celebrities involved should have thought of all that before they unbuttoned the mutton, waved the pork sword, and brandished the beef bayonet.

Yet as Lord Wakeham said, 'the Courts inevitably err on the side of the applicant'. Meanwhile, what about the discarded mistresses, cheated-on wives and cuckolded husbands? Where is their protection? They aren't even being accorded sympathy. That's probably because they can't stump up the £60,000 fees.

Parenthetically, Mr Justice Tugendhat and Mr Justice Eady – I can't help but picture them as the equivalent of Statler and

Waldorf from *The Muppet Show*. It also amuses me that Mr Justice Tugendhat is virtually an anagram of *I'm a silly old cunt*.

But what's not funny at all is the way that Twitter is being compelled to yield up to the authorities the names and addresses of its members who have breached the super-injunctions, even though the company is based in California and is not covered by our jurisdiction. This is very sinister – like the secret police demanding to see everyone's documents.

As much as I dislike the cocky and conceited Giles Coren, who is a sort of unshaven food pundit, he shouldn't be persecuted for making jokes on Facebook about another of these wretches who has purchased a super-injunction. Yet the Attorney General got involved. It looked like an example was going to be sought, as in that Kubrick film *Paths of Glory*. Coren risked a fine, the seizure of his assets and a jail sentence. He became a Twitter Martyr. Unless of course now every Twitter user is to risk dawn arrest and a one-way journey to the gulags? Imprisoning everyone wasn't thought impractical in Stalin's Russia.

And what exactly have the twits and tweets and twerps *done*? People have only been exchanging data and notifying each other of the truth – and in my view laws that prevent the public from knowing the truth (and telling jokes) must of course be overturned.

It's not so much that the judges are allowing the rich to sin in secret that worries me – who cares about their squalid afternoons of adultery?* – it's more that by banning anyone from

* Squalid afternoons of adultery are nevertheless the subject of Harold Pinter's play *Betrayal* (1978), which was based on his affair with Joan Bakewell, Dame Joan Bakewell CBE as she became, The Right Honourable Baroness Bakewell of Stockport in the County of Greater Manchester, as she currently is. When *Betrayal* was revived at the Comedy Theatre, Panton Street, in June 2011, Joan wrote a chirpy article about the background to the play ('now I look back on it all with fond memories' etc) in the *Sunday Telegraph*. The following week, the paper printed this interesting letter from an enraged reader:

even reporting or discussing the legal hearings that have taken place, by keeping the identities of the lawyers involved a secret, by insisting that details of the order granted remain a secret, by ensuring that the case name is kept a secret, we are in the realm of Kafka, Lewis Carroll and the KGB's Lubyanka cellars. Imagine what Gilbert and Sullivan would make of it all?

Indeed, when Lord Mackay of Clashfern affected to be outraged that anyone should question the implications of these super-injunctions, huffing and puffing that judges operated 'without fear or favour, affection or ill will', he seemed simply to be providing a gloss on the Lord Chancellor's song in *Iolanthe*: 'The Law is the true embodiment/Of everything that's excellent./It has no kind of fault or flaw,/And I, my Lords, embody the Law.' To which of course the only reasonable and measured response is *Jesus Christ, what balls*.

How long will it be before defendants are not given any details of the charges they face? How long before we all risk unexpected detentions? Plus the detention of our families – guilty by association. Somebody needs to point out to Mr Justice Eady and Mr Justice Tugendhat that just as a vein is not a neck gland, privacy is not the same as secrecy. I'd tell them myself if I still went in the Garrick.

Sir – Further to Baroness Bakewell's article ('Love, Loyalty and Betrayal,' June 12th), if I found her merriment off-putting – 'Sixties London was a good place to have an affair . . . People always smile on lovers' etc – it is perhaps because I cannot forget or overlook the agony of Harold Pinter's deceived wife, the actress Vivien Merchant, who was the tragic victim of Pinter and Joan Bakewell's adultery. She deliberately drank herself to death and died in 1983, aged 53.

Furthermore, what Joan Bakewell calls 'the right to privacy' – which according to her seems to have prevailed in earlier days – simply meant a cover up for the right to behave as selfishly as possible.

It is a fact that once Vivien Merchant died, Pinter never again wrote anything of consequence. He descended into mad political ranting.
Yours faithfully,
Doctor Roger Lewis,
Bromyard, Herefordshire.

Secrecy is abhorrent in a democracy. Transparency is what our judicial system is meant to be about. Also, if it catches on, newspapers may as well fold. Historians and biographers can pack in their tasks. Nobody will be allowed to find out anything about anyone. Even to print that (say) a person takes sugar in their coffee will be a gross invasion of their privacy and human rights. Because how can you define the limits of privacy? Non-fiction is over.

I'm screaming the place down most days already, when I need to talk to course tutors about Oscar's syllabus or his university fees and loans, and they won't talk to me because of 'data protection'. Balls to data protection. Up the bum and no babies with it. *I'm your student's fucking father!* If I said I was Oscar's pre-op lesbian transgender one-legged black vegan Mohammedan partner on asylum-seekers' benefits, no doubt all doors would immediately be opened and everyone would be courtesy itself.

Do you know, I've never sent a tweet or a twerp in my life, so I won't be arrested on this occasion. I've never received a text. I can't use my mobile because I'm foxed by the Keypad Unlock function* and I've lost the instruction booklet. I am the last man alive who uses a Waterman's fountain pen. I became a writer, indeed, because I loved ink and paper and stationery. I love calligraphy – yet cheques are to be phased out because nobody now knows how to sign their own name. Nobody writes essays in exams – it's all copy-and-paste course work.

What I dislike about twerps and twits is that our glorious English language has been reduced to a few badly spelt words, ungrammatically assembled. A chimpanzee grunting with a stick is more sophisticated. The more advanced the technology, the stupider the people using it have had to become. Tragic.

* I'll keep on mentioning this until one of you offers me assistance.

That religious morality is no longer allowed as a guiding precept in the Royal Courts of Justice or anywhere else was rubbed in again recently when the General Medical Council officially reprimanded a Margate GP for mentioning God during a consultation.

Well, I'd not particularly want the subject of the Holy Spirit's mysterious ways to come up during a prostate examination, but 'talking about spiritual matters', which is what Dr Richard Scott stands accused of, might be an enlightened way of treating, for example, the patients who traipse in with their depression, drug abuse, alcoholism, and obscure aches and pains. A lot of what makes us feel wretched isn't always physical. Also, as a doctor used at one time to be a person whose job was to make us feel better, a bit of prayer, touching wood, putting your faith in a miracle, could be an element contributing to recovery.

Nevertheless, the grim quacks on the board of the GMC have accused the good doctor of 'harassment' and of bringing the profession into disrepute. Dr Scott may even be struck off, if he fights back. His mentioning God 'must not be repeated'.

I wonder – would they tick off and bully an Islamic GP in this way? They wouldn't dare. Harley Street would be burned down.

I hate these official bodies that boss us about and lecture us on 'standards'. Soon it is village fete time, if you can cope with the 'risk-assessment' forms warning against the sheer horror of coconut-shy balls going off-course, children exploding because they are allergic to face paint, old folk being poisoned when they chew on firelighters from the barbecue, and the crowds of people doing the sponsored walks collapsing in a heap with broken limbs because the path was strewn with rocks, which somehow they'd failed to notice. Common sense is dead.

Dead as the dodo, indeed, in Bury St Edmunds, where magistrates handed Alexander Purser an eighteen-month conditional discharge and ordered him to pay £500 costs, all because he cycled naked through a Suffolk village.

Such an action, said Joy Watkins-Ellis, chairwoman of the bench (I picture old trout Dame Margaret Rutherford) could have caused 'alarm and distress' – to whom? Nuns?

What happened is that Purser saw a 'community speed watch group' – i.e. a bunch of do-gooders, peeping toms, curtain twitchers and crypto-fascists – hanging about in a lay-by at the side of the road and decided to have a bit of a lark. So he nipped home, stripped off, and whizzed past on his Chopper.

The curtain twitchers immediately called the police, fearing that 'children at a nearby primary school might see a naked man'.

If the naked man in question was fruity astrologer Russell Grant or the late Bernard Manning I could understand the alarm, at least on aesthetic grounds. But Alexander Purser is twenty-three and rather cute. He ought to do it all again for charity – though health-and-safety officials may first want to check his helmet.

Anyway – back to the *MV Gustav Holst* and matters more rewarding. What a small world. One old lady, from Malpas, used to be a nurse at St Joseph's Hospital and knew Sister Columba, who was there when my grandmother had her hysterectomy. That's forty-odd years ago. It was only when my grandmother went in to have her hysterectomy that she was excused cooking/cleaning duties, so she always talked fondly of Sister Columba. To give you an idea of how ancient this former nurse was, she began her career working for A. J. Cronin in Tredegar. So she had to be at least a hundred and twenty years old. She'd also once seen Marianne Faithful in Penhow.

Slimbridge – after two hours every duck looked the same.

I've been there before, actually, in the long ago. Forty years have passed, I think, since I last looked at a duck with any degree of care or interest. We used to go on an annual daytrip to Slimbridge from Bedwas Junior Mixed with Mrs Rich, Mrs Tippens, Mrs Bullen, Mrs Dunnicliffe and Mrs Rayo. A frightful old poof was in charge – Peter Scott. He was once married to Elizabeth Jane Howard, Kingsley Amis's second wife. She left him (Peter Scott) because he wasn't (how can I put this?) wholeheartedly in the vagina business. I hope I've got that right and I don't mean Coral Browne.

॰

Which brings me adroitly to Vincent Price in *Witchfinder General*. Can there be a more misogynistic film? It must be the top favourite video in the video rental shops in Tehran, particularly on the nights before a good stoning.

It is all about women screaming in dungeons, with lashings of ketchupy blood. Ranting about 'the foul ungodliness in womankind', Vincent apprehends and defiles virgins, then burns them. 'We must thank you for your good work, Master Witchfinder,' says Master Loach – played by the epicene Wilfred Brambell, old man Steptoe himself. Wilfred was the sort of chap who, the minute he was born, must have looked back from whence he'd come and said to himself, 'I'm not going up one of *those* again.'

॰

I've wanted one for years and have always kept an eye out in hospice shops and the like – and last Saturday suddenly there it was: a Goblin Teasmade. There's something very *Terry and June* about a Teasmade. I can see now why they went out of fashion. It's not the fact that it is just as easy to nip down to the kitchen and boil a kettle, or the fact that it is a pain bringing the cups and saucers and milk jug upstairs and then having to take the cups and saucers and milk jug back downstairs for the washing-up. It's the fact that when the device is starting to get going – gurgling, spitting steam, whistling, clearing its throat – you might as well have The Flying Scotsman in the bedroom. The first morning we were wide awake ages before the off, watching it warily and suspiciously. That's right. Warily *and* suspiciously. The second morning we were woken up by the noise and then blinded by a bright light that flashed on. The third morning Anna forgot to set the timer. Tomorrow morning it is going to be back in its box.

↜

'When a thinking man reaches maturity and attains to full consciousness he cannot help feeling that he is in a trap from which there is no escape,' said Chekhov. Yes and no. The trap is of his own manufacture; sometimes the trap is more of a cocoon – job, house, friends, tastes, hobbies. Is where we find ourselves living a trap?

Well-meaning people always ask me am I glad to be in Bromyard, situated as it is in a fold in the map in the remote Herefordshire Balkans. 'Do you not pine for walking about the place in London with the feeling something might happen?' To which I always reply that I'd love to lord it in London, of course I would, but have never had the money – and I'd not want to be there and be half-skint, living in some distant region that's a slum now but in another fifty years will be gentrified, like Penge or Croydon, where the only white people are the Irish.

Perhaps it doesn't matter *where* one is really. 'Something like nothing happens everywhere,' said Larkin – or maybe he didn't and it's 'Nothing like something happens nowhere'; or fuck me blue perhaps it's even 'Nothing like everything happens anywhere' . . . Anyway, you get the picture. Hull, Leicester, Loughborough were his haunts. Not on the face of it the Boulevard Montparnasse.*

* The correct quotation is 'Nothing, like something, happens anywhere' – from a poem called 'I Remember, I Remember', written in January 1954 and published in *The Less Deceived* (The Marvell Press, 1955). Any *clearer* now? Any *happier* now?

What we truly cannot escape are responsibilities. Though Charles Strickland in *The Moon and Sixpence* leaves his City job and his family to try his hand at being a painter in the South Seas, Maugham is clear that this is a self-destructive fantasy, even an inhuman one. But I always liked the letter Strickland left for his family to read – something along the lines of 'I've supported you for twenty years. Why don't you support yourselves for a change? You've had many years of comfort . . .' When my children stay in bed all day and booze and wench all night, I often dream of cutting them off like this. So what is it that stops most of us from clearing off? Conscience? Duty? Love perhaps?

୨

Philip Larkin told his paramour Monica Jones – she was like the Miss Jones in *Rising Damp* and he was definitely Rossiter's Rigsby – 'The only good life is to live in some sodding seedy city and work and keep your gob shut and be unhappy.' Apart from the fact that it is a township and not a city – that's me in Bromyard, *n'est ce pas?*

୨

Tracey Carter of South Wye has been 'hitting a brick wall' trying to identify her six-headed tulip.

୨

Spike Milligan, Chaplin and Hitler shared a birthday – 16 April. What a joint birthday party they could have had. Spike and Charlie were always dressing up as Hitler. They could have been triplets. Except that the Führer would probably have dressed up as Eccles from *The Goon Show*.

୨

'Give me the sun!' I'd been howling during my illness. Hepatitis, gastritis, iritis. So to Seville by Easyjet from Bristol. (Vernon Dobtcheff! He's off out and about again!) The city was filled with the smell of pungent sickly sweet orange blossom – so what colour's an orange? I can tell you. It's not the trick question it may seem. Easyjet orange, Opal Fruit orange, burnt orange, sunburst orange, any variety of ochre and umber and sodium flares and the saffron that gives paella its tint. Seville is an orange city. The streets are lined with orange trees, heavy with fruit. The sand in the bullring is yellow with an orange tinge. The food is orange and blood-red – peppers, pimento, paprika. I can't shake the colour off. Since we've been back I have been buying Anna orange scarves and bags, beads and cardigans. I found an orange glass vase in IKEA. Anna's dad made a jar of marmalade from an orange we smuggled home from the Alcazar gardens.

The desert is not far off – there is a ferocity to the heat. There are tall tapering palms with their plume of frayed, stiff leaves. You can see why David Lean used Seville for Cairo and Damascus in *Lawrence of Arabia*. The Arab heritage can be heard in the bleak wailing of the flamenco singers; a Muslim call to prayer. It gets into the blood, the stamping, the clapping, the beat. The swirls and barbs; the representation of domination and submission. The dance suggests the fighting bull – just as the Morris Men, here in the Herefordshire Balkans, suggest going ratting.

I've watched these people for hours. Each and every song or routine is about hatred, abandonment, love and death. Seville – the flamenco. 'I want more!' they seem to be saying, as they stamp their sturdy polished patent-leather shoes. As for the bullfight, I'd like to introduce the bullfight to England. To Uxbridge, say, or Reading. The corrida on the M4 corridor.

I avoided Spain for years. I expected it to be corny – castanets, mass tourism and sangria, like in *Carry On Abroad*. Yet it is the only country in Europe that is distinct and odd and exotic. It is an old-world country, where the past is alive to people – as it no longer is in England. No wonder Orson Welles was besotted. (His ashes are interred near Ronda.) Welles stayed every Easter at the Alfonso XIII, a hotel that is like the Xanadu set in *Citizen Kane* – top-heavy marble fireplaces, polished staircases, cloisters, empty antechambers, ducal escutcheons. There is a Moorish influence in the architecture, in the ceramics and intricate geometrical designs. Herbie Kretzmer told me he once saw Princess Grace of Monaco arrive at the Alfonso XIII in a horse and carriage – it is that sort of place.

I like the astringency of Spain. Picasso, Almodovar, Bunuel. Did Bunuel ever make a film that wasn't about fucking the maid? I never saw it. In Seville, the men and boys were wearing suits. Hair is oiled and neatly combed. Women had mantillas. It's like before the war. There are no displays of public drunkenness. It was Easter and there was something spooky about the cowled penitents, in their Klansmen attire. Something pagan, too, in the notion of Easter as a fertility rite. Easter Sunday is celebrated with the first bullfight of the season.

I ate like a fool: wild boar stews and oxtail soups, slices of raw ham and bowls of olives – I've returned to the city three times in less than a year purely for a plate of *Jamón Ibérico*, which is made from pigs fed on vipers and acorns. I love the atmospheric tapas bars decorated with old bullfighting posters, which serve toasted rolls rubbed with garlic and tomato, which are to be dipped in olive oil.

I made a study of the food scenes, the domesticity, in the pictures of Murillo.* The boys feasting on grapes and melon, with the peelings and prawn shells scattered around their bare feet. The depiction of wine glasses and stone jars. The thirst and hunger of lost civilisations.

When I get back to Britain, after all those meals in Seville or Venice, what confronts me always is a plate of sandwiches at the Holiday Inn – glue-flavoured bread, chemical butter the colour of baby shit, processed cheese, a pile of cheap crisps – £6.95 and served grudgingly by an asylum seeker at the end of his shift.

* Another project I have underway – I'll have to live to the age of 300 to complete everything – is a book about appetite and greed, called *Hog Roasts*.

My father was drawn to inland Spain. It is one of the few places beyond Bedwas he ever went. I wonder was he reminded of the Wales of his own childhood – the agricultural traditions, the backwardness? He read up on it all – histories of the Civil War, books by Gerald Brenan, Norman Lewis, Jan Morris. Imprisoned in the butcher's shop, he dreamt of getting away – and he only did once or twice.

In the spring of 1976 we went to the Royal Academy of Arts to see an exhibition called 'The Golden Age of Spanish Painting'. One of those Day Returns from Newport to London that filled my parents with such apprehension. The taxis, the waiters in restaurants . . . My father was so taken with or by Zurbarán's still life of four jugs or vases he ordered a print of it – it remains on the wall in Wales above my mother's sewing machine. It seems a simple enough painting, even an austere one: ordinary empty cups and sharp-edged vessels, nothing fancy, arranged in a line on a table and surrounded by a lot of darkness. So why should a picture of a few utensils be so moving, so beautiful?

It is because what we are looking at is not only a kitchen, it is an altar. This could be the Holy Grail and associated accoutrements. The lack of ostentation is what gives added mystery, and the intensity of the black suggests a lot of dread. Scholars squabble about provenance and attribution. There are replicas in various galleries throughout the world, one of them by Zurbarán's own son. Perhaps even the one at the Royal Academy was a copy of a lost original – so the print now in Wales is a copy of a copy of a . . . But at least the Royal Academy had borrowed the version from Madrid.

Wandering through the Museo del Prado, in Madrid, one hot afternoon I came across it again, after a gap of thirty-five years. The same one that had been exhibited in London. I wanted to phone my father and tell him, but by then he was already dead.

Members of the Hereford Allotment Association have been much inconvenienced by the installation of bollards near their site off Belmont Road. 'This route has never been a public vehicular right of way and it was always planned to install bollards as part of the improved infrastructure for the area,' said a spokesman from the council.

Wouldn't you like to punch that spokesman from the council in the mouth? I don't know where to begin. The jargon, the mealy-mouthed sentiments, the gobbledegook, the sod-the-public stance . . .

❧

In the middle of the group shot – my own grandfather, Clifford Tavener Lewis, who was born in 1903. It was a strange thing to be named after, as Taveners was a brand of confectionery. Taveners' Chocolate Limes and Chocolate Eclairs, tangy boiled sweets with milk chocolate centres, are still on sale today, if you look.

Clifford took over the running of the butcher's shop and was a total misery. Really quite formidably furious and brooding. He adored me and I adored him. I was completely spoilt. If I wanted six ducklings as pets, an Aberdeen Angus bull calf or a new walking stick – what was I doing wanting a walking stick? – he'd despatch a member of staff to fulfil my whims immediately. I later sold the bull calf back to him for £100, with which I bought a Sony cassette player and the tape of *Jesus Christ Superstar*.

He was ill a lot. Hernias, prostate trouble, cancer. He died in 1973 and I sobbed and sobbed at the funeral, which was like Churchill's funeral for Bedwas, with the shops shutting and a policeman in white gloves in Bedwas Square to stop the traffic. No women attended – a Welsh tradition. They stayed back at the house, cutting sandwiches. Actually, Auntie Hilda and her sister Auntie Jin sneaked in and sat at the back, twisting their handkerchiefs and dabbing their eyes, but fair play no one slung them out.

My father never got on with him – and this blighted his life. My father wanted to go to university and generally get away, but he was told he had to stay at home and 'take over the business' – a sacrosanct duty, it was made to sound, as if it was like taking over the running of a country approximately the size of the Austro-Hungarian Empire. (My father did go to Cirencester – he's buried in his Cirencester blazer.) But it was a chain of five butchers' shops, a farm in Glamorganshire, and a slaughterhouse. Like King Lear, or Kaiser Franz Josef come to that, my grandfather was very bad at giving up his power. He wouldn't sign stuff over, so what my dad did mostly inherit were crippling tax bills.

Every Saturday, my grandfather would sit at the dining room table in Troedyrhiw and 'do the books' – poring over these huge leather-bound ledgers with their columns of figures, adding and subtracting and dividing, writing out bills by hand in ink and preparing the following week's meat orders. This was the pre-decimal, pre-pocket-calculator age. Unless my mother has had a clear-out, these old volumes, with columns of figures going back a century or more, are still in the airing cupboard.

Meanwhile, I sat in a big brown Art Deco armchair (an armchair that years later I saw covered with dust and stuck in a barn), watching television – colour television. My grandparents had the first colour television in Bedwas, a huge cabinet with sliding doors, like an altar-piece, bought from Shattocks, the electrical goods shop. When colour televisions were originally put on display in Shattocks' window, crowds would gather after dark to watch the shifting shapes.

I didn't watch television like people watch television today, glancing at the screen while they do ten other tasks, flicking over from channel to channel in a casual, flippant manner. I was rapt. I gave things my absolute attention. As my grandfather concentrated on his columns of figures, I was concentrating on *The Two Ronnies* or on Richard Greene in *The Adventures of Robin Hood*, which was repeated interminably.* *Sez Les* was another firm favourite. Slightly off-stage, my grandmother was busy in the kitchen preparing egg and chips, which I'd eat from a little table set up in front of me, like in the First Class cabin of a KLM jumbo jet. I've never known such happiness.

♎

Newport Cattle Market, where I'd go on a Wednesday with my grandfather. Let's be frank. No point in mincing words. The pervading colours were green and brown – the green and brown of shit. Everywhere you looked, it was shit. Pellets of sheep shit. The olive-green pools of cattle shit. The animals were nervous and shitting themselves non-stop, particularly when the herdsmen slapped their flanks with sticks. The colour tones were picked up by the farmers, who went in for brown and green tweeds. They must have said to their tailors, 'I want to look like shit.' Their boots were caked with shit. The only bright colour came from the blood – the sheep had holes cruelly punched in their ears, to show that their owners had claimed the lavish EU subsidies. And beyond the colours – the noise. The auctioneer's ululation. The herdsmen's yelps and oaths. The

---

* *The Adventures of Robin Hood* was repeated interminably *and* there were lots of episodes – about a million, I think. It is not generally known that one of the directors was Lindsay Anderson. He kept that quiet.

ramps thudding up and down on the lorries. The clicking and clacking of gates. The bolts and locks in the maze of pens and paddocks. The honk of the calves.

∾

What I hate about Jeremy Clarkson, on television and in his newspaper columns (which become his books), is his affected twang of indignation. He pretends to be worked up about caravans or family cars. He has this puerile keenness for speed. He's like the pub bore who knows at a glance the difference between that Cortina and this Vauxhall Viva; the trim and livery and engine specifications. It is utterly adolescent – the mentality of someone who has yet to kiss a girl.

Loud and brash, it is also so obviously put on. Like Alan Titchmarsh, who can talk quite normally and properly for seconds at a time – but then he has to drop his aitches and shove in a few Yorkshire tropes, to remind and convince us of his man-of-the-soil working-class credentials. Again, it always strikes me as a deliberate, calculated performance. What do people see in them? Yet Jeremy and Alan are a million times more popular than I'll ever be if I live to be a thousand.

Fred Dibnah was also always giving a deliberate performance, too, but for some reason he convinced me he was being completely natural, in his eh-by-gum way. There was no phoniness. The enthusiasm (unlike Jeremy's disdain) wasn't being faked for the cameras – so I found myself enthralled by his descriptions of old boilers and broken brick steeples. Somebody is going to spoil it now and tell me that in actuality Fred wore a purple cravat, painted his nails, collected French Impressionist paintings, and was so la-di-dah he was offered Life Membership of Boodle's and maybe even Pratt's. Perhaps he stood as a candidate for the Oxford Chair of Poetry? I was sad when the prostate cancer got him.

∾

The Morris Men are at large in Bromyard, their excuse being that it is Folk Festival Weekend – though they don't need much of an excuse to show off their serious bellies and beards, their open-toe leather sandals, their bright three-quarter-length socks. They wear top hats woven with hops and weeds. They jig about a lot and wave handkerchiefs. Harmless and twatty. Yet the origins are in pagan ritual, fertility dances and blood-sacrifice – the world of *The Wicker Man*.

You'd have a hell of a search on your hands if you wanted to round up any virgins in Herefordshire today. Even the ugly birds have babies in their teens. Yet I do like the way the mysticism of Old England has survived, with corn dollies, holy wells and fairy verses.

୨

George Orwell – there's another one, like Jesus, Jimmy Savile or Wittgenstein, who wanted to transcend his background (he was an Old Etonian) and who set about suffering on purpose, having a go at being down and out in London and Paris, serving as a policeman in Burma, and so forth. Why do such people so dislike themselves, so dislike who they are, that they feel self-obliteration is a highly necessary step? And where has this idea come from that extreme poverty will somehow be more *truthful* and that reality is to be found in the unadorned basics of existence? No possessions. No material things. No relationships. Strip it all away.

As I've seldom been solvent and was raised in industrial South Wales, you won't find me searching for the poor life, which has no nobility that I can see.

୨

Crime Wave Corner. The Filth won't leave that gatepost collision incident alone. 'Police would like to speak to anyone who saw a car hit the gatepost . . .' we keep being told in the local paper, week after week. 'The metallic blue car damaged the post on the junction of Sheridan Road and Cliveden Grove . . .' It's getting to be like the Bloody Sunday Enquiry.

✏

I've been looking at Annie Leibowitz's pictures lately. Everyone in them is asleep (and look dead) or they are actually dead. Poor old Susan Sontag laid out on the funeral director's slab is a ghoulish subject to say the least. Illness wasn't a metaphor to Susan at the finish, was it? Here she is, bloated with cancer and turning green. The only person such a portrait would appeal to is Charles Addams.

Annie's landscapes are dead, too. Leafless trees or war zones. Gravestones, shells, pebbles. It is post-apocalyptic. Venice is vanishing in a black fog. Yet then of course there is Annie's public art (if photography can be an art) — the film stars she shoots for Condé Nast. That side of her work is jokey, silly. Oprah or was it Whoopi in a bath of milk, Barry letting his Edna make-up run, Steve Martin covering himself with paint. I've got a (signed) print of Leonardo DiCaprio with a swan draped around his neck — a homage to Ludwig II of Bavaria? I wonder what stunt she'll dream up when she comes round here, because I am *pestered* by photographers. My guess is that I'll be done up as a matador to fight a Herefordshire bull.

✏

The Jesus story is magic realism.

✏

With Helena Bonham Carter in *Dancing Queen* it was an achievement of sorts to make Rik Mayall look as if he is underplaying. She sent an old video to me — so I watched it wondering how she was going to follow this particular path in her performance, i.e. going full pelt from bad to worse. The kooky costume — including a coloured plastic umbrella; the way she waltzes in the rain; the absurd Fanny Squeers accent. It made no sense at all that Rik Mayall's character was enchanted — she's

103

just a pub stripper. Except it is Helena Bonham Carter as a pub stripper.

Dancing Queen was either remade as Martin Clunes's film *Staggered*, or else Martin Clunes's film *Staggered* came first – I can't be bothered to check. Here's the premise: a groom has been abducted on the night before his wedding and is trying to get to the church on time. Er, that's it.

So: why doesn't said groom (stuck in Scarborough – seems quite nice) start getting on the phone to people? Hasn't he heard of reverse charges? The set-up is so contrived and infantile I got cross. For instance, Helena Bonham Carter promises to get some cash. She makes Rik Mayall promise not to turn up at the pub until after six-thirty. But why exact this pledge? He knows how she makes her money. She'd been the entertainment at his stag-night do. When he does blunder into the pub early, there's nothing to discover – nothing happens.

Rik Mayall, like a magician, can fool you into thinking that something is afoot – that a relationship is forming, when it is not, or that the story has poignancy, when it does not. Like *Cactus Flower* or *There's A Girl in My Soup*, when Goldie Hawn used to play the befuddled character that Helena Bonham Carter does here, i.e. women who keep tantalising their square co-stars – you wonder why Rik Mayall (or Walter Matthau or Peter Sellers before him) doesn't simply knock out his tormenter with a tent mallet and be done with it.

Trivia: Martin Clunes has a bit part here as a co-conspirator with the Best Man. Martin Clunes is very agreeably misanthropic, isn't he, in *Doc Martin*? I'd be like that if I was a GP in Cornwall. It is bad enough being a DLitt in Herefordshire.

ᔥ

Anna's Auntie Hepworth at The Swinburne Arms. Tiny as a bird, quiet as a mouse, ate like a horse. Not completely quiet, though. 'I'M THE CHEESE TART!' she near-bellowed when the waiter was taking the orders – it wasn't even her turn. But they might have run out, see. I only wish she'd gone for the stuffed marrow and had got her megaphone out to announce that to the world. Though in appearance as fragile as a hairnet, Anna's Auntie Hepworth wouldn't share her marrow with not nobody no how, not even in wartime.

'*THAT'S* FOR THE SOUP!' she bellowed again in a Regimental Sergeant Major's parade ground voice, when Oscar went to take a slice of wholemeal bread. Other than this she made absolutely no contribution, neither conversational nor financial. It's a mystery to me how little old ladies obtained this reputation for sweetness. They are rapacious. They have killed off their husbands, whom you can be sure saw them left more than right. The devil in Dreyer's *Vampyr* is unmasked as a sweet little old lady. The wealthier they are, I have noticed, the more mean they are. The very wealthiest cut their own hair. They have the chopped, cropped pudding bowl appearance of Iris Murdoch or Lady Penelope Betjeman.

౿

London audiences have a very low (or anyway very different) standard for what they find uproarious. They guffaw away and I'm stony-faced. *Noises Off* – stony-faced. *The Play What I Wrote* – stony-faced. I went with Birmingham fabulist Jonathan Coe – we were both stony-faced. Bored to tears. *Boeing Boeing* – stony-faced.

It's happened again with Dion Boucicault's *London Assurance* at the National. A dreadful, laborious would-be romp in my opinion – but not according to John Peter in *The Sunday Times*, who went on about 'this comic masterpiece . . . Sparkling . . . Bursting with elegant, biting but warm-hearted wit and revelling in its own mastery of theatrical skill.'

Was I in the wrong auditorium? 'Wonderful, outrageous, stylish, hilarious and unmissable,' he continued. Steady on, John Peter, what's put *you* in such a good mood? Those words may be said with some justice, and without fear of successful contradiction, about (say) *me*, but not about this production, which was so bad I wanted to go backstage and give everyone involved a good spanking. Even a bad spanking. Which can sometimes be good.

Unless, of course, what John Peter thought was that when full-of-beans Sir Simon Russell Beale was playing Sir Harcourt Courtly he was indeed playing me — because in his curly black wig and velveteen suits the resemblance was uncanny and all too believable, if unflattering. People during the interval were similarly confused — what was Sir Beale doing mingling with the crowds? During *London Assurance* itself — how come Sir Beale was on the Olivier stage and sitting in Row E Seat 32 of the Circle simultaneously? It baffled science.

As for the others in the show — Fiona Shaw laughed heartily as she delivered her lines, as if that made them funny. Richard Briers came on for the sole purpose of showing us that Richard Briers is still alive, though I still need some convincing. He's at that as-he's-ninety-and-can-still-eat-a-boiled-egg-give-him-the-Nobel-Prize time of life.

I enjoyed the set. I like elaborate sets. I like seeing money really *squandered* on a set. Here we had a life-size Cotswold stone Toad Hall. But it was short of rooms. The inhabitants appeared to have taken up residence only in the entry hall. There didn't seem to be an upstairs. References were made to a billiards room, a dining room, a drawing room, a library. There was meant to be a chase sequence. The cast would go through little curtains and vanish, but from the angle of my seat I could clearly see that where they crept or dashed away to was only into the wings. My disbelief didn't get to be suspended.

❧

I wanted to be one of those cynical and sophisticated people who sniffed, 'What Royal Wedding?' I'd have settled for looking at photographs of the Royal Wedding in the newspapers a day or so later. At 6.30 a.m. on 29 April I was turfing Anna out from under the eiderdown with the injunction, 'Come on, come on, we don't want to miss a moment of Huw Edwards's informative commentary. Fiona Bruce and Sophie Raworth will already be on duty outside Westminster Abbey!'

To get her going, I served Anna breakfast in bed – grapefruit, a boiled egg with Mrs Toze's egg cosy, toast and marmalade made from the orange we picked in Seville. After that start, I've never known the woman have a day like it. Normally Anna is out and about at meetings, seeing patients, or customers as they are now called, dictating reports, swapping frocks at East, the newish boutique that's opened locally. Then there's her Church Warden stuff and her charity trustee stuff. If she's not totally busy all the hours there are, she's guilty. On this never-to-be-forgotten-day, however, she sat down to watch the Royal Wedding coverage at about eight o'clock and didn't move from the sofa until *The One Show* came on. She didn't even get up to *pee*.

Angela Rippon was such a tremendous bore on *The One Show* I had to phone up Gyles and ask him to shoot her dead. 'You are funny,' he said – which is what Gyles would say to Fred West, if he'd gone along to Cromwell Road for *The One Show* to discuss laying a patio. 'You are funny, Harold Shipman. When did you first start wanting to kill old ladies?' That's another thing he'd say.

I made a champagne picnic lunch, with salmon, new potatoes and salad. I invented a cocktail called The Prince Harry Plunger: port, gin, dark Navy rum, shaken and poured over ice. Strain and serve in a Martini glass with a few blueberries and a slice of lemon. Sounds elaborate – basically it was whatever I could find in the fridge. If there'd been cheese in the fridge, The Prince Harry Plunger would contain cheese.

I drank a bottle of claret at lunchtime and slept for three

hours in the afternoon. When I came round, the Royal Wedding was still on. Prince William and Princess Catherine were still saying their vows and going up and down the aisle. Oh Christ, I thought, they are doing it all again. There must have been a hitch. But Anna was cleverly switching channels from Sky to BBC News 24 to ITV and back again, hence creating this Bermuda Triangle effect.

What I remember from my own experience in Westminster Abbey, when I went with my father to Ted Hughes's Memorial Service in 1999, was the power and volume of the organ and the choral music. The BBC seemed to tone this down so that we wouldn't miss Huw say of a lady in a hat, 'There's a lady in a hat. Mag-ni-*f-f-f*-i-cen-*t*.' I do wish my fellow countrymen wouldn't elongate words.

It was like a film, the good bits – the bride and groom walking down the aisle to the William Walton music, the bride's nipples sticking out like chapel hat-pegs. Walton scored Olivier's Shakespearean adaptations – and with the dashing military uniforms, the scarlet and gold, here was Britain at its best: when it looks like Ruritania. Horsemen, coaches, swords drawn, polished helmets flashing in the sunshine.

My other observations on the day are few and brief:

(a) The naff mini-buses were a comical touch. A mini-bus is suitable for a bunch of rugby lads off on a spree, but these mini-buses emerging from Buckingham Palace and proceeding up the Mall contained lords and ladies out of Shakespeare's history plays – the Kents, the Gloucesters, the Yorks, even Old Norway, last seen or anyway mentioned in *Hamlet*, Act I sc. ii, where Claudius calls him 'impotent and bedrid'. A slander – as King Harald V, covered with orders and decorations, tottered to his place in quite a sprightly way.

(b) Did you see those leather-clad men on police motorbikes, leading the Royal Wedding cars up the Mall? Keeping to a steady

15 mph on a flat empty road, lined by the Household Cavalry and with snipers on the rooftops, the police escort was utterly without function. I mean, didn't the chauffeurs know how to get from Buckingham Palace to Westminster Abbey without assistance? Were they new at the job – indeed, this their very first day? It is not a complex route. The police had such a look-at-me-in-a-stab-suit mentality, I think the motorbikes (with their headlights on) were there simply to make the cops look important. They fancy themselves like anything, the Filth.

(c) Old Norway in *Hamlet* is the uncle of young Fortinbras, who is described as being 'of unimproved mettle, hot and full'. Can there be a better description of Prince Harry? He had a shagged-to-death demeanour, as if he'd been forcibly dragged from the harem to be at the Abbey and was bloody well heading straight back to the harem the minute it was all over. I bet he even had a couple of quick ones in the vestry.

He is a captain in his cavalry regiment, but was covered with such an elaborate tangle of bright gold frogging, his commanding officer – even a field marshal – couldn't possibly look more adorned. From what I understand, the protocol involving these aiguillettes, to give the proper name, is pretty complex – but basically in the presence of a member of the Royal Family an officer is meant to be in full-dress mode. As Harry is a prince of the blood royal, he therefore has to wear this elaborate costume in the presence of himself – hence the thickly corded loops and tassels and ropes. But he does look like a successful porn star, doesn't he?

(d) I wasn't sure about these trees they'd planted in the Abbey – it had the air of an expensive department store 'installation', when they are promoting shoes for Easter or new handbags and accessories for the forthcoming season. If there were white bunny rabbits hopping about and butterflies flitting through the dappled glades, at least the cameras didn't pick any of it up.

(e) I was annoyed at the brevity of the balcony appearance — don't these people know about curtain calls? I thought that the sad middle-aged provincial women (from e.g. Burnham-on-Crouch) and clueless foreign students who had camped out for days to watch the events were rather short-changed. And it wouldn't have hurt for a camera to have been allowed into the Reception. I felt that one way and another the public was being kept at a considerable and very decisive distance, the gulf between *them* and *us* unpalatably feudal and vast. I believe that the cost to the taxpayer was £20 million.

❧

I'm not a political person. We've had those polling cards for the Local Council Elections — and unless there is The Dog Lovers' Party or Monster Raving Loonies, I'm stumped. On the day of that big 'Don't Attack Iraq' demonstration in London, I went to see *Chitty Chitty Bang Bang*. The old dears in the audience swooned for rosy apple-cheeked well-fed Michael Ball. The man who does Lily Savage was The Child-Catcher — how dull he was. Yet when Robert Helpmann created the role in the film he was so terrifying I still wake up screaming. As Baron Bomburst, Brian Blessed didn't have to worry about over-acting on this occasion. Understudies were on for Anton Rodgers and Edward Petherbridge. A suicide-inducing horrible afternoon, with everyone having to clap along merrily to 'Oh, you, pretty Chitty Bang Bang/Pretty Chitty Bang Bang, we love you!' Oh I longed to sell the thing on Mucklow Hill for scrap. I came out of the theatre so cross I wanted to attack not only Iraq, but Iran, Afghanistan, even fucking *Belgium*.

❧

I've been thinking how Francis Wheen's book about the bizarre Charlotte Bach — a burly fraudster transvestite — would make a brilliant film for Stephen Fry. I mentioned this to Francis, who agreed. I mentioned it to Stephen, who went quiet. Lynn

Barber told me that she has done Stephen three times and that he relies on his charm – and when his charm doesn't work he gets defensive and prickly. Apparently Jeffrey Archer is the same. (*I'm the same.*) Jeffrey Archer would also be ideal for Charlotte Bach. He'd be better as Charlotte Bach than James Bond, which is the role he covets.

When Charlotte Bach died, the funeral directors, laying out the corpse, discovered that she was a fella. Bach (real name: Doris Klunt) was a confidence trickster who, to perpetrate his scams, changed his identity over and over again, eventually believing he'd changed even his gender – and (dottily) that this amounted to a great scientific breakthrough in the history of human evolution. He/she wrote pamphlets on the subject. In his deluded way, Bach was heroic, because indefatigable. Though he'd totally taken himself in, the joke is – he always looked like a burly bloke in a frock. In wig, padded bra and panties, he still puffed on a pipe.

৯০

To the Hippodrome in Birmingham for the Birmingham Royal Ballet. I always find the classical ballet highly artificial and cool – almost cold. Brittle, like icicles. The unflattering white tutus and tights. Yet ballet (surely) is about heat – sex and pursuit. All dance seems to involve pursuit and capture: a bit of writhing and conjoining, and then separation and parting. It's the geometry of courtship and possession. I love the ritual of it, but there's something snowy and frozen-in-time about it all.

৯০

An actor I'd best not name – let's call him Stretton Sugwas – keeps calling me when he is so drunk he slurs his words, which come out at a slower and slower pace, like an old-fashioned horn gramophone winding down. Stretton recently phoned me to talk about Arthur Lowe. 'When Wilson looked quizzically at Mainwaring, that was Le Mes looking quizzically at Arthur.'

Stretton must have been using a primitive mobile or remote control device, because there was a huge amount of distortion and disturbance, deafening blasts of white noise and negative feedback. I don't think he could have been orbiting in a spaceship or signalling from the moon, but I did wonder. In the end the line went dead. I found Stretton's number and called back. He didn't know who the hell I was and put his wife on, another piss artist. She said that all that noise was her dog whining, which cannot be possible. I could hear Stretton crashing and mumbling in the background, pulling corks and dropping bottles from shoulder-height on to what was without doubt a stone floor.

My month ended badly. My blood pressure is up. I need a Church of England witch-doctor to put me right. But I had this call from the Huffington Puffington website people, who are starting up a European arm. I got the soft soap treatment. Would I be a contributor, as 'we hear you are very good at what you do. Blah-dee-blah . . .' All very jolly. Then, suddenly, after fifteen more minutes of this, 'There's no fee however. It's self-promotion.'

At which point Roger Clifford Lewis, MA, PhD, DLitt, FRSA (though *not* FRSL) saw red. Because what other professionals are treated in this way? I mean do people go up to lawyers, surgeons, vets or architects and say, 'Please handle a case for us/perform an operation/bring my pooch back from the dead/build an entire fucking house plus conservatory extension, but there's no fee. It's *self-promotion*'?

No, it is not self-promotion. It is *earning a living*. Anyway — nice to have official confirmation that what a full-time writer does is officially *worthless*.

On a happier note, a man in Horsham crashed his quad bike into a tree when he was chased by a goose.

It is already eighty-three years since Spanish poet Federico Garcia Lorca took the train from London to Hereford, in order to visit a friend who worked as a teacher in Leominster. But what of it? It is four years since Jeffrey Holland was last in Malvern, appearing in the hit play *By Jeeves*.

May

What am I still doing here? With the great geniuses, the beginnings and ends of their careers are far apart; they've traversed galaxies. Picasso's early works, his final paintings – the man who drew pinkish pigeons and blue clowns was by the Sixties depicting himself as a lubricous, drooling baboon; Olivier's Heathcliff and the lightweight magicians he portrayed in his last films; Pound's Pre-Raphaelite verse and the abstractions of *The Cantos*. With Anthony Burgess, there he was, fully formed. No evolution. And me? I was a prize-winning Junior Research Fellow at Oxford University and today here I am sitting at the kitchen table in the Herefordshire Balkans, thumbing through a pamphlet calling itself *Lifestyle Solutions*, seeing if there is any comic mileage in Magnetic Knee Straps, Home Chiropody Shears, Extending Garden Tool Sets ('No More Pain From Bending and Kneeling') and a Spill-Proof Portable Urinal ('A Must for the Elderly or Bedridden, Children on Long Trips, Boaters, Campers and Travellers'). I don't know whether to laugh or cry.

The last time I saw my parents together was in London in May 2001, for *The Lion King* and Patrick O'Brian's Memorial Service. What big babies they'd become, or enjoyed being. The provincials up in the big city, like Joe Gargary in *Great Expectations* – standing out, gauche and clumsy. My mother waddling, too fat for her shoes, not really quite coping with pavements, with crossing the street, with the speed and action of a town; complaining endlessly about her ankles, her knees. Huffing and puffing in ill-fitting best clothes; saying she was only comfortable in boots. Complaining about money. Convinced taxi-drivers were cheating her, taking us miles out of our way. At the Lansdowne she misread 'Continental Breakfast Included' as 'Full English Breakfast For Free' and so (though I couldn't bear to be there to witness this) she bolted down a gargantuan platter of eggs, bacon, sausages, grilled tomatoes, mushrooms and fried bread. Confronted with the £4 supplement later she was most indignant – indeed sulked and muttered for several hours – and told the poor embarrassed reception clerk, 'I only forced it down because I was told it was free.' She refused to eat lunch later because of the expense and (as she continued to have it) the earlier outright deception. She cheered up when we went to Aspreys and there were free catalogues.

Then we all of us got depressed because *The Lion King* was in its tenth or eleventh cast by now and it was like painting-by-numbers. I wonder if anyone on the stage that night had even met Julie Taymor, let alone been rehearsed by her? And the story, the Disney rip-off of C. S. Lewis's rip-off of the Easter myth, is trite and the ecological undercurrents are banal – they'd have us believe that the lions are *vegetarians*.

I took them – my parents not the lions – to the Garrick for supper (in those days I was a reciprocal member through the Players Club, New York), and they had a hard time crossing the cobbles of Covent Garden. My mother complained that she wasn't able to finish eating her salmon – though I could tell she was pleased with herself for not polishing it off and not looking a greedy pig; she was pleased with her restraint. She tut-tutted when I ordered more wine. 'Save your money, Rodge. Save your kidneys.' I should have listened. Oh *God* I should have listened.

The next day – the Docklands Light Railway to Greenwich. They couldn't easily get their balance on the escalators. When the trains halted or pulled away, over they nearly went again. After the (thinly attended) Memorial Service, there was a Reception in the Painted Hall. My mother made sure she tucked into the canapés, made sure she had a good feed, 'so as not to need to pay for any dinner', she said, meaning luncheon. She had this peculiar habit of talking loudly about people as if they (or she) is in another dimension, cut off from them, where they can't see or hear. 'Only one in every four people is English,' she observed on the Tube. I was exhausted when I finally waved them goodbye in Paddington. I went to bed for two days. My father was never well enough (bum cancer) to visit London again.

૭

A fire crew from Malvern leapt into action after a 'report of a fire on open land'. When they got there it was out.

૭

Anna and I went down to Devonshire to see Oscar, who is studying art at Dartington – not that he does much art or studying of any kind, needless to say. Anyway we decided to stay not far away in Torquay, where I've never been. It is a dump for impoverished OAPs and the disaffected young.

The first thing to greet the casual visitor to Torquay is a sign directing you to the Crematorium. That sets the scene. There seems to be a sharp division between the gentility of the place (though the gentry have long since left – their villas now dental surgeries, multicultural bed-and-breakfast establishments or sex cinemas) and the nasty cement centre of town, with junk shops, pound shops, aromatherapy salons and art galleries selling original prints of pouncing leopards by Rolf Harris.

The modern buildings here – council flats and derelict office blocks, bungalows and leisure facilities – are real *disfigurements*. Whenever I see a gasoliers being discarded or a Georgian sash window ripped out and replaced by a UPVC frame I feel the same sense of impoverishment and catastrophe – the same anger at the fiery destruction of the things that matter – that other people may feel when they see animals becoming extinct.*

Here in Torquay there is an ugliness that is evil. Someone must have been in charge that absolutely hated stucco and wrought-iron verandas, and who was determined that never again could anyone sit down to high tea on a croquet lawn.

The alleged palm trees that the local council planted are dead cabbage stalks. On the quay were lobster pots but no fucking lobsters. If you are peckish what you have to choose from are Cantonese takeaways, chip shops, and burger establishments that will be responsible for the stink of frying. Microwaved curry from Chittagong seems popular. I had a beef sandwich and pot of Earl Grey, but they had to hunt for a slice of lemon and I felt I'd put them out.

I took my refreshment in The Pavilion, perhaps the one edifice hereabouts that hadn't been kicked to death. Outside were still balustrades and pagodas – Edwardian Oriental. The interior had been ripped out, however, and converted into what they call retail outlets – brightly lit glass booths selling scented candles and handicrafts. Many remain empty.

The Pavilion (constructed in 1912) used to be a theatre and concert hall, a place in the evenings for lantern lectures and a

---

* The most depressing books I have ever seen in my entire life – and I mean no disrespect to the brilliant author, Gavin Stamp, who is as agonised as anyone – are *Britain's Lost Cities: A Chronicle of Architectural Destruction* (2007) and *Lost Victorian Britain: How The Twentieth Century Destroyed The Nineteenth Century's Architectural Masterpieces* (2010). The vandalism was wanton. It was evil. The only explanation I can think of is Freudian: that the town planners and developers had somehow to strike back at their forefathers, remove the symbols of their influence, literally grind them into dust. Like in Dublin, when Georgian buildings were wrecked because the English had constructed them. No other reason. Town halls, stately homes, grand hotels, assize courts and railway stations were mutilated and flattened. One of the sad joys in watching old films is to see a lost London in the background.

palm court orchestra. Hattie Jacques appeared here in a show, as did Dickie Henderson, whom I once saw falling out of the beer tent at Wimbledon at eleven o'clock in the morning. If you want any entertainment now you'd have to make do with *The Laughter Party* at Babbacombe, starring Ruby Washington ('Divine Diva'), Andy Oakley ('Nationally Acclaimed Comedy Star') and Louis Naylor ('Rising Talent'). It's not the same.

In London the London Marathon was on, but here in Torquay I was flaking out trying to make my way along the Coastal Path. The better to admire the yellow tufts on the broom and gorse, I made full use of the many benches conveniently left there by dead people. Down on the beach there was a gull the size of an emu – the size of the city of Gloucester – picking at a starfish. Other gulls sat intently by, like eBay watchers. It was a greyish hazy day, the ash light never getting up the energy or enthusiasm to be blue.

We were staying at the Headland Hotel, a bargain at £48 a night including dinner and breakfast. At dinner the vegetables were potatoes, served three different ways. There was tinned soup, tinned fruit salad. My favourites. Cheddar and cream crackers. Nothing silly. No sign of any Elizabeth David muck. The professional waitresses were on duty again at breakfast because few of the guests would ever master the getting up and sitting back down part that a running buffet involves.

We were surrounded by OAPs on a coach tour who could and did knowledgeably compare and contrast the aisle-width of various supermarkets, and who then, chirruping for the sake of chirruping, discussed which supermarkets welcome mobility scooters and which ones don't. Prizes were awarded accordingly. Then they got on to buses and their sod-the-public timetables. Then there was a seminar on knitting. 'I spent three years making that waistcoat and I never finished it,' said one old lady to another old lady.

The heating was turned up to greenhouse strength and the old ladies were going bright red. Some old ladies, the ones who were quieter than the rest, wore easy-to-wipe bibs, plastic monsoon rain capes really, and were fed by what these days are called carers. In previous eras, the oldsters had daughters.

You imagine that getting on will mean serenity – these brochures I keep getting sent in the post are filled with soft-focus photos of white-haired figures, their unfinished knitted waistcoats casually unbuttoned, strolling in flower meadows or wind-surfing. I thought all the chaps coincidentally resembled Michael Parkinson – then I looked again and it *is* Michael Parkinson. But far from being a placid and calm time of life, slowing up and caving in to decrepitude actually looks as if it will be busy and frantic, with a lot on one's plate to do with illness and medications, walking sticks, crutches and paraphernalia. Deaf aids. Blood pressure pills. Inside everybody must be screaming.

I don't mind any of it. I'm used to screaming. I was in my oils, as we say in Wales. I wanted to move in here to the Headland Hotel permanently, like the Major in *Fawlty Towers*, which of course was set in Torquay. Though it smells of old carpets and cardigans now, once upon a time the Headland Hotel was the holiday home of the Russian royal family, according to the leaflet. I thought the Romanovs had perished in the cellar at Ekaterinburg, but another theory apparently – though disputed by the experts* – is that they lived out their exile on the English Riviera. Unless these were a remote branch – the *Devonshire* Romanovs? Would I find Rasputin in the Neptune Bar?

* Frances Welch tells me that the last Tsar's family came to the Isle of Wight around 1911 – that was the closest they were allowed to the British mainland. Tsar Nicholas's sister, Grand Duchess Xenia, once visited Bognor. She had seven children, six of them sons – so maybe here is a connection? The Tsar's mother, the Empress Maria Feodorovna, Princess Dagmar of Denmark as was, bought her wigs in London. 'Torquay does seem to claim links with the Romanovs . . . But I'm stumped,' says Frances.

No, but there was a magician called Peter Baffle on in the Tsar Nicholas Lounge after dinner, though by then I wanted to go to bed early with Barbara Windsor's *Book of Boobs*. When I came down for breakfast the next morning I saw one or two feathers on the carpet. Had the dove act not gone wholly to plan? I'd heard cooing noises coming from a suitcase.

I never sleep well in hotels, and in Torquay the night air was rent with the wild and spontaneous barnyard squeals – the high-pitched oinks and prolonged excited grunting – of Young Farmers on a regional convention, drunk on cider and shagging their own fat sisters.

ॐ

Even when it was a salubrious place, there was demure Miss Agatha Mary Clarissa Miller, working as a nurse for the Red Cross Hospital set up in Torquay Town Hall, learning about poisons and inculcating thoughts of murder and violence. She first clapped eyes on Archie Christie, her future husband, in that Pavilion place I liked.

Outside The Agatha Christie Shop & Tourist Information Centre there was a bust of Agatha Christie that looked like Sir Frederick Ashton in a huff. Or, as Groucho would say, a minute and a huff. Old Agatha was born in Torquay in 1890 and I wanted to look around that place of hers at Greenway, nearby on the River Dart.

But first Anna had to move fast, gunning and reversing the car like Steve McQueen in a film, otherwise we'd still be stuck outside the Headland Hotel now. A crocodile of OAPs had started to emerge from the Grand Duchess Anastasia Reception Area to get on their charabanc, and they were creeping so slowly – some of them doubling back of course as they forgot which way is straight on – it was like when those columns of ants are on the march in the jungles of Ceylon. Days and days they can take to go past. Anyway – we escaped.

At the cost of only £5 million, the National Trust have cleaned up the muddle and clutter Dame Christie left behind at Greenway, quite eradicating any atmosphere. The house is so spanking new-looking, it could have been put there yesterday morning. It is like a replica, a sterile cube, with here and there a few floppy sun hats and an empty bottle. Hopeless.

The lush flowering magnolias on the banks of the river, the bushes dripping with moisture, the tangled foliage and secret paths going off in all directions, the rotting trees filled with fungus, did suggest Dame Christie's world to me, however. The tangled gardens in the wet air are almost tropical – the camellias and magnolias, the crimson blooms and deep pinks. There is a very sinister boat-house, with a pool that's more of a black pit. Just the place for a murder.

Even though I am not one of those nutters who thinks Captain Hastings was a real person, I did see Julia Mackenzie in the gift shop – I wonder if she is paid to hang about and be Miss Marple? They probably have David Suchet on duty in the disabled toilets.

❧

I thought the oddest fact I knew was that Richard Ingrams's grandfather was Queen Victoria's gynaecologist – hence, you might say, his intimate knowledge of high places. But that was superseded by the news that Peter Cook wore a gendarme's hat in bed – I thought that pretty hard to beat. Then I discovered something more unlikely still: that Peter Cook was a member of Minehead Golf Club. Apparently, when one of his wives tried to dry him out, she moved him to Exmoor – but he quickly discovered a nearby nineteenth hole.

Peter Cook was born and raised in Torquay, which explains everything about him. *Everything*. So important was Torquay to Peter Cook, the old satirist married his third wife in the town. The third Mrs Cook was a Chinese lady from Kuala Lumpur – and Torquay was easier to get to than Kuala Lumpur.

While it is probably not the case that Cook was 'a promising junior amateur wrestler for Devon', it is verifiably documented that he was the upper-middle-class son of a Colonial District Commissioner who'd been awarded the CMG for running Nigeria. Cook, said Jonathan Miller, 'was the most upstanding, traditional upholder of everything English and everything Establishment'. Cook's Soho club was of course called The Establishment – a combination of homage and piss-take. Alan Bennett told me that Cook was always amazingly solicitous towards his venerable mother, whom he (Bennett) would take to tea, and John Wells never forgot Cook's extravagant politeness, his drawing-room manners.

These are Torquay virtues – but they became Cook's vices. The gentility and the drink and the guilt. Cook never escaped the prejudices and concerns of his refined background. The languidness, the drawling voice, the rituals and decorum that are intended to kill time, keep boredom at bay. Sir Arthur Streeb-Greebling could be living in Torquay retirement. Torquay would account for Cook's idleness, his amateurishness. The unopened mail, the overflowing ashtrays – Cook couldn't be bothered.

Idleness, indeed, was his chief occupation. He ought to have been in Chekhov, he was so filled with inertia – the futility of life is of course the theme of the classic Pete and Dud *Dagenham Dialogues*; and while still a student Cook was providing monologues for Kenneth Williams, a man who similarly found life intolerably dull and stifling and who was also a chain-smoking insomniac.

Agatha Christie, as I have outlined, was also from Torquay – her father drank himself into an early grave in the yacht club. If beneath her genteelisms there is horror, so beyond Cook's charm there was contempt for humanity's sufferings and impurities. His philosophy or settled conclusion about the universe was that everything is equally ridiculous, and that when it came to comedy you should be 'completely and utterly unfair'. There's a certain rigid morality to this.

❦

A man in Hereford said he saw otters 'near the city centre'. Doing what, he didn't say. They definitely weren't mink, however, 'as they were too big'. So that's another thing to keep me awake at night: giant fucking otters.

❦

My sister's wedding in Chepstow. I have not seen or heard from my sister in seven years, so it was thoughtful of her to phone up to say I wasn't going to be invited to her wedding in Chepstow. I did a rain dance. Which worked.

❦

One of my editors wanted to meet me for a business lunch. I'm good at lunch – probably none better – but Special Needs when it comes to business. As my next toilet-book masterpiece – *My Hairy Aunt and Other Misprints* – is years and years late, I took along Tristan, by way of a decoy.

The plan worked better than expected. My editor turned out to be a very pretty twenty-four-year-old called Camilla Mence. By the following weekend Camilla Mence was visiting Tristan regularly at the circus. Within a fortnight Camilla Mence was baking him cakes – and he was in High Wycombe by then. Most people in the literary/publishing/arts field have to get to the Frankfurt Book Fair on full expenses and spike the minibar drinks with Rohypnol before they can cover a tiny fraction of that distance with the likes of Camilla Mence.*

❦

She had dire news to impart, did Camilla Mence, the employee of a conglomerated house. She confirmed that no publisher wants these antiquated things called books – what they

---

* Once the circus left High Wycombe to spend the summer months touring the Scottish Highlands, the romance ended. Camilla Mence has since moved to another publishing house, and is no longer the editor of *My Hairy Aunt and Other Misprints*.

want is celebrity-packaged shite and that anyway these days commissioning ideas come from marketing and accounts, who think they are the ones who can spot a trend or niche. I asked why then that being the case did a publisher pay a reputed £2 million to Peter Kay, when any fool could see his moment in the limelight had passed, that he was already repeating himself . . . Meantime you begrudge paying me £3,000 for *My Hairy Aunt and Other Misprints* and I can't wrap it up because I am skint. We changed the subject, to bread and circuses.

I made my first return to The Thorn since the New Year and asked for a slice of lemon in my Bloody Dani. 'Tell him to fuck off back to London with his fucking London ways!' cried a falsetto voice from the cellar – Zany Antony, the landlord. Nice to be back.

Barmaid Dani is a white-witch, who collects nuts and berries from the hedgerows at night to make what she calls chutney. Except after one spoonful you start levitating. Dani invented a drink for me, The Bloody Dani – and again, you start levitating after a few sips:

> Coat the inside of a brandy glass with Lea
>   & Perrins and Tabasco
> Coat the rim with Celery Salt
> Fill completely with ice
> Pour in vodka pretty much up to the brim
> A dash of tomato juice to create a pinkish colour –
>   the colour of a light wound
> A slice of lemon for garnish purposes

Being off the booze and on the water-wagon for virtually six months, though with weekends off, I'd become addicted to carrot cake – which shows how much sugar I was getting from booze.

My hands and fingers went tingly, so Dr Twelvetrees told me to get back on the *vin de table* properly. My carrot cake addiction had triggered Type 2 Diabetes.

On my grandfather's left – Richard Francis Lewis, born in 1908, always known as Dick or Dickie. I know little about him, except that he was a staff captain in the Royal Engineers and in a letter home to his parents felt the need to tell them that 'by the way there are two "I"s in liaison'. He went to live in Brighton ('Hove actually'), where he married a frightful snob called Gladys Cully. Her family were art dealers, though I suspect that what they did was frame pictures. I saw a lot of her. She had quite a bit of style, went on planes to America – that sort of thing. She wore a bracelet with charms on and when amused would say, 'I say, that is *frightfully killing*, darling!' as if she was Dora Bryan trying to be posh in a play. Gladys worked briefly as an infant-school teacher, and thought the only important thing to teach the children were the words of the National Anthem. I'm with her there. She had very big hands, and when playing tennis could hold two balls at once. Or was it three balls at once? Four? Up in the attics at Troedyrhiw, along with the morning coats and piss-pots, were old tennis rackets in their presses. What was once the tennis court had become a pot-holed paddock for Emily my donkey.

Great Uncle Dickie and Gladys's two boys were called John and Richard, and they spent the war years in Bedwas, as it was feared Hove might be invaded – though Gladys would have got on well with the Nazis, as her views on the working class, on foreigners, on coloured persons (workers on government sites) were a little, shall we say, reactionary. 'Have *you* been to Heathrow and leant over the rail and seen them *coming in?*' I heard her challenge an aghast Mark Rylance. The distinguished Tony Award Winner and founding director of The Globe Theatre smiled glassily. Actors to Gladys were also socially suspect – on a par with gypsies and fast women who went to nightclubs without a chaperone. She'd have made Sir Laurence Olivier use the Tradesman's Entrance.

In the event, Hove survived intact but a bomb fell in the vegetable garden in Bedwas and shrapnel was found in Richard's cot. Auntie Hilda's sister Auntie Jin was blown clean up the chimney. She emerged looking like a worker on a government site. John later ran a publishing house called Wayland, which specialised in children's history books. He lived grandly in Possingworth Manor, Sussex, got into debt when he built a fountain, went bankrupt, lost everything, got oesophageal cancer, and died in May 2001, aged fifty-eight.

I went with Oscar and Sébastien to the funeral service, held in St Margaret's, Buxted. The church was situated halfway up the drive of a stately home, where the Queen Mother's brother, the Honourable Fergus Bowes-Lyon, briefly lived – before he was killed in 1914. Richard gave an amusing eulogy: 'We were woken each day by the sound of burnt toast being scraped. Our mother was a woman of considerable talents, but cooking wasn't one of them. We were the only boys in the history of the British public school system who looked forward to going back after the holidays to be properly fed.' Afterwards, the undertakers executed an impressive three-point turn with the coffin by the altar.

Richard is still in America. We used to see several of his ex-wives now and again, when they passed through Oxford.

Mark Rylance's wife, who considers me 'England's best-kept secret' – a kindly meant remark but when I look at the whirlpool of red ink that is my bank account I can't help wishing I was a *very badly kept secret* indeed – tells me that she is composing a full-length score for the Carolina Ballet and finishing a musical, 'an alternative version of *Brief Encounter*'.

Can they dance in the Carolinas? Or is it more that they *stagger*? There is such a thing as the Royal Winnipeg Ballet. One pictures moose.

An alternative to *Brief Encounter*? *Long Encounter*? Trevor Howard and Dame Celia Johnson actually run off together and *do it*? 'I married a girl to stop her getting away./Now she's there all day.' Terrifying. Who wrote that?

The Rylances are also in a panic about what frocks to wear on the red carpet – Mark gets a Tony Award every year. I suggested they pick out frocks made of red carpet and paint their faces red and be invisible. That would be scary and surreal – it would suit Mark. The only time I was on the red carpet the paparazzi thought Truman Capote was back.

෴

The Two Ronnies were perfectly amiable, but difficult to write about – difficult to engage my interest – because there was no darkness or danger. I am discovering this as I research *Growing Up With Comedians*. Their programmes pass the time, but little of it is nutritious. Like snacking on salted peanuts. They went home afterwards, did Ronnie B and Ronnie C, to Pinner or Cheam. There was the charity golf and hobbies such as collecting Edwardian postcards. Professional. But compare them with Russell Brand, say, who'd single out a member of the audience, fling them in the back of the van and shag them until their ears drop off. Plus their friends. And their friends' mothers.

෴

I've been thinking about cockerels – because Brand is a reincarnation of one. The crowing of a rooster was a pagan portent. St Peter (was it?) heard the cock crow thrice. *Thrice* he heard it. In one of D. H. Lawrence's stories, the crowing of the cockerel awakes the dead – it brings Jesus back to life. There's a Gabriel Garcia Márquez story, too, about a Colonel waiting for a letter about his pension, which never arrives – so all his hopes become vested in a fighting cock and gambling.

Hemingway went in a lot for the same sort of suggestiveness – about animal spirits that are not to be tamed or domesticated, but are perhaps to be killed, ritually slaughtered. Marlin, bulls, lions. Beasts and creatures, who are alive to themselves, until hunted down. I like the one about the aged matador and the bull called 'The Undefeated' (in *Men Without Women*), because what Old Hem is suggesting is that his kind of hero – grizzled, wizened, drinks – has a rapport with animals and with their destruction that he, the Old Hem hero, doesn't with anything feminine – women are what men find truly alien. War, confronting big game, and so forth, brings out the best in them – facing up to savagery. It is then that their instincts are working automatically, when they operate without thought. As a State Registered Sissy, I haven't got *a fucking clue* what any of this feels like or means.

❧

You can see the Crucifixion in bullfighting terms. A ritualised death.

❧

When Elvis Presley died, he was on the toilet reading a book about Jesus.

❧

Everything I love that has been made (buildings, books, bibelots) has been made by a process of individualism. I hate anything that might deny individuality or eccentricity – there'd be no more Mr

Toads, no one with unique visions, however daft. I can't abide Political Correctness. It is like East Germany under the Stasi. No freedom of expression.

ॐ

Matt Lucas as Toad in *Wind in the Willows*. What a disappointment. It never ignited. One of those projects that looked good on paper – 'Let's get Matt Lucas in! Let's get Lee Hall in!' – that ended up flat. The costumes were good – elaborate tweed Edwardian-era motoring togs in shades of mossy green, pond green, weed green. Toad Hall itself was decorated throughout in greenish and mildew tinges. But Matt relied on voices and mannerisms that were reminiscent either of *Little Britain*'s Sir Bernard Chumleigh or of the distinguished actor Sir Simon Callow, who might now have grounds for litigation. Toad here was a gigantic retarded baby. Mark Gatiss,* usually reliably good, played Ratty as vaguely queer – though that element was in the adaptation Alan Bennett did for the National Theatre years ago, where Ratty and Badger pined pederastically for a young Mole.

ॐ

Mark Gatiss has the shortest scene or role in the history of cinema – in Woody Allen's *Match Point*. He is playing ping-pong with Scarlett Johansson, and we see him dart through a door. A chronometer has yet to be devised that can gauge the duration of his appearance. It is the tiniest trace, less than subliminal.

By cutting everyone else back to nothing (John Fortune is there, I think, driving a car; and I believe Steve Pemberton walks down a flight of steps; and wasn't that Paul Kaye as a

---

* Wearing a newly bespoke suit, Mark Gatiss attended my splendid party for Charles Hawtrey at the Groucho Club in 2001. This was also my father's last-but-one appearance in public before the bumhole cancer began. 'Who are all the poofs?' asked Wyndham Gardner Lewis. In fairness, there were one or two. Fenella Fielding was there, in a comedy wiglet. Dame Barry Humphries wouldn't remove his coat in case it was stolen.

landlord?*), Woody, at least, was able to give more time to the true stars of the show — not Scarlett Johansson and Jonathan Rhys Meyers exactly, but Scarlett Johansson and Jonathan Rhys Meyers's lips. Woody's camera isn't interested in anything else except those two luscious pairs of lips.

Though they do have amazing mouths — almost freakishly over-scaled, as if they are white blacks; and as with Billie Piper, you look at Scarlett and you think *she could get your balls in* — when they start kissing, Scarlett and Jonathan, you fear they will never again manage to pull apart without medical intervention, such will be the suction.

༄

When Sébastien said he was doing the First World War at school, and asked me if there are any films on it, I said of course there are — there's Frankie Howerd's *Up the Front*. It is full of dreadful old jokes, done properly. 'It's so dark, you can't see your hand in front of your face.' — 'What's that?' — 'Oh, it's my hand in front of my face.' Made me laugh anyway.

༄

Crime Wave Corner. You don't have to do a lot these days to be incarcerated and made to break rocks and sew mailbags. Kyle Price stole £10 from his grandmother's purse and spent nearly a year on remand, mainly at his grandmother's insistence. 'She wanted him to have professional help.' Not only that, he 'needed structure in his life'. Kyle's grandmother had 'no lasting animosity' towards him, however.

If she's one of those helicopter/abseiling grannies, I hope she falls off a cliff.

* I find it slightly annoying — the way Woody Allen, in his series of London films, *Match Point*, *Scoop*, *Cassandra's Dream*, among others, uses our splendid local actors, Penelope Wilton, Richard Johnson, Selina Cadell, Robert Bathhurst, Julian Glover, among others, as glorified extras. It is peremptory. It is like Peter Rogers casting Burt Lancaster in *Carry On Again Up the Doctor* and putting a potty on his head.

Audrey Hepburn! Even in a terrible meringue-like film like *Paris When It Sizzles* she is wonderful — she radiates happiness. William Holden is a drunken writer — but everybody is happy! It's the Sixties! The Beatles are about to happen! When Audrey Hepburn is around, nothing can be bad.

I've been reading about Audrey Hepburn and looking at loads of coffee table books about Audrey Hepburn. She was gauche and odd as a youngster — and of course she experienced God Knows What in Occupied Holland — but went on to be one of the world's great faces. Did anyone ever look better in those Givenchy outfits? It's like a piece of music, Audrey's interaction with her clothes.

❧

Herbie Kretzmer told me that Mel Calman died while watching *Carlito's Way* with his girlfriend, Deborah Moggach. He'd been moving from seat to seat, to get away from people who were talking, and he had a heart attack and died. The manager stopped the film — asked everybody to leave. I hope they put on some suitable Soviet-style funeral music.

I know how Mel would have felt. I stopped going to the cinema years ago because I can't stand the presence of other people in the auditorium. Nor can I watch DVDs with the family about. Which is why I am up all night on my own, with my boxed-sets. I think it was unsporting of the cinema manager to stop the screening. They should have simply thrown a blanket over Mel and carried on. You're dead, you're dead. *Carlito's Way* isn't any good, though.

❧

I saw Herbie's new one, *Kristina*, at the Albert Hall. Fuck me gently with a wire brush. How can I put this? Ingmar Bergman with fewer laughs? It was all about Swedish immigrants who haven't seen the sun for eleven months heading for Minnesota. The crops fail, the wife miscarries, children die, everybody gets malnutrition, there are storms, the barn is hit by lightning. That's before they leave Sweden. The ship takes three months to get to America. Scurvy, lice, tempests, starvation, claustrophobia, prostitution get a look-in as they sail across the ocean. Interval. Act Two, more of much of the same, with the one interesting character dropping dead because he wants to go prospecting for gold in California – and somehow The Lord disapproves of this, or anyway of the one interesting character. Like Elizabeth Taylor, Kristina suffers from one illness after another, including scarlet fever, but she never gives up her faith in The Lord, even though He seemed to me to be leading her up the garden path. 'God, isn't God a shit?' as Randolph Churchill said, when he was found leafing through the *Bible*.

It ended around ten-thirty. The Scandiwegians present applauded heartily, Lutherans lapped it up, and there was obviously a following for full-throated Russell Watson, if the middle-aged bags in Size 20 Boden frocks were any clue. One nice element – Herbie had laid on catering in the box, so we had a wee multicultural lady from Leith's topping us up with drinks and serving canapés. Except I was still on the water-wagon.

Anna and I then to Rules, where they'd had a refit and got rid of the choir stall seats I loved. Nobody there except the waiters hoovering and stacking chairs on the tables, which was unatmospheric. In such instances I always feel I should lend them a hand.

❧

I'm told Monty Don lives in Herefordshire, though I've never seen him locally. I saw him coming out of a Royal Garden Party with a camera tripod over his shoulder once, looking sheepish. *Tim Wonnacott won't have to lug the equipment about*, you could almost hear him thinking. He, Monty, used to have a jewellery business, but even then I'm sure he did the macho gardener act. Moody Monty with a spade. He'd liked to have been the male

Charlie Dimmock. He'd have settled for being Percy Thrower in the *Blue Peter* Garden. Perhaps he will end up selling plastic gnomes and ornamental wishing wells to couples with health issues who've taken early retirement and have got a lump sum and a Bovis Home. But at least he's better than that Alan Titchmarsh, who always reminds me of John Mills's Oscar-winning goblin in *Ryan's Daughter*.

What's with the *Monty*, though? Montgomery? Montmorency? Python? In Bedwas Junior Mixed, a monty was a knob. 'Miss! Miss! Clive Curnow is showing Derek Cheasty his monty!' was a cry you'd hear in the gravel playground at dinner time. Another word for knob was brolly – though these days that would now have to be *knwb* and *brwlli*.

❦

A headline in the local paper: 'Quentin Letts to Speak'. I am immensely relieved to hear it. I hadn't known little Quentin was deaf and dumb, or that in his moated grange at How Caple he had for many years and without uttering any coherent sound been jumping up and down in a friendly way for chocolate buttons. But at least now I know his silence is to be at an end. It is a sort of miracle.

❦

Quentin and I have both contributed to the Boden catalogue. We were paid in Boden vouchers. I had to write a paragraph about the one earth-shatteringly amazing book that had changed my life. Other hacks nominated *Middlemarch* or Enid Blyton – predictable classics of English Literature and so forth. I saluted *The Life and Death of Peter Sellers*. I have got to the stage where if I don't bang the drum for myself, and loudly too, no other bugger is going to do so, *ever* – so, lights under bushels and all that. Still, it was a bit shameless. Not that I care about shamelessness.

The Boden catalogue was (is) like a very jazzy and lavish school mag or prospectus for a fine art degree at the Slade. Terribly bitty

133

and busy and migraine-inducing, every page a calligraphic riot. 'Fun' is what they'll be wanting it to be, a 'hoot'. Imagine what it must be like in the Boden office, if this object is any clue – compulsory jollity. Puke. The Virgin office used to be like that. Parenthetically, Richard Branson's casual attire, his beard and his planes and hot air balloons annoyed me, too. Still annoy me, in fact. Informality can enrage me to such an extent, I sometimes think I must have been stickler King George V in a previous life. Or a sniffy head waiter.

Quentin said he's got his Boden copy, also, in How Caple. 'It made me feel a bit pissed, just looking at it.' So it wasn't just me.

But nevertheless, it is a sign of the times – symptomatic of the way childhood is getting to be infinitely prolonged. The design of the Boden catalogue is bright and glittery and teenagery. This is the trend everywhere today. Folk in their thirties dress like adolescents, with sloppy shirts, baggy trousers and baseball caps on backwards. *Doctor Who*, sci-fi nonsense, computerised escapist claptrap – alleged adults watch it. One of the things I can't stand about *QI* is Alan Davies pretending to be the naughty schoolboy. Davies is *forty-five*.

When back in the last century Jon Pertwee and Patrick Troughton played Doctor Who, the programme was for nine-year-olds. After that age, you started wanting something more demanding and nutritious. Not any longer. Our culture is geared towards perpetual infantilism. Childishness is so encouraged, *Last of the Summer Wine* was axed because old people are not officially allowed to exist.

Almost worse than dead-headed youngsters deferring adulthood – they carry on living at home and never tidy their rooms, contribute to their keep or do their own laundry on principle – are grown-ups trying to look young, e.g. by going to Glastonbury and squirming in the mud. Plastic surgery and expensive hair colouring treatments are all the rage. Everyone is trying to knock thirty years off their age — with the upshot that though still chronologically old they are psychologically immature, and start going on tablets.

✌

Crime Wave Corner. Vandals have smashed a shed window and ripped branches off a tree on a Bromyard allotment. The sheer evil of some people.

✌

Lynn B. tells me she has been in Rome interviewing Rafa Nadal. I said who's Rafa Nadal? A dress designer? 'Rafa Nadal is a tennis player, in fact World Number One,' said Lynn, as to a backward child. Am I thick or which? The only interesting thing that ever happened to me *vis-à-vis* tennis, or indeed sport taken in its totality, was seeing Dickie Henderson at Wimbledon falling out of the beer tent at eleven in the morning.*

✌

There's a go-ahead company that calls itself Incontinence Choice. But isn't that the very *last* thing you'd have if you were incontinent, a choice? If you've got to go you've got to go. I enjoy leafing through the cheerful brochures, with the advertisements for 'almost undetectable' pads and absorbent king-size nappies. The 'whisper-quiet' plastic knickers are an absolute must this season, though the word they surely whisper is *piss*.

✌

Have you noticed how many references there are to hunting dogs in *Twelfth Night*? Orsino says his sexual desires are like 'cruel hounds'. Sir Andrew, talking about singing and dancing, says, 'I am a dog at a catch.' Maria is called 'a beagle, true bred'. When Malvolio is about to be trounced — 'I'd beat him like a dog,' Sir Andrew says in anticipation. Fabian, wanting Feste to hand him Malvolio's letter, says 'to give a dog, and in recompense desire my

---

* As that is my sole sporting anecdote, I repeat it at every opportunity.

dog again . . .' There are lots of images about following the scent, sniffing things out.

I don't know what little theory I can advance here, except Shakespeare was specific about King Lear's dogs who are called Tray, Blanche and Sweetheart, and in *Two Gentlemen of Verona* the clown, Launce, has a long speech about his pooch, Crab.

What perhaps we have a glimpse of is sixteenth-century England, with manor houses and adored domestic pets, the rough domesticity. Exactly like my home in Wales, where there were always beloved dogs under the table, waiting for scraps – Tog, Clyde, Tosca, Pogle. They were like brothers to me.

It is already eleven years since *Carve Her Name With Pride* star Virginia McKenna opened the Violette Szabo Museum in Wormelow, though it is over two millennia (399 BC) since Socrates took hemlock.

June

What am I still doing here? My mother had loads of Enid Blyton books, preserved since her childhood in The Gelli – and I too sought such a world, where goblins and elves lived in flowers and under ferns. Where streams and magic woods and castles of adventure were all about. What Enid Blyton's books promised was a life of incident. Well.

⁊

The River Wye Preservation Trust has revealed that woodland in Herefordshire may be 'older than was thought'. This is a common enough discovery. Anne Robinson, Sophia Loren, Barbara Windsor, Britt Ekland – all of them older than was thought. Most of them have had so many facelifts, when they sit down their hat falls off.* When Faye Dunaway bends her knees, her eyelids clamp shut.

---

* Sophia Loren, it should be noted, has denied ever having gone under the scalpel, attributing her contemporary appearance to 'a love of life, spaghetti, and the odd bath in virgin olive oil.' If she threw some tomatoes over herself, we could eat her for lunch – *Pomodori Farciti al Forno* (serves 4).

Joan Rivers, however, is unimpressed by this explanation, and on *Parkinson*, in May 2007, told the chuckling host, 'I hate it when they say "I've done nothing." Sophia Loren, God bless her, allegedly has done nothing. She's been pulled and stretched so much she shits through her ears. And she says to me, "I've done nothing." And I'm like . . . they took all the extra parts and made another woman who walks beside her. I see her in the garden walking with a Mini-Me.'

I prefer the tomato theory myself. But I don't know why people get cross if plastic surgery is alleged, as it compounds their vanity. It would be easy enough to get them in a rugby headlock and search for sutures. I myself am in urgent need of total body plastic surgery, though with my luck if I issued instructions to turn me into Rob Lowe, I'd emerge from the bandages as Arthur Lowe.

Susan Sontag claimed to have read the multi-volume *Les Miserables* by the age of seven and the novels of Mrs Aphra Benn by the age of eight. Whether Mrs Aphra Benn read the novels and uptown essays of Susan Sontag at any age, I really have no inkling. But what of it? Here's what I wrote at the age of four. Unknown to myself, I was fluent in Chaucerian Middle English. Though these disorders hadn't been invented back then, I was also possibly dyslexic, with a tad of ADHD (Attention Deficit Hyperactivity Disorder), autism and Asperger's thrown into the pot for luck:

The Tael of Teddy and Foxy and Rat

Onec upon a Time There was aer Teddy Bar and a Fox and Misur Fox sed that he wood see Teddy and Teddy sed that he wood go to see Foxy and thay Met at the pine WooDs and thay thot thay WooD see Rat in his hol so they Did.

Thay had a ras and Teddy came pharst and he noct at the Dor.

'Coming' said Rat. 'How is it Teddy? Wot Do you wont?'

'Something to eat.'

'All yull get is nothing.'

So Teddy grorlD and Rat gav Teddy some ches. So e et it. He lickt it.

To the question that always gets asked – 'Did you always want to be a writer?' – I can now point to the above and say, 'Well, what do you fucking think?' Though there are holes in the narrative – whatever happened to Mr Fox? Why was Rat so inhospitable at first? What kind of cheese was it? Caerphilly? – this is the sort of thing that nowadays gets a person elected to the Oxford Chair of Poetry. I shall ask my friend Sir Ricks for an exegesis.

෨

Ah, the Oxford Chair of Poetry. Vernon Dobtcheff! One of my more *significant* catastrophes. As Willie Donaldson may well have conjugated it – you want to be the Professor of Poetry at Oxford University. You'd settle for being chosen as an official candidate for the post. You end up in fifth place, below people no one has ever heard of and poll only a handful of votes more than a busker.

To explain: every five years, the graduates and fellows of Oxford University are invited to elect a Professor of Poetry. Previous incumbents have been W. H. Auden and Robert Graves. It is a prestigious post – though, thank God, with light duties. The Professor simply has to turn up and deliver one lecture a term, for which he (or she) gets paid an annual salary of £6,000 – a sum that hasn't gone up since the post was first endowed in 1696. That wouldn't keep me in vintage port for a weekend.

Quite often, the election descends into farce, which is Oxford's traditional way of capturing the attention of the wider world. Derek Walcott, the Nobel Laureate who was the favourite to win a few years back, was revealed as having once been at the centre of sexual misconduct complaints at Harvard. Ruth Padel, Walcott's rival, was instead elected – but she resigned after nine days, when it was noticed that she had volunteered information regarding ancient scandals, digging up the dirt about Walcott, and this was deemed bad form. Which it bloody well was. I'm told that these days Ruth can still only go round in disguise. She has to wear a wig and one of those plastic all-in-one Groucho Marx false noses-and-spectacles sets.

So there was a re-run. When it was realised that the outgoing Professor was Sir Christopher Ricks – that is to say, a leading critic and not actually a practising poet – I was asked by various people in the media if I'd agree to be nominated. Word seemed to have got round that, like Tristram Shandy, old Roger Lewis can't be accused of keeping his opinions to himself.

Of course I agreed with alacrity. As I sit here in the Herefordshire Balkans watching mid-afternoon repeats of *Songs of Praise* and *Cook Yourself Thin*, I sometimes forget I was a Junior Research Fellow in my younger, more promising years. I really was. My gown and mortar board are still in the attic. It seems like another existence. But I'd write for learned journals (for no pay) and teach undergraduates at Magdalen and St Catherine's. I shared the stage with Dame Kiri Te Kanawa at a University ceremonial, conducted in the Latin.

So – I possessed every qualification to be the Professor of Poetry, except I've never written poetry. Indeed, I don't entirely approve of those who do. There is quite enough English Literature already, don't you think? Philip Larkin would have agreed with me. He once told Douglas Dunn, a colleague at the Brynmor Jones Library, at Hull University, 'There's too much poetry on this campus. I'm relying on you to stamp it out. Come down *hard* on them.' These Creative Writing courses that are springing up everywhere – my vow to help close them down will assure my seat in heaven, even if it didn't at Oxford.

For my sincere belief is that to write one mostly needs to read – read everything, from the classics to magazines. And it is my additional belief that criticism and commentary can themselves both be imaginative and mercurial, passionate and finely observed.

That was certainly the case with the outgoing Professor of Poetry, Sir Ricks, who has spent the last twenty-five years in Boston researching the lyrics of Bob Dylan. I bump into Sir Ricks at Zippos Circus. During the summer, he travels with the Big Top and I turn up to prepare picnics and cook barbecues. One of his many daughters, Julia, is married to Zippo himself, Martin Burton. My son was the apprentice clown. But more than this, Sir Ricks in his books shows he has a circus personality: colour, courage, acrobatics, and dazzle of a verbal kind. He is the critic-as-artist. Someone to emulate, definitely.

From the first, however, I feared I was teetering on the brink of the most ignominious defeat and massive public humiliation. But then if there's a wild goose chase afoot, I'll fetch my fowling-piece. When I heard that the fuddy-duddy dons were assuming they had it all sewn up to elect either bearded seventy-eight-year-old Geoffrey Hill or seventy-five-year-old kazoo-player Michael Horovitz to the position, my heart sank. Though I'm sure they are nice old codgers, splendid in every way, I'm afraid I personally find their work serious-minded to the point of pain and obscure of purpose.* But then I alone believe Alan Bennett is more worthy of the Nobel Prize than Harold Pinter, as it is surely better to laugh at life than to lament it?

I just don't see the point in unintelligible modern verse that requires footnotes to explain it. I prefer John Betjeman and Philip Larkin — with their elegies about everyday life, church-going and hospital appointments, train journeys and bicycle rides. As John Betjeman said, sophistication is always phony — and that would have been one of my key lectures: 'The Lost England of Betjeman, Waugh (Evelyn and Auberon) and Larkin and the Advantages of Being Unfashionable'; another possible subject: 'The End of England — Eric Ravilious, Barbara Jones and Edward Bawden'.

Keen on finding true poetry in unexpected quarters, determined to bridge the gap between high literary culture and the popular arts, I'd also have prepared talks on the graphic world of Osbert

* Until his retirement, Geoffrey Hill was a Professor of Literature and Religion at Boston (having been invited there by Sir Ricks), and before that he taught at Cambridge and Leeds, where his career began in 1954.

Hill's as-expected election made the Oxford Chair of Poetry the equivalent of a Lifetime Achievement Award at the Oscars. I've never gone for his poetry, I'm afraid. It is difficult, dark, dense. Academics love that sort of thing, of course. They think it is *serious*. I think it leaves the reader out. Hill, indisputably, has real academic weight.

Lancaster and Ronald Searle. I've never understood why cartoonists and illustrators are never accorded much respect. I wanted to rhapsodise about Elizabeth David and the invention of appetite. What are the connections between the biblical translations of M. R. James and his ghost stories? I'm fascinated by the nineteenth-century view of Jesus, Shakespeare and Great Cryptograms – the codes they decided to find in ancient texts.

Then there's 'Sex, Violence and Difficulties with Girls' – quite a topic – all these poets who are rascals when it comes to sex. Strong-willed and with a volatile temperament, there's Lord Byron, of course – boasting about his adventures in gondolas, against walls, under tables and in hackney carriages. Nearer our own time, Ezra Pound kept two women on the go, his saintly wife Dorothy and a mistress called Olga Rudge, who proudly told me how she'd once played the violin for Mussolini. T. S. Eliot was torn between the mad Vivien, shut away in a mental home, and his secretary at Faber & Faber, Valerie Fletcher, who is now his widow. Larkin had Maeve and Monica. Kingsley Amis had Hilly and Elizabeth Jane Howard. John Betjeman had a wife in the Black Mountains and a mistress in Radnor Walk, Chelsea. Nevertheless, his true idea of erotic bliss, he said, was to be given 'a real wigging by Lady Harrod'. Ted Hughes, tragically, had the distinction of not one but two people gassing themselves on his behalf – poor old Sylvia Plath and Assia Wevill, who also killed their child.

Compared with all this, the Oxford Chair of Poetry is rather a sober institution. I doubt whether my old chums John Wain and Peter Levi, who held the post in the Seventies and Eighties, ever did much damage. John went blind and stood in the street waving a knobbled stick, as if he were Homer or a Celtic hermit. Peter Levi was an ex-Jesuit, if it is possible to be such a thing. He married Cyril Connolly's widow and went to live on a mudflat near the River Severn.

By indulging my catholicity of taste – the saga of Richard

Burton and Elizabeth Taylor coming to Oxford in the Sixties to put on a production of Marlowe's *Doctor Faustus* is a subject I still intend to explore – I hoped I could have communicated my enthusiasm, my curiosity. I always see my job, as a writer and commentator, as conveying the real and instructive delight I get from reading and looking at things, from the established masters and classics to dim artists and actors and poets who lie on the far horizons of unfamiliarity – L. Cranmer-Byng, Percy Pinkerton, Edgar Saltus, A. E. Coppard, or Matthew Phipps Shiel. And I am attuned, I hope, to poetry wherever it may be found, whether in opera libretti (Sullivan's non-Gilbert works are worth recovering), in follies and grottoes, fairgrounds, waxworks, and in unusual personalities.

Artists of all kinds interest me because of their unknown compulsions. I agree with Soho resident Jeffrey Bernard, who said, 'All people who are more or less interesting are more or less their own inventions.' They get clear of their roots, and then they can flower. My first book – swiftly remaindered by Lord Weidenfeld: indeed I think it was *pre-remaindered* – was a collection of profile essays about actors and actresses, the self-destructive Robert Stephens, the urbane fusspot Alec McCowen, vinegary Ian Richardson, the sainted Judi Dench, and so forth, called *Stage People*. (I'm embarrassed by it now.)

It was here, nevertheless, that I began my lifelong study of investigating kaleidoscopic selves, celebrating people who are just different from everybody, and asking – as a biographer must – how people live their lives and behave as they do; how they embody their passion and imagination in literature, painting or performance; how improbabilities, dreariness and unworthiness are transformed, and gain momentum, gain freshness.

With Peter Sellers as my specific subject, I covered 1,200 pages exploring all this. The project took five years. I was living with Anna and the children in a falling-down farmhouse in Normandy and we were completely broke. Then *The Sunday Times* bought the serial rights and I got up to zero at the bank. Years later *The Life and Death of Peter Sellers* was made into an award-winning film by HBO. I was promised five per cent, which has yet to materialise. As *My Little Chickadee*, made in 1939, didn't start earning royalties for Mae West's Estate until 1977, I am not sanguine about receiving riches, though maybe great-grandchildren yet unborn will receive a cheque.

I wrote further books on Laurence Olivier, Charles Hawtrey, of *Carry On* fame, and Anthony Burgess, my hero. Critics thought I was being nasty about him, when I said that Burgess was less the heir to James Joyce and Goethe than a Manchester music hall act, a glorious charlatan. But by being vehement I was expressing my affection – or is that a Welsh thing? My intention throughout, however, has always been to bring the sophisticated and the unsophisticated arts together, to talk about (say) Samuel Beckett in the same breath as Laurel and Hardy – and *Waiting for Godot* is *about* Laurel and Hardy. But where Roland Barthes could discourse on Greta Garbo, Japanese food, the Eiffel Tower, wrestling and Racine, and the French loved him for it, try being eclectic here and see where it gets you.

I was like this as a tutor, so my best students would all get Firsts, then go into the City and never open a book again. I recall that when I pontificated about T. S. Eliot, I got the students to look at his correspondence with Groucho Marx and his essays on music hall – for are not Eliot's poems filled with comical voices, overlapping jibber-jabber, snatches of song and recitals from the classics; a nightmare gas-lit theatre effect? Ezra Pound, another enthusiasm of mine, is full of masks, imposture, disguise, impersonation – his work resembling a scratchy newsreel, the soundtrack a mad babble. Pound and W. C. Fields were children at the same time in Philadelphia. I'd still like to explore the ramifications of that.

Left to my own devices, a quarter of a century ago, I ran the tutorials as I pleased, like gymkhanas. Can you dare do that now? If anyone were to hand me an Equal Opportunities Monitoring Form or a sheet requesting my Stated Learning Intentions, I'd rip it up and shout *up the bum and no babies*. The only possible comment to make about a Research Assessment Exercise is that it sounds like resounding balls. For the point of intellectual adventuring is you don't always know where you are heading. It is only in retrospect that I can see how my classes on Eliot and Pound evolved into my lifelong interest in actors and circus personalities – Peter Sellers, Laurence Olivier, Orson Welles, Anthony Burgess.*

However, when Dryden, three centuries ago, said that 'the chiefest part of the business of criticism is to observe those excellencies which should delight a reasonable reader', I have to ask myself, *where the hell are reasonable readers to be found in this day and age?* They have been throttled by dogma and cant, students and lecturers alike. People seem bound by accepted rules and politically correct conventions. Academics are drained by accelerating bureaucracy and administration. The world of

* These days, as I prowl around the Herefordshire Balkans or linger over a plate of fattening *Kaisergugelhupf* in the Café Ramsauer, Bad Ischl, it is indeed all too easy to forget I was once an Oxford don myself – so what did Oxford do for me, eh?

One of my problems was that in my time you couldn't study the subject I was most interested in – *theatricality* – because the syllabus stopped with Tennyson. I knew I'd have always had to fend for myself, as a freelance author. Even the appointment of my supervisor Richard Ellmann to a job at New College was considered immensely daring, because he knew about James Joyce.

Like Sir Ricks's playful virtuosity, the natural humanity of Ellmann was well worth emulating – but his scholarship left much to be desired. There are over 1,500 inaccuracies in his biography of Oscar Wilde, for example. He gets Wilde's parents' full names wrong, confuses Eights Week with Torpids, misquotes everything, confuses dates, and even buries his subject in the wrong spot. Nevertheless, Ellmann as a biographer sparked my interest in trying to understand the inner lives of artists and performers. I'll always be grateful to him for that.

publishing and media, which should contain the guardians of our culture, is run by marketing and accountants, philistine characters who are by nature cautious and constricting.

Turn on the television or flick through a magazine – it's filled with the things that don't count, imbecilic talent shows, the wrong sorts of heroes, airbrushed photos of pneumatic models who give us information about their divorces and pregnancies. I'm really not interested in Vanessa Feltz's gastric band. In Waterstones all you'll find are the ghosted memoirs of celebrities, and my own little memoir, *Seasonal Suicide Notes*, is to my chagrin hidden miles away in the basement under Toilet Book Humour. No wonder sales are meagre. When did you last see Anton Chekhov by the lavvy?

It is against this landscape of intellectual and imaginative desolation – and the cruelty and stupidity that go with it – that I am and always will be in furious revolt. Believing as I do that the moral importance of literature and literary study is that it expresses and embodies human freedom, human independence, had I won this election it would have been a victory for life-enhancing joviality and the grand style. 'Let's see some passion and candour – no more solemnity and pompousness, please,' I told everyone.

ꟍ

Asked by several people what I thought poetry might entail, I came up with the following catalogue – my own personal manifesto. I obviously don't bother to mention *The Sonnets*, Wordsworth, Milton, the Romantics etc. I take the A Level and First Year English Literature BA syllabus for granted.

My intention was and is to open out the definition of poetry beyond the linguistic, to embrace music, painting, architecture and acting.* Oscar Peterson playing jazz, Picasso's free-flowing

* I was astounded at the backlash from little poetasters and academics about my catalogue – which all helped to confirm for me that people who devote or anyway use up their lives, in the security of institutions of higher

lines, St Pancras Station – all the things I have jotted down –
are to my mind every bit as poetical and part of the intellectual
adventure as Shakespeare or the iambic pentameter.

The Lewis Manifesto

The sea foam in Homer; the *Sea Symphony* of Vaughan Williams; the
Sea Drift of Delius, to the words of Walt Whitman.

Hearing the 'chimes at midnight' in Verdi's *Falstaff*; Orson Welles's
film adaptation of *Henry IV* Part One and Two, *The Chimes at Midnight*,
which he made in Franco's Spain. One of my longer-term projects is
to follow Welles's footsteps around Europe, retracing the locations
for *F For Fake*, *The Trial*, and his peerless Shakespeare adaptations. (So
far what I've mostly managed to do is follow Welles's footsteps into
his favourite restaurants.)

The Alcazar in Seville, where Lean filmed the Damascus and
Jerusalem scenes for *Lawrence of Arabia*; Peter O'Toole's diaphanous
robes, as designed by Phyllis Dalton.

The mustard-yellow sand in the Plaza de Toros de la Maestranza,
Seville. Though we all have to disapprove of bullfighting, we can still
marvel at the eighteenth-century architecture – at the real setting
for *Carmen*.

Gogol's *The Overcoat*; Nabokov's book on Gogol. I studied all this
with my beloved tutor at Oxford, John Bayley. Gogol's short story
was, said John, crammed with 'complex meanings and a deeper
resonance'. Gogol makes his overcoat stand for 'all the poetry, all

---

education, to the teaching of culture, to the humanities, who are meant to
propagate nice civilised things, nevertheless generally tend to be, in their
own behaviour and outlook, *nasty little creeps*. One particular shag seemed to
think that my enthusiasm for the circus and my use of circus metaphors was
derogatory and facetious – whereas I find the circus idyllic and absolutely
see how Fellini couldn't leave it alone. Yet they always astound me, what
Betjeman called The Friday Pharisee and The Sunday Prig.

the love, and all the romance that has been missing from the main character's life'. Nabokov's biography of 1944 is one extraordinary Russian writer discoursing on another. A prime example of a work of dazzling criticism that is creative and topsy-turvy. It ends with Gogol's birth and begins with his death – a structure I stole for *The Real Life of Laurence Olivier*, when the book concludes with Olivier's first spoken word: *Damn!*

The characters eating the watermelon in Chekhov's *The Lady and the Little Dog* – sheer mysterious ecstasy.

M. F. K. Fisher's description of the restaurant-buffet at the Gare de Lyon. I prefer Fisher to Elizabeth David as a passionate scholar of food and of the appetites. She was an American who lived in France before the war and in *The Art of Eating* she said, 'When I write about hunger, I am really writing about love and the hunger for it, and warmth, and the love of it . . . and then the warmth and richness and fine reality of hunger satisfied.'

The colour of Elizabeth Taylor's evil eyes.

The tilt of Garbo's face in profile.

Judi Bowker – everything about her.

The bend of Chaplin's cane.

W. C. Fields's juggling routines.

Peter Sellers as Inspector Clouseau – the stiff walk, the alertness, the misplaced confidence.

Milton's Satan – what a role it would have been for Laurence Olivier.

The Surrealist Manifesto of 1925. As teenagers, we all want to be Surrealists – my copy of the Pelican *History of Surrealism* is dated May 1978, when I was sitting my A levels. 'We are Specialists in Revolt,' declared Louis Aragon, André Breton, Max Ernst and the rest of the boys. 'We intend to show the Fragility of Thought, and on what

Shifting Foundations, what Caverns, we have built our Trembling Houses.' Of course, one grows out of this – and then as we grow older, going against the current becomes an attractive option again.

Beckett's book on Proust; Proust's book on Ruskin; all of Ruskin – and not only his rhapsodic prose about Turner and Venice's stones, but his watercolours.

Gerard Manley Hopkins's 'Hurrahing in the Harvest' – though he was a Victorian priest, his poetry is like syncopated jazz. 'Summer ends now; now, barbarous in beauty, the stooks rise/Around; up above what wind-walks! What lovely behaviour/Of silk-sack clouds!'

Samuel Palmer's harvest moons and weird skies – 'Had wilder, wilful-wavier/Meal-drift moulded ever and melted across skies?' (to carry on quoting Hopkins).

Pinter's pauses – not his words, only his pauses.

Rules restaurant in Maiden Lane, Covent Garden, on a winter afternoon, half empty.

Agatha Christie's knowledge of poisons.

Sergeant Troy's business with the sword in *Far From the Madding Crowd* – Terence Stamp gives it everything in the film with Julie Christie. To be blunt, it's symbolical of his cock. But you'd have been ahead of me there.

Cruikshank's elaborate signature – like a seismograph of a significant earthquake. George Cruikshank illustrated Dickens's novels, depicting the moods and grotesqueness of the characters. 'There was about Cruikshank's art,' said G. K. Chesterton, 'a kind of cramped energy . . . His drawings have a dark strength.' His drawing of Fagin 'does not merely look like a picture *of* Fagin; it looks like a picture *by* Fagin'.

Chesterton's writings on Dickens, particularly the little book he wrote in 1906, which was in its twelfth edition thirteen years later. 'All roads point at last to an ultimate inn, where we shall meet Dickens and all his characters: and when we drink again it shall be from the great flagons in the tavern at the end of the world.' I'm not entirely sure I understand what this means, but it is certainly rousing.

Walter Sickert's music-hall etchings and prints.

The photographs of Alvin Langdon Coburn. Bostonian Coburn took the frontispiece pictures for the revised editions of Henry James's novels at the turn of the last century. His non-representative works are printed in a sort of faint sepia and silvery wash and resemble Whistler paintings. He was still alive in the Sixties, living in Harlech, North Wales, of all unlikely spots.

The severity and beauty of Britten's church parables, *Curlew River*, *The Burning Fiery Furnace* and *The Prodigal Son*.

Charles Conder's silk fan designs. Conder was an Australian artist at large in the London and Paris of the 1890s, a friend of Oscar Wilde and Toulouse Lautrec, and the illustrator of Balzac novels. His creepy, decadent works, watercolours on fragile silk, are collected by Dame Barry Humphries. I've got a dozen or so myself, including Conder's portrait of his wife, Stella Maris. No great beauty. Conder died of the absinthe and is buried in the grounds of the Virginia Water asylum.

The *Letters* of Oscar Wilde, as edited by Sir Rupert Hart-Davis.

D. H. Lawrence's *Birds, Beasts and Flowers*.

Illuminated missals.

Magic lanterns.

Hockney's swimming pools.

Robin Askwith's arse.

Ezra Pound and Olga Rudge in Venice. When he was set free from the Washington mental hospital in 1958, Pound returned to Italy, where he had been arrested by the Allies during the war for broadcasting in favour of Mussolini. If we can separate politics from poetry, Pound's descriptions of Italy and his writings about Venice are beautiful. He died in 1972 and is buried on the island of San Michele, next to Diaghilev and Stravinsky. I met Olga Rudge, his ancient companion, in the city in 1988, on the centenary of Pound's birth. 'Look at this,' she said, moving to the wardrobe. 'It's the blouse I wore when playing the violin for Mussolini.'*

The pier at Clevedon – where 'There is no colour but one ashen light' (Andrew Lang).

Andrew Aguecheek's line, 'I was adored once, too.'

Dame Barry Humphries as Sandy Stone, but not as Edna or Les Patterson.

Roland Barthes's book on Japan. Barthes is pretty impenetrable, I agree, but his monograph about The Land of the Rising Sun, *Empire of Signs*, written in 1970 and translated by Richard Howard in 1982, is a haunting meditation on the meaning of signs and symbols. Trust a Frenchman, however, to turn literary criticism into *algebra*.

Buster Keaton's flat hat.

Monsieur Hulot's striped socks; the architecture in *Playtime*.

An Osbert Lancaster cartoon.

A Ronald Searle drawing – also Ronald Searle's calligraphy: the sharp fine nib and his clear, neat hand.

John Betjeman's rhapsodies about girls' bicycle seats.

---

* As this is my sole anecdote about Ezra Pound and his world, I repeat it at every opportunity.

Philip Larkin's lines, 'Look at the pictures and the cutlery./The music in the piano stool. That vase' . . .

Black and red circles and spirals – suns and moons – in Sir Terry Frost.

The gigantic fraying blocks of black and red and orange in Mark Rothko – the Earth seen from space.

Picasso's free and faultless line.

Matisse's drawings and paintings of fruit and odalisques in summer gardens.

Braque's birds in flight.

The house Ludwig Wittgenstein built for his sister in Vienna. It is not widely known that the philosopher was also an engineer and an architect, fully trained and qualified. He designed everything for his sister's house, right down to the window catches and the radiators.

Philip Langridge's voice (though not when singing Britten) – also Peter Ustinov's and Richard Burton's.

Sir Ralph Richardson.

Glenn Gould playing Byrd's pavans and galliards.

Mark Rylance as Peter Pan. I first met Mark when he was in the J. M. Barrie play at the RSC in 1983. He is one of my most beloved friends – and my eldest son Tristan's godfather. Tristan is now an apprentice clown at Zippo's Circus and Mark got him into that. Mark has always had this other-worldly Peter Pannish quality, especially when he was Ariel or Hamlet. There Peter Pan was again in Rooster Byron, in the award-winning *Jerusalem* – Peter Pan grown old and arthritic but still a force to be reckoned with in the wild wood.

The darkness in a still life by Francisco de Zuraban.

The baroque filth in Peter Cook and Dudley Moore's *Derek and Clive* recordings.

Molly Bloom's monologue.

Sullivan's orchestration for *Iolanthe* and Sir Charles Mackerras' *Pineapple Poll*.

❧

Barring any unforeseen calamity such as an invasion from Mars, it was always going to be odd-on favourite Geoffrey Hill's day. So well done, old lad, with your landslide victory, your 1,156 votes.* Pretty decisive, I'd say, even if you will insist on using words like *offertorium*, *atrorubent* and *claustral*. My own Inaugural Lecture, to have been entitled 'Give Up Literary Criticism!' (which is what Wittgenstein said to F. R. Leavis when he bumped into the Ghoul of Downing College in a Cambridge street), will now never be delivered. Well. Shucks.

Nevertheless, because in a piece I wrote that went off into cyberspace, a sub-editor removed the word 'If' from a sentence of mine that had begun 'If by some miracle I have won the Oxford Chair of Poetry,' the next thing I knew the garden was full of photographers from Italy, who believed I'd been made Poet Laureate. I was so shocked, my pubes went white, then went black, and then settled down as a sort of off-putting shade of mouse.

Nothing I could do changed the Italians' minds and a flattering profile duly appeared in a Milanese fashion magazine. In the pictures I look like a mass murderer. My destiny clearly is to try and hide in woodland, glimpsed in jerky long shot by a camera focusing on me and zooming in and out from a police helicopter.

My chief disappointment was that Mavis Nicholson promised to embroider a cushion for me, had I won. Mavis took the word 'chair' literally. But it was hardly plain sailing, gathering support,

* According to the statistics, less than 1 per cent of the people who were eligible to register and vote bothered to register and vote. Of the people who did vote, all but a handful were lecturers and other academics still within Oxford itself. Clearly to the graduates out there in the world at large, nobody gave a flying fuck.

to be frank. Look what happened at Michael Winner's house. Michael has highly educated people on his staff, but when I asked him to get them to vote for me, one of them 'secretly ordered endless glasses of port, was sick all over my lovely assistant Dinah and others, had to be carried up a long flight of stairs by the chauffeur and others. Then never even apologised to Dinah or offered to pay for the dry cleaning. So I don't think you can rely on him to get you the job which you clearly deserve. These are the travails of my life. I know, like me, you bear them bravely.'

That's Michael Winner, advising me on how to go about matters with calm, dignity and grace. I also had an urgent message from Boris's sister, the madcap Rachel Johnson. She'd asked her brother to give me his vote, so he fell off his bike, talked exclusively in Latin for three days, and a poultice had to be applied to his fevered brow. 'He erupted,' said Rachel, whose manner oscillated between sisterly concern and hilarity. 'He declared in a Ciceronian manner that he would do anything in his power to prevent you from claiming the Poetry Chair.'

Boris's initial idea was to get the Johnson paterfamilias, Stanley, who himself was once the winner of the prestigious Newdigate Poetry Prize at Oxford, to stand against me. Stanley burst out laughing and became one of my official nominators instead – but it must nevertheless be rather riotous, when the Johnsons get together in one room. It shouldn't be forgotten that they are descended from Turkish brigands.

My crime, it transpired, was that I'd 'written ungraciously' about Boris in a newspaper years ago. 'He's very Sicilian when it comes to these little matters,' said Rachel cheerily, using her own powers as editor of *The Lady* to cut my fee in half for an article I'd contributed on unrepentant pederast Jonathan King.* Andrew

---

* We have since made up – I adore the woman, and when she comes towards me at parties with her unmistakable swaggering cowboy gait, my spirits almost rise. Jonathan King is another of my Rules luncheon companions

Gimson, Boris's biographer, tried to be mollifying. 'Boris cannot bear to be disliked and . . . would not forget whatever you may have said. His memory is astonishingly good, but he is not a man to let a feud fester.' That is good to know. I have been going in daily fear of one of his bendy buses chasing me along the pavement and up the stairs at Rules. Boris's was definitely a vote for Geoffrey Hill, though, wasn't it?

But oh my and oh dear. For thirty years I have been snortingly rude about everyone in print, nipping and biting at the flanks of the self-serving, and with their chance now not to vote for me, revenge was offered them on a plate. Melvyn Bragg is not likely to have voted for Lewis, the things I say about his hair. I called the literary biographies of Hermione Lee, the President of Wolfson College, as much fun as swimming upstream in mud. I called Professor John Carey's book on William Golding as suffocating as a tombstone. I wrote at length that Magdalen College ought to be sold off and turned into a Travelodge. I don't seem to have gone around winning influential friends.

Paradoxically, some dons applauded my bad behaviour. An Emeritus History Fellow said I had his vote because, 'and I can't avoid a football metaphor now the World Cup has started, you are the bloke who throws bottles on the pitch'. I've also had the thumbs up from Mr Know-All Stephen Fry, who again appreciated

---

incidentally. He is a modern Norman Douglas. Norman Douglas (1868–1952), after a Foreign Office career, settled in Capri, where he wrote travel books about Italy (*Siren Land*, *Old Calabria*, *South Wind*) and bummed the shepherd boys. According to Anthony Burgess, when Douglas came across a postman who'd knocked himself out cycling into a tree, Douglas bummed him where he lay. Anthony Burgess would have stolen the bike. Jonathan King would have bummed the bike and the postman.

Literary encyclopaedias elliptically refer to Douglas's 'engagingly cheerful pagan outlook and his limpidity of style' and to the way he celebrated 'the liberating effects of southern temperament and temperature upon Anglo-Saxon Puritanism'.

the rough and tumble: 'For the first time ever I'm almost wishing I was an Oxonian so I could vote for you. The ticket on which you are campaigning is one that should unite anyone who cares for literature, art, honour, humour, delight – all the proper virtues. Such a position is liberal and liberating, kind, wise, funny and alive to all the dark, strange, ludic and improbable glories that poems and especially poets should embody. Bravo, mon copain.'

He's looking for a part in my next film, *Seasonal Suicide Notes*. He wants to shuffle about on his knees as the diminutive Welsh housekeeper, Mrs Troll. He'll say anything to get the role. Though a Cambridge man, and hence not having any vote, Fry nevertheless went along to All Souls for dinner last month, 'to plead your cause with all the eloquence I can muster'. More votes for Geoffrey Hill there, then.

As for my own campaign strategy – should I have emulated James Fenton, who held a garden party at his house in Cumnor and organised a mini-bus to ferry people to the polls? Or C. S. Lewis, who gave doddery clergymen a bibulous lunch and shepherded them up the High to the voting booth? As Geoffrey Hill is seventy-eight, murder wouldn't have been too onerous a scheme. I'd simply have to leap out from behind a bush in his garden and shout *boo!*

I mentioned this at the black-tie Annual Dinner of the Herefordshire, Brecon and Radnor Branch of the Oxford University Society, on 21 May 2010. Not a vast throng, as you'll have surmised, but votes are votes. The first rule of public speaking is know your audience. I didn't know this. I made the crack about my murder plot and said that as this is a five-year gig, there is a very real possibility that Geoffrey Hill's last lectures will be delivered through a spirit medium and a ouija board, should he fall out of his bath-chair. As the Oxonians in the Welsh Marches were each of them nearly eighty, my remark was met with a stony and disapproving silence and went down, as Mrs Troll would say, like a lead baboon. Support lost there, I fear, and in spades.

It has taken up a great deal of time, calling in favours, persuading people to support me, bringing the election to people's attention. I racked my brains and tracked down farmers' sons who went to Oxford and are known to my late father – one of them runs a vineyard in Monmouth. I have located my grandfather's brother's son (he's in his seventies himself), who drives a Rolls-Royce for weddings in Washington DC. He once read Roman Law. I found a vote or two in an orang-utan sanctuary in Borneo.

Michael Gove said he'd 'do everything I can to support you' but then he got sidetracked by being made Minister for Education and I've never heard from him since. Tristan Garel-Jones dragooned the Oxonians at UBS, the merchant bank he runs, to rally to my cause. He also campaigned for me among the Taffia, the Welsh ruling class. I pinned a few hopes there – possibly a mistake.

My old English teacher in Newport, Phil George, who went to Christ Church and is now a television producer, never replied to my appeal. Nor did the chap who runs Welsh Water – yet I was the best man at one of his weddings. Nor did one of his ex-wives, Carys, who was a high-flyer at Jesus College and wrote speeches for John Major. Leaving aside the possibility that they always hated my guts, why did they give me the cold shoulder? The Welsh aren't entirely comfortable with success if it is achieved in England. Failure they love – so I'm sure they'll pop corks, embrace me and commiserate like crazy, should I ever venture back across Chepstow Bridge.

Oxford people have class – but they are indolent and woolly. Many people said they'd vote and then forgot. Furthermore, the online electoral procedure foxed nearly everyone. The University website is a labyrinth and you can see how Oxford encouraged Lewis Carroll to invent Alice falling down rabbit holes or going through a looking-glass. First people had to register to vote – which meant remembering their date of matriculation and girls remembering their maiden names – then, days or weeks later, they had to actually vote, if successfully sent an online ballot paper in the meantime. Most of my team lost heart and patience.

Others discovered, years after going down, that they weren't technically Oxford graduates after all and couldn't vote. Though they'd sat their exams and got their results, as they'd not bothered with the official Graduation Ceremony, putting on a cap and gown to go to the Sheldonian, they weren't listed in the University Records. Gyles Brandreth discovered this. 'If you lose by one vote you can blame me!' he said. If I'd lost by one vote I'd have killed him.

Several people were afraid to register to vote for fear of past misdemeanours coming to light – which they did. One friend was reminded by her college that her library fines were still outstanding, another that his unpaid bar bills had been accruing interest since 1978. Bevis Hillier, author of the definitive biography of John Betjeman, divulged that though he won the Gladstone Historical Essay Prize, which forecast a First, he never got around to sitting his exams at all – when at Magdalen (1959–62) he discovered champagne instead, an excellent move. Richard Ingrams also muttered about not being eligible to vote for some forgotten reason or other, such as leaving to set up *Private Eye*.

Though Duncan Fallowell got his Second in History in 1970, he'd never officially graduated either – so to Vote for Lewis he took his degree *in absentia* at a ceremony a fortnight before polls closed, God bless him. It cost £10 and he was given an upgrade to an MA. Duncan has been my most stalwart supporter, even virtually taking a bullet for me. When my candidacy was announced, he told a diarist, 'I support Roger because he believes in literary culture. You'd be surprised how few of them do. I was going to discuss the campaign today with Roger but he has a date with Sharon Osbourne at the Dorchester.'

This was true – and Sharon promised to drive my Campaign Battle Bus. Even I could see that that would play right into

Geoffrey Hill's hands. But Duncan's jokey remarks were taken ill by another elderly candidate, Michael Horovitz, who attacked him verbally in a public swimming baths. He said the job should be his because he needed the money more than me – that's debatable, Christ knows. Spittle flew. It is probably not true that armed assistance had to be called.

I'm sure he's a nice old codger really, but in general the less said about self-proclaimed genius Horovitz the better. He hands out leaflets in the street. His big moment came in 1965 when he played the kazoo for Allen Ginsberg at the Albert Hall. He also published an article in the *Guardian*, during the campaign, his idea of high-pressure salesmanship being to big himself up by doing me down. Quite right. I was doing the same. Word had reached him that my tongue had not been wagging in his praise.*

---

* Sometimes (not often) you encounter a person and nothing can be done – you simply dislike and exasperate each other instantly and abidingly. You can barely manage being courteous. Thus it was (sadly) between Michael Horovitz and myself. He didn't think I had a right to be a candidate – and I didn't think he had a right to say I didn't have a right. Our ding-dong filled the letters pages of the national press for weeks. He (more or less) accused me of effrontery. I thought he was a silly old fool – but then my refusal to be quite serious about anyone is my chief weakness. At least you can say this, however: both Horovitz and Lewis preferred being themselves. They cannot be accused of dishonesty.

One of the things Horovitz accused me of is being 'a pseudo-intellectual' – so I hasten to reclaim the phrase. Who wants to be an intellectual anyway? This seems a good point to toss into the cauldron a letter sent by Kieran Grant to the *Daily Telegraph*. Interest declared. When Kieran was reading English at Exeter University, he wrote a dissertation on my approach to the art of biography, with particular reference to Peter Sellers, so he has been familiar with my work, and has championed it, for many years, God bless him.

'Sir, To Lewis's inspired and inspiring list [of what he deems poetical] I could add a thousand things: the glint in Alastair Sim's eye, sunset at Wadi Rum, the chill gloom that descends on the last line of a Robert Aickman short story, Tom Waits's throat, half-melted snowmen . . . These things are, as Horovitz points out in despair, completely indefinable – but so what? Isn't that the point of art?

Actually, I am so inscrutable and capricious, I wish Catweazle-lookalike Horovitz, who fair play polled more than twice the number of votes as me at the finish, had been duly elected, sending Hill back post-haste to his retirement home. Nice Michael Palin, for example, told me he'd been asked to vote for Horovitz – and I only remembered a lot later that I was waspish in the press about both volumes of Palin's diaries, and I've made no secret of the fact that in my opinion *Monty Python* is dire and unfunny, like bank managers and accountants being daft.

At least the upshot of the cabals, stratagems and secret alliances is clear to me. When, in the year 2040, I am the age Geoffrey Hill is now, and if people seek me out in Bad Ischl, eager to find the venerable magus, Sir Roger Lewis CBE, or Pope Roger as I may well be by then, if still living of course, and should they be begging me to stand for the Oxford Chair, and deliver that Inaugural Lecture, 'Give Up Literary Criticism!', then I know *exactly* what to say: *Up the bum and no babies!* In the meantime, let the last word on my present fate belong to Jan Morris, the veteran travel writer. 'Dear Roger, even if you lost that silly contest, you're the real winner.' There's Welsh logic for you. She wouldn't vote for me because I'm not a poet – and to think I've only ever given Jan Morris glowing reviews.

If Lewis's rapturous celebration of poetry in all its unexpected forms is 'pseudo-intellectual', as Mr Horovitz claims, then pseudo-intellectualism is clearly the way forward, at least if poetry is going to mean anything to anyone in the twenty-first century. Too long has the appreciation of this art form been exclusively reserved for fusty intellectuals . . . Is it any wonder that poetry has become a laughing stock? The final addition to my list of wonders would be Mr Lewis's book *The Life and Death of Peter Sellers*, a magnificent 1,200-page elegy that smashes into dust any accusations that this magnificent writer and critic has never written poetry. Yours faithfully . . .'

I remember the first time I heard a piece of classical music. I was a Mixed Infant in Machen and we had a temporary teacher called Mrs Higgins, because Miss Graham was off at a golf tournament. Mrs Higgins put an LP of Dvořák's New World Symphony on the record player. Suddenly it was all there – the sounds of America and the pull of the peasant dances, the pull of the composer's homeland, the shock of the new. It was lovely. There's an untranslatable Spanish word that means a sort of cosmic, unassuageable nostalgia: *enyoranca*. I am sure what I felt back then was related to this – but what *was* it exactly that I felt, that I hankered for? I was eight, maybe nine.

It set off fragmentation cluster-bombs in my head – in my viscera, aorta and Eustachian tubes. It was almost erotic – my first erotic experience, i.e. my first heightened feelings of arousal.* It awoke a need. A wave of sensuality overwhelmed me, or anyway my pep glands. I was keyed up. But I only had four or five seconds to become an aesthete suffused with Beardsleyesque melancholy, before it vanished like a breath and I was tugged back to reality. The other unripe twat-shaped twats in the class, the South Welsh *jeunesse dorée*, Ian Gough, whose mother was Arthur Askey's niece, Clive Fussell, Pansy Banfield, Ronnie Pudding, Friskin, Fatty Prescott, Russell Hawcutt, whose mother burned to death – I could name them *all* – started pretending to conduct an orchestra, waving their arms about and taking the piss. It is true to say that the biggest blight on my childhood was other children. I couldn't stand them. I couldn't stand their silliness, their shallowness and pack tactics.

୨୦

The thing about a picture – for example, Matisse's cut-outs and dancing men or views through windows; Picasso's portraits of his

* 'Let me play to you some mad scarlet thing by Dvořák,' says Gilbert in Wilde's *The Critic as Artist*. His piano recital over, Gilbert then says, 'Education is an admirable thing, but it is well to remember . . . that nothing that is worth knowing can be taught.'

wives and mistresses; Chagall's sheep and goats: how come there is such energy and life in an object that doesn't move and has never lived; how come there gets to be this private strangeness? Because a picture is nothing more than a flat surface.

❧

It will make you dizzy, Matisse's *The Dance*, which is in The Hermitage in St Petersburg. Everything is in motion. There are the five dancers themselves, of course, twisting and revolving – bodies without costumes, without historical association. There seems to be a pagan energy at work here, something primitive. The reds of the earth, the violet of the sky. The picture is full of circles – the interlocking discs of the green stage or field; the roundness of heads and buttocks and leaping legs. The quick strokes of Matisse's brush make leaves and flowers. Everything curves, everything tilts. It is called *The Dance* and was painted in 1910, but perhaps it should be called *The Flight* – because in this picture the forms are flying, as if spun by a propeller. In 1909, Louis Blériot was the first man to fly an aeroplane over the English Channel.

❧

Superdrug have withdrawn Katie Price's fragrances from sale 'for ethical reasons'. Workers in the Indian factories where Stunning and Besotted are brewed 'have been given less than twenty-six pence an hour by the Pragati Glass Company', according to reports. After a few moments jabbing away at my pocket calculator I can tell you that for a project that recently consumed eighteen months of my life, I was paid getting on for nearly double that.

I wouldn't mind concocting my own perfume brand – I'd call it Minge or possibly Bile. I'm told there is already a popular pong called Poison. Or was that Poisson? Who'd want to spritz themselves with fish? Parenthetically, 'eau de toilette' I've always found a most off-putting idea.

When you uncork Lewis's Minge or possibly Bile, a trail of

greenish dry ice will emerge, as in a Jekyll/Hyde transformation scene. Perhaps I can distribute it among my enemies, who'd choke to death. Now I need to track down those dear little Indians and offer them twenty-seven pence an hour.

❧

Now let's have a little peep at the Lewis finances, shall we? I have received a royalty statement from Faber. A grand total of twenty-two copies of my Anthony Burgess biography have been sold since 2003. One copy went abroad, but was returned – I'd like to find the fuck-stain joker who went to the trouble of doing *that*.

In total, a mighty £16.82 has been trimmed from the advance, which means that at the current rate it will take only another 1,733 years and the book will at last be in the black. To put this in perspective, that's like a volume coming out in the days of Jesus Christ and the Roman Emperors showing a profit round about now. And Our Lord and the Emperor Caligula didn't have to sign copies in Daunts on Marylebone High Street and go on *The Alan Titchmarsh Show*, though they'd surely have been quite a draw at Hay-on-Wye.

I'd be way better off sitting at the bench next to the little Indians, helping to make Katie's pongs. Have Mr Justice Eady and his friend Mr Justice Tugendhat imposed a super-injunction to ensure *nobody knows I exist*?

❧

Here's a story that only works if read out loud, owing to the what is/what does confusion. Anyway. A child is lost. Goes to find a policeman. 'What's your mum like?' – 'Oven chips and big cocks.' Perhaps a northern accent is also needed.

❧

Another one that only works if heard rather than read: 'Is that Fanny Greene?' – 'No, it's the reflection from the stained glass window.' A favourite of mine, that.

163

A little girl goes into a pet shop, wanting a rabbit. 'Well, little girl,' says the friendly and obliging pet-shop owner. 'Do you want a black bunny rabbit or a white bunny rabbit?' – 'My python doesn't give a fuck.' You could tell that anywhere. I have.

I have had a letter from my babysitter. I don't mean the person who babysat for my babies, as we could never afford one of those and didn't go out for twenty-four years. I mean *my* babysitter, Mags Curnow, who used to pitch up in Bedwas when my parents went to a St Mellons Agricultural Show Dinner Dance. She'd tell me about Christopher Lee and Peter Cushing horror films at the Workmen's Hall and about how sad it was that Jimi Hendrix had died. God's honest truth, I only found out that Jimi Hendrix was a black man in 2004.

Mags has heard that I am a Registered Diabetic, so tells me I must wear flip-flops where possible, eat garlic, avoid corn plasters, and walk a lot. What, walk a lot, in public presumably, stinking like a Frenchman and wearing comical beach shoes? I've got my pride, Mags Curnow. I'm not going to be mistaken for a Midlands chemistry teacher who has taken early retirement and a lump sum 'due to stress'.

Oscar has a Bolivian chum whose has got a Chinese girlfriend. The Chinese girlfriend has her own four-by-four and a degree in jewellery design from Plymouth. Meanwhile, the Bolivian boyfriend's parents who live in Switzerland and work for Greenpeace are trying to get themselves Italian passports. This is an international mix. I was reminded of when Spike Milligan decided to become Irish. He went to the Irish Embassy to get an Irish passport. 'Oh, hell, yes, Spike, come in. We are terrible short of people.'

If you want to irritate the hell out of me put 'Hi Roger' at the beginning of an email. A stupid slangy fake jolly Americanism. Up the bum and no babies with it. Also, any post addressed to Mr Roger Lewis through Her Majesties' mails gets returned-to-sender immediately, or shredded. There is no such person living here. It is *Doctor* Lewis, I'll thank you to remember, as in Johnson, Miller, Seuss, Jekyll, Frankenstein, Zhivago, Strangelove, Doolittle or Who. Anyone who called Anthony Powell 'Pow-ell' rather than 'Pole' was similarly absurdly rebuked. Prickly even for a Welshman, the credibility of Powell, aka. the Horse-Faced Dwarf, wasn't helped a jot.* Nor should it have been.

In the same or similar strain, try-anything-once well-known character actor Hugh Bonneville is really Hugh Williams. His Welshness will be why he was interested in acquiring the rights of Byron Rogers's brilliant memoir, *Me*, in which Byron related how someone had once assumed his identity and ran amok having wild sexual adventures. The phone would ring, Byron would answer, and a woman, different women all the time, would thank him for the good time had by all. The episode would indeed make a good film – about doubles and doppelgangers.

We had these monsters from the deep called gurnard for supper. You can see evolution at work. They look as if they are about to hop on land, take a breath and turn into reptiles. Hard skulls. Horses' eyes.† I've not had anything so frightening on my plate

* The Horse-Faced Dwarf was Philip Larkin and Kingsley Amis's unkind private nickname for the appallingly snobbish and untalented though still popular Powell. The nickname stopped being private when Larkin's letters were published, edited by Anthony Thwaite for Faber in 1992.

The aggrieved Powell wrote in his dairy, 'Larkin's unfriendly comments on myself are all but insane. They are absolutely inspired by jealousy.' Because Powell pronounced his own name in an affected way, Evelyn Waugh and his family mocked him by exaggerating it to *Pow-elle*. Excellent.

† Gurnard, or *Eutrigla gurnadus*, of the family *Triglidae*, is always on the

since my mother boiled a bullock's tumour. Chewy, but mighty fine with mustard.

During my childhood I got quite used to eating lumps of steaming grey fibrous antimatter, e.g. camel humps, haunch of brontosaurus or roasted seal. My father a butcher, we were fed on what couldn't easily be sold to the public.

❧

Choral Evensong and Prayers of Thanksgiving for the Life and Ministry of the Reverend Prebendary Gerald Rainbow were said in Hereford Cathedral on Saturday, because the Reverend Prebendary Gerald Rainbow was Vicar of Leominster in 1957.

❧

In the spirit of politically correct equality and suchlike totalitarian gobshite, it has been decreed by a jack-in-office at Worcestershire County Council that the administrative assistants (as secretaries are now always called – there's an annoyance *right there*) must no longer make tea or coffee for people, as this is apparently 'demeaning' – even though they used to love doing this; it was a highlight of their day. Nor must Anna and her properly qualified professional colleagues leave folders and papers about for the administrative assistants to file away – this also somehow infringes their human rights. Nor are rubbish bins allowed. I thought this was in case al-Qaeda come along and hide bombs in them, but no – everything has to be carted off to the recycling dumpsters. So everywhere is always a mess.

❧

---

menu at Rick Stein's place in Padstow. Though Jane Grigson in her *Fish Book* warns that 'it can be confused with the red mullet', this is not a mistake I myself have made.

Another prehistoric-looking fish that has appeared in the Bromyard fishmongers and hence on your author's table is megrim, or *Lepidorhombus whiffiagonis*, of the family *Scophthalmidae*. But of course you knew that. A megrim is like a translucent plaice or lemon sole, but its beady little eyes look as if they have gazed on mermaids and other secrets of the deepest sea.

Francis John Kenvyn Lewis, born in 1896. I only saw him once, when he was on his deathbed, his barrel chest heaving. I remember the oxygen tanks lying about the floor. Great Uncle Ken was a second-lieutenant in the Royal Welch Fusiliers, being commissioned in August 1914. He was ordered to France and fought on the first day of the Battle of the Somme. He was on the Somme for six months. He came though all that, plus Ypres, plus Passchendaele. He was finally invalided out with typhoid and put in hospital in Wandsworth. He next went with his regiment to Ireland. On 10 October 1918, intending to travel home from Ireland on leave, he boarded the RMS *Leinster*, which was sailing to Holyhead at 9 a.m. He went to his cabin, began to get sorted out, when the purser appeared with a telegram from the CO in Limerick, telling him to get back to base. So he disembarked.

Sixteen miles out of Dublin, 43 miles west of Anglesey, the German submarine UB-123, which had sneaked around the Irish coast from Scotland, fired two torpedoes at the *Leinster*, which in a rough sea sank with the loss of 529 lives – most of them officers and other ranks from the Royal Welch Fusiliers. Until Reinhard Scheer, Admiral of the German High Seas Fleet, signalled his vessels to return from patrol, the signing of the Armistice the following month was jeopardised.

After these adventures and near misses, Great Uncle Ken was demobilised with the rank of captain, which no one was allowed to forget. His uniform and kit, specially made by C. L. Coles of 3 Queen Street, Cardiff ('Gentlemen's Hunting Coats and Breeches, Uniforms & Liveries') had cost £41 6s 8d. During the Hitler War he commanded the Bedwas Home Guard, which meant patrolling the railway bridge and taking up prime position in the saloon bar of The Church House. When *Dad's Army* was first broadcast in the Sixties, everyone said Arthur Lowe was Ken to a tee.

Ken was given by his father a small dairy farm on Bedwas Mountain called Llynllynfa, which even Welsh people found hard to pronounce – we called it Ling Ding. The charming little house was situated in a dell or dingle and slap bang opposite was a massive pylon. The outside lavatory had two wooden seats, side by side. Nobody ever explained how or why two people would ever want to go and have a cosy crap like that, though it is true that even now girls at parties vanish into the bogs together and spend hours and *hours* there. Doing what? No man knows.

Great Uncle Ken married my Great Auntie Vi. She was a Woodruff from Machen, a family of iron foundry owners who had a mansion called The Vedw. This was already ruined by the Sixties of the last century and Vi spent her married life washing milk bottles in Ling Ding. It was a tragic existence. The first child, Richard, tipped a kettle over himself and died of burns after a pioneering skin graft treatment went wrong. The other child, Rodney, had muscular dystrophy and died in his teens. Great Uncle Ken used to lug Rodney upstairs to bed by carrying him on his back. Rodney was put down for Taunton, but he eventually went away to live in a Cheshire Home. 'You did not state the age of your son,' the Taunton School secretary scribbled on a With Compliments slip, when sending the prospectus. I find that an excruciating detail. So that's the First World War, two children dead, lung cancer . . . No wonder, when it was harvest time,

Great Uncle Ken thought to hell with it and stayed indoors to watch Wimbledon.

Vi lived on her own in Ling Ding, a widow for a quarter of a century. I say she lived on her own. At the bottom of her drive was a tin shed where a shy little cowherd called John Burt lurked. He worshipped Vi, did all her shopping, did her garden, did the odd jobs on the farm. Neat and elderly, like Firs in *The Cherry Orchard*, he was her manservant. Let's leave it at that.

Vi got to resemble Dame Edna Everage as she aged, and she died in Caerphilly Miners' Hospital, where I'd been born, listening to what we'd hoped was a tape of Monteverdi but was actually Mantovani. My mother threw a big party for her eightieth, made a cake, made cream horns. Asked to bring a bottle, Great Uncle Ron's contribution was a bottle of Co-op liebfraumilch, the cheapest grapes ever trodden. It's a miracle he didn't take the request literally and turn up with a bottle of HP Sauce. The real miracle is why Vi wasn't insane with horror and depression after all she'd been through during her married life, but she was cheerful and sparkling. It was as if, blessedly not of a fractious disposition anyway, she'd deliberately cut herself off from her woes, which were never mentioned. People don't do that now. They have counselling and are encouraged to open up and let it all out. A mistake.

Interestingly, my parents would never let me go and stay at Ling Ding, an antiquated model farm like a farm in an Enid Blyton book. 'Auntie Vi would forget you are there,' said my mother – correctly diagnosing Vi's blitheness and abstraction as a protective amnesia, a disturbing repose.

❧

Crime Wave Corner. A man in fancy dress was beaten up in Hereford. He got his jaw broken and his face punched. 'The victim was wearing a fairy suit,' according to the report.

Now that's truly unfair and appalling. A fairy suit in the name of Sweet Baby Jesus and all the Sainted Orphans. 'The victim would have been very distinctive,' said the Crimestoppers spokesman, helpfully.

⚮

For some reason – maybe no reason at all: pure chance – the following letters were preserved, folded inside *The Philips' Junior Historical Atlas*, a book that came my way in childhood. What we have here are notes from one maid to another, the one in Bedwas, the other in Caerphilly, the town with the castle in it that lay a mile or so distant, across the Rhymney and in Glamorganshire. Bedwas and Caerphilly, along with Machen, Trethomas and Newport, have all long since merged and blurred – into a single big South Welsh conurbation. Also here is a painful exchange with a jilted boyfriend.

It could all have been written by James Joyce. Oddly enough, there was a first edition of *Ulysses* in the attic above the butcher's shop. It is on my shelf now – purloined originally from a lending library in Cardiff, I suspect. I place this in the chronicle today because 16 June is what the academics call Bloomsday – the twenty-four hours that Joyce's book covered, back in 1904. A Thursday.

> Dear Old Gert – Tis now I find the pleasure in writing these few lines to you hoping they might find you quite well and happy as it leaves me I must say I am sorry you won't be coming home next week with Rosie for it would have been great especially now that Evelyn is home too but still I don't quite know what Rosie intends doing for she might not go back to Bournemouth how are they in your place any more dying gee if Miss Tutting dies won't it be great you shall be your one and only boss all the Lewises are long livers well kid I must tell you after I had sent you my last letter I realised what a fool I must have been as I couldn't keep my . . . [*The rest of the letter is lost.*]

Dear Rosie – Girl of my dreams I love you honest I do. Life is so sweet. Can I hold your charms again in my arms. Since you have gone dear life don't seem the same. Please come back again. Ivor.

Dear Ivor Jones – Returning the watch but shall keep frock. For this last six weeks you pretend to make me understand you cared for me. Now I understand everything. Rosie.

Dear Ivor Jones – I have come to the conclusion that it would be best if we parted. For this last seven weeks you pretend you cared but as time alters ideas perhaps it would be best for us both last night I wanted to tell you but you know I am a baby. You'll understand I am sending your watch. I wish you the best of luck and prosperity. Rosie.

Dear Old Gert – Well dear I am so pleased to hear you are getting on all right in your new place you seem to be very lucky up till now and I hope and trust it will continue as for me I am honestly getting fed up it really seems a waste of time since there are so many situations idle Rosie and I are thinking of getting to Cardiff writing for a post tonight hope I shall be lucky enough Gert I must say Mam is much better she was supposed to go under an operation last Friday with her eyes but Doctor thinks it is not necessary she seems a bit tired the Baby is cutting his teeth and is very cross what you have to put up with married life won't come to seriousness with me yet awhile I am busy just lately have turned over a new leaf started making my own underclothing tis rather a surprise to them at home glad to say Ivor is all right of course Rosie is working for Mrs Lewis's sister she is a little difficult to get on with but still if we succeed in Cardiff she won't be there long Rosie will probably write to you first well has love tried its torture on you yet I should be pleased if I could see your boy's photo give my love to Olive and the children we are having splendid turns down here at the cinema we are keeping one good turn for you at August it seems a long time away but still dear it will soon slip I am putting soap on each week now please do the same it is now bedtime and I am taking a kiss of you the children are running all round the bedroom hoping I shall see you in my dreams so shall now close with tons of love and kisses and I . . . [*The rest of the letter is lost.*]

∾

Who exactly was writing to Old Gert – and it can't have been Molly Bloom; who Old Gert was in any event; who Rosie and Ivor were – this will never be discovered. They are gone with the wind. There's such poignancy here, in the little declaration of love and loss, the yearning for freedom. On top of everything else, these characters will later on have had two world wars to live through. If they lived through them.

∾

Crime Wave Corner. Thieves have stolen a horsebox in Hay-on-Wye. The horsebox 'contained several books on horses, cookery and law' – well, good God, there's only one person with all those interests. Clarissa Dickson Wright. Frisk her immediately! See if she has a horsebox about her person.

∾

In Tony Palmer's documentary about Salzburg, somebody – I think it is seasoned old warhorse Inge Borkh – talks about the structure of a work of art, about finding the shape and the pace – and about how this can differ and alter from performance to performance, exactly as the weather shifts imperceptibly from hour to hour and from day to day and can never be identical or repeated identically. And though in Tony's film they are discussing musical compositions and orchestral rehearsals, I understand this. (One of the things that is always shifting and evolving is my relationship with the past.)

172

Playing Her Majesty the Queen, Dame Mirren's voice squeaked like new shoes. Nevertheless, for turning herself into a washed-out frump padding about Balmoral in a winceyette nightie and carrying a hot-water bottle, she won the Oscar. Michael Sheen OBE is better at being Blair than Blair is at being Blair. He's nicer – if he does flash the cartoon grin a bit too much. He should be in an advertisement for Colgate.

What was the business about stalking the stag about? I didn't get it. Was the Queen sad or pleased when it was shot? The symbolism was confusing. Diana the stricken deer? *The Queen* presents the Queen as the victim, though, not the Princess of Wales. The Queen is pushed about and bullied by the press, by her government, by her husband, by her mad old bat of a mother – all of them with their contradictory advice. You got a sense of the loneliness of the woman, who is happy only fleetingly, when the Land Rover breaks down in the river and she is stranded on her own. She is briefly away from her cares.

Paradoxically, Dame Mirren is more regal – bossy and commanding and unsmiling – when she is Detective Superintendent Jane Tennison in *Prime Suspect*. 'Don't call me ma'am!' she snaps at a sergeant. 'I'm not the bloody Queen!' Oh but you *are*, Dame Mirren, you *are*.*

* That's why she could never be convincing as the insecure and victimised Karen Stone, in *The Roman Spring of Mrs Stone*, which was made in Dublin in 2002. Dame Mirren can't play subservience, so she attempted to play dimness, blankness. When Vivien Leigh starred in the role, in 1961, she all too convincingly portrayed madness – Karen Stone as delirious. That's the way to do it.

Also in the Hallmark Entertainment production was Roger Allam, who in *The Queen* was Her Majesty's private secretary – the man caught in the crossfire – Sir Robin Janvrin. Here Allam was a Tennessee Williams figure, with the worst Deep South accent I have ever heard. I misunderstood at first. I thought Allam was being an Englishman in Rome, putting on the

One of the first grown-up books I bought ('Roger Lewis, Troedyrhiw House, Bedwas, September 1978' it says in a flourish of turquoise ink on the flyleaf – I throw nothing away) was Freud's *Jokes and Their Relation to the Subconscious*. It cost me – well, my father – precisely £1. No doubt I minced about at school with it to give the impression of erudition. What forgiving teachers I had.

Forgiving – or indifferent. A lot of them could never disguise the fact they were in the job for the long holidays and the short hours. (This was before the League Tables came in, which brought the profession out in a muck sweat.) At Bassaleg Comprehensive the staff would race to get out of the car park before the buses, which meant they'd be home by four o'clock, four-thirty, even if they lived miles away, e.g. in Pontllanfraith.

There was little Verdun the poppy-eyed music teacher, who had a new Triumph every year; Ivor Philips, who taught woodwork and seemed to think he had to behave like a NCO bossing National Service recruits about, who had a red sports car he was proud of; John Knowles, a Special Policeman, JP and Lay Preacher in charge of compulsory sex education, who probably caught the bus; and a flotilla of cookery teachers who had the airs of minor members of the Royal Family, and who had top-of-the-range Minis. Another one, the Senior Mistress, who reminded me of Annette Crosbie, had a husband who won a Rolls-Royce in a raffle in Howells (or Morgans) in Cardiff. They sold it after a year and went on a cruise on the *Canberra*.

In front of this lot, I confess I went through a long phase of speaking in a silly German accent and behaving like Peter Sellers as the psychoanalyst in *What's New Pussycat?* It is mortifying to think that this is the abiding memory many staff members (if alive)

Deep South accent as a joke, and that sooner or later he'd snap out of it and everyone would laugh.

174

and fellow pupils – old now, bald or with grey hair and sagging boobs – will still have of me. Christ. But what I did grasp, I'm pretty sure, was that comedy, according to the Viennese witch-doctor, was dangerous. Jokes imply disorder, misrule.

✀

What I also grasped was that life is one long performance, a lived fiction.

✀

One of the problems I had with the academic world – there is too much decorum; not enough *aliveness*. Why can't a biographer (say) be *disrespectful?* What is the convention that when writing about and describing what has been observed and thought, what has been strongly felt, you have to be hushed, reverent, subservient? Not me – though I have never been admired for this. Only rebuked and mocked. Roger Lewis is so *opinionated*, opine the root-faced reviewers, the condescending twat-shaped twats. But I am unwilling to share any consensus, which is the lesson I'd din into my students when I was a tutor at Oxford in the Eighties. Whatever it is everyone else is for, be against it. Occasionally what one wants is *delirium*.

✀

Crime Wave Corner. Eighteen months after Brian Powell's cat was poisoned, he's still so upset he has put his house on the market. 'There are a lot of cat lovers around here and I have told them to be on their guard, particularly at the allotments.' Deb Large from the RSPCA said she is 'keeping an open mind'.

✀

Though I will make an exception for Dame Barry Humphries (a brainy well-read bugger) and my beloved Dame Beryl (who was always needing to be scooped up from under the table where she'd go for a snooze), it a mistake to meet literary or artistic heroes in real life. Such a let-down. Actors and actresses, in particular, and

175

on the whole, are pretty dim. That'll be why they need a script, of course, to compensate.

But take all this a little further – works of art are always better (nobler, more enigmatic) than the real life they depict. I don't much like knowing about Monica Jones, Maeve Brennan or Betty Mackereth, Larkin's women, because this makes the haunting poems less haunting, more like autobiographical vignettes. The air of edgeless mystery is reduced.

It's like when A. L. Rowse sought to identify The Dark Lady of *The Sonnets*. The entire exercise was limiting. The fish and eggs and flowers in Spanish paintings, to give another example, the play of light and shade, can't possibly be found anywhere out in the real world, search though we might. (Search though I have.) I suppose it is because art is about essences and real life is just a fucking mess, with no beginning or end.

᪣

There's nothing in the Kenneth Tynan diaries, the James Lees-Milne diaries, the Alan Clark diaries or the Evelyn Waugh diaries about domestic chores, cooking, cleaning, shopping, children, the maddening things that pack my sort of day. It's all Cyril Connolly up Noel Coward's bum while Alvilde wonders what time Princess Margaret is going to arrive for drinks with Paddy Leigh Fermor. Take today for example. I had to clear up the breakfast things; empty and refill the dishwasher; tidy the bedrooms and gather up the laundry; clean the bathroom – especially the toilet seat. You'd have thought a horse had been using it. I wrote 1,000 words on Mae West. I prepared luncheon; served and cleared up from luncheon. I spent £200 on groceries in Asda in Hereford. I put the groceries away in the fridge and the cupboard. Made supper; served and cleared up from supper. Put the washing machine on. Got the laundry out of the drier (twice) and carried it upstairs and folded it. Every day it is like this. No wonder I am at screaming point. Why couldn't *I* have been Princess Margaret, lying on the Mustique beach while slaves lit my cigarettes and popped them in the holder and poured me endless drinks?

◈

I never understand why *A Midsummer Night's Dream* is prettified. At the end of the play, the tolling of the 'iron-tongue of midnight' is surely ominous. And Oberon and Titania's quarrels have been perilous, discordant, upsetting the weather, upending the world, causing floods, fires, miscarriages, birth deformities.

Alexander McQueen, the troubled frock designer, had a line from the play tattooed on his arm: 'Love looks not with the eyes but with the mind.' Ugly people always try to believe this is true – and McQueen, found hanging from the neck in the wardrobe by his cleaner, had problems with his weight, subjected his models to perverse experiments (they had to wear clothes made from shells or bird skulls), and said that he'd sought inspiration 'in the most disgusting of places'. He should have given me a tinkle. We could have gone back to the slaughterhouse in Bedwas together.

◈

Sometimes I can't sleep – because of the dangerous fragility of things. Everybody else is asleep and safe – for the time being; for how long? They are off in different directions, to different destinations, during the day. Back here in the hen-house at night. I'm like one of those people who can't relax on a plane. They think that their will-power is needed for it to stay aloft and keep flying. If they relaxed it would crash. I'm like this with family life. If I relax it will crash.

◈

At Maggs' Bros, By Appointment to Her Majesty the Queen, Purveyors of Rare Books & Manuscripts, on the wall alongside the staircase there are all these portraits of worthies called Edward Maggs. They are in periwigs at the top of the stairs, and

177

as you go down the stairs we slowly reach the modern era – the Edwardian Edward Maggs in frock coat and wing collar, the Twenties Edward Maggs in a bowler hat, a contemporary Edward Maggs in skateboarder gear . . . I made that one up. It would be funny if suddenly there was a dyslexic Edward Maggs, the last of the line, not interested in books, manuscripts or the Queen, who turned 50 Berkeley Square into a Betamax Video Store.

✤

Quimby* came across a dignitary in Peshawar called Anil Valvekar. When he first overheard people talking about Anil Valvekar, who as it turned out just happened to be a retired lieutenant-colonel and presently Head of Security, though in fairness at a motor factory, he thought they meant an anal valve car, and that vindaloo had become a new power source. 'Do be looking for our anal valve car,' is what Quimby genuinely thought he'd been told.

Furthermore, he was told that the ambassador in Pakistan was dick shit – actually Dixxit. 'I'll make my own mind up on that, thank you,' Quimby had retorted, diplomatically. I said that on the road to Delhi I saw a garage with a sign saying Anil Lubricants. Quimby said that in Istanbul he was handed a business card that had printed on it Mustapha Kunt.

* I met Quimby on my first day at St Andrews University. He was finishing a doctorate on William Plomer, I'd recently had my A Level results. Despite this gap in age and maturity, we began a conversation about art, life, the cosmos, literature, vintage port and W. C. Fields films that continued without interruption for over thirty years. Quimby was always travelling to exotic places on behalf of the Crown. He was like Mycroft Holmes, with a dash of Professor Moriarty.

The other person I met on my first day at St Andrews University was Anna Margaret Jane Dickens, to whom I became engaged to be married on the spot.

I wonder if anyone else has ever sorted their entire future life out at such top speed? The Duke and Duchess of Cambridge?

By my second day at St Andrews University I was ready to leave.

In Afghanistan, Keir Hardie's first name would mean penis. So it goes.

⁊

Minor writers have eventful lives – Anthony Burgess in Malaya and so forth; Simon Raven and his carousing; all those Elizabethan and Jacobean playwrights who got into brawls. Philip Larkin sat in a small room and got on with it. Fucked his loaf-haired secretaries, however. Ding-dong! Not wholly monastic. My life is so spectacularly uneventful – shall I get drunk or shall I get very drunk – or am I drunk already? Shall I go to the Co-op now or go to the Co-op later – or am I drunk and in the Co-op already? – I ought to by rights move to Pearson Park, Hull, and gaze in a forlorn way from high windows.

⁊

With Picasso, sexuality and art were the same thing. Not only in his subject matter (nymphs and shepherds, artists pouncing on their models, the minotaur and his maidens), but also in the form of his work, in the way his lines and shapes are always flowing from one thing to another thing, interpenetrating, burgeoning. This prodigal growth and form is erotic. It has sexual heat, does Picasso's turbulence.

⁊

Olivier: his style of striking acting is out of fashion. Actors now play Hamlet as Hamlet – he played Hamlet as Fortinbras or as Claudius. He would have made the definitive Claudius. He was his own man on the stage – which is always a threat.

⁊

How to Eat, How to be a Domestic Goddess, Nigella Bites . . . All of them stuffed in my cupboard. The woman is wasting her time in the kitchen. *How to Give a Tip-Top Blow-Job* is the book she was born to write. I suppose that is her secret. Programmes and books ostensibly about food that are actually about sticky fingers and sucking the egg-beaters. The softest of soft porn. Jamie

Oliver when he started out was similar: *The Naked Chef*. I know somebody who is immensely aroused by Jamie's thick tongue – turns him on. I'm a *Fat Ladies* man, me.

✺

Asked, as one so often is these days, to specify any 'dietary requirements,' I use this Fusspots' Charter as a champion opportunity to point out that if rich Burgundian wines don't flow in my direction like the mighty Zambezi, I will deliberately die on the spot, choking to death very dramatically in front of gluten-free vegans of both sexes and shiftless lactose-intolerant foreign-looking gay people without partners.

✺

Being one myself, I am fascinated by ugly blokes. Ugly blokes in art never get the girl. They are rejects – ignorable, without love. So they turn to the Dark Side of the Force. Scarpia in *Tosca*, Don Pizarro in *Fidelio*, or Eddie Robinson in gangster films. Ugly blokes – people don't want to go near them. I look like Joan Sims in a polo-neck, since you ask.

But look at Edward G. Robinson in (say) *Key Largo*. He is relaxed about his bad behaviour; how easy being evil is! Lolling in his bath, or adjusting his tie, or shooting a wise guy in the guts: he is having a wonderful time. He has a majestical scene (and has a long speech to deliver) where he is being shaved – the rasping voice, his flickering tongue. He is reptilian. In *Key Largo*, he is a toad that has crawled out of the Florida swamp. John Huston's camera can't get enough of that Somerset Maugham-ish face.

Eddie Robinson belonged in the Roman baths, swathed in towels or a toga, though it was Romania he actually came from originally. He had that same broad menacing peasant face as Nicolae Ceauçescu – big cheeks, a huge petulant downturned moist mouth, an angry squatness. But despite this, there was a strange beauty to an Edward G. Robinson performance, because there was nothing apologetic about him. He had a dancer's confidence (as Cagney did); a relaxed energy. I like the way, as the villain in *Key Largo*, he doesn't live on his nerve-ends – he's not intense. Just imagine how 'Bobby' de Niro or James Gandolfini from *The Sopranos* would do it – or overdo it. According to reliable reports, Edward G. Robinson (real name: Doris Klunt) amassed the biggest collection of Impressionist paintings outside France.

'Julia's [that's the late Julia Trevelyan Oman] worst nightmare was to be Lady Strong. I remember saying to her, "We're going to lunch at Clarence House. You're going to have to be Lady Strong."' Her *worst* nightmare? *Really?* That's quite a claim. Perhaps she'd have preferred *Lord* Strong? Julia Trevelyan Oman did look like a little bloke – a battler, almost Welsh. When I first met her she reminded me of Mrs Arthur Mallett, the wife of the Bedwas coal merchant who had a depot on Pandy Road.

Nevertheless, Sir Roy Strong actually did make this remark.* It is not one of Craig Brown's parodic inventions. The anecdote annoys me for several reasons: the fact it's not funny, though advanced (presumably) as wit; the snobbery; the name-dropping and social climbing; the smugness and sense of entitlement – all in the name of attracting attention, like those ghoulish 'businessmen' one sees heading ostentatiously for the First Class carriage on the Paddington – Hereford 'Cathedrals Express.'

The shrill and sycophantic high camp that pervaded anything to do with the Queen Mother would make a good subject for a modern Firbank. It was a toy theatre world, charming to the eye. Clarence House; Royal Lodge, Windsor; Birkhall, near Balmoral; Walmer Castle, Deal; the Castle of Mey, in Caithness. How that old queen was indulged in her many hives.

* In the *Telegraph Magazine* on 18 June 2011.

Someone ought to do a ballet version of *Vertigo*, to Bernard Herrmann's score. The theme of doubles, of losing somebody twice. The beautiful Givenchy suits. Like *Swan Lake*, it is all about disguise, deception, and suffering over an obsessive love. It is very enigmatic – and hypnotic – as a film; it's already more than halfway to being choreographed. It is immensely stylised. Think what the deep feeling of dance could reveal. A Hitchcock ballet. Has anyone done one?

∽

And has Benjamin Britten ever been sung *properly* – so that the inner-secrets of the music are revealed? Britten stayed in East Anglia and got tighter and tighter emotionally. Look at the photographs of him – the over-combed crinkled hair, the collar and tie, his preference for cold baths.

The operas are full of a controlled frenzy. They are about sexual non-fulfilment, which go close to the edge of the abyss, but won't ever go over. The agony of restraint – which is not the same as the guilt about licentiousness, or even temptation.

I wonder what an Italian tenor would do with the roles – Grimes, Quint, Oberon, Captain Vere, Aschenbach? Peter Pears's voice was cold and chaste, a desiccated hoot, mischievously parodied by Dudley Moore's rendition of 'Little Miss Muffet' – and such was the accuracy of the parody, Pears and Britten, who adopted the personae of repressed prep school masters, were much offended.

Ian Bostridge's voice is the same, also the late Philip Langridge's, whom I otherwise much respected. I am convinced there is something in Britten still waiting to be released – something more potent and passionate than the music of Clare College Cambridge choristers, where the effect is etiolated.

∽

Though the Black Death began nearby in 1348, it is already twenty-three years since Keith Chegwin materialised in Hereford. The *Multi-Coloured Swap Shop* star visited the Leisure Centre and participated in a Summer Skills Workshop.

July

What am I still doing here? Why can't I be famous? Because I have had an ace idea for a television panel game that will surely get me on nodding terms with the chieftains who executively produce *So You Think You Can Dance Live*, *The Million Pound Drop Live* and *Piers Morgan's Life Stories*. I'll be up in Noel Edmonds's helicopter before I know it.

It's called *Fatal Celebrity Mishaps*. Rod Hull and Emu fell off the roof; Derek Nimmo fell down the cellar steps; Stirling Moss had a lucky escape when he fell down a lift-shaft. There's Roy Kinnear toppling off a donkey in Spain, while shooting *The Return of the Musketeers*. Marvin Gaye was shot by his father. Roger Delgado, the original Master in *Doctor Who*, drove off a cliff in Turkey, as did Princess Grace, though in Monaco. Roland Barthes was run down by a garbage truck. Nyree Dawn Porter had a stroke after receiving obscene letters. Dorothy Tutin fell off a camel during a camel race at Chipperfield's Circus. Questions were asked in Parliament – about the extent to which a camel could be considered domesticated under the terms of the Dangerous Wild Animal Act (1976). 'What about ferrets?' asked one MP, and the Deputy Speaker had to intervene. Trevor Bannister dropped dead on his allotment in Thames Ditton.

Instead of *Fatal Celebrity Mishaps*, a request for an interview from Kimberley Hunt, producer of the BBC's *Breakfast* programme, forwarded to me by Claire Daly of *The Oldie*:

Hi Claire

Thanks for your help just now. If you wouldn't mind passing this on to Roger I'd be very grateful.

We're looking for someone who might be able to help us with an interview at 0810 on Wednesday morning.

The Royal College of Psychiatrists are releasing a report advising people over 65 to drink half the amount of younger adults. That would mean an upper safe limit of 11 units a week for older people. It suggests that an increasing proportion of older people are drinking above existing safe levels.

We have someone who will explain the research and talk about the benefits of drinking less but what we'd ideally like is someone who can talk alongside them about their personal experiences and whether we should be telling people of this age what to do when they're not drinking excessively, are healthy and it seems we've heard before that some amount of alcohol can be beneficial.

I hope you might be able to help . . .

So the bastards think I'm an alkie, do they? Bastards. In the grip of the grog. A turps nudger. Bastards. As the message had been sent c/o *The Oldie*, where they run a Honeysett cartoon of me looking like Robbie Coltrane swigging from a hip flask, I guess Kimberley had assumed (a) he's an OAP and (b) he's pissed all the time except when he's asleep.

I don't think I'd have accepted this gig even if I was living in London and it wouldn't have been a huge hassle getting to the studio at dawn. (Except for a £5,000 'appearance fee' of course – that would have swung the balance.) Indeed, I don't want ever to appear on television. I go all self-conscious whenever there's a Kodak Instamatic around.

But what a scream, anyone believing I could be a suitable spokesperson for inebriated people over sixty-five. It's like putting Tess Daly on to talk about the menopause. I replied to Kimberley as follows:

> Doctor Lewis presents his compliments to Miss Hunt
> but regrets that as he is always already drunk at 8.10 on a
> Wednesday morning (it is a regular Wednesday morning
> tradition of his – has been for years), his answer is a regretfully
> slurred *no*.

Gyles told me that when the crew on *The One Show* saw my email – which found its way around the Corporation in a flash – they fell about laughing. *Evil* bastards.

❧

The highlight of our year was the agricultural show. In fact, there were several, which run together in my mind. Machen Show, St Mellon's Show, Bedwellty Show, the Royal Welsh Show, a whole world of passes, tickets, badges, and silk rosettes. There'd be endless committees all year to organise, print and distribute these. The rabbit tent, the dogs, goats, caged birds, horses, cakes – each had its own group of fiercely loyal and on-the-brink-of-falling-out helpers. The WI flower arrangers were competitive to the point of being psychopathic. The way they crossly jabbed prickly stems into the powdery green oasis cones – it was their husbands you felt sorry for.

I loved being inside the cool marquees, with the yellowish pale light filtering through the canvas on to trestle tables, which were covered with jam pots, seed cakes, and onions that stood in saucers of sand. The smell of sweet mown grass. The horses and the finery of the riders. The cattle, shampooed and combed. The rasping voices from the loudspeakers: a man called Michael Bishop did the commentaries – for hours, for years, he'd chirrup away from his vantage point in a little caravan, explaining the jumping scores ('Four faults!') and the goings-on in the gymkhana ring.

The Author wins prizes

I used to be in what's called Leading Rein. I sat there on a Welsh Mountain Pony – absolutely immaculate – while I was led about the ring. Hay bales were dumped around the ring as benches, and there'd be polite applause. I was also Andy Pandy (still talked about) in the Fancy Dress Parade. I think I retired from being Andy Pandy only because I went to university. My Grandpa George, in his bowler hat, was often a judge, so I could guarantee I'd at least be Highly Commended. I don't know if they still hold these, but there used to be a Formal Luncheon for Members, laid on in a long tent, with caterers and speeches and silver cups given out. There was always a mass exodus after the raffle, and a scraping back of chairs.

We'd always be first at the site, and the last to leave, the field by then a mudbath. My mother was in her absolute element. Horses, spectacle, atmosphere, display. My father tottered from trade-stand to trade-stand, accepting more and more of the hospitality and rashly agreeing to buy sheep-dip, ploughs and combine harvesters, seed drills and quad bikes. I myself bought a lawnmower from a man called Bunny Philips. Bunny was later shot by his mistress, who then turned the gun on herself.

✆

Clevedon I like. I mean the pier Betjeman saved. Lots of commemorative brass plaques inset into the planks and benches. I'd like to put one there for myself, but you probably need to be dead first. I picked up an application form anyway. Prices start at £85. The steam launch *Waverley* (or was it the *Balmoral*?) arrived, pulling up alongside the wrought-iron pavilions – the light feathery galleries and walkways – glass and metal and sky. At the toll booth end, the buildings are made from greenish-brown rock – including a boarded-up hotel. It was as if they'd grown out of the cliffs – neglected and severe.

Clevedon is wintry even in summer, the dusk dipped in grey. There were old ladies creeping into the tea shops. Clevedon is where, in 1963, Betjeman made a film about a residential hotel – an entire hotel full of silent widows, left behind. The town is suffused with cold damp melancholy.

✆

We called in at Clevedon on our way to Bigbury-on-Sea, where the Art Deco elements of the restored Burgh Island Hotel suggest sunshine and sunbursts – whiteness, yellowness, brightness. It is the setting for at least one Agatha Christie novel. But the atmosphere of her tales is much more gothic – overgrown gardens, romantic ruins, weeds and wildflowers – like that place of hers on the River Dart, which is a place for secrets and lies.

✆

I was not staying in the Burgh Island Hotel, but in a bungalow owned by Anna's family nearby. What a (diplomatic word) beyond-basic place; a (undiplomatic word) shithole – I doubt if £50 had been spent on the decor and maintenance since the Second Ashanti War. Broken beds and chairs. Anna's Nan's old fridge and carpets. A kitchen so old you could charge people an entrance fee to tour the historical exhibits.

There was a coffee morning at the Bigbury Old Folks' Home. Though they'd put the posters up, there's always the fear that they may well have forgotten all about it. But it was rather wonderful – the hopeless raffle prizes and stalls set out in the lounge, selling broken lampshades, jigsaw puzzles with the pieces missing, copies of *Reader's Digest* condensed novels, a book on how to build a patio by Cyril Fletcher, the Odd Ode man, lots and lots of straw dollies and ornaments made of driftwood. The staff came round with glasses of Bristol Cream Sherry. No coffee in sight. There was a big colour television set, of the earliest vintage. An upright piano, with the vocal score of *Showboat* open on the music stand. A small yellow parrot in a large cage. Photographs of the late Queen Mother. The residents in their favourite armchairs already looked very dead themselves. A twilight atmosphere – also very warm. The heating was turned right up, which surely is not good for the corpses? I pretended that Nanoo* was with me in order to drop her off. We roared.

* My mother-in-law, Iris Grace Kelly Margaret Rutherford Angela Lansbury Elsa Lanchester Dickens, b. 1880 or thereabouts. Retired balloonist. Goes in for purple tweed capes and red hats with feathers. The original for Noel Coward's Madame Arcati, though Coward may not have known this. Macular degeneration has not impaired her ability to drive, because she never looked where she went anyway – she always drives very fast and with total confidence. Indefatigable flower-arranger. Invented cake-scapes – cakes so elaborately iced they are sculptures. Did the catering for my Fellini Party in Zippo's Big Top on Hampstead Heath in 2009, when Dame Beryl Bainbridge, wearing a velvet tutu, went on the trapeze. Nanoo is as deaf as a stone and because she can lip-read knows what rude words the Royal Family are saying when they make balcony appearances at Buckingham Palace. The name comes from Robin Williams saying *nanoo-nanoo* in *Mork and Mindy*.

Ivy Trembley (eighty-seven) tells me that she went on this vibrating treadmill thing at the gym the other day up in Oswestry where she lives, and 'It did more for me than Reg ever did' . . . And her Reg rode a Raleigh in the Tour de France. My mother invested in a vibrating treadmill when she wanted to lose weight, even though there is plenty of Glamorganshire near at hand, fields and woods and that, that she could walk around in if she wanted, if only because she owns a lot of it. But anyway, she put her new treadmill into reverse gear by mistake, did my mother, and was catapulted backwards against the far wall with such force she came bouncing back, ending up spreadeagled like a cartoon cat against the wardrobe. There was then that the earthquake in New Zealand we all heard about. What you didn't hear was that in Ellesmere Road, Bromyard, an ornamental plastic swan fell off its plinth into the garden pond.

I'm sure a lot of mad mullahs were disappointed when that woman was not stoned to death for adultery in Iran. It is the subject of so many Victorian melodramas – Tess of the D'Urbevilles being hanged, for instance. You can picture those grumbling bearded holy warriors, having to rebuild the rockery in the garden, under the baleful eye of their wife/wives.

'Specialist incident response crews' and the 'environment protection unit' were called out to Weston-under-Penyard because chemicals had leaked on to the road from a farm sprayer. No one was injured and the chemicals had already been swept up.

Beryl Bainbridge obit. I loved her mournful clown face – those huge sad eyes, the downturned mouth, the little girl haircut, the St Trinian's fishnet stockings. Her expression was always startled, the manner withdrawn. There was something about her of Stan

Laurel, who of course was also from Lancashire. She was an actress first and foremost – a lot of novelists have a smack of theatricality about them. Burgess put on plays, when a teacher at Banbury. Paul Bailey worked at Stratford, as did Margaret Drabble. Jean Rhys went on the stage, as I think did William Golding. Arthur Machen performed with Sir Frank Benson's company for eight years. Jerome K. Jerome toured the provinces as an actor, and wrote a book about his experiences – *On The Stage & Off* (1885). As an undergraduate, Iris Murdoch toured with a theatrical troupe. Harold Pinter famously appeared as an actor, under the pseudonym of David Barron – except of course Pinter wasn't a novelist. He was the greatest cast member *Crossroads* never had.

A lot of my enemies mustered at the funeral – Sue MacGregor (who was disdainful about me on *A Good Read*), Mark Lawson (who was disdainful about me on *Front Row*), many others. They only needed sad mother Julie Myerson (forty-nine) to turn up – she's the woman who *can never be forgiven* for asking me 'Is writing what you do full time? Sorry, I ought to know that' – and we could have had a brawl, an affray. Luckily I stayed at home.

There's a Larry Grayson Museum in Nuneaton, which is closed Mondays. Also in the same building – a reconstruction of George Eliot's drawing room. What a strange juxtaposition or conjunction across time and space, Larry Grayson and the author of *Middlemarch*. What I most remember about Larry – one of the first celebrity gayers – was his perspiring upper lip. He had in abundance the cross exasperation, the prickliness, of a harassed gents' outfitter measuring inside legs. The museum, situated in Riversley Park, Nuneaton, contains Larry's 'trademark gold bentwood chair'.

You can still find these nellies, though they are a dying breed, on the shop floor in department stores, in hotel restaurants folding napkins, organising the flowers at society weddings, and in charge of the Purser's Office on cruise ships. They are fuss-pots who are convinced their staff will let them down so they have to do everything *themselves*. 'Look at the muck in here!' was Larry's cry. They always still live with their mothers.

❧

Bruce Forsyth is an interesting figure. He is very proud of his CBE, as I should be if I get mine. His writing paper has 'Bruce Forsyth CBE' across the top in huge letters. Under his signature it says 'Bruce Forsyth CBE' as a reminder. I wonder if he has monogrammed slippers with 'Bruce Forsyth CBE' on them, a quilted dressing gown, pillowcases . . . He could emboss everything. His golf clubs, his golf buggy, his wig stand, his ego.

The Prince of Wales is the same. I believe there's not a chattel at Highgrove or in Clarence House, from top hats to teaspoons, that is not smeared with the Prince of Wales feathers and related Prince of Wales insignia, just in case anyone is in any doubt about the identity of the master of the house. Poor old Brucie, though. If he is upgraded to a knighthood he'll have to unpick the stitching, re-gild the Goblin Teasmade, and start from scratch. It would be a hell of a time-consuming task. He wouldn't mind it. He's very organised. He is the kind of man who times how long his teabags are to stay in the pot.

Sir Bruce Forsyth – why not?* It is Sir Wogan, Sir Frost, Sir Gambon, Sir Caine . . . On his coat of arms he can put: *Dulce Te Videre, Te Videre – Dulce!* I've always been frightened of Bruce, I have to confess – he sucks you in against your will; like the rabbit with the snake you are powerless to resist his charms. 'Aren't you glad you are not married to me?' I once heard him ask with unironic menace – and who did he imagine would possibly disagree?

In sketches with Roy Castle (Brucie annoyed at the trumpet

---

* Lo, it hath verily come to pass. For his 'Services to Entertainment and to Charity,' Bruce Joseph Forsyth-Johnson was made a Knight Bachelor in the Queen's Birthday Honours List, announced on 11 June 2011.

solos – understandably), Norman Wisdom (Brucie exasperated at the wallpapering – glue everywhere), or with Sammy Davis Jr (Brucie leaping out of the way of clashing cymbals), there's always this moment of sheer irritation. Though the joke is that Brucie is the straight man and these others are acting the giddy goat, for a second he genuinely isn't amused, the warmth is switched off. It would not be surprising to learn that Brucie is a bad loser at golf – sullen, bossy, prone to sulks. I had an uncle exactly like this. He'd play energetically with the nieces and nephews at a party, putting on this huge public act, and then you notice he's pink with annoyance.

Brucie's a bully, snapping at the studio audience and snarling at co-stars and getting irritable with the (admittedly drippy) people on his game shows – and then he'll suddenly be nice. He'll smile and glow. Yet you can never be sure where you are with him. It is impossible to predict when his niceness will curdle, whether he'll get bored and dismissive, or whether maybe he'll start loving you again.

He always makes an entrance as if he's on the point of rushing off somewhere else, and will only stop and stay if we interest him. He's in a hurry, racing about. He hops about and tap dances, plays the piano, does his little twirls – and what long legs he has, what polished shoes, what long arms, and then there's that jagged Punchinello profile. He has a mouth that finds it easy to sneer (and is half hidden by a thin moustache); cold beady eyes. He is like a crane or heron or egret. (Egrets, I've had a few, but then again, too few to mention.)

He ought to be thoroughly camp – and he's full of campy, dainty mannerisms – but it is too carefully choreographed for camp; too determined, as when Olivier is Richard III. He doesn't have the self-conscious artificial quality of camp. There's no nervous distance or shield. He has none of camp's evasions. And you can tell he is attracted to women – the flirtation, the utter self-belief. He doesn't skid away. There's no aversion he has to disguise or put himself out to overcome (as with Dale). I never think of Brucie as effeminate – just as I don't think a pantomime dame is a woman.

He's been on the box my entire life, yet his appalling game shows and television card games are forgettable – literally ephemeral. I can't remember a single contestant, so they were wasting their time. The absurdity of the wigs and toupees, the irritating catchphrases, the vanity – yet Brucie fascinates me. I am fascinated by the looks of genuine loathing he shoots at the audience. Frankie Howerd would also sneer at the audience – affect to fall out with them – but Frankie was much more exaggerated and arch, cawing, womanish, affronted. With Brucie the aggression is real.

Postscript: After I'd invented a totally silly and regrettable little fantasy that what's on the top of Brucie's head is a trained Arctic fox (*Vulpes lagopus*), which when not needed lives in a small cage and is fed on earthworms caught by Wilnelia, the current Mrs or Lady Forsyth, Brucie said I'd so vastly increased the number of sympathetic fan letters he'd been receiving, I felt I was absolutely honour bound to send him nothing less than a booklet of second-class stamps. I haven't heard from him further.

❧

I had another of those letters – 'If you die unexpectedly how much cover do you need? £150,000, £350,000, £550,000?' But if I died unexpectedly I'd be *dead*, wouldn't I? I won't be able to go on a spending spree *then*. This is the one cheque you'd not cash. The first thing my mother did when my father died was cancel the insurance policy connected to the Will Trust, which would pay out in the event of the second death (hers that is to say) to cover the taxes that then become due – she couldn't see the point in paying the premiums on a policy she'd not personally derive any benefit from. She also cancelled the subscription to the *Spectator*, though I could see the sense in that.

✦

Maggot, Double Barrelled Dave, Croaky, Gumsie, Strawberry Blonde Karl, Ginger Shane, Petrol Pete, Andy from Bedford . . . Soon the regulars will all have gone from The Thorn, either dispersing to university or because they are old and stupid and will be dead.

✦

Charlie would have us believe that since Elsie croaked he has been beset by elderly widows who want to keep him company. They way he talks he's Casanova. One widow came all the way from France on the Bromyard Twinning Scheme. Parenthetically – what is this keenness for English towns to form these links with towns abroad? There's one or two I know that should be twinned with Dachau. Anyway, this Froggie woman billeted herself on Charlie and annoyed him by calling him Charles, 'as if I'm bloody Charles Aznavour. Then she complained about the state of my pots.'

✦

The highlight of my week is to totter along to the WI Country Market in the Public Hall, known as The Pubic because someone stole the letter 'L'. Here old ladies in green tabards sell free-range eggs and tomato plants. The knitwear specialist is Mrs Pepper. But it is Mrs Toze's egg cosies that have caught on with me. I have sent heaps off to friends. Stephen Fry, Sir Simon Russell Beale, Sir Francis Wheen – they honestly don't know how they have survived this far in life without one of Mrs Toze's egg cosies.

I estimate I have despatched about a hundred, the latest pair having been posted to Ronald and Monica Searle. Ronald told me that it is 'so damned cold' where he lives, 2,000 feet up a French mountain, that he uses his egg cosies 'as ear warmers. They really look rather nice.'

However – consternation. An egg cosy was stolen the other

195

day from the WI Country Market. In Bromyard terms – where the clocks stopped round about 1955 – that's like the Brinks Matt Robbery, where, as you may recall, thieves (always thieves) made off with £26 million in gold bullion.

Each week now, as a consequence, Mrs Toze's husband, the dapper Mr Toze, stands guard over the egg cosy stall like Arnold Ridley's Private Godfrey. I for one don't half blame him.

❦

It is always kicking off at The Thorn. Last night a woman fell down the steps, got concussed, so Barmaid Jodhi called an ambulance. When the ambulance came the concussed woman was already fighting with a gypsy. There are always fights. The evening is punctuated by thuds as bodies hit the ground. Mark Pointy Shoes, whose sister sells wet fish on Hayling Island, and Barman Jason have regular soda-siphon duels. Police cars come and go, the town arsonist wanders in with a petrol-soaked rag asking for a light – it would be good training for Helmand. I find myself stepping over the bodies without a qualm.

❦

Consternation in a local school. The infants were making and signing a card for one of their number who has leukaemia. One little lad wrote 'Drop dead Fred!' for his message, which I thought hilarious when I heard about it. I'm still laughing now. But no – the psychologists and psychiatrists were called in. No doubt they arrived like a SWAT team, leaping from helicopters and armoured vehicles. The social services people would lock up that little lad in a home if they could, take him into care, for what could possibly have been at the root of his 'inappropriate behaviour'? So that's another budding satirist squashed.

❦

Why do I find foot spas funny? I don't know the answer, but I do. My friend Woo tells me she's got one that I can have, but I don't fancy a second-hand foot spa.

I'm less clued up about the womenfolk, to my regret. My father said they were 'a bunch of cows', who'd march off to bed in single file, 'with pisspots under their arms'. An intimidating procession, and it's true there were a lot of potties in the attic. Disappointed in love, the sisters sat in the bay window of the upstairs sitting-room, sneering at passers-by, calling them common. Downstairs the father of these self-appointed Grand Duchesses was chopping meat for the common folk, whose custom kept everyone in fresh hardback books and hairgrips from Harrods. It was in that very same room, in that very same bay window, that I'd listen to Gilbert and Sullivan and Stravinsky, while my own father laboured underneath. So that's where I get it from. Or get some of it from.

There had been things going on that were never to be talked about – I was not even aware of discreet whisperings. The woman in white is Kathleen Mary Lewis, born in 1905. She had an affair with Great Auntie Nancy's husband, Dennis, and when this all went wrong she put her head in the gas oven. Among The Lewis Papers is the invoice from the funeral director, who'd had to collect the body from Swansea: 'Drawn to Williams Bros, Undertakers, Tydfil Road, Bedwas, 10 May 1952: Best Oak Coffin and Gown, Conveying from Swansea, Hearse and Three Cars to Cemetery – £47 14s 6d.'

What had happened is that Nancy and her daughter Sheila moved back to Bedwas because of the war. Kathleen went to Swansea to help Dennis with his business – he'd made tents, but now the government wanted him to mass produce canvas shrouds for the Royal Navy. One thing led to another.

Sheila later danced with Michael Heseltine at a Conservative Party fundraiser and went to India to find herself. She had found herself sufficiently to attend my father's funeral, in January 2004, when she told me, 'The planet is slowing down.'

I remain thrilled by this saga of passion and violent death.

෨

Crime Wave Corner. A flasher has been at large in a Hereford park, 'exposing himself' to elderly female dog walkers. An odd detail. 'He did not speak before exposing himself.' Why mention this? Do they usually have a chat, recite a monologue, quote poetry? What is the normal flasher's protocol? Someone must know.

෨

Keeping an eye on my parents during their infrequent London trips was nothing compared with Judy Campbell, the actress for whom Eric Maschwitz composed 'A Nightingale Sang in Berkeley Square', and who had toured with Noel Coward during the Hitler War. She came with me to a Faber party – in the long-ago days *when I was fucking invited*. Perhaps I was barred after I'd mistaken Julian Barnes for the butler? It's not my fault if he looks like Lurch from *The Addams Family*. He must get this a lot. Anyway, I introduced Judy, who among other things was Jane Birkin's mother, to Verity Lambert, little Germaine Greer, Simon Gray, and Joanna Mackle, who was in a black rope and cord arrangement or contraption that simultaneously squashed her tits and made them pop out.

By eight-thirty Judy said she was flagging. We had twenty minutes of a 'Now where did I leave my car?' performance. Her Renault, filled with magazines and junk, was parked on the pavement at a 45 degree angle against the plate glass window of a casino on Great Russell Street. It was being guarded by Noah, a big black bouncer. He was one of the many people who, every hour of every day, Judy got eating out of her hand. She wasn't imperious or bossy in her manner; it was a sort of charismatic elegant grandeur. It was a bit like being plunged into the world of Mrs Wilberforce in *The Ladykillers*, as there I was with this elderly fairy, who was decked out in a long linen frock and a summery hat. Judy was about ninety-two.*

She drove like the clappers — very fast and nippily back to Chelsea, racing through the lights, overtaking taxis, shooting along alleys and back lanes and, if memory serves, even through shops and market stalls, with baskets of oranges flying through the air and costermongers diving for cover. She lived in a tall narrow house with a green lush secret garden. Pictures on the walls in the sitting room by Edward Ardizzone and Merula Guinness. Off we then went to Thierry's Restaurant in the King's Road, a walk that was virtually a run. Again — the waiters made a big fuss, plied her with complimentary champagne, the works. But I found it hard work. It was hard to keep judging how much she wanted to be indulged, how much it was up to me to make conversation, how

* Yet she was still only eighty-eight when she died in 2004. It baffles science.

much she wanted to take over completely. I insisted on dropping her off in a taxi. I wasn't up to another route-march.

Dr Harold Shipman – will he be remembered as a Crippen or Jack the Ripper or Christie? His crimes (though numerous) were not macabre – just putting old ladies to sleep. A calm, muted murderer. No blood or gore. It's like *The Ladykillers* – getting rid of sweet little old ladies, the Herbie Lom part. Harold Shipman must have had a lot of self-loathing. He was (as I understand it) rather friendless, and with an ugly fat wife, the wonderfully named Primrose Shipman. He practised alone – no colleagues at the surgery. Methodically getting rid of people – happy, jolly, sweet little old ladies.

For some reason I was reminded of Travis in *Taxi Driver*: his disaffection and friendlessness, and need for sex; his complete loneliness and rejection. The build-up to the killing spree at the end – which redeems him; it's a purgation – a moral crusade. The De Niro character is desperate to love – and to get laid.

A giantess here in Bromyard, Vera Moxby, said she saw me going into the florists and had said hello and that I'd probably not heard her because I hadn't said hello back. I said I was probably in the clouds. Another reason may have been that I didn't want anyone else thinking I knew the big fat cow. Anyway, that settled, I said I was actually buying a funeral wreath, which cost me £74.50. Instead of putting on a sympathetic face, which I'd have done in the circumstances, fat woman Vera Moxby said I was ripped off and that did I know they recycle them at the hospice? I said that's nice. She said, yes, they make flower arrangements out of left-over funeral wreaths at the hospice. Everyone knows that. That'll really cheer them up, I remarked, my irony going for a Burton. Lo, another day passes in the Herefordshire Balkans.

When I think of Bedwas Junior Mixed – it's where I was to be found while the successful men of my generation were at Eton and Harrow – what comes back to me are the smells, the flavours. Rancid milk on the milk crates, the biscuits available at playtime, the reek of dumpy coloured wax crayons, pencils and satchels. I was always well-equipped. My mother had my leather satchels and music case specially made by a saddler called Mr Hunt in Blackwood. I had a new woollen coat each autumn from Howells (or Morgans – Cardiff's department stores were indistinguishable) and highly polished brown shoes from the shoe shop in Church Street, Bedwas, that was known as The Shoe Shop. I was what was known as well turned out. I also stood out. My schoolmates were urchins in bare feet with rickets.

Luckily I was the eldest. By the time my hand-me-downs reached my sister, Angharad Frances Lewis, born in 1972, my rubber pantaloons had perished and were crinkly and yellow. My mother ensured that the big white nappy pin lasted for all four fruits from her womb. (Regarding fruit – I was the kumquat.) She's probably still got it, the safety pin. She's a hoarder, like me. My rubber pantaloons are doubtless also somewhere about, if not already on proud display in St Fagan's Welsh Folk Museum.

My mother had very strict standards in certain areas – standards that I rigorously adhere to myself. Correct table manners. Holding cutlery properly. Replying to letters promptly and sending thank-you cards punctually. Pulling out all the stops at Christmas. Looking after one's fingernails – I have an abhorrence of anyone with bitten nails. I literally can't look at them. She'd dust and scour the house from top to bottom every day, sometimes twice a day. But on the other hand she was always shouting and it was as if she was trying to reach you from across a large distance, though she'd only be in the next room and not down a ravine. She also swore to an extent that would make Roy Chubby Brown blanche.

It was always bloody this and bugger that. This was the influence of her father and brothers, who were gross.

She could also miscalculate the mood of an occasion spectacularly – as when she donated a 9-inch chocolate penis as a raffle prize for the Bedwas NSPCC. Who should win it but spinster Gwyneth Edmunds, the old maid who ran the Bedwas St John Ambulance Brigade, and who resembled Queen Victoria at her severest and most vinegary, complete with plump quivering jowls.

Well dressed in her black paramilitary uniform, Gwyneth Edmunds was always on parade at any gathering of five persons or more – perhaps turning up on spec in the average kitchen now and again – ready to spring into action and dab iodine on an abrasion. Gwyneth put the cock in her bag and an embarrassed silence fell.

Gwyneth later let on that she'd taken the cock home and had stamped on it in the garden. I believe you, Gwyneth! You quiver those jowls, girl! As a family we laughed about this for years. I'm still laughing now.

৯০

We've had all these anti-religion polemics from The Dawk and The Hitch. Yes, I quite agree with them, religion is the very devil. But it is still not how I feel about the world, which has its definite poetical moments, its lyrical moments – the suggestiveness of ghosts, haunting, visions, omens, magical stillness. The Dawk and The Hitch offer only empty panoramas. There's a higher (or a deeper) plane to be found, as in Shakespeare's last plays, with the theme of regeneration out of death. The cyclical structure of the seasons – nature's recurring circular patterns. The rites of spring, which triumph over the wasteland.

৯০

My family had no brushes with celebrity – except when my Grandma Lewis saw Mrs Mills in a motorway service station, Gordano or Leigh Delamere. 'Are you Mrs Mills?' asked my

Grandma Lewis. 'Yes, that I am, love,' said Mrs Mills. Mrs Mills! There's a topical name. She was a fat and jovial novelty pianist, whom I much preferred to Tessie O'Shea, who was a fat and jovial novelty banjolele player. Mrs Mills used to plink and plonk at the keyboard in a Blitz party-spirit manner or a family sing-a-long manner, her hits being 'No! No! A Thousand Times No!' and 'Let's Have Another One!' She resembled suburban clairvoyant Doris Stokes.

❧

Did Noel Coward ever return to Teddington or André Breton to Tinchebray? That's my excuse for never re-visiting Bedwas, though Cary Grant was forever walking the streets of Bristol, where he was greeted as old Archie Leach. 'Do you still think you are Doktor Fritz Fassbender, then, Rodge?' is what the Welsh would be asking me. Not that I'd have anyone there to go and see.

❧

Have any of you heard of Clifford Fishwick? I saw a painting of his in a catalogue – blood-red pillars of flame, a pyramid of piled-up blocks of red and reddish-black: it had an atmosphere. I was very taken with it. A volcano? A red sea? Maxim de Winter's house in flames? Mr Rochester's? Poe's masque of red death? The red of red meat in a butcher's shop? The picture could be the sun – fire descending from heaven – or hell.

There was something about the picture that spread through me. Knocked down for £450 (so our council tax goes unpaid), it is now in the Lewis Collection. I'd like to start a Fishwick Revival. Clifford Fishwick (1923–97) was the principal of Exeter College of Art and Design. He went in for abstract depictions of mountains and mists – tilted planes and colossal hewn shapes. The sky. The sea.

❧

I had another argument with one of my editors. No, I didn't. I keep my peace. If there's one thing I've learned – when these people sound off just let them carry on. You can't change their mind because they haven't got one. Or at least not one of their own. Not in the way that I understand having a mind. Also I'm a coward.

Anyway – I was told that my reference to Glenda Jackson's appearances in Ken Russell films and a mention of the Bavarian castle in *Chitty Chitty Bang Bang* were 'abstruse and cerebral'. No, you dopey minge-tunnels, I wanted to say (but of course didn't), Ludwig Wittgenstein's *Tractatus Logico Philosophicus* is fucking *cerebral*. Bertrand Russell's *Principia Mathematica* is fucking *cerebral*. I'm talking about Glenda getting her tits out in *Women in Love* and Gert Frobe as Baron Bomburst singing 'You're My Little Coochie Face' to Anna Quayle.

But what can you do about people who also say things like 'the peg has moved on'? The tragedy is that newspaper editors think their readers are stupider than they are which is (a) patronising in the extreme, and (b) impossible.

If it's any consolation, television commissioning editors and producers are worse again, as is apparent by a glance at the schedules. So:

Doctor Lewis Glances at the Schedules.

One of the reasons I as a rule don't watch television is that I can't abide the people who are on it. Actually that's a bit of a lie – there's a television set on full blast somewhere in the house every hour of the day, so by a process of osmosis I see everything that's ever broadcast, from *CBeebies* at dawn to *Animal Rescue Squad Highlights* on Five when insomnia sets in. I have also never missed a *Poirot* and I like *Question Time* if there's a chance I might know someone in the audience. They are in Brecon soon. David Dimbleby will be mobbed by my aunties.

But they are so cheerful, the presenters, so determined to make me join them in having a hilarious good time. That's what gives me the hypertension, drives me to drink, and makes the liver go bang. The *Top Gear* team remind me of Fourth Form geeks, keen on engines and speed. I didn't like them much when I was in the Fourth Form and I certainly don't like them now. The arrested development is a bit alarming – like seeing Terry Scott dressed as a schoolboy in those Curly Wurly adverts. One just wishes these chaps would move on to discovering *girls*. I like James May, though, in fairness. He plays the harpsichord.

Alan Titchmarsh is another grinning Dinner Monitor, self-consciously dropping his aiches while telling us about the latest horticultural trends and 'the initiatives in support of the International Year of Biodiversity' at the *Chelsea Flower Show 2010*. Don't you watch these programmes – *The Seasons With Alan Titchmarch* is another one – and yearn to run amok with a bucket of weedkiller? The man puts me off my radishes. My purple sprouting broccoli positively wilts when I hear him pipe up – which is every blinking minute this week. When I look out at the patch of poison ivy and dead geraniums that constitutes my own garden, I sigh with pride. I wonder if it might win a medal at Chelsea next year? The shed with the broken strimmer and the rusty barbecue – if Tracy Emin's unmade bed is art, so is my patio.

It must be wholesomeness that sets me off, as I was cast into a bilious temper at the prospect of *Halcyon River Diaries*, in which 'Charlie, Philippa and their family follow the fortunes of kingfishers, moorhens and dippers as they try to survive the spring'. Why can't Charlie and Philippa do what normal families do – argue, slam doors, get drunk, storm off, come back, eat a takeaway and watch *Three in a Bed*, in which the owners of B&Bs from Bournemouth, Sussex and the Peak District compete – though compete for what exactly, or indeed why, I haven't worked out yet. I love it when the competitors tick each other off – last week one of them complained about the lack of a full-length mirror and so the other one got going about a missing toilet brush.

When I'm having luncheon, *Bargain Hunt* is on, so I'm always exposed to the Blue team and the Red team rifling through a skip. If only the competitors would drop a few china figurines I'd have a real laugh. But day after day they waste money on buttonhooks and broken telescopes, chipped Royal Worcester soup tureens and pipe racks carved by Polish POWs out of biscuits. The competitors are quite clueless – barely articulate, giggling and simpering. Haven't they got proper jobs to go to instead of proudly appearing on daytime TV? Well of course they haven't. They belong to England's vast dreary platoon of white-collar retirees and dispirited redundancy victims, whose children still live at home and whose own parents refuse to die.

Tim Wonnacott, the presenter, can barely conceal his impatience. What is it about him I like least? I've thought about this for a very long time. I've given more thought to Tim Wonnacott than to Laurence Olivier, and I wrote Laurence Olivier's biography. Is it the Terry-Thomas moustache? The spectacles on coloured ropes around his neck? His newly acquired twatty panama or trilby hats, spiv's waistcoats and forced jocular air? He reeks of minor public school. In the old days he'd have worn gloves to drive the Riley. He's no fool, though, or at least once wasn't. He's a former Sotheby's director and ran charity auctions for the Blairs at Chequers.

It's just that he is trying *so hard* to be a television presenter, making the glee of Gyles Brandreth seem sombre – though he'll never be the next Arthur Negus. Does anyone remember former air raid warden and antiques expert Arthur Negus? He used to paw and caress chair legs and wardrobe doors, murmuring in a Gloucestershire burr. He moved so slowly and heavily, he was like an old oak table himself – it's a surprise no one threw a cloth over him and laid out the plates for tea.

Arthur wasn't the kind of man you'd want to strangle with his old school tie, yet like art gallery people, antiques dealers generally hate themselves for being – when all is said and done, at the end of the day, no word of a lie, we've got to be honest with them – *in trade!* They are shopkeepers, no posher than butchers like my father, God rest his immortal soul, when he was summing up and appraising pigs and bullocks in Newport Market.

Yet your antiques 'experts', on all the time in David Dickinson's *Real Deal*, *Flog It*, *Antiques Roadshow*, *Cash in the Attic*, *Put Your Money Where Your Mouth Is*, among others, like to pretend they are scholars and academics, that they have dropped into the studio from the Senior Common Room at All Souls.

What amuses me about *Loose Women*, which again is always on when I'm taking luncheon, is that I have never heard of their guests, even vaguely: Shappi Khorsandi, Stacey Solomon, Katrina Leskanich. The whole thing could be an ingenious spoof. If I'm in the right mood, the old bags talking gibberish and moaning about men can be quite soothing. Claire Sweeney and her mates ought to team up with Clarkson, The Hamster and nice James May and let's see what happens. We don't always want to watch *Panorama* documentaries about the work of bomb disposal experts in Afghanistan or listen to Mr Know-All Stephen Fry on BBC Four give a lecture on Richard Wagner. Sometimes all the heart yearns for is piffle.

I know Stephen – who doesn't? He was miscast as Maurice Woodruff the soothsayer in my little HBO Peter Sellers biopic. He's been taking a camera crew around the opera houses of the world for years, making his programme about how you can spot the difference between Richard Wagner and Robert Wagner. Only one of them was married to Natalie Wood, apparently.

According to old Fry, Wagner's work 'is on the side of the angels'. I'd rather say it is on the side of goblins and ugly giants, as the inspiration for *The Ring* was the *Nibelungenlied*, a sort of pre-Tolkien saga, out of which I may have sprung – or at least my Pembrokeshire grandmother, who was as short and squat, rotund in a misshapen way, as a rugby ball, with floppy bosoms and tiny legs and ghastly whiskers.

It is not generally known even to Stephen Fry that Wagner derived much inspiration from Wales, finding there in the old castles and myths the origins of *Parsifal*. My friend Byron Rogers says the Holy Grail is kept in a safe in a NatWest bank in Cardiganshire. The manager had assumed the cup was 'something to do with horseracing'. One day it'll turn up on *Bargain Hunt*, going for a song. Yes? *Yes!*

❧

It is not generally known that *custle* or maybe *kustle* is the Norwegian word for cunt. So I had a lot of fun with that. Roy Custle, the Custle of Mey, Barbara Custle, Caerphilly Custle. I am so easily amused it's frightening. *I Capture the Custle* by Dodie Smith.

❧

How can one cross the magic line and gain access to power and privilege, money and honour and respect? Because some folk do and some folk don't, just as some make it in their careers and others can't, regardless of apparent talent, let alone 'qualifications', in my case two doctorates. Working-class women from northern townships mistakenly claim benefits and go to prison. Politicians and bankers who swindle billions earn a mild rebuke – and are in addition given massive pay-offs and pension benefits, even a seat in the Lords.

Though £1.46 million was repaid by MPs following the expenses scandal in 2010, the 'resettlement grants' (whatever they may be) handed out to the MPs who have now stepped down – mainly due to the expenses scandal – have cost the taxpayer £10.4 million. Resettlement grants my arse. Where's the guillotine?

Meanwhile, the rest of us, to get through the day, are heating up old baked beans, metaphorically speaking. Being from industrial South Wales I'll always *already* be one down.

During luncheon, my father-in-law went off and dismantled the cooker. I know he doesn't much like small talk, but this seemed extreme. There were screws and parts of old cooker hob everywhere. But the joke is, he did manage to fix the grill, which hasn't worked for months. So not the onset of Alzheimer's story you were expecting.

Parenthetically, I love small talk. It's big talk that bores me — religion, politics, Concorde flying faster than the speed of sound. I also suffer fools gladly. Very gladly indeed. I cherish ineptitude, clownishness — that's where my sympathy lies. Flaws are what make a person.

In our world of misunderstanding and accident and anguish, when people are unselfconsciously foolish they are vulnerable — and paradoxically that's when they thrive, when they are most themselves. Look at Morris Men. Look at Bromyard's chief 'character', Everard Cuncliffe, who has a dressing-up box and is always dressing up and being photographed by the local paper. I can't get enough of people like that. Shag Harris and so forth. Zany Antony.

'If people did not sometimes do silly things,' wrote Wittgenstein, 'nothing intelligent would ever get done.' Saying all this, I wouldn't want to be on the receiving end of an inept or silly surgeon, but otherwise my point holds.

❦

Crime Wave Corner. Thieves have stolen all fourteen shirts and shorts from a garage in Hafod Road — the entire kit from a school football team. Squirrels.

❦

The silly Catalans have outlawed bullfighting. One of the reasons I love Spain is that on the whole it has not yielded to squeamish political correctness. Yet there's been a typical celebrity-led campaign to suppress bullfighting throughout Spain, starting with a petition handed in to the regional parliament in Barcelona. 'A ban on bullfighting in Catalonia will encourage the movement to keep growing,' chirped Ricky Gervais – and I wish someone would land a pair of banderillas in his ample flanks, because yesterday the ban was indeed officially approved in the region, with 68 votes in favour and 55 against. Gervais proudly says a ban will 'save 100 bulls from inhumane slaughter', starting on 1 January 2012.*

Does it really need to be pointed out that such bulls wouldn't ever have been born – wouldn't have existed in any shape or form – unless they'd been bred for the ring? They are splendid mythological creatures, nurtured for their aggression and intent on seeking an adversary. What I stand in awe of is precisely their wildness. Not Gervais or Pamela Anderson or any other sweetly intentioned protester is going to tame them and turn them into daisy-munching cattle in an orchard. They are killers. If bullfighting is banned, no one is going to keep one or two as *fucking pets*. They will become extinct.

The spectacle of a man standing there on foot in the sand with

---

* As Jonathan Meades painstakingly explained to me, however: 'The Catalan opposition to tauromachy is an assertion of its separateness, of its longing for secession. I suspect Mr Gervais will be disappointed. Madrid will not follow suit. Indeed, Catalonia's preoccupation with its "identity" has been the re-making of Madrid. The intelligentsia which grew up in the Franco years spoke Castilian. The only people who spoke Catalan, which was banned, were the workers and immigrants (mostly from Murcia and Andalucía) who learned it in the barrios. Under Pujol, who was in power for a quarter of a century after Franco's death, a sort of linguistic authoritarianism was practised and Castilian speakers were disqualified from jobs teaching, working in the executive etc. So a huge number moved to Madrid. I did a filmed report about Barcelona in 1985 and wanted Ricardo Bofill to participate. He was embarrassed because he didn't speak a word of Catalan despite having lived in Barcelona all his life. Eventually he did it in French. The effect on Barcelona has been to turn it into a glamorous hick town.' Got that, everyone?

nothing but a red flag and a short sword, while half-a-ton of sleek angry bull whirls and spins and hooks with its horns, used to inspire the likes of Ernest Hemingway and Kenneth Tynan. Orson Welles so worshipped the corrida, his ashes are scattered on bullfighter Antonio Ordonez's farm in Andalucía. Picasso painted images of the bullfight non-stop.

But nobody dares speak up for the corrida today, certainly not since Hemingway snuffed it. Indeed, four years ago Adrien Brody starred in a biopic about Manolete, the bullfighter who was killed in the ring at Linares in 1947, but owing to pressure from Alliance Anticorrida, a French anti-bullfighting group, the £20 million production has yet to be shown on the screen, only on DVD. 'It is inadmissible to release a film in which the hero is a matador,' argue the protestors. I watched it the other day – it is so over-edited, the bulls are barely to be seen. Manolete could be pointing his sword at the empty air. It's as daft as playing Othello white or pretending that in James Mason's final film *The Shooting Party* what they are firing at are clay pigeons. So quite what is going on?

It is more than an animal rights issue. If you are against animal cruelty, then ban horse racing. Ban putting horses in harnesses to pull carriages. Stop keeping cats and dogs – that's all unnatural. Free your goldfish. Become a vegan. Any step short of that is hypocrisy. Wear hessian half-hose and sandals made of lettuce.

As I never cease pointing out, my family were farmers and butchers in Wales for over a century. I grew up next to the slaughterhouse, so I've never understood sentimentality about animals. I don't think of them as little humans. We ran what would now be heralded as an organic business, where the sheep and beef cattle were pampered up until the last moment – as is the Spanish fighting bull.

The *toros bravos* is a breed native only to the Iberian peninsula. Traditionally they have been bred by the rich, who possess the required land and capital – though these days with bulls costing £5,000 a piece to raise, estate-owners earn more from sunflower oil and olive harvests. There are only about 200 bull-breeding ranches left throughout Spain, continuing and controlling the bloodlines that date from the seventeenth century. Kept in herds for four or five years and never seeing a man on foot, the bulls have a pretty majestic free-range existence up until the final fifteen minutes. By law, the matador has to complete his task within that fifteen minutes, or else the bull is returned to the pens.

This happened in Seville recently, where a bull overturned seven horses and was set free to father other splendid monsters. And who doesn't cheer when one of those cocky tourists comes a cropper in the streets of Pamplona?

Hemingway first went to the bullfight expecting to be 'horrified and perhaps sickened' by the 'stupid brutal business' – but he found himself transfixed. He was able to see that the primitive and passionate ritual isn't about the bull but about the man facing it, who is seeing and learning to appreciate genuine danger.

The bullfight is about mastering fear. It is a display of sheer courage that puts one in touch with Roman gladiatorial games. It is very visceral. I have myself been to the world's main bullring, Las Ventas in Madrid, and to the Plaza de Toros de la Real Maestranza in Seville, built in 1761 and the setting for Bizet's *Carmen*. The first thing to note is that the corrida is undeniably amazingly exciting – and second that it has nothing to do with sport. It is an ancient ceremony, re-enacting the bloodletting and death of an innocent victim, in which Welles saw parallels with *Othello*. But surely a closer analogy is with the savagery of what happens to Christ. It is a sort of primeval Mass.

I am not being facetious. In Seville, Holy Week is celebrated with the first bullfights of the season. During the night there is a procession of black-cowled penitents. An effigy of the Virgin of Macarena, to whom the matadors pray and who they then decorate with jewels, is carried through the streets. It is all very devout – simultaneously Catholic and disconcertingly pagan.

But this is Spain, not Islington. It is ridiculous to impose the sensibility of Islington and Hampstead on a place which, if left to itself, has a ferocity and a formality. Look at the paintings of Goya and El Greco and Velásquez – the portraits of the hanging body of Christ with gaping wounds – and at those sinister baroque churches with wrought-iron gates. Or consider the stamping and wailing and howling in flamenco music – the songs about love and loss, with postures that mimic the weird intimacy of man and bull. Southern Spain with its yellow soil is so hot it is like being on fire. The contrast of light and shade has an intensity I've seen nowhere else. Bullfighting comes out of this frenzy. There is blood and danger and a cruel beauty in Spain's landscape and temper. We in the north can't begin to identify with it.

The matador with his passes and stances, the tossing and goring, is participating in a grotesque ballet. Strong emotions such as fury, horror, loss, fear and pity are involved. And in our own society here in the British Isles, where, as in America, no one can cope with the basic facts of death and pain, this is felt to be very threatening. We are too pusillanimous. The dark aspects of humanity are suppressed – and it is even not allowed to leave earth on our vegetables any more. Carrots and apples are rinsed and put in a supermarket plastic box.

Cigarettes are banned, hunting is banned, boxing they want banned, and sensuality I am sure will soon be banned. Enjoyment will be illegal. We are so uptight. Everything is bland and nothing is challenging. Everything has to be virtual, kept inside the head or on the computer screen, like the violence in children's computer games. Politically correct persons want to obliterate or muzzle any evidence of the link between modern man and our urges to be bacchanalian. The bullfight is a massive threat to this.

No wonder we are going mad and are pumped full of

antidepressants. We are socially anaemic, insect-like and machine-made, with no energy. Bullfighting, maybe, is a sign of a healthy culture, one with, as Hemingway would say, *cojones* – i.e. balls.*

✑

In point of fact I'm less pro-bullfighting than I am anti-insipidity and anti-Ricky Gervais, which is just a poncey way of spelling Jarvis.

✑

There is something far more evil than bullfighting. Fish pedicures, in the name of God. *Fish pedicures.* Why don't those people who want to ban bullfighting turn their attention to fish pedicures?

---

* When I essayed the above arguments – in *The Times* as it happens; and I don't mean *The Hereford Times* – I fully expected the animal rights brigade to have my bollocks for a bow-tie. But not a peep. I suppose they never saw the article because on principle they only read the *Guardian* or the *Fortean Times* (aka *The Weird 'Un*). It would have been funny to have published a pro-bullfighting piece in the *Guardian* or *The Weird 'Un*, which is devoted usually to aliens, crop circles and the Knights Templar. Why didn't I damn well think of it?

Anyway, apart from having to fob off invitations to go on *The Jeremy Vine Show*, what I did receive was this nice letter from a Mrs Bickler from Allerton Park, Leeds. She sounds a formidable woman:

'Dear Mr [sic] Lewis,

[. . .] Like me, you are an aficionado of the *Corrida de Toros* – *Es mu Grandes!* [Eh?] I truly enjoyed reading your article and share your passion of the ritual, knowledge and excitement that the whole scenario of the *corrida* can bring. Applause and white handkerchief-waving directed to *El Presidente* on behalf of the matador, who in his suit of lights arrogantly struts as he acknowledges the crowd's delight. *Viva cojones!* Yet not forgetting to applaud the bull, who died with honour on his part.

The simile here is that you too show *cojones*, Mr [sic] Lewis, daring to take on the many non-believers [. . .] *Bravo!* I throw my rose at your feet. Ernest Hemingway would be as proud of you as I am.

I have been to many bullfights all over Spain, as I have friends living in Barcelona. How could the Catalonians be the first to ban this cultural heritage? I trust that the Andalucíans will square up to the fight.

At seventy-seven years of age, I still enjoy the spectacle of courage and also re-reading *Death in the Afternoon* . . .'

When Nanoo went for a fish pedicure in Merry Hill I saw my chance to slip in a piranha, but the opportunity never arose because once she saw the tank of squirming tiddlers she ran a mile. She hid in Costa Coffee. Anyway, the only piranha I've got to hand is mounted and stuffed – a souvenir of my expedition up the Amazon with Rosie Boycott.

When Nanoo saw the fish, we feared for every pane of glass in the West Midlands, because she is not good with animals of any kind. She hates them – phobic. She screams like a banshee. She won't go in the garden if it's reported there's a frog in it.

So Anna took her place – and she screamed and shook, because the tiddlers went on a feeding frenzy. I thought she was in danger of falling off the chair and landing in the tank, where the tiddlers she hadn't squashed to death would eat her alive.

It is a bizarre set-up. You expected the person in charge to be Vincent Price, but the overseer was a smiling multicultural babe who gave off serenity rather than menace. There are these large white padded seats that surmount cubic white lavatory pans. You put your feet in the lavatory pans and paddle about while the fish mob your flaky skin. Bluish light plays across the room. Forest warblings played on a Peruvian nose flute waft from a loudspeaker.

How disgusting, inflicting old smelly feet on harmless tiddlers – which apparently come from a river in Turkey. If they came from a river in South Wales they'd poison you; you'd start craving male voice choirs and Brain's Dark. French fish, you'd wear a beret. I plan to mount a protest and will march up and down outside Merry Hill with a placard. *Down With Fish Pedicures!* I will never be able to eat whitebait again. Nor will you, having read this far.

❧

A mobile home caught fire in Much Birch. Two fire engines arrived top speed from Hereford, 'but there were no reports of any injuries'. What a bore.

As it is possible to be at one with Nature, let's just say I am at two – at sixes and sevens – with technology. I can't use my mobile because I can't work the Keypad Unlock function. Of course I've lost the instruction booklet.* So don't start trying to convince me about the merits of a Satellite Navigation device.

We got lost in East London recently. An hour after going past Shoreditch tube station we went past Shoreditch tube station. We were trying to get to Stansted from Mile End Road. Dante's deepest circles of Hell are where we found ourselves.

So Anna said we had to have one of these satnavs. Trust us to get a satnav that has mental health issues, i.e. the advice it gives is fucking nuts. We were trying to get from Looe to Plymouth and ended up in a field near Bodmin. Anna paid that field a second visit when she had a meeting in Wolverhampton. Then Anna said it was my fault anyway because I'd been holding it upside down, rotating it, confusing it, looking underneath – the satellite up in space was as a consequence spinning and throbbing and probably fell to earth on a small township in Chile. Not many dead.

It is already almost a year since Sir Roy Strong, wearing a wide-brimmed straw hat, was seen chatting to Boo and Oliver Vaughan at St Bridget's Church, Skenfrith.

* Still no assistance. I could be in real peril here, with my rape alarm going off, and you wouldn't give a bugger.

August

What am I still doing here? I am in Buxton. It is August. It is pouring with rain and cold enough for a coat and scarf. I'd never been to the Peak District before – and by heck, over there are the peaks, over there is the district. The brownish rock and remote undesirable cottages put me in mind of the Moors Murders, particularly as depicted in a sinister little book by Edward Gorey called *The Loathsome Couple*. ('Mona lured a little girl named Eepie Carpetrod to the villa with promises of a doll wearing a green satin frock.') Aren't there still meant to be dead children buried hereabouts?

❧

The Devonshires own Derbyshire, so Buxton is unspoilt. There was an antique shop selling dinner gongs and a stuffed stoat. There are bowling greens. There are arcades. There are pump rooms, with sinister plunge pools and marble slabs, with straps and hoists, drains and sluices, where colonic irrigation once went on in what looked to me like a version of my family's slaughterhouse.

During the week of my visit, a casual observer will have assumed that a medical conference was underway, perhaps something to do with clinical obesity, goitres, Bell's palsy and thyroid deformities, and that the surgeons had helpfully brought along their patients to illustrate the lectures.

Not so, it was the annual round-up of Gilbert and Sullivan fans, as a glance at the posters will have told you. The coquettish stout old ladies with golden ringlets were the Poor Little Buttercups of yesteryear; the huge plain ones were the Katishas, the Ruths, the Duchesses of Plaza-Toro; the fat bald men with goatee beards were the Poo-Bahs. There were hundreds of them, the lame and the near-dead and the wobbly – so many immense bellies that for once I fitted in and felt normal. It was also faintly frightening, because everything these good people do, whether it is walking through a door or saying hello, is done in a slightly exaggerated amateur operatic way and is always accompanied by mugging and gusts of laughter. They never stop being on a stage.

Gilbert and Sullivan – whenever the operettas are put on I detect a last gasp of Victoriana. The works are crisp and dapper and light and filigree – yet also cobwebby. They are put on by schools and in church halls. But has anyone noticed the bottled-up sexuality? All these little maids and shepherdesses, randy sailors and gondoliers? The pulchritude, the lubricity? Nabokov would have had something to say about the nymphets. How come Major General Stanley in *The Pirates of Penzance* has all those 'daughters'? I bet a lot of surreptitious shagging goes on between the men and women choruses in provincial amateur operatic societies. There's a sitcom there.

They put on Gilbert and Sullivan in Upper Machen Church Room, before the Craig Secondary Modern was built and operations were moved there, nearer Newport. The village nancy took the patter roles. The painter and decorator Cyrus Hughes painted the scenery. The scores and libretti were hired from D'Oyly Carte, who made a killing. People made their own costumes, in clashing colours. They'd scour James's Emporium in Bedwas for ribbons. I'd spot local old hags and dinner ladies as the fairies or as Sir Joseph Porter's cousins and sisters and aunts. Tradesmen or those who'd gone a short distance up in the world and worked in an office – possibly even one or two games teachers – would be policemen and pirates. Elaine Jenkins, the ironmonger's wife, who had a big friendly smile, was always the soprano. I bought an aluminium watering can and a pot of Dulux

Emulsion from her. The conductor was my Uncle Verdun, with his hostile eyes.

I'm not a fan of Gilbert's lyrics, which are arch and forced, but Sullivan's music has been a revelation to me lately. Those juddering cellos and worried strings, the fanfares and Wagnerian chords. Lots of motets, too, anthems and close-harmony unaccompanied trios and quartets, hidden among the tarantara-zing-boom-zing-booms – you can see/hear Sullivan's training as a choral scholar, when he was a soloist at the Chapel Royal. Sullivan was also a church organist and composed the hymns 'Onward Christian Soldiers' and 'Nearer My God To Thee'. Mrs Harrington told me that when I was a Mixed Infant in 1969.

There's more going on in Sullivan than there is in Gilbert, who was a bore. 'Grim's Dyke', Gilbert's house near Harrow, where he drowned in the pond, before it became a hotel, was used as the setting for horror movies, including *The Blood Beast of Terror* and *Curse of the Crimson Altar*, which was Boris Karloff's final film. Mrs Harrington didn't tell me that, however. To be told that you'd needed to have gone to Eton.

I particularly wanted to go to Buxton to pay my respects to the late John Reed, who died in March 2010. When I was growing up in Wales an annual treat was the visit to Cardiff's New Theatre of the D'Oyly Carte troupe. I'd insist on being taken along, usually by my Grandma Lewis, and John Reed was the masterful patter man – the Lord Chancellor in *Iolanthe*, the Major General in *The Pirates of Penzance*, Koko in *The Mikado*. I admired his dainty precision. What I didn't know (aged eight or nine) was that what I was also admiring was will-o-the-wisp Reed's immaculate camp. He had pathos too.

The D'Oyly Carte Company was like the *Carry Ons* at Pinewood – Dame Bridget, exactly like Peter Rogers, keeping everyone in penury while amassing millions for herself. The cast couldn't afford digs, so stayed in circus caravans in car parks. Those ossified, ropy worn-out productions, tatty costumes and collapsing scenery –

and the singers, God bless them, were uncomplaining stalwarts. Male and female members of the Chorus were kept chastely separate – separate travel arrangements and so forth in reserved train carriages.

What a drag it must have been touring endlessly for little money, the clothes and the sets falling to bits and the management too mean to provide replacements. John Reed was ninety-four when he died, having retired first to Bournemouth, where he ran a hotel, and then to Halifax, where up until his final months he was still directing productions for the Harrogate Gilbert and Sullivan Society and the West Yorkshire Savoyards.

At the Memorial Service we saw some home-movie footage of him, near death and blind, teaching youngsters how to play Jack Point in *Yeoman of the Guard*. It was rather moving – this visible handing on of the tradition. I wept actually. Someone produced from their pocket the paper flowers Reed had handled during his final performance as Koko – the actual flowers that had bloomed in the spring, tra-la.

Ancient people with collapsed features and rodent ulcers stood up to remember Reed, who seems to have been a nicer version of Kenneth Williams, filled with nervous energy, a dapper pixie. The speakers were revealed as former principals and the surviving members of the chorus from the D'Oyly Carte Company.* So I'd seen them all before – forty years ago in South Wales. Thomas Round, who must be nearly a hundred himself, was present, as were Valerie Masterson, Cynthia Morey, Gillian Knight and Peggy Anne Jones. These artistes were on the LPs I bought as a child with my birthday money and knew by heart. I was in a room with ghosts.

Between the speakers and the video clips there were bursts of song. The audience was encouraged to join in, and bloody

* Which disbanded in 1982. As sad a day as when Beeching axed the steam railways.

hell they did, and very good some of them were too. During the rousing extract from *The Pirates of Penzance*, when the pirates and the police are singing one thing and the women are singing another thing – everybody at it at the same time and at full blast – I found myself joining in (you had to), but with the women. 'Go ye heroes, go to glory' and so forth. When Anna looked at me strangely it was not because I was singing with the women's chorus but because I was openly enjoying myself.

To crown it all, that night there was a full moon.

୨

A missing man from Ross-on-Wye was found safe and well. He'd gone for a walk in Tintern.

୨

These drawings and paintings of Cy Twombly – what is going on? These ridiculous scribbles and scrawls, like graffiti on whitewashed outside walls, semi-erased messages, most of it inscribed in long-lost alphabets. But I am transfixed. I've bought a pair of his books – *The Rose* and *Bacchus*, published by the Gagosian Gallery. I'm reminded of the peeling, flaking walls in Fellini's *Satyricon*. The poetry and the pastoral images jostling with obscenity and coarseness – a deliberate jumble, crumbling and messy, but vibrant.

I saw a series of huge pictures called *Lepanto*, which filled a gallery at The Prado. You could make out ships and sea-battle shapes in the runny paint, just about. So if the title was any clue, what we had here was a massive frieze illustrating the clash between the Ottoman Turks and the Holy League (the Spanish, the Venetians and the Pope) that took place in the Gulf of Lepanto in 1571.

Twombly's work seems to call out for decipherment – and yet defies it. Is he still alive?* Lives in Italy I think, though is an American. Kentucky? His pictures are pastiche runic stones

---

* Cy Twombly died on 5 July 2011.

and fragments. He's hyper-modern and archaic simultaneously. Infantile and senile-seeming daubing, ancient and archaeological, and yet belonging, too, to a world that is still to come.

Actually, I'm not sure pure abstract art exists – I always try and make sense of what I am looking at, generally finding it representative of *something*.

ဏ

Invited to judge a dog show at Ocle Pychard – I may never have been asked to judge the Booker, but I have been *invited to judge a fucking dog show in Ocle Pychard* – I awarded the rosette for The Dog That Most Resembled Its Owner to Mr Swainshill and his splendid Airedale. How was I to know that in fact there was no such class and that Mrs Swainshill has had her ovaries and uterus removed, hence the unfeasible hairiness? I must make that appointment with Mr 'Mint' Jelley.

ဏ

August Bank Holiday Sunday – *The Life and Death of Peter Sellers* was on BBC Two. I've not seen it for several years, and I'm glad to report that I found it immensely powerful, particularly the Peter Pannish subtexts and undercurrents, with Sellers as the boy who would not grow up. This hadn't been totally apparent to me before, when I saw the HBO film in London or inserted the DVD. Like a true work of art, it is revealing different things about itself.

I normally give up watching after my own name has flashed on the screen, so at last I can agree that Emily Watson plays Anne to perfection. She's playing Anna in fact, and can do so again when they do my life story. (Though who can play me adequately, now Don Estelle is dead? Why, Sir Simon Russell Beale!) For into my Sellers book I crammed all my own dilemmas, tantrums, and problems with personality and identity; I was always interested – am still interested – in how we go about fashioning a character for ourselves.

Oscar Wilde said that any portrait painted with feeling is a portrait of the artist more than the sitter – biography as disguised autobiography – and that's what is going on here, though I admit that is not a wholly flattering admission or confession, is it? Sellers was fucking nuts, but through Sellers I began to find out who I was and what I felt.

Miriam Margolyes, who plays Sellers's mother, can play my mother – there is a distinct physical resemblance, what we might call the thunderball effect. (Actually, old Miriam could play *me* without too much trouble and without the need for expensive prosthetics, either.)

❧

Nanoo has been to an Abba Karaoke Night. I long to know how it went, but she's as deaf as a stone and didn't know the songs anyway. Last month she went up in an air balloon with her friend Edna Cockin (as God is my judge), and Edna fell over in the basket. It was a veritable sight to see, Edna Cockin's stockinged feet pointing to the sky as they floated over Clent.

❧

Barry Cryer has phoned me with a good joke. 'I'm worried about my hearing' – 'You've come to the right person. I'm a healer! Now, let me put my hands over your ears. Concentrate. Start humming. Now, feel any better?' – 'A bit, but I'm still worried about my hearing. It's Tuesday'.

❧

Non-Gay-Al from The Thorn thought he was on for what is known in Herefordshire as a Sporting Double, i.e. a mother-daughter combo. She was about forty, not too raddled, still quite nice. Non-Gay-Al went back with her to her house and she shouted up the stairs – and that's when he realised he'd hooked up not with the mother as such but . . . Apparently this crone was quite put out that she'd been disturbed from her foot spa, even though she'd squeezed herself into a boob-tube.

❧

I think I am going mad. I sacked my agent, cancelled a book contract, dumped my publishers, and sabotaged a column I had in a Sunday tabloid by making fun of Bob Monkhouse and his Bikini Atoll suntan, which (so the editor told me) upset Bob's widow, 'who is a good friend of the paper'. But Jackie Monkhouse died two years ago. I remain the sole person in the history of journalism who was officially reprimanded for upsetting someone who is dead – but editors are such megalomaniacs this is just insignificant nitty-gritty. On top of this, I don't speak to my mother. I never go out. I dine alone. I work at night, when I don't have to see anyone. I have this craving for solitude.

Oscar is in Athens, theoretically. You never know with Oscar. His sense of direction is not good and his ability to get to places is hit and miss. Meant to go to Gatwick South Terminal, the place to find him is in Gatwick North Terminal. He went to Paris and had a pleasant weekend in Charles de Gaulle Airport. He couldn't find the way out. I've been there myself and have every sympathy with that one. So – I don't know if he is in Greece or Inverness and if that bouzouki music we hear on the phone is a CD of the *Zorba the Greek* soundtrack.

My holiday present from Greece: the Audio CD of *Zorba the Greek* by Mikis Theodorakis.

To The Thorn for my nightly dose of variegated drivel. Billings said, 'What's the difference between eroticism and pornography? Eroticism is when you are tickled with a feather and pornography is when you have the whole feather shoved up your arse' – 'I think it's when you have the whole chicken shoved up your arse, Billings,' corrected Strawberry Blonde Karl. 'I can never tell jokes, me,' said Billings. By now I was falling about.

Vanessa Redgrave was allegedly seen going in The Falcon. Perfectly possible, as she and little Corin were evacuees in Bromyard during the Hitler War. The Kempsons were local landowners. 'She's a lesbian,' said Billings.

৩

It's like an outbreak. A woman with an emphatic clumping gait came up to me in the street. 'Agatha Christie was a lesbian,' she said, as bold as flipping brass. This in Bromyard, mark you, where like espresso machines and slices of lemon in drinks, gays haven't come in yet. Oscar told me that when a woman with a laptop went into The Thorn and asked for a Skinny Latte, everyone in unison, as if they had been in rehearsal for weeks, flapped their wrists and said, 'Milky coffee! Milky coffee!' Coincidentally, my informant was of the same dumpy shapeless build as Dame Christie, with wrinkled brown stockings. Was it a ghost – a visitation? A message from the far-beyond?

But it would explain a lot, sexual guilt – the failure of the newly married Agatha to satisfy war hero Archie Christie, hence his desertion; her fleeing to Harrogate in a state; the sheer number of bitter old maids in her books – and evil slender young girls. Poirot and Miss Marple are single. Passion sublimated as problem-solving – and as interfering.

Having rehearsed these hypotheses in the *Daily Dacre* – adding for good measure that Max Mallowan, Dame Christie's second husband, seemed a bit of a nancy* – I received death threats from Dame Christie's fans (nothing unusual there), including the following, which I toss into this chronicle because the letter came from South Wales:

---

* Sir Max Edgar Lucien Mallowan CBE (1904–78) was an archaeologist who dug up a lot of Iraq, then known as Mesopotamia. Agatha Christie accompanied him on his expeditions, hence the many stories set in the Middle East.

225

'Dear Mr [sic] Roger Lewis,
What a sick little man you are! I have just read your article about the biography of Agatha Christie. Quite interesting, but presumably to shock us you imply she was a lesbian in the last paragraph. Just because her life wasn't full of sex I presume?! People like you are quite pathetic – you get your kicks implying others are inferior. I expect you were the one at school calling classmates lesbians or gays if they hadn't had sex by the age of 1 2! A typical bully. I doubt if you will ever remotely reach the heights of literature or money that Agatha Christie did. The only way you have decided to make a name for *yourself* is to try and blacken hers. Get a grip. Have you thought she may have been just normal? I haven't given you my address. I don't want anything *you've* touched coming through my letterbox.
Mrs L. Waters.

I wouldn't come through Mrs L. Waters's letterbox with a stolen dick. But actually she's the one who has taken it upon herself to decide that lesbianism = a bad thing to be. What's inferior about the gays? I don't make that assumption. Mrs L. Waters is the one being homophobic, I fear. She's the one doing the degrading and the humiliating. Furthermore, when I was twelve, I was still very much in South Wales, where as Mrs L. Waters will be well aware, gays and lesbians are stamped out by the Methodists and the Baptists. No one is allowed to have sex in the Valleys before the age of thirty, let alone twelve – so where's she got that from? She gets herself into quite a little lather, and I bet writing *lesbian* and *gay* gave her a delicious hot flush. The handwriting gets tremulous, the biro digging into the notelet. Anyway, up the bum and no babies to you, love.

Vanessa Redgrave played Agatha Christie in a film about her Harrogate disappearance – when she went mad after Archie

Christie left her for a younger woman. Thereafter, as I've said, story after story is about adultery and sexual double-cross.

Who was it that Vanessa Redgrave used to be with, Timothy Dalton or Franco Nero? What a name, Franco Nero. Two mad dictators in one. Like Stalin Caligula. I didn't know until the other day that Timothy Dalton was Welsh – but it's obvious really: short legs, long body.

✇

I saw Claude Rains in *Phantom of the Opera*. What a beautiful voice, with a faint hoot to it, a dryness, a delicacy that's not mincing. He's a violinist in the orchestra who is brutally sacked when he starts getting arthritis. So this is what starts to make him cross. Worse, when he shows a publisher a symphony he has been toiling at for years, everyone laughs at him. I can't remember how it happens, but then he gets acid thrown in his face – the acid is a tray of green water. Somehow the accident leaves him with a livid red duelling scar. Apparently the studio didn't want to overdo the grossness, so as not to upset disfigured ex-servicemen. The next thing we know, Claude is running around the opera house in a big cloak – you'd think the cloak would get in the way. He moves into the obligatory crypt and the twist – rather touchingly – is that he is Christine's father, the diva a daughter he could never acknowledge. I don't want to *begin* contemplating the Freudian reverberations of all this.

✇

My belly is bloated and misshapen, like I've swallowed a Space Hopper. I am a bulging, sprawling person. I was up in the night with acid reflux agonies. Despite swallowing every pill and potion in the house, sleep evaded me. At four in the morning I was at the kitchen table reading a biography of Germaine Greer. I'd put good money on the fact that I was one of the very few people in a population of 60 million (far too many – we need a war or a plague) to be found doing *that*. Certainly not above a score.

227

Germaine has managed to create quite a career for herself based on a single idea – that men are bastards. She has this hectoring, Amazonian tone. She's a bit of a disciplinarian, laying down the law, dominating her environment. She thought of herself as progressive in sexual matters, but her own experiences sound unencouraging – wasn't she tied up once by a research student at Warwick? Didn't she marry a plumber briefly – like for a fortnight? I find her prose hard going. Her arguments are vague and generalised and she lurches about angrily. But in person she is flirtatious and teasing, her jugs on display under lacy tops. She swept up to me at a Faber party – *back in the days when I was fucking invited* – and said she'd overheard me use the word popinjay. She's like a mad Mary Warnock.

❧

I can't stand it when the window cleaner is about. I feel invaded. I know what a medieval gentleman felt like when he was (for the sake of argument) composing a madrigal or illuminating a manuscript and some gonk with a siege ladder appeared at his casement. I was in bed just dropping off when there the window cleaner suddenly was. Then he appeared at the window of the bathroom. I was being pursued. I couldn't have a shit in peace. Then he wanted £10 and I didn't have change. The glass is falling out anyway because the blue tits go for the putty.

❧

I had to do some Silly Season cobblers in the *Daily Dacre* on Teddy Bears. Even *Woman's Hour* wanted me on to discuss the subject. Presumably Gyles Brandreth was unavailable, as he is the world Teddy Bear expert, and indeed is the curator of a Teddy Bear Museum, which used to be in Stratford-upon-Avon. I don't know where they moved – Penge or Croydon I suspect, where the only white people are still the Irish.

It is not generally known that the Teddy Bear cast as Aloysius in *Brideshead Revisted*, and carried about Oxford by Anthony Andrews, was owned by the fruity old character actor Peter Bull. I suppose he is forgotten now, but Peter Bull is in *Dr. Strangelove* as the Russian ambassador, standing behind Peter Sellers and glowering. Indeed, he was capable of one thing only when acting – *glowering*. He was very good in drag in an *Alice in Wonderland* film with Fiona Fullerton. His 'Moral Song' was cut from the finished film but is on the LP.

Yesterday for the first time in ages I lost my temper with a non-family member. The photographer the *Daily Dacre* sent – to capture me cuddling my Teddy Bear collection – was a moron, and anyone who spends more than ten minutes trying to take pictures of me is wasting their time and mine. I freeze with self-consciousness and get more and more tense.

Anyway, this bloke spent over an hour getting me to simper with my Teddy Bears and in the end I just flung the bloody things away and said, 'I'm sorry, but I'm not having any more of this!' and walked out – that is, I walked out of my own house and hid in the Leisure Centre on Cruxwell Street. I had to creep round to the back garden half-an-hour later and shout up to Sébastien's window, 'Has that [*expletive deleted*] gone?' Luckily the fucker had. But I was white with rage. *White.*

༄

I was on a high level of anxiety all week. Really in a quite grotesque condition. And I had good reason for my forebodings. I am never wrong to be paranoid. A motorcycle courier arrived to hand-deliver a letter from the editor of a Sunday tabloid, saying that because I'd persisted in poking fun at Bob Monkhouse's butternut squash suntan and upsetting his widow, even though she is still dead, I was to stop submitting copy, which in any event they always chopped, changed, toned down – like Jonathan Swift finding that when *A Modest Proposal* came out his editor had changed *babies* to something 'less offensive' such as *cabbages* or *custard.* The courier was rather sinister, standing there in the pitch dark with his helmet and clipboard.

I was told that it is all very well to sound off in my books (which nobody buys or reads anyway), but that my splenetic and opinionated style was out of place in a family newspaper, where what is required (by implication) are mediocrity and pap, or in the columns of Petronella Wyatt, both at once. I disagree – there is a hunger for people who know their own minds; a need for a little light vituperation. Newspapers have a duty to be provocative, not to seek out what they anticipate is the thickest person in Britain – a northern housemaid, say, or a raving ratbag of a Wesleyan who gets her notelets out to complain if she sees the word *knockers* in print,* or a researcher on *The One Show* – and aim everything at them.

It is my belief, in any case, that the ordinary reader is much smarter and more humorous than the features editors in London – who exist in their horrible self-regarding media bubble – dare to imagine. I was hired to be me (if you follow), then they tried to stop me being me, reined me back on my haunches. It's like enlisting a war photographer and then being disappointed when he doesn't submit cute pictures of a kitten in a brandy glass.

The minute the courier started back to London the phone rang and it was Barry Cryer. 'Love your columns, old love!' – 'I've just been sacked!' I yelped.

The coda to this sad episode is that the editor who gave me the heave-ho retired and moved to a part of Ireland where people can still catch leprosy, though paradoxically (given how reactionary Ireland can be) leprosy is no legal bar to either marriage or divorce.

* If the Wesleyan is a South Welsh Wesleyan, then of course it is not knockers but *cnocwrs*.

I generally don't get on with editors, not unless they treat me as if I'm of Air Commodore or Lieutenant-Colonel rank, with a CB. (Most do, to be fair.) I haven't come this far to be regarded as an NCO. V. S. Naipaul, even before he got the Nobel and the knighthood, expected to be treated as if he were the equivalent of a very good society vet or a QC, payable in guineas if not doubloons. Because if we don't stand up for ourselves as writers we'll be ground down and told to use the Tradesman's Entrance. Like little Sir Vidia, I won't be anyone's subordinate – which is tricky because I want their money.

I particularly loathe it when editors say they love my work and then don't give me work. That doesn't pay my Barclaycard bill. It's patronising and empty. Dylan Jones of *GQ* used always to be saying he wanted to 'cover [me] with love' – but the plain fact is that he hasn't commissioned an article from me for four years, keeps me away from his parties, and has rejected every idea I've sent in, claiming 'lack of space'.

Lack of *space*? A Condé Nast production is bigger than the Tokyo telephone directory and surely readers would rather something to read than have to look at those acres of homoerotic advertisements for luggage and wristwatches?

When I published something in *Esquire* he sent me a ferocious email, really not very nice. Here it is:

I see you have a piece in another men's magazine. You can either work for us exclusively, or not at all. So let me know which it is to be. Obviously I'd prefer to have you contribute to *GQ*, but not if you're going to work for magazines that think they compete with us.

I reminded him that he'd never offered me any exclusivity contract; secondly, that I hadn't heard from him for donkey's years; and thirdly, that as a freelance I sold my wares where I could. I also pointed out that the piece in *Esquire* was one I'd offered him for *GQ* first, but that he'd turned it down *sight unseen*. That would have clinched it surely?

Furthermore, man-of-influence Dylan Jones himself, in addition to editing *GQ*, has columns in the *Mail on Sunday* and the *Independent*, so he's the servant of at least several masters. But no – he wouldn't back down. All he'd keep saying was 'as for exclusivity, obviously I want and expect you to write for us exclusively'. *Expect*, eh? Who does he think he is? Horatio Nelson? I never heard from him again. I didn't even get a Christmas card this year. Ooo, he knows how to *wound*. Incidentally, what is a magazine called *Gentleman's Quarterly* doing coming out *monthly*?*

᳀

Another one who decided to fall out with me recently without any just cause that I could detect is Wendy Wallop, a (oxymoron alert) literary editor. That's definitely not her real name by the way. For years I contributed book reviews to Wendy's pages. Hundreds and hundreds of them. I was diligence personified. Then – suddenly – nothing. Dropped me completely, like I had a contagious cancer. No explanation.

These people have the morals of the Borgias. They are capricious, vindictive and disloyal. I'm told that Wendy Wallop (still not her real name) keeps having to move desks because she gets into feuds.

᳀

There have been any number of Wendy Wallops in my life. Thin women in offices who use words like *pardon* and *toilet*. Nothing in the fridge at home save a bottle of nail varnish. They possess 2:2 degrees from provincial universities. They come across people like me – a winner of The Fucking Chancellor's Fucking English

---

* I was going to disguise the names here – Dylan Jones as Gwatkin Pillbox, *GQ* as *Le Bourgeois Gentilhomme*, and *Esquire* as *The Toff*, but then I thought: the story loses its point unless names are named.

Essay Prize at Fucking Oxford Fucking University – and the strategy is to pretend I'm a naughty little boy in the back of the class who has to be curbed. Here's a typical Wendy Wallop email:

> Just one thing! I know you're very sensitive so please don't take this the wrong way, but sometimes you become a little too crude or flippant in some of your reviews. Recently for example we've had to change quite a lot, e.g. Lynn Barber not being able to spell diarrhoea; Otto Preminger being like a Nazi; and in the David Niven review, the reference to Prince Rainier preventing Hjordis from toppling into the grave . . . That's not to say your reviews aren't always very entertaining; but I feel that in putting your own funny spin on things you stray too much from the content of the book or indeed occasionally from accuracy. Hope I haven't ruined your weekend . . .

One day I must publish the Original Director's Cut of my articles. The world will discover a new writer. Anyway – that's quite a Grand Remonstrance. It didn't spoil my weekend. It spoiled *my life*. Can you believe that *diarrhoea* is taboo? Or mentioning that playing Nazis in films was an odd thing for the Jewish actor/director Otto Preminger to do? Or that Prince Rainier had to offer Niven's widow his arm at Niven's funeral because she was pissed and couldn't keep upright?

As usual I kept a dignified silence, though inside my liver throbbed, my prostate fizzed, my spleen pulsated, my gallbladder sang the blues. Oh I'd so love not to need these dreadful people for my bread and butter money, because isn't what Wendy Wallop is saying really is, 'Roger, *please* be mediocre! Then everybody will be happy'?

I'm beyond caring sometimes. Wendy Wallop can lick my love pump. But what *next*, in the name of Jesus H. Corbett?

☙

Old people. Not that I'll get to be one myself. Lilian Summers (ninety) has been taking helicopter lessons in Shobdon. Next year the 'plucky pensioner' is going to 'try abseiling down a cliff'. Last year she 'rowed fearlessly up the Thames'. During the war she worked in a munitions factory. Prior to that, she no doubt participated in Viking raids.

❧

Friskin, an old friend from industrial South Wales, turned up on my doorstep. 'Let me take you out to lunch!' Nobody ever takes me out to lunch. As The Falcon was full of Christians eating sandwiches, we found a café up the road. 'If it comes to more than £20 you'll have to help me out,' said Friskin, my old friend from industrial South Wales.

❧

Laura Ashley died after falling down the stairs, but was she pushed? Was it murder? A Radnorshire neighbour of the Ashleys tells me that the late Sir Bernard was a maniac when drunk. And he was drunk a lot. All the time in fact. The week before Laura was killed he'd kicked a fridge-freezer down the stairs – the same stairs. Perhaps he simply couldn't stand seeing any more of those frilly frocks.

❧

A Magdalen mate, the music scholar John Jones, was an extra in that film Madonna is making about Wallis Simpson, Edward VIII and the Abdication Crisis. Though we are all brought up to assume Wallis was A Bad Thing, Madonna is very pro-Wallis – an American broad who infiltrated English High Society. The parallels are not hard to seek. It's a mystery really why she hasn't cast herself as Wallis Simpson, instead of Andrea Riseborough, an actress who already has one Iron Lady under her belt, having played Margaret Thatcher in *The Long Walk to Finchley*.

Anyway, the call went out for Welsh-speaking extras as they were shooting that scene set in November 1936, when the feckless Prince of Wales (played by James D'Arcy) met the poverty-stricken unemployed miners in Dowlais and notoriously (though vacuously) said 'Something must be done.' As John Jones, my Magdalen friend, speaks the lingo, he was asked if he'd come forward and jabber a bit to add colour to the proceedings.

He suggested that what he could say to the Prince was 'Shwd i chi, Syr?' – 'How are you, Sir?' John assures me that what he said doesn't translate as 'Up the bum and no babies!' – a bloody missed opportunity.

It went down a treat. Madonna – Madonna of the Valleys as she'll henceforth be known – was in raptures. Kept repeating it. *Shwd i chi, Syr! Shwd i chi, Syr!* 'Oh my!' squeaked Madonna, who in reality is a registered midget, 'Is Welsh a *Celtic* language?' As opposed to what? Igbo? Inuit? Zulu?

I was reminded of when Richard Burton was asked if he was Celtic, the inquirer pronouncing Celtic as *Seltic* – 'It's *Keltic*, you *c*unt,' said Burton, with impressive speed. This anecdote works better if spoken aloud.

❧

The Pumpkin Eater. I knew the novel but had never seen the film, which was on late on BBC Two. As the book is an unflattering portrait of John and Penelope Mortimer's marriage, I wasn't too keen to start watching. But there is something about Peter Finch that is alluring. He's the only man who truly rivalled Larry Olivier for Vivien Leigh. There's a gentleness about him – and a harshness, a masculinity. He was Australian of course – but I've never been able to detect an Australian accent or inflection in his voice; so his voice (at least) has to be a thorough invention. His combination of nonchalance and authority – is that what's Australian?

There's a brilliant description of him by Gudrun Ure, who was on stage with him in Welles's *Othello* at the St James Theatre, where he played Iago: 'Peter often seemed to be crying inside, not in any obvious way, but being in a state of terror your awareness and perception often become heightened and you observe more deeply.' You can see why Finch was excellent as Oscar Wilde, who shared these traits.

Pinter did the screenplay adaptation and *The Pumpkin Eater* contains the best Pinter performance I've ever seen – given by James Mason. I didn't recognise Mason at first, with his nasty little moustache and glasses. He was ideal for the Pinteresque insinuations and half-concealed threats, and he really got at the genuine pain and cruelty underneath the mannered, repetitious dialogue, which is like a sort of chanting. I've not seen that managed before. Usually when actors speak Pinter's dialogue they might as well be reciting Congreve, it is so artificial. But perhaps there was never anyone better at conveying malice than James Mason. The scene at the zoo, with the animal screeches mixing with children's noises, was as fine as anything people always claim is in *The Caretaker* or *No Man's Land*.

Anne Bancroft – mad from start to finish – was a deadening presence. In furs and turbans, she even had several Norma Desmond moments on staircases. Her character (like Penelope Mortimer in real life) had lots and lots of babies, but she didn't seem much of a mother. There were nannies to take over. Children actually gave her no pleasure – she keeps complaining that her life is empty and a waste. When she sees her eldest boys, who are home from boarding school, she's blank and awkward.

The film was pretty much two solid hours of Anne Bancroft's miserable face. Perhaps this was all less Penelope Mortimer brooding on her relationship with John Mortimer than Anne Bancroft thinking she had to go home and listen to Mel Brooks's constant yakking.

❧

As well as the groceries, I had to go to Asda to get some clothes. My father had his suits made at Gieves & Hawkes. I have to make do with XXXL black T-shirts that cost £3 and shrink in the rain. Anyway, I started at one end of the shop, Anna started at the other end of the shop. We met in the middle of the shop and we'd both put large yellow sunflowers in our trolleys. We roared.

❧

What a day. I had Bernie Winters's brother Mike (still alive and in Florida) complaining that I'd said he'd sunk to managing bars when in fact he owned at least one bar and was a hotshot. I also had said that Bernie Winters's career only took off when he ditched Mike for Schnorbitz, a St Bernard dog – so Mike was accusing me of all-sorts, including (bizarrely) anti-Semitism. Then I had my ex-agent's henchperson – a former Turkish wine-waiter – sending me aggressive emails. Then I went to The Thorn, where everyone was falling over drunk.

Andy From Bedford got down on bended knee and proposed to a paramedic from Barton-le-Clay. She accepted, but turned around and pulled a face. Not a good beginning. Andy From Bedford then sat on Zany Antony's pussy, the sixteen-year-old Goodnight Vienna. Barmaid Jodhi was in a state of shock because her ex-boyfriend The Viking is shagging somebody he met at Nozstock, which is the Bromyard version of Glastonbury. The new curate came in and took his dog collar off so that he could say *fuck* and *bugger*. Adam says he has split up with Sarah, who has gone off to design jewellery in the Black Mountains. Charlie told the story of Elsie's chemotherapy, which we've all heard before. Then Andy From Bedford sat on Zany Antony's pussy again. Then he and his new fiancée, the paramedic from Barton-le-Clay, started slapping each other in what was almost an affectionate way. Finally the window came crashing in. The parasol had been shoved through the glass by a gypsy who was upset that time had been called. Zany Antony went upstairs and refused to come down.

❧

237

Blind football. They play blind football in Hereford apparently. I thought it was a wind-up, a Python sketch. There's a bell in the ball and they run around after the noise. But what if a church clock chimed the quarter-hour? Or a herd of Swiss cows went by with cow bells on their way to summer pasture? Helpers run up and down the touchline, shouting instructions. This is human Subbuteo. They'll have blind darts next or javelin throwing and everyone will have to dive for cover. On Channel 4 in Wales they have the wrestling in Welsh, so every disability gets catered for today.

Next to Kath is Linda Margaret Lewis, born in 1898. All I know of her is that she used to swear. 'You do the buggers and I'll do the bitches,' she'd say of the pots and pans during the washing-up. She was remembered for being unladylike. The men she'd loved were killed in the war, so she devoted herself to dog breeding. There were kennels and sheds galore in the fields and compounds surrounding our house, verminous and deserted and overgrown. On the walls, pinned up and disintegrating prize certificates and faded rosettes from Crufts. The doctor forbade her marriage to a man she'd met at Crufts called Ryland, because Ryland had the syphilis.

Linda died before I was born – but was often talked about as a fiery spirit.

✎

Crime Wave Corner. It's getting as lawless as the Wild West here – scrap metal has gone missing in Kington, a trailer was pinched in Leominster, oil has been nicked in Yarpole. Police are increasingly confident that 'thieves' are to blame.

✎

I've been watching the films of Carl Theodor Dreyer – Joan of Arc and her visions; another one about vampires and witches. He hated his actors acting and almost preferred to use amateurs, as they'd not be striving for their effects, or so he believed. He assumed amateurs would be less artificial. 'The important thing,' he said, 'is not only to catch hold of the words they say, but also the thoughts behind the words, the expressions that lie in the depths of the soul.' That's asking a lot from any actor, professional, semi-pro or just in off the street. Tati also used amateurs – and it shows. It mars his work. These people are always wooden, obviously just copying what Tati has previously devised for them. It's a bit despotic, only to want amateurs – a crowd the maestro can control.

Sellers could do what Dreyer would have wanted, a suggestion of a character's weird psychological make-up – but Olivier? There's conscious technique with him always – a vulgar phoniness; he's *all* acting. I adore that. Sellers was all instinct. I

239

adore that too. But my point is – Dreyer planned to make a film about Jesus.

❧

When the third-rate biographies started being published with all the rumours about Olivier being a sausage jockey, Geraldine McEwan allegedly said, 'Well, he certainly wasn't when he was with me!' They'd toured Russia in some play or other. He also had a liaison with Anna Carteret. Allegedly.

❧

When Patrick Garland directed *A Doll's House*, the company was very friendly off-stage – picnics in Central Park and so forth. When they did *Hedda Gabler* – all was rancour. Because the play is about disappointment, death, bitterness. The actors pick up on these things and it affects the relationships they then form with each other, in rehearsals and during the run.

❧

Arthur Mullard to Jonathan Cecil: 'Our careers are alike. You play all the upper-class silly fuckers and I play all the working-class silly fuckers.'

❧

Alice Thomas Ellis was an interesting woman, if *affected*. 'Wales! How strange!' she seemed to be saying all the time. Even when she lived in Camden it was as if she was in the depths of a Welsh forest, with the weeds and overgrown sooty house. She was both a witch and a nun, full of darkness and melancholia, clinging to Catholicism because she believed it would enable her to be reunited with her dead son. Her husband Colin Haycraft was banging the dinner gong with Dame Beryl for years. When he died, Dame Beryl lost the ability to write, though she blamed the block on giving up smoking.

❧

Young people know fuck fuck-all about anything. Amy Tortue the Montmartre tap-dancer and Tristan's occasional squeeze said that the government weapons inspector who killed himself over the dodgy dossier business was Dr Harold Shipman. Another one of her beliefs is that astrology is a real science.

※

Raiding the fridge for cheese at three in the morning, I saw that Powell and Pressburger's *A Canterbury Tale* was on the television. I thought I'd stay and watch it until Charles Hawtrey's scene as the railway station porter came on, but stayed until the credits rolled.

What a mystical film it is – all about *blessings* and *cursings*. Eric Portman is a sinister magus, who creeps about at night chucking glue in young girls' hair. That's weird. It is a celestial film, though, rather than a horror film, and it caught me at the right moment – a bit drunk and hung-over simultaneously. I loved the shots of the cathedral soaring above the bomb sites, symbolic of an enduring England, which was also an endangered England. When the soldiers are in the procession at the end, accompanied by the Canterbury dignitaries in their medieval robes, it was as if everyone was marching towards death. Dennis Price is playing the organ.

There was a delightful scene set in an oak-panelled hotel bedroom – and a boy appears to be standing in mid-air outside the window. It is like a vision. It turns out he is on top of a hay-wagon – but for a moment it is miraculous.

If I was in the wrong mood, I'd find *A Canterbury Tale* irritating – pretentious. I met Michael Powell. Rather a broken figure, bankrupt, bad-tempered, arrogant, lost.

※

On seeing *Special Kay* and the DVD outtakes of *Phoenix Nights* – he has an immensely irritating high-pitched laugh, in the falsetto register. He is so pleased with himself, it's nauseating. When he corpses, everybody sycophantically joins in. Other actors get the giggles – you sense his irritation, his impatience. The deleted scenes were other people's set-pieces for the most part. You sense that he is like Sellers at his most arrogant and self-obsessed.

Yet they love him Up North. Can't get enough of him. He's a funny man who hasn't moved to Hampstead, didn't go to Oxford or Cambridge. He has the chubby chops that make people think he's lovable – a face that'll break into a grin. Yet the best thing he did was Brian Potter, who is churlishness personified.

❧

One of the most truly horrible women I ever came across was Liana Burgess, Anthony Burgess's widow. Liana Wilson, as she correctly was, because he never officially changed his name from John Wilson. Burgess was the pen name – as le Carré is for David Cornwell. Liana made a huge mess of the Estate, alienated publishers, got everyone in a knot, fiddled the taxes, pretended to be in Monte Carlo when she was in Twickenham, caused kerfuffles in a boring Italianate comic opera way. In a film she would have been played by Anne Bancroft.

Her sole identity was being The Burgess Widow. She was so devoted to his memory, she resented anyone else having a part of him – even his readers and fans were somehow competition. So imagine what it was like for me, being the biographer. It was as if I was stealing him away from her. I was the enemy. I once asked where Burgess was buried – in Monte Carlo, or Manchester, or in West London? She reacted as if this was the most intrusive inquiry ever made, a shameful invasion of privacy. When Burgess died, she refused to allow the press to be informed for several days. She wouldn't organise a funeral – and the hospice got fed up of having the corpse underfoot for weeks and weeks.

Strangely, she resented Burgess too – for she was smart enough to be aware that he was all she had in life, and it wasn't much. He wasn't the new James Joyce, the new Goethe. He was a rambunctious Northern music-hall act, full of histrionic airs and fol-de-rol effects. (He can be read with enjoyment again once you realise this.) Freddie Jones could play him perfectly in a biopic. So that's Freddie Jones and Anne Bancroft, except one of them is dead. (Anne Bancroft and Mel Brooks – I never understood it.)

Liana was a paranoid person, who'd get involved with shady foreign lawyers in tax havens, who'd flatter her and cajole her – which deepened (and justified) her paranoia and anxiety.

✃

Twenty years ago. To the very hour. We were attempting to move to France. The Ascott-under-Wychwood mortgage had got on top of us. Utility bills. Day nursery fees. So we sold up and decided to decamp abroad, thinking it would be cheaper. You can only plunge into these adventures when you are young. We were young. Also, on top of everything else, on top of the baby-minding and writing begging letters to banks and building societies, as if that wasn't enough, I was working on the Sellers book, which I fully intended being my lasting masterpiece.

We left Oxfordshire, put everything in storage, and became refugees, shuttling between Anna's parents' house and my parents' house, wearing out everybody's patience and welcome. This strange floating state. We found a property we loved in the Lot, but for months on end we were messed about by a bent estate agent whom I'll call Windy Spasm.

Throughout that summer of 1991, I was trying to do business with Windy Spasm, who kept altering the conditions, hiking the price, prevaricating about signing important documents, making promises, breaking promises . . . Whether he was a French estate agent based in Britain or a British estate agent based in France – or whether he was an estate agent at all – weren't questions I asked at the time or found answers to later. He came to see me once in Ascott-under-Wychwood – he literally said he was in the neighbourhood 'seeing a man about a dog' – and from having been all smiles, and accepting my food and drink, he'd turn sour on the phone. Always the phone – he was careful not to put much in writing.

One of his tactics was to somehow make it seem as if the delays and problems were of my own making. So we'd fall out, make it up, start again. I don't know why I didn't pull out and realise he was a crook. I think it is because Anna and I loved the house we were hoping to buy – but it didn't dawn on me until ages later that maybe the house wasn't Windy Spasm's to sell? He'd mention his wife, who then became his ex-wife or his sister, according to mood or whatever yarn he was spinning. She may even have been his mother at one point. Wanda Spasm I'll call her. They had a daughter, who was also a step-daughter and a granddaughter, maybe an adopted daughter or a foster daughter. Ownership or part-ownership was complicatedly often in her name. Or so I gathered.

I think perhaps part of me was simply transfixed by this man. I wanted to see how far he could go with his bad behaviour, how many lies he'd tell that he'd have to keep whirling in the air – the lies-within-lies, the lies he had to tell to back up earlier lies. It was an impressive performance. He no doubt thought I was an unworldly academic, the Junior Fellow of Wolfson College, who could with contemptuous ease be hoodwinked and flummoxed by sharp business practice. I'm sure he never once thought it was business malpractice, for the first person a con man cons is himself. Once he's taken in, the rest follows. And anyway Windy Spasm was right about me. I'm the one born every minute. The sucker that should not be given the even break. The thing is – I can never quite believe that people are as evil as they actually are until it is too late. I am a disappointed romantic, always being caught out.

Everything was in storage with Luker Brothers in Headington. I'd made the mistake of being completely open with Windy Spasm about our plight, how desperate we were to get going, how I couldn't get on with my work, with my research papers packaged up. He used this information to turn the screws. So we killed time, Anna, Tristan, Oscar and me, waiting for the day when we could move, by paddling in rivers, watching videos of *Dogtanian* and *Honey I Shrunk the Kids*, and visiting dinosaur museums. When my children were small, I could have passed a stiff examination in dinosaurs. I have surely seen every dinosaur bone and reconstructed dinosaur skeleton in the British Isles. I read every book in Halesowen Library – and I don't mean only the dinosaur ones; I mean even the novels of Julian Barnes and the memoirs of Ned Sherrin. For a fee of £1,000 I wrote the Introduction for an Everyman edition of Hogg's *Confessions of a Justified Sinner*. This was my sole income for some years.

I spent a lot of time on the Quinton 9 (a bus) going in and out of Birmingham – to see the dinosaurs in the Birmingham City Museum and Art Gallery. What you notice on the Quinton 9 (a bus) going into Birmingham – the coloured people always had little headphones plugged in. They inundate themselves with music. It must be like walking around in a movie – this continuous soundtrack. Also, single people tend to shift seats to stay by themselves. There were newspapers and tickets and empty crisp packets carefully folded and pushed down the sides of the seats. Why bother to do that? *Why not find a fucking litter bin?*

There was an array of video cameras and mirrors, for the driver to monitor malefactors. On buses, I had more than enough leisure to notice, there are a lot of old ugly people who don't wash properly; their folded-up faces as brown as the colour of the tea they drink. Plastic teeth. Terrible clothes. Surgical stockings. Too poor to afford cars. It was a glimpse of the future. Then the non-driving teenagers with inaccurately applied make-up, too much jewellery and wrecked fingernails. Giggling Asian girls with jewels in their nostrils like shiny pustules. The places we chugged through had wonderful names – Bearwood, Gornal, Bangpit and Wombourne.

Within weeks, Windy Spasm was demanding another £3,500. It always crept up by these sorts of amounts. This involved contacting banks and building societies all over again, to see what I could do. Having mesmerised me, Windy was relishing re-negotiating the original deal, seeing how high he could make me leap. Perhaps it wasn't about money any longer, but about his need for greater and greater stimulus. Remember that this was pre-mobile, pre-email, pre-fax. Letters had to be written and photocopied and posted off. Meantime the children would be arguing and needing to be fed and entertained.

Another little gambit of Windy Spasm's – we'd sign the *compromis de vente*, i.e. the official document committing us to the purchase, but he'd not countersign it, because that would commit him to the deal. He'd lie that he had signed – but he hadn't. Then he'd up the price. Again. Then the document would lapse. He'd pretend that we could proceed again 'on the original terms' and he'd vanish for a few weeks. There was not much more we could do, except the obvious thing – which was to walk away and start house-hunting afresh. But I don't think we had funds for such an excursion. We were getting to be trapped. Every day, Anna took the children to Halesowen Swimming Pool and I read Iris Murdoch and Muriel Spark and watched television programmes about mass murderers.

Windy Spasm's new problem – as if he didn't know this already – was that he'd be facing a Capital Gains Tax bill. He didn't like the thought of this at all. So he wanted to raise the price to cover it – he said that the price has been kept unrealistically low up until now, as a personal favour to me. Anna, meantime, was showing the world her own credulousness – or her own ability not to think the worst of people. She bought a tenth-hand Fiesta from a swarthy man on Mucklow Hill, paid for it in cash, insured it, taxed it, and the engine fell out in the giraffe enclosure of the West Midlands Safari Park. We had to organise the hire of another car to get us back home. Anna's parents then returned from Hong Kong and we went to Wales.

First, though, Anna was off to the police station in Stourbridge, to report the drama of her Ford Fiesta. She did some sleuthing and tracked down a previous owner, who'd sold it to the Mucklow Hill characters for scrap. It was not roadworthy. Well, we'd soon found that out. Anna was also determined to get her money back. When the game's afoot, she has no fear, that woman. She personally questioned the slimy second-hand car dealers, who made the mistake of telling her one or two fibs, so they were demolished by her cross-examination. She went back to the police station, gave a full statement – and of course the police did nothing, even when she produced the car's log-book with the forged dates and phony service history. They didn't think they 'had a case'. Meanwhile, the dodgy Fiesta had to be collected by us from a garage in Kidderminster. We had to pay quite a lot for having had it patched up. On the way home, it caught fire.

It was still not clear – no doubt deliberately unclear – whether Windy had signed the necessary forms. The uncertainty was agony. Meanwhile, Anna went back and forth to Mucklow Hill to confront the crooks about the car, getting to know the place quite well. I said, 'You'll be on each other's Christmas card list next.' She got them to agree to take it off her hands for £850. Windy Spasm was now saying that he wouldn't sign anything before a deposit of £12,000 had cleared in his account. An impossible demand. None of the lawyers I instructed to help me out were of the slightest use, by the way. Windy could fool them as he fooled me, with charm, threats and baloney. I collected a Transfer of Funds Form from NatWest.

The crooks said that they'd give Anna the money in cash – but at home. She was as nervous as a kitten about this and hid upstairs with the children, leaving me – who has all the physical courage of Charles Hawtrey's Private Widdle – to face this lout who turned up at the door with knuckle-dusters and tattoos. He started to crap on about his own car having just been broken into, but I said 'Just let me have the money,' so he produced £850 in damp notes from his sock. He then had the fun of driving a scorched and wheezing wheels-falling-off Fiesta away along suburban, curtain-twitching Alison Road.

At Thomas Cook three people working double-shifts sorted out our travel arrangements to get from Birmingham to Montpellier. I couldn't settle to write. I couldn't read. I ended up watching *Billion Dollar Brain*, for the third or fourth time. It still doesn't make much sense, though next to *The Boy Friend* it is the best thing Ken Russell did, because he's not knocking himself out to be flamboyant.

I translated and typed up an inventory of our sad possessions, for the Customs formalities at Le Havre. Sent this in triplicate to Luker Bros, the removal men. Returned library books. Windy Spasm assured me that he'd send us immediately a written guarantee and cast-iron promise that he would hand-on-heart sign the forms once he got his up-front £12,000, which he was now saying was for (non-existent) fixtures and fittings. Of course, as Neville Chamberlain said of Mr Hitler, I have to tell you that no such assurance was received and that as a consequence . . .

I sorted out three boxes of extra papers to take to Luker Bros. Collected a Conder fan that had been mended for me by a conservation expert in a gallery in Warwick. Anna's mother, who drove me to Warwick, amazed me during the journey – and still amazes me – by being able to recite the dates, times (to the nearest hour), and give full chapter and verse, for all of her own five children's potty training experiences. I can't even remember when my children's *birthdays* are meant to be, which obviously makes me *a thoroughly terrible person*, but Nanoo remembers everyone's weight at birth, when they first took solids, when the first tooth was cut, what size and colour shoes they wore, and when they took their first faltering steps.

Anna's dad was a physics teacher at Menzies High School in West Bromwich – where John Cleese's *Clockwise* was filmed – and when Nanoo on the way to Warwick described it with pride as '*the* best school in West Brom', for some reason I laughed and laughed. I only saw my father-in-law at his place of work once, as he has been retired for donkey's years. He's almost been retired for as long as he worked. I was astounded at the way the teaching staff in the science block looked the same. Moustacheless beards, awful fawn jackets, brown socks with open-toe sandals.

Everything was finally packed. Very heavy cases and bags for two adults and two children. No porters, of course. No servants for the middle classes these days. To a coach in Birmingham called The London Liner. Thence to Victoria, the boat train to Calais, the night train to the Languedoc. We were moving south.

ʖ

No we weren't. Having arranged the appointment with the Notaire, predictably Windy Spasm failed to turn up. We sat there waiting and waiting, the children on the floor colouring in colouring-in books. When he was tracked down by phone, he ranted and raved at me for having the temerity to be sitting there 'with my Notaire' – whereas in fact in France (a) the Notaire acts for both sides impartially and (b) this was an appointment he had known about well in advance and had helped to set up. Windy Spasm wouldn't let us meet him at the house – an old presbytery – that we were intending to buy. He said he'd come round to our rented place that night.

Well, he did, with Wanda Spasm as back-up. He came clean. He laughed in a humourless way and pretended to apologise for the fun and games, as if it had all been a bit of a jolly jape between gentlemen. He said he wanted £12,000 in cash immediately on what is called an 'under-the-table basis' — *dessous la table* — i.e. cash passed by the purchaser to the vendor surreptitiously, so that the officially declared price is lower than the actual amount of money that is changing hands, thus reducing the amount of money (the capital gain) that will get exposed to tax. Windy Spasm said everyone in France did this. That the Notaires turned a blind eye. Oh yes — and he was also increasing the officially declared price, to cover all his unexpected costs . . . He also revealed that he was a French *duc* and that his full name was what I'll call Windy Spasm de Sorbet.

Now what would you do in such circumstances? Remember that we had been hanging about for several months, with babies to look after and no income coming in, trying to survive on dwindling capital, getting under our respective parents' feet. I had a book to write. Everything was in storage. Windy Spasm had sold me down the river, as the saying goes.

I knew the man could not be reasoned with. I knew I would never get anywhere trying to sue him for breach of contract, breach of promise, breach of being a human being. There are no statutory bodies to regulate these characters. Anyone can put an advertisement in the *Daily Telegraph* — as he had done — claiming to be an estate agent brokering foreign property. He'd have the last laugh.

In a flash it became clear to me that here there really was a very definite Wrong 'Un. I thought you only met villains like this in films, where they'd be played by silky types like George Sanders. Or that they'd be signalling a comic caddishness, like Terry-Thomas. Why hadn't I run a mile from Windy Spasm when I saw that he wore a cravat? But the psychology of the confidence trickster is fascinating. Underneath, there must be a lot of hatred, with the urge to destroy. They play upon one's weaknesses and needs. They know what they are about.

What I mostly felt, in that instant of realisation, was used, cheapened, dishonoured. And the next minute or two still seems like a hallucination – as if I'd stepped aside from being me and a different me altogether was acting on my behalf. Sir Toby Belch, perhaps, in *Twelfth Night*: 'I would we were well rid of this knavery,' he says when the baiting of Malvolio has gone too far.

I grabbed a copper bedpan from over the fireplace and thwacked Windy Spasm on the noggin. He threw a glass of wine over me and I chased him around the room. I have never been so angry with anyone in my life. I chased him, he chased me, and when his big fat wife or grandmother, or whoever she was, Wanda Spasm, started to run out of the door, Anna gave her a push up the arse.

Ten minutes later the lady from next door came round. It was Windy Spasm on the phone. He wanted to speak to Mrs Lewis. He didn't want to speak to Mr Lewis 'because Mr Lewis keeps hitting him over the head with a bedpan' – the word for bedpan being *un bassin*. Our neighbour was wetting herself laughing and within half a day the news had spread throughout the entire *Département*, where wholesale merriment drowned out the noise of the cicadas. '*Le jeune homme Gallois, il vraiment a cassé l'immobilier avec un bassin! Oh, la, la, la!*' I think I was nominated for the ribbon of the Legion d'honneur.

Anna took the call – and you won't believe this, but though out for the count, Windy was still trying to negotiate, still trying to fix up a deal. He was indefatigable. We never saw him or heard from him again, though I believe when he next returned to England, the finest tax inspectors from Her Majesty's Customs and Revenue flung him in their torture chamber.

ço

Anna is very cross with me even now, twenty years on, when I say I'm glad I smacked the cunt. Even Flaubert would agree that *cunt* is *le mot juste* on this occasion. Perhaps it is a man thing? A male thing? Or a Clouseau galloping after Cato with a shovel thing? Anna believes in sweet reason and in trying to chivvy out a person's ultimate inner goodness and compassion, even if it was Hitler. Twenty years on she still can't see that, though I may have not done the right thing or the admirable thing, when you look at the matter soberly and objectively, it felt very much the right thing for me to be doing under those circumstances, when I'd been put under such pressure and was intolerably provoked. Well she can see all this, of course she can, but slapstick violence mustn't be condoned, in her view. Otherwise what would society be? It would be bedlam. So I then remind her she slammed the door on Wanda's arse and we have a good laugh.

But now and again – as when the British Army went into Iraq after Saddam or started this no-fly zone thing with Gaddafi – only a little bit of physical force will do the trick. Nothing else gets through. The message hasn't got across through diplomatic channels. As Laurence Olivier says in *That Hamilton Woman*, when he is Nelson, and Napoleon is on the high seas, 'You cannot make peace with dictators!' By having a showdown straight out of a *Carry On* film with a corrupt so-called estate agent, I felt I'd got a smidgen of my integrity back – and I also taught Windy Spasm a lesson he'd not forget in a hurry, i.e. even worms turn. But he was shameless and nothing would have registered, I'm sure. Another lesson I've learned in life – you can never change people. He'd have blithely gone on to seek another dupe. Francis Wheen still calls me Raging Bull Lewis.*

---

* You'll be gagging to know what happened next. After the farcical denouement, as described, we got into our Europcar hire car the very next morning and drove north, staying the night at Thiers, which is nothing but dagger shops, and at Blois, where Peter Sellers made a forgotten film called *Mr. Topaze*. We then arrived in Normandy and set up Operational Headquarters at the Hotel de la Post, Mortain. We were now in *'Allo 'Allo* France, having escaped from a *Clochmerle* France. With the help of the Notaire in Sourdeval, we found a granite farmhouse called Le Haut Gué in the hamlet of St Jean-des-Bois, near Tinchebray. Kestrels and jays nested in the roof. We lived there for five years, though we never had the money to patch it up.

ॐ

It is already thirty-three years since Chris Tarrant in his capacity as an ATV reporter judged the fancy dress parade at Eardisley Carnival.

I finally got to write *The Life and Death of Peter Sellers*. Despite what the horse cocks who leave unhelpful comments on Amazon and some dimmer critics may say, it was all I wanted it to be. If that opus has a distinctly *possessed* feel to it – a frenzy that is not totally unsuitable given the subject-matter – then perhaps you now know part of the reason why.

I spent years on Peter Sellers, thinking about Peter Sellers, building a big book about Peter Sellers. He pulled me about. My book is over a thousand pages long. If you just only knew the effort that went into it, *you* should be exhausted after reading it. You should be on *tablets*.

This time there was not a scintilla of the nonsense and hoodwinking we'd endured with Windy and Wanda Spasm. Perhaps one day I'll write a book about our five years in rural France, entitling it *Normandy Landings*.

September

What am I still doing here? It's a miracle surely? A miracle of *survival* and *persistence*. Because being a Chekhov character myself, I can never get enough of Chekhov. When I was young I never saw the point of these tedious turn-of-the-century gentlefolk in linen suits and straw hats complaining about how bored and ill they felt – inert, arid, excruciating. Well. Yes. However. Though. Here I am, suddenly half-a-hundred years old, and I myself am the one wearing a linen jacket and a panama hat, always complaining about boredom and illness – about how my life is *inert*, *arid* and *excruciating*.

And so now Chekhov has become electrifying. The interaction of the characters – everybody affecting everybody else, usually not for the better; lost chances, missed opportunities; the massive self-importance and self-hatred. Cupid missing his mark: nobody is in love with the right person – they all want the person who is unattainable. They are highly sexed plays actually – the erotic charge; the sense or feeling of violence bubbling under the surface of the slow, sluggish end-of-summer/early autumn mood. They are at *boiling point* – sexually tormented. They'd fuck the samovar, give them half a chance. Yet in the English theatre, Chekhov is always performed so tastefully, so elegantly, as if shot through with sepia and set to music by Chopin, with a nocturne or an étude.

❧

Louis Malle's *Vanya on 42nd Street*, my father's favourite film incidentally, gives a clue to the real dynamic – those morose Russians aren't the about-to-be-dispossessed minor English gentry; they are (temperamentally) New Yorkers – and New Yorkers love nothing more than to be able to talk about themselves, loudly and at length, even if they are also aware that nobody is really listening. Dialogue overlaps. Everyone is fretting. Everyone is emotionally in a knot. (They enjoy their misery.)

Perhaps the artist who is closest to being a modern Chekhov would be Woody Allen in his long-lost prime – *Hannah and Her Sisters*, *Interiors*, *Crimes and Misdemeanours*. They are school-of-Chekhov. The self-absorption is Chekhovian. It is emotional farce, like the Marx Brothers, if the Marx Brothers' ancestors had stayed in the Ukraine. It is emotionally helter-skelter. Olivier loved what he called the tension of playing Chekhov – the taut bow-string of *The Three Sisters* – how, if you alter *this* in performance, you alter *that*. His Astrov in *Uncle Vanya* is one of his great roles (I have a video of the Chichester production) – the good doctor, with his scientific charts of the forest, and the way he knows the forest faces inevitable destruction.

Nina in *The Seagull* has a long speech about the end of the world, too. Actually *The Seagull* is frequently a terrible play. Too many characters – too many people to care about; and the symbol of the beautiful young girl, used and discarded by the callous poet, Trigorin, the way she's 'the seagull', and then Constantin shoots a seagull – all that we could do without. I like the role of Doctor Dorn, wandering about being wise and reflective. It is Astrov grown old.

Another interesting theme: Nina and Constantin have the sensitivities to be artists, but they are too swamped by their sensitivities to be any good. You need the cold hard detachment of Madame Arkadina to make it in the theatre; and what makes her good as an actress makes her disastrous as a mother. She's always attitudinising; she's stopped having real or authentic reactions to events – even to her son's suicide.

Another thing about Chekhov: seeing people from all angles

– the ensemble scattering and colliding, like the balls on the billiard table in *The Cherry Orchard* – nobody is ever wholly evil, or wholly good. You love one person – you'll torment another; there'll always be hurt.

❧

I lived in Alberta for a while and was told that Canadians won't go to orgies because it takes too long to write all the thank-you letters afterwards.

❧

What amuses me about Karloff in *The Black Cat* is that he says of his wife, 'She is the core and very meaning of my existence,' and ten minutes later he kills her. Furthermore, you've got to respect the libido that guy had in *The Mummy*. They burn him. They kill him. They bury him under a pyramid. Yet when Imhotep is resurrected, the first thing that happens – *after 2,000 years* – is that he wants to fuck Princess Ankhesenamon again. Fair play to the man.

Compare Karloff's Imhotep with George Zucco or Lionel Atwill, when they finally get the girl in *The Mystery of the Wax Museum*. They get Fay Wray, for example, strapped down on the table in the laboratory – and what's all this fuss about granting her Eternal Life? *Eternal Life?* They should simply want to fuck her. Well, that's what I would have done.

Princess Ankhesenamon was played by Zita Johann. I met her at The Players. She died in 1993, aged eighty-nine – or if *The Mummy* is to be believed, aged 3,700.

❧

September 11th – that never-to-be-forgotten day, since when we've all learnt to be nice to the Islamic lot, otherwise you'll (a) get accused of racism by newspaper columnists and (b) become a target for religious reprisals. But I will simply say this – it wasn't Welsh Baptists flying those planes; it wasn't a C of E Parochial Council. It wasn't disaffected Buddhists learning to fly in Florida or Hindus hiring the cars in Canada.

What a good job I'm not the American President. I'd have bombed Mecca. I'd have used up a few nuclear missiles and destroyed Kabul, Baghdad and Vail, Colorado – like Japan was destroyed in August 1945.* They would have rebuilt afterwards, like Japan rebuilt. Otherwise – and hasn't this been *exactly* what has happened? – there would be inconsequential shilly-shallying for years, for decades, which exposes only our impotence. I sound like Doctor Strangelove – the man, not the movie.

Anyway, I was in London to see my old chum Arne, who for years played the flower seller in *Little Shop of Horrors* on Broadway. Now his old mother had died, aged about a hundred, and released his inheritance, and his only son had died from the drugs, aged about thirty, so there were no more rehab bills to meet, Arne often treated himself to a transatlantic trip.

Lunch went on until 10 p.m., because Arne is such a slow talker. My usual fare when I am in funds – champagne, oysters, partridge: you can see why I am never in funds. Arne had put on a bit of weight, and in nautical white trousers, a navy blazer with anchor-shaped buttons, a crimson shirt and a red spotted tie, he looked like a cross between Captain Nemo, a circus clown and a billiard ball. His moustache partly disguised a pretty disfiguring hare-lip. We chatted amiably about this and that – about a beloved mutual friend who cadges $20 loans that will never be repaid; about Hy Anzell and his litigiousness – Hy was always getting new doctors and new lawyers and setting them off against each other. Hy was another one who played the flower seller in *Little Shop of Horrors*. He also appeared in a few Woody Allen films. He

* Vail, Colorado? Agatha Christie appeared to me in a dream and told me that Osama bin Laden was disguised as a ski instructor in this pleasant winter resort. Maybe he did hide there for a while, though of course when the Americans finally located him and shot him dead, on 2 May 2011, the al-Qaeda mastermind was residing in a suburb of Abbotabad, in the Khyber Pakhtkunkhwa Province of Pakistan.

had prostate cancer for years and when I said to him that that must play hell with the libido he said, 'My libido! I don't even feel like jerking off!'

Then the Irish waitress came in and said that terrorists had flown two planes at the Twin Towers of the World Trade Center – that there'd been huge explosions and the buildings had collapsed. Everyone else in the room hurried off – Rees-Mogg, Simon Heffer, others. Their huffing and puffing articles were to fill the papers for weeks. Is everyone who churned out their ghastly 'the world has changed forever!' polemics now ashamed? Is chagrin the lingering emotion? Because I mean – has the world changed forever, apart from irritations like airport security measures? It seemed to be forgotten in the week of 9/11 (what the fuck happened in November?) that in Britain we'd had IRA atrocities for decades. Birmingham. Hyde Park. Omagh. Enniskillen. 'For those thousands in the South Tower,' wrote Martin Amis, 'the second plane meant the end of everything. For us, its glint was the worldflash of a coming future.' Vernon Dobtcheff! What's 'worldflash'? Another casualty of war: good prose. The future comes about anyway.

Arne and I found we weren't the slightest bit concerned, or interested. I can't even claim we were dumbstruck. It wasn't as if the whole of Manhattan was in flames. I called for the wine list and we went on drinking claret until they were laying the tables for dinner and putting out the candlesticks. If the entire city of New York had become a crater, I concede that Arne may have started getting worried – he lived (lives) on Eighth Avenue. Otherwise – how dare those Mohammedans interrupt luncheon.

There was nothing self-conscious about the way we carried on boozing. We weren't making any sort of point. It was more that if this was the beginning of the end of the world, what better place to be in than in the Garrick? I look back and I am surprised at how cool we were – like Basil Radford and Naunton Wayne in

The Lady Vanishes. Or Sid James and Joan Sims as Lord and Lady Ruff-Diamond in *Carry On Up the Khyber*, carrying on dining as the fort is shelled.

When we were prevailed upon to watch the television bulletins, it was like a badly edited special-effects movie – we are all familiar with fireballs and famous landmarks being destroyed in blockbusters; it was hard to be impressed by this at first. When was Bruce Willis going to swing into shot? Or Arnie? Or Sly? *Towering Inferno, Airport, Die Hard, Armaggedon, Independence Day* . . . The meaning of that genre only now becomes apparent years later, and it's chilling. Blowing up New York, Washington and national landmarks: it was arrogant; America thought itself invincible, so it indulged itself with these games of make-believe oblivion, this apocalyptic let's-pretend. And so I wonder now – underneath, in the national subconscious – was there a desire, expressed in these films, for annihilation, a mad urge to tear the place down and start again, the ever-new New World? It is possible – analogously – to look at the art of the 1890s – the *fin de siècle* – and in the Decadent movement, when Peter Pan, for example, says that to die will be an awfully big adventure, the guns of the Somme start to be heard. Art can be a premonition.

Compared with even the schlock of Hollywood disaster epics, real-life tragedies, as they unfold, are rather meaningless and chaotic. They lack a narrative arc. I only started being shocked and emotional days later, when we began hearing the eyewitness accounts: the stories of husbands and wives lost and found; the way Mayor Giuliani hastened to the scene and insisted on looking at the destruction; the exhausted firemen caked in dust and debris.

How easy it is to destroy human life. How vulnerable we are – how easy we are to dispense with. The planes sliced through the towers like a knife through cake. The buildings collapsed in a pile of grey powder – they dissolved. I loved those Twin Towers and had ascended them a dozen times. The Sixties lattice-work windows, the burgundy carpets, the wide stairways, the height, space, grandeur. I thought they were architectural wonders, and still grieve for them. Yet I never thought them indestructible, either – far from it. The glass and airiness was always fragile. They were kept aloft by magic. They didn't have the stony, massy solidity, the rocky rootedness, of a medieval cathedral. The Twin Towers were gorgeously (hubristically – hence why a target) man-made. Medieval cathedrals seem organic. They have grown out of the earth. They are geological. Even the marble halls of the Empire State Building belong to that tradition – mineralogical.

People were quick to leave candles and posies outside the American Embassy in Grosvenor Square. Ever since Diana, at the drop of a hat it's like the Mexican Day of the Dead, with shrines and make-shift altars. Armed policemen wearing yellow tunics were on patrol – they've never gone away, have they? And when I look now at the pictures of what got to be called Ground Zero, what strikes me is the strange beauty of some of the images – the crumpling tower, with the mast remaining perfectly vertical as it descended; the volcanic ash or dust, like snow; the great billowing grey clouds rolling up Fifth Avenue and Broadway, pursuing the fleeing townspeople – like dragons or Godzilla. 'Sometimes we see a cloud that's dragonish; a vapour sometime like a bear or lion, a tower'd citadel . . .' as Shakespeare says (eerily – a prophecy?) in *Antony and Cleopatra*.

We kept hearing everyone say – all the officials, all the columnists – that 'this was a cowardly act'. I think that to have steeled yourself to pilot a plane that'll explode, to have prepared for this, to execute this mission – *that* showed immense courage and determination, surely? Cowardice is to retreat, to become querulous, ineffective, weak. The problem the West went on to face is that Islam showed itself to be the opposite of weak. At the Memorial Service in St Paul's Cathedral, Prince Philip's reading – 'If God is with us, who can be against us' – might just as easily be a text or rubric for the Islamic fundamentalists.

The *Daily Dacre* printed the stars-and-stripes: 'As a mark of respect, cut out this flag and display it in your window at home or at work' — and of course I did, sticking it to a jug of flowers, and on either side I placed my *I Love NY* ashtray and my *I Love NY* money box. I also lit a scented candle, which kept guttering and never amounted to much. So I had my personal shrine and make-shift altar, and had fun assembling it. I was reminded of when I made a miniature garden on a tea tray for St Mellons Show.

Months later, fragments of the towers still protruded from the heaps of rubble and moon dust, which quickly resembled ancient ruins — the tapering gothic windows and arches, 'Bare ruined choirs where late the sweet birds sang,' as Shakespeare said of the sacked abbeys and monasteries. Unlike a movie, 9/11 (what the fuck *did* happen in November?) never seemed to end satisfactorily — people's hope and blind terror yielded to the fullness of despair, as it became clear that absolutely nobody was ever found alive, as at Aberfan. Wristwatches and a few rings: that is all that was left.

⁍

It goes without saying that the autumn weather is turning the leaves to flame and that the days are growing short and dwindling down to a precious few (look — do I *look* like Lotte Lenya?), but if you are thinking of taking Sunday luncheon in the Herefordshire Balkans, think twice.

We went to a pub the *fuck* and *bugger* curate recommended called The Red Lion near Malvern and did an immediate about-turn. A carvery, the menu on a blackboard, sticky uncleared tables, unruly children and dogs, and men with tattoos on their heads.

We then went to the township of Malvern itself. Everywhere was either shut, or they stopped serving at 2 p.m. That's worth repeating. *They stopped serving luncheon at 2 p.m.* We ended up in a teashop next to a craft centre, where I bought an Advent calendar. I went to bed for two hours when I got home as my nerves were that shredded.

One of my chums from Bassaleg Comprehensive, Gareth Von Jones (his Bavarian-Celtic ancestry must be unique), was taking as his latest wife a scrummy Russian girl called Natalia. She really did look like Julie Christie's Lara, complete with a coat with a blue fox-fur collar. I was greatly honoured to be asked to be the Best Man at the Wedding Reception in Hampton Court.

I got lost – not in the maze, but trying to find Hampton Court. There are so many Hamptons about the place. Hampton Wick, Hampton this, Hampton that. A Bermuda Triangle of Talbot Rothwell Hampton gags. I raced around on trains, buses and cabs, breaking out into a malarial sweat. My knee came back.

It all went as you'd expect. Topless KGB full colonels chugging vodka and selling football clubs, other KGB officers behind the walls listening with stethoscopes, babushkas whizzing about in Zils and wanting to buy up everything in the Burberry shop on Bond Street, and at the buffet, lashings of tench caviar shipped from Shropshire.

The wedding ceremony took place in a terraced house in Richmond – the Richmond Registry Office. The bride appeared in an outfit that required the aisle of St Paul's Cathedral to get its full effect. Natalia had to clamber over chairs and a potted fern. When she sat down, the hoop holding down her chiffon petticoats sprang over her head and she and Von Jones the groom were lost from view for quite some minutes. I didn't know where to aim the ring.

At the reception later a shooting war broke out with water pistols. One of the KGB full colonels kept saying 'A penis!' when what he meant was 'Happiness!' He told me that when in England he always drank Scotch, which he pronounced in Hollywood central casting B-Movie villain style as *Scooottttccccchhhhhh*. He held up a half pint of Bells. 'Your eyes look beautiful in the moonlight, dear,' I said. 'Here's to 'em!'

I had to leave early to attend London Fashion Week.

I covered London Fashion Week for the *Daily Dacre*. Suffice it to say, I fully comprehend why Isabella Blow swallowed the weedkiller. One knows *exactly* how she felt. I was the fattest person ever to be seen at such an event. I drew crowds. Anna Wintour was delivered to the catwalk shows in what looked to me like a hearse. I almost needed to borrow it. Oh Christ, if I don't diet I will die. I look like roly-poly astrologer Russell Grant — and at the London Fashion Week, after I'd demonstrated what a good sport I was by being photographed covered with powder and paint, I looked like roly-poly astrologer Russell Grant *as a corpse*.

I also had to have these 7-foot tall supermodels draped all over me. Oh it was very confusing. They are beautiful (like a modern sculpture by Brancusi is beautiful) but have no passion, no *heat*, and absolutely no bosoms or bottoms. As sterile in their way as nuns.

I accord it a great triumph that I got the word *muff* into the *Daily Dacre*. Admittedly I was talking about a furry hand-warming fashion accessory and not a front bottom, but the sub-editors are so amazingly prudish, they like to do the equivalent of putting covers on chair legs and disguising what might look like ankles. Little gets past their censorship. Nipples still don't exist, for example, as far as the pious sub-editors on the *Daily Dacre* are concerned.

The colourful Russians aside, a lot of the other guests at that wedding were (are) sensible people in the corporate world, businessmen who go on business trips, who wear suits and know about hotel dry cleaning. They have pension plans and are adequately insured. It doesn't really matter what their companies produce — it could be yoghurt or garden implements — as the marketing mechanisms behind it all are the same, and this is their area of expertise, for which they are well remunerated. Next to these serious sorts of fellows I feel so utterly inadequate and unmanly, self-indulgent and vulgar – which I am. So up the bum and no babies!

✍

It was a hell of a few days. As well as my knee, my liver came back, so I'm taking it slow for a bit. There was the Russian wedding, London Fashion Week, and then Quentin had a party at the Savile Club, at which one of his little girls sang 'Over the Rainbow', very creditably. Every verse. I said to Oscar bitterly, 'That's why your father's career never took off. I didn't get you to sing "Over the Rainbow" at my launch parties.'

Oscar and I went to The French, the great Soho drinking den, and who should pop up but Joe McGrath. Joe said that when he was directing Spike in *The Great McGonagall*, Spike wanted to do a scene in black face. Joe talked him out of this, as it would have been offensive even in 1974. So Spike turned up with a green face. 'Okay, let's offend the fucking Irish!'

✍

Friskin my friend from Wales tells me he met a colleague on a software course in Urmston who is tighter than a mermaid's Tampax. All he thinks about is not spending money. For his wedding he didn't want to send off invitations unless people planned definitely to be there – though in the event the invitations weren't beautifully hand-crafted cards but emails, which included the bank account details and sort codes of both bride and groom. They didn't want actual gifts, only money drafts, which had to clear in the bank before the big day. Invitations were not extended to husbands or partners – so Friskin's wife Mrs Friskin was excluded. There was a cash bar. No food. Because there were four years left on the bride's passport before it expired, she decided not to pay the £92 it takes to have it updated with her new marital name. So on honeymoon in Peru the happy couple had to pretend they were not together and travelled as single passengers. They also took their rings off.

264

During the Notting Hill Carnival, Duncan danced in his upstairs window for the crowds. 'I now know how Hitler felt!' he joked. I did not know that the Fuhrer had ever visited Leamington Road Villas, though Dame Beryl was convinced she saw him, Hitler not Duncan, in Liverpool.

But I think what Duncan meant is that one can be carried away with the adulation of the seething crowd below, catching the wave. 'Hitler doing the rumba!' added Duncan. What I think the scene was probably more like was Evita Peron on the balcony in Buenos Aires, as portrayed by Elaine Paige.

❦

For the Bromyard Folk Festival Weekend, when people from all over the world come to gape at authentic Herefordshire *Herrenvolk*, I ought to take a leaf out of Duncan's book and do the twist in my lounge-room casement. Except bricks would be hurled at me.

Oscar was on duty in The Thorn from noon until 2 a.m., refreshing the Folkies. Needless to say, fights broke out among rival Morris Men, and stand-in barman Strawberry Blonde Karl told one traditionally bedecked Morris Man, 'That's £6.20, but as you look like a total twat, a fiver.'

More relationships are going tits-up. Andy From Bedford was so broken-hearted when the paramedic from Barton-le-Clay left him he spent the night with a lesbian. The next morning he was sick. 'It was that lesbian I ate last night,' he explained. Barmaid Jodhi said that the paramedic smelt of Playdoh anyway. Which she did, now I think of it. Odd. Or was it Anais Anais?

❦

We drove miles through the Herefordshire countryside to find a place called The Hutch or The Hatch, where an exhibition forming part of the Herefordshire Art Festival was being mounted. What a magical part of England this can sometimes be, with the dark-green trees concealing what's left of abandoned parks and lost stately homes. There are gatehouses and lodges and grassed-over drives.

Local art usually means basket weaving, ethnic pendants and recycled glass earrings. Maybe there'll be a woodcut of an owl. Anyway, we get to this place, The Hatch or The Hutch, and it's funny how you can take an instantaneous dislike to a person. We went in and there was this snooty shag and his posh-voiced chums standing in front of these daubs drinking very diluted punch. I went to pick up a Xeroxed price-list sheet. 'Oh, you'll not want that,' said Lord Snooty. 'My works are too expensive – the most expensive in the show!'

Hatred rose in me. 'How do you know how much I can afford?' I asked him – Ferdinand Aniseed was almost his name. He wasn't even attempting to be amusing – probably if I'd been wearing my father's Gieves and Hawkes suit rather than my George at Asda T-shirt it would have been a different story. I wanted to buy up every single fucking picture in the room and take them outside and jump up and down on them and piss on them and then chuck them in the ornamental lily pond. The sheer *presumption*. Though there wasn't an owl, there was a hand-printed neo-primitive woodcut of a vole (£600).

Next to Linda, looking a bit squashed and uncomfortable, is Violet Nesta Mary Lewis, born in 1901. I know nothing about her, except she married a man with shell shock and the MM,* who took a knife from the shop, went upstairs to the bathroom and cut his throat. The district nurse, Nurse Dann, had to come and clear it all up. My father remembered her rushing out from her house behind Garfield Coslett's, the grocers' – the building that is now the Bedwas Post Office. The knife was swilled and returned to the shop, where it carried on being used to slice fillet steaks. That's the same bathroom – a room where something very nasty had occurred – where I sailed my rubber ducks and started wanking. I was eleven, since you ask, and had been told about it by a boy who is now a (retired) Detective Chief Superintendent.

୬

I've been to a wedding. No names. No pack drill. The congregation weren't singing the hymns, not because they didn't know the tune but because they couldn't fucking read. The rotund, indeed spherical, bridesmaids, shoehorned into their rented frocks, had misspelled tattoos on their shoulders. There were loads of babies and toddlers slithering around – a network of stepchildren and step-parents so complex that my late chum Rodney Needham, Professor of Anthropology at Oxford University, would have had his work cut out explaining the kinship patterns. There's modern Britain for you.

୬

An 'urgent alert' has gone out across the Herefordshire Balkans as food safety officers try to trace stocks of a sausage 'that could pose a serious health risk if eaten'. If eaten, eh? I mean as opposed to shoving the sausage immediately up your arse? Thwacking people across the bonce? Hiding sausages in the bed and, when the wife screams, saying, 'How's that for a conservatory extension!'

* Military Medal, one down from the MC, or Military Cross. Awarded to other ranks for bravery in the field.

The food safety officers – self-important chaps whom one has to picture in full riot gear or in those spacesuits qualified scientists wear when fiddling with radioactive isotopes – are making no bones about the sausage danger. No siree. This is a red alert.

If you come into contact with evil sausages, you can expect headaches, a stiff neck, confusion, loss of balance and convulsions. As most days in my field I encounter people with at least several of these symptoms, particularly if I am attending a literary party in London, I can now say to them with authority – *you have met with the fatal sausage.*

႟

James Cagney in *White Heat*. It is grand opera, his chuckles and snarls. There's something about his pigeon-chested strut – the way he tilts himself forward, so he's always about to break into a run – that reminded me of Norman Wisdom and Freddie Starr. The boxer's crouch. Cagney goes up in flames at the end – like an atomic explosion. You don't see that again until Sellers finishes off the world in *Dr. Strangelove*.

What vitality and animation Cagney possessed – there's an extraordinary scene in the prison canteen, when he is told his mother has died, and he screams and roars. He is demented.

Cody Jarrett, Cagney's character, is only truly joyous when he is behaving badly – shooting people or robbing a train. That's his *element*. How I envy him.

႟

Steptoe and Son, Bottom, Peep Show . . . The list is long: so very many sitcoms are scenes from a (male) marriage; two men locked together in a nasty little flat, incapable of happiness, unable to move out or on. Humiliation and non-fulfilment underpin the laughs, which are uneasy laughs.

Peep Show seems improvised and cobbled together – a video diary, with spoken thoughts and voice-over reflections – but it is adroitly done and my children adore it. Try as I might, I cannot remember the names of the characters or the actors. Or when I'm told, which character is which, what actor is whom or why or where. There is a podgy one, prematurely middle-aged and repressed, and he has a friend who is a bit better-looking, even though the one who is the better-looking one is always twisting his face into a sneer and hence resembles Huckleberry Hound. The lads could be Stephen Fry and Hugh Laurie in their younger years.

୭

Crime Wave Corner. Because Carly and Philip Payne were having a violent 'domestic', the cops were called – so Carly and Philip immediately joined forces and attacked the good officers who'd only come to sort them out. Detective Sergeant Andrew Duckworth had his finger bitten off. His fellow officer, PC Wendy, had her hair pulled. As a result, PC Wendy has been 'withdrawn and emotional' and only recently felt able to return to the station. The Paynes have been ordered to pay her £250 in compensation. That'll cover the cost of a nice new coiffure at Toni and Guy's.

୭

Laurence Olivier and Herbert Von Karajan: they both had a chiselled implacable quality. You sense they'd be capable of murder.

୭

Laurence Fox in the *Morse* sequel, *Lewis*. He's what Don Quixote would have been like when young. That's quite a dynasty of Foxes. Edward Fox, James Fox, Emilia Fox. Like Redgraves and Cusacks and Mitfords. I wonder if there is a Zeppo Fox and a Gummo Fox.

୭

Emilia Fox is bang tidy beyond belief and when her scenes as Lynne Frederick, Sellers's last wife and widow, were cut from *The Life and Death of Peter Sellers*, though don't ask me why, because it meant the story was left dangling, she sent me a very sweet note, saying she'd enjoyed the experience all the same. Her scenes survive in the extra bits on the DVD.

269

I had high hopes of *Gavin and Stacey*. A charming love story. *Romeo and Juliet* without phials of poison. The blue-eyed Billericay boy and the grinning, giggling girl from Barry Island, her pretty face creased with smiles. Joanna Paige also has champion tits.

The geography is a bit peculiar, however. Getting from Essex to Barry Island seems to take them half an hour – yet they'd be ages in actuality. The townships are 204.8 miles apart. And the Essex scenes seem a bit suspiciously damp – I think they are pulling a fast one and shooting the whole thing in Llantwit Major.

Ruth Jones as Nessa is my ex-sister-in-law's neighbour Nerys Dunt to a tee. It's a common South Welsh type, these hefty valkyries, chopsy, sarky, sex mad but impossible to impress. They have a full quiver of put-downs. 'You're a cracking bloke, but let's face it. You're riddled.' They tend to speak in the present tense – I does, I loves, I goes, I wants – as if the past and the future can't exist. They also have a way with clichés. 'At the end of the day, when all's said and done, not a word of a lie, I got to be honest with you . . .'

I'd not seen such a character in a play before, and the recognition was instant. It was also a pleasure to have South Wales on the screen with no mention of rugby or coalmines or leeks or Brains Dark or harps or love spoons or male voice fucking choirs. Because that's normally all you ever get.

Rob Brydon's Uncle Bryn – we all have an Uncle Bryn. Creepy, pedantic, bossy, queer, repressed, annoying, intrusive, and blithely unaware about how boring they are. They keep the car in tip-top condition. They wear special driving gloves. They insist on showing you their holiday slides. They keep their back issues of subscription periodicals in chronological order.

I've been to Barry Island once or twice. I remember it as run-down and faintly sinister. There was a graveyard of scrapped steam trains, hundreds of them. But not here. Not in *Gavin and*

Stacey, where there are candyfloss colours and blue skies and the sand is sand and not dog shit.

And then it all went wrong. You want comedy to be kept real (somehow) and it grates when there are unlikely elements, starting with Alison Steadman who whooped and created like Madame Arcati. (Larry Lamb got the comic tone right.) Nor can I stand that James Corden, who is getting to be too pleased with himself by far. I saw him once in the Groucho. I wanted to go over and say how much I'd enjoyed his performance in *The Return of Martin Guerre*, in which he was a boy soprano. It was on at the Prince Edward Theatre and so bad it closed halfway through opening night.

A little tip – when meeting these sorts of people, self-important celebrities, always congratulate them on something very minor that they did ages and ages ago, that's all but forgotten and erased from the resumé. My biggest bullseye here was saying to Corin Redgrave (and what a humourless party *he* was), 'You were brilliant in *Crooks in Cloisters*' – in which he'd appeared with Dame Barbara Windsor and Wilfred Brambell in 1963. Because what Corin wanted people to tell him was that he was smashing as King Lear, much better than his father ever was, and *Viva la Revolucion!*

So – Series Two of *Gavin and Stacey* was a disaster. The fairy story was already flagging and faltering – because what do you do after the happy-ever-after bit? What is there to explore, except disappointment and disillusionment? *Gavin and Stacey* was not going to be a drama about the sudden loss of romantic ideals – though Matthew Horne, as Gavin, has an attractive gloom, which suggested feelings and thoughts the script didn't get around to providing him with. Instead there were too many indulgent scenes with James Corden as Smithy – scenes written by James Corden – who was (preposterously) meant to be jealous that his Best Friend had got married and had moved away. This was *milked*. It wasn't even done as *gay*.

Smithy had stopped being a peripheral character, Gavin didn't have much to do except look troubled and defeated, Stacey had become a shrew, a nag, a scold, and in a nutshell too much was now not credible – e.g. Ruth Jones as Nessa (in scenes written by Ruth Jones) speaking Italian, reading the *Financial Times*, knowing about stocks and shares. It wasn't *Gavin and Stacey* any more really, it was *Smithy and Nessa*, like when *Man About The House* became *George and Mildred*.

Also annoying: Stacey's mother's omelette fixation; Uncle Bryn being 'lovable'; and Alison Steadman was so broad she could have been at the New Theatre, Cardiff, in panto. Exaggeration at the expense of being natural. I felt that everyone had given up trying, particularly when sentimental stuff about babies commenced and Nessa stopped being slaggy. I think there may have been a Series Three by now, or Thirty-Three, plus Christmas Specials. I haven't a clue.

But there were compensations, such as Joanna Paige's beauty. It shouldn't work – and in some shots it is as if the camera crew were trying to make her ugly. The crinkled forehead and wave-shaped eyebrows. Teeth that don't seem to fit. Unsymmetrical nostrils. Chopped hair. But it comes together, her skin and bones and her imploring look. When she's under the duvet, sexily half-awake, or briefly glimpsed in the shower – oh my and oh dear! Vernon Dobcheff!

As she shows when she flares up after being jobless too long in Essex (or Llantwit Major), when she'd rather be back in her beloved Barry (which is 10.8 miles down the road from Llantwit Major), Joanna Paige is not soft-centred. You feel she could be very unsettling – I hope she does proper things in the future, not simply cameos in *Poirot* or *Marple* as a scarlet murderess or a co-starring role in one of those drama serials filmed in blue light about secret agents with sci-fi powers. Cleopatra is within her range.

I see that our first home in Oxfordshire is for sale. An attic flat in Stratton Audley Manor, near Bicester, now priced at £209,000. We bought it in 1985 on a 100 per cent mortgage for £28,000 – a mortgage raised on Anna's salary. I wasn't earning anything. Haphazard journalism and hack teaching at Oxford colleges brought in as much then as writing my wonderful books does now. The difference being: back then I had *hope*. My coveted Junior Research Fellowship was non-stipendiary – which meant exactly what it said: no wages. The Governing Body must have assumed that the younger dons moonlighted as cat burglars or footpads.

How chi-chi and piss-elegant Flat 7, Statton Audley Manor, looks in the estate agent's photographs. Dinky spotlights on thin wires. A fitted kitchen. When we were there it had woodchip wallpaper and tenth-hand furniture from dead Welsh relatives. What is now a bedroom with a four-poster and ivory-coloured curtains wafting in the breeze used to be our dining room-cum-my study. Mark Rylance and the late Katy Behean ate with us there a hundred times. Juliet Stevenson, Miranda Richardson and the late Bob Peck used to call in. I had nothing to offer them except a tomato. My friend Ronnie Pudding came from Jakarta – he peed out of the window without opening the double glazing and left his underpants in the spare bed.

But most of all, Iris Murdoch and John Bayley turned up on a regular basis. They'd accept any invitation that involved free food and drink. People said Iris was like the Mother Superior in *The Sound of Music*, but I never took her quietness and absent-mindedness for serenity or shyness. 'Can I have some more red wine?' or 'Can I have some more potatoes?' were what I remember her saying. She ate heartily and knocked back the drink, and now and again she'd smile in her enigmatic fashion (wind?) – but she was on edge, I felt, despite the benignity – which I think was her camouflage. She was too wary to have a sense of humour, and would certainly not have appreciated the story about a production of *The Sound of Music* in the north of England. During rehearsals, Maria suddenly burst into tears. 'The Mother Superior just called me a cunt face!' – 'No she didn't,' explained the director patiently. 'What she said was her line, "What is it you can't face, my child?" She's from Chorley.'

The brilliance and exuberance were wholly supplied by John Bayley, against whom let no man say a word. His width of learning and sagacity remain unparalleled in my experience. Enormously well read and faultlessly discriminating, John always served as my model of how real criticism is creative, poetic at a stretch – and in my own books there are such elements of exaggeration and fantasy, I wonder if they are more than halfway to being novels.

John taught me everything I know – without teaching me anything. As he himself said, 'I was reluctant to advise too much or to press recommendations on students.' He simply created this atmosphere in which words and books were paramount. He gave me confidence in myself.

He gave me confidence in myself – yet when he said to me that English wasn't really an academic subject, should never have become one, and that in the end lecturing and giving tutorials will hardly *do* – and that a thesis and 'research' was only to be embarked upon for the sake of appearances only – while this made (and makes) perfect sense, and was why I left Oxford for France, and the life of *being a writer*, I still think: lucky old John Bayley with his professorial salary, CBE and index-linked pension.

❧

As for Iris's novels . . . Vernon Dobtcheff! What high-minded pricks her characters are. If anyone else had written *Henry and Cato* it would never have made it to the printers. Henry Marshelson wants to sell his stately home and build a council estate. He wants to give his money away, though of course he doesn't. Somewhere else in the novel, Cato Forbes, a homosexual priest, is kept prisoner at knifepoint by his boyfriend. Interspersed with all that – lots of chopsy philosophy derived from the Oxford University Literae Humaniores degree syllabus circa 1955.

Another ghastly one that springs to mind – and of course there were dozens – is *A Fairly Honourable Defeat*. More homosexual civil servants and conceited, idle Oxford dons with private means. The assumption always is that if you are not from the landed gentry or a foreign aristocrat – if you don't have *breeding* – you aren't ever going to be very smart. In her outlook Iris was formidably reactionary.

Has anyone remarked on how anachronistic Iris's books are? Women wear hats and gloves to go out. Yet we were ostensibly in the Oxford and London of the Sixties, Seventies and Eighties. Characters write letters, not phone. They turn on lamps instead of switching on lights. Iris stopped noticing the world during the Hitler War. She was immensely incurious about the contemporary world, and this is what I'd noticed with her as a person – she'd ask questions, but you could say 'Up the bum and no babies!' and she'd not be bothering to listen – though she was very good at giving the appearance of listening.

Bedrooms in her books have dressing rooms leading off them. Bedrooms are actually called boudoirs and have doors that lock. Downstairs, adjacent to the terrace, people come in and out through French doors. Husbands and wives keep their own apartments, with unseen maids and valets doing the domestic chores, like with the de Winters at Manderley in Daphne du Maurier's *Rebecca*.

Daphne du Maurier is probably the author Iris most resembles: there is a similar log-jam of hysteria and inertia; they were both aroused by tyrants and sexual sadists. There is a taste for violence. In Iris's books, Canetti, Fraenkel and crew, mentors of hers who really did (according to the biographies) jump on her during tutorials, became magi, enchanters, evil wizards.

It is a cruel thing to say, but when she got the Alzheimer's, for the first few years, and until she started leaving her shit on the mantelpiece, *how could they tell?* In her later novels, for example, descriptions of the London Underground are wrong – Sloane Square is not on the Circle Line (or it is). Her books were antiquated and artificial and, well, *vague*.

❧

Anna loaned Tristan her credit card *for emergencies*. He used it in the upstairs bar at Rules.

'Thou hast raised the boy well, Kimosabe!'

❧

It is already seventy years since cheery-looking mass murderer the late Fred West was born in Much Marcle.

October

What am I still doing here? The universe is standing still. Today was one of those dates and times that appeal to wonks: 10.10 a.m. on the 10/10/10. I remember sitting next to David Huw Harries in the duffers' O level Maths set at Bassaleg Comprehensive on 7/7/77. I did O level Maths twice and still only scraped a C. On the 8/8/88 I was a Fellow of Wolfson College, Oxford, writing articles for the *Spectator* and the *Standard*, and so basically up the bum and no babies to a grade C in O level Maths. As for today's particular chores, like those of 9/9/99, when according to the record I was gazing at bills I couldn't pay, I am stuck here in the Herefordshire Balkans wondering quite when it was that things started to go wrong.

To Cornwall. I'd never been. The brochures and cheap picture postcards suggest sunshine and blank blue skies – whereas what I found (Mevagissey, Fowey) is rain and darkness – a wilderness. Everyone is completely mad – A. L. Rowse; Peckinpah's *Straw Dogs*; Daphne du Maurier, who wore big wide leather belts – lesbian! Manderley in flames. Laughton in *Jamaica Inn*. Piracy, shipwrecks and fearful apparitions. The clifftop hotels look like Dr Seward's asylum in *Dracula*.

I've been mugging up on Daphne du Maurier, the Catherine Cookson of Cornwall. The paperbacks I've amassed have dated 1970s bodice-ripper covers. Surely they ought to be re-done? On the other hand – the jackets are not utterly misleading.

My, she loved her turbulent landscapes, the moorland, broken trees, and tempests, did old Daph. *Rebecca* is her version of *Wuthering Heights*. Interesting that Olivier is associated with both, having in Hollywood played Heathcliff and Max de Winter – bringing to the roles his own passions, inner fire and psychological bad weather.

The rain drives harder, the sea is angrier, the birds are more vicious-looking here – the gulls are threatening. They could grab a toddler. You can see why old Daph wrote *The Birds*. What a shame Hitchcock transferred it to California for his movie. But Hitchcock was drawn to her mixture of nightmare and dreams – *Jamaica Inn*, *Rebecca*, *The Birds*. Cornwall is a place of mists and ghosts – the interpenetration of a spirit world or supernatural world with our world. Old Daph explored that, too, to perfection – though she set it in Venice, with *Don't Look Now*.

Having bought nineteen slightly foxed but still desirable first edition Dame Daphne books in local bookshops, which are not slow to spot that she is their local author, we went to see if we could find Menabilly, her stately home and (surely) the inspiration for the Manderley of her novel. Sure enough – the fogs were rolling in off the sea; there were owls and sea eagles and crashing waves. We found a tiny church or mausoleum where Daphne du Maurier's funeral was held. Locked. Dripping leaves, a slippery moss-covered path, and rhododendron bushes with big blue blooms. Or is it purple blooms they had and I mean hydrangeas?

Yet all this *atmosphere* was the setting, in *Rebecca*, for what is essentially a squalid and nasty and ultra-modern (what was it – 1930?) tale of upper-class adultery. Rebecca is a character whom we don't actually see, yet all the other people in the book live through her. She is still powerfully alive, in many ways.

ॐ

The art of Cornwall – Sir Terry Frost's black or blood-red discs, his moons and blooms, rocks and plants. Frost's pictures are also full of boats or, to be more accurate, shapes that suggest masts and prows and decks and sterns.

❧

Polperro is inhabited entirely by goblins, hunchbacks, and hunchbacked goblins, each with epilepsy, cramps and a mandatory clubfoot. In the bar, Robert Newton is showing off. In the fields, ancient stones, twisted trees, hermits' cells. In the sky, owls and ravens and creatures of ill omen. There are people here who'd put spells on cattle, give hogs the mumps, and horses the staggers. Cornwall is a place of dark pagan customs. Worse than Wales. The Brontë sisters' mother came from Cornwall – Maria Branwell.

The tram driver – the tram a glorified milk float – at Polperro was (I am convinced) Bob Todd. Then I remembered Bob Todd is dead, so it was evidently his ghost or identical twin. As we were getting aboard, Bob asked us for our passes. 'Eh?' we said. 'Your passes. You can get them from any library.' He meant our OAP free bus passes.

To get into the spirit of *being old* I decided to make it look as if I'd pissed myself, and had wee stains down my leg. Actually it was sprinkled Malvern Water.

❧

Are bras banned west of the Tamar? Cornish women have these huge swinging udders. They wear swirling skirts and have strong hips, as if they are about to carry pails of milk or encumber themselves with a yoke. There also seems to be a shampoo shortage.

❧

Trying to get advice on the best seafood restaurant in Falmouth: 'I've lived here all my life and I only ever get my husband to take me for a balti,' was what we'd typically be told. The seagulls eat curry too. They shit brown. Brown streaks down buildings and doorways and splashed across windows. But anyway, Rick Stein must despair.

The madness of Cornwall – as depicted in the personality of A. L. Rowse. He fascinates me. His grudges and bitterness – and he was proud of his censoriousness and conceit. Twisted and savage. He delighted in being nasty to people to their face. A working-class man wanting to mix with the posh folk, so he went in for acts of self-aggrandisement. (Emlyn Williams was a Welsh equivalent.) He never let anyone forget that he'd been elected to All Souls as a young man. It was tragic that after his early twenties the rest of his long life was a waste.

The only thing academic success proved to me was the meaninglessness of academic success – it led to nothing.

⚘

Oscar's twenty-first. I hired the Falmouth–St Mawes Ferry and the invitation stipulated black tie, ballgowns, no kilts. On the day of the do it was blowing a gale. The coastguard forbade anyone from casting off. Vernon Dobtcheff! What to do? I had a hundred people in full mess-kit descending on Cornwall, including Maggot, Double-Barrelled Dave, Croaky, Gumsie, Spoon, Strawberry Blonde Carl, and his twin, Ginger Shane, Chirpy, Andy From Bedford, Wozza, Mozza, Curly Ben, Creepy Ian, who likes to invite girls to Gloucester 'for a curry', and Mark Pointy Shoes, whose sister runs a whelk stall on Hayling Island. The Bromyard township had closed for the weekend.

Anna's mum, i.e. Nanoo, had made cream horns, bean and bacon pie, forcemeat balls, cheese straws, and rissoles *a la mode*. It was quite a panic – church halls were unavailable, there was not time to de-convert Oscar's house from being a crack den. So I commandeered an old folks home. I was like Mickey Rooney or Judy Garland marching in and saying 'Let's do the show right here!'

The old ladies loved it. They were doing the hokey-cokey with their zimmers. They helped light up the spliffs and reminisced about their own young days, in the Fifties and Sixties and earlier, when no one would think twice about doing anal for tabs. 'I did oral, actually', said Mrs Dirkin. 'Fancy!' said Miss Hinch eventually, ending the minute or two of silence that had fallen. 'We didn't always only suck barley sugar you know!' Mrs Bipsham then said, rather loudly and brightly. 'I had five children on half an ovary,' she added, with pride.

Mrs Dirkin sought to become the centre of attention again by explaining that the beauty of treating her arthritis with Esterene was that 'It's the trade name for crack cocaine.' Miss Hinch claimed that when fire-watching during the war, 'I shelled peas in my overcoat.' Mrs Bipsham said, 'I was fingered by a rough lad in Budleigh Salterton. Such a nice night, it was. So many stars.'

The party went on for days. Jodhi locked herself in the bathroom, climbed out of the window, fell in a bush, and came back in covered in bruises. A week later, a couple tumbled out of the cupboard under the stairs, where the Hoover is kept. The chap had been in hiding because he was wearing a kilt. They were lucky to find privacy, as there were hundreds of twenty-year-old men *gagging for it*. Lissom lasses were *lezzing off* in the Warden's oubliette. I was all day Sunday with my sky-blue Marigolds on cleaning the mirror with Dual Action Multi-Purpose Lemon Fresh Flash.

There was a truly apocalyptic atmosphere to it all. Strawberry Blonde Carl told me the police came five times, or seven times if you count when they stopped by for drinks. The neighbours switched the mains water off in protest, which we thought a pathetic gesture, like leaving the car door open or the glove compartment so the little light runs down the battery. Croaky managed to break the rotary clothes line, the Edwardian bell-push, the stained glass in the front door, and the curtain rails. We had to forgive him. He'd taken such trouble hiring Size 15 patent leather dancing pumps, which I think were eventually located in a theatrical costumiers. Proceedings only ground to a halt when Mrs Ebnall had to go and deliver her Christian Aid envelopes.*

ᕒ

I was therefore hopping mad over ghastly Lord Browne of Madingley's comment that 'the benefits of studying away from home are exaggerated' and that 'we live in straitened times and the priority is education'. When you look at what politicians, bankers and hedge funds persons make, it is only straitened times for some people. *The Sunday Times* 'Rich List' is still a substantial document.

And *resounding balls* to all that being away from home isn't a plus-point argument – I rather enjoyed the wonderful debauch in Falmouth, a useful 250 miles from the Bromyard township. Like *Animal House* crossed with a Bright Young Things party out of Evelyn Waugh. On top of everything else, I personally provided forty-six bottles of Côtes du Rhone and 180 pints of lager and that went in a flash.

In my view – and I've got two doctorates, don't forget, and I was an Oxford don – it is essential that youngsters have a few years of mad freedom like this, well away from Mummy and Daddy, otherwise we are living in a totalitarian community like North Korea, with homework, endless slog, and then straight to work as wage slaves for the state.

* When we received a letter from the landlord of Oscar's diggings, later in the academic year, complaining about 'your son's riotous behaviour', I wrote back saying that as he was in his twenties he was rather off my hands – and that owing to the Data Protection Act, Oscar couldn't be discussed with third parties in any event. Indeed, it is not for me to confirm or deny whether Oscar is in Falmouth or on the moon.

I further pointed out to the landlord that should he wish to complain about me at any stage, then here's my mother's address in South Wales, though she will be as surprised to hear from him as I was. Furthermore, I asked if I could please have his, the landlord's, parents' address, because I wanted to tell them to tell their son to please keep all his pissy remarks about 'standards' to himself in future.

Youngsters have a right to a rite of passage – though I didn't have one myself. I was too busy reading every book ever written, from *Beowulf* to *Gabriel's Lament* by Sir Paul Bailey. What a lot of missed opportunities. As John Betjeman said, reminiscing in old age, 'I wish I'd had more sex.'

I only decided to become a delinquent – well, only the other day, in fact – when I woke up and realised I'd been a Surrealist all my life, though I'm not sure this is the only reason I get enraged by insurance premiums, broken washing machines, brown envelopes, insolent tradesmen, cleaning the kitchen floor, brown envelopes, picking up dirty laundry, buffet luncheons with Rotarians, brown envelopes, being sold software by men with pens clipped in their top pockets, personal pension plans, pre-paid funeral schemes, brown envelopes, health checks, flu jabs, diabetic 'screening', bank charges, the end of silver-service dining carriages on trains, health and safety regulations, gender studies, bunions, varicose veins and brown envelopes.

V. S. Pritchett – a genial old stick; I knew him – said in the end everyone wants to be respectable. I am going in absolutely the opposite direction. The rewards of good behaviour, compliance, diligence, politeness, have *not been enough*. There is no pleasure to be taken in any of it in the least. Once people become settled in adult life, moving next door to, say, computer analysts in Tottenham Hale, where the only white people are the Irish, they will quickly realise there's nothing left except for disappointment, counselling and support groups.

Lord Mandelson also, in his autobiography, had some High Puritan shithouse comment about students knuckling down to study – in his case studying tomes about politics and economics and, I surmise, flower arranging. I was like that as an undergraduate and it got me exactly where I am today. My gas jet has gone out and Anna's kettle has furred up. So think on.

ഔ

A large number of junk political memoirs have been rushed out. Tony Blair's autobiography was gripping – in a bindweed sort of way. Like the way he gripped the throat of Lord Falconer on Millennium Eve, when everything went tits up at The Dome. But a lot of his book – economic analysis, political analysis – was tedious beyond. And no mention of Cherie hardly, or the family.

I thought Blair came across in his own book as one of those madmen in Stendhal who becomes a priest. I was going to say 'or like Alec D'Urbeville becoming a hellfire preacher' – but there's oddly no sex or passion with Blair. Ice cold.

*

I've been as bad as that woman in *The Waste Land* who keeps complaining that her nerves are bad tonight. Perhaps it is because I find travelling – leaving the security of my burrow – so filled with anxiety, so crammed with the possibility of disaster, that I teeter along the edge of a panic attack?

Being at the mercy of timetables, the queues, delays, general inconvenience: it is all so ulcer-inducing. There was a long queue for the bag drop facility (as they call it) at Stansted and a Ryanair weight fascist made me pay a £40 supplement because my case was 1.8 kg over the 15 kg limit. Perhaps if I offered to eat it instead? They'll be charging extra for fat people soon. Then I'll be fucked.

How nice to have been the Queen Mother, whisked around by helicopter or private train, with equerries and her Clarence House team smoothing one's passage. Where's my equivalent of Sir Ralph Anstruther or Sir Michael Adeane? A lot of republican feeling, I am sure, is pure envy. I'd live to be 102 if someone wiped my arse with gold foil.

As it is, I arrived in Bad Ischl having not slept for three nights. My hands and fingers tingled from diabetes. I had heartburn, a sore throat, throbbing eyeballs and throbbing piles, which made me walk with the comical chimpanzee gait of Sir Norman

Wisdom. The previous evening I'd been to Craig's party to launch his parody collection at the National. Let's hope they took my crouch or gait for eccentricity or a venerable stoop.

What I loved about Edward Fox impersonating people in the dramatisation of Craig's book they put on in the Cottesloe was that he did every voice the same, whether it was James Lees-Milne, D. H.Lawrence or Julie Burchill. I thought this was brilliantly subversive, doing even the Mitford Sisters as Edward VIII – particularly as Jon Culshaw and Eleanor Bron were more conventionally doing their level best to convince us it really was Clive James or Nigella speaking. Craig himself said *fuck* and *cunt* in a loud voice – you can't beat his Harold Pinter. He is often requested to do his Harold Pinter at children's parties, as it goes down better than (say) Mr Twisty and his novelty balloons.

During rehearsals, Fox had said quite firmly that what he hated about directors was that they were these little men who kept pointing out the obvious *at boring length* – surely the last word on directors? Francis Wheen and I sat on the side of the stage like Statler and Waldorf in *The Muppet Show*, heckling merrily. At the drinks-do afterwards on a parapet above the Thames, Sir Peregrine Worsthorne wore a big purple hat and looked as though he'd come as Quentin Crisp. Or did he inherit it from George Melly, whom he'd known since their days at Stowe? Mary Killen was in a big red pixie costume. The message they seemed to be giving off was – *Look at me before I vanish and the waters close over my head for ever!*

Victoria Hislop said she thought Sir Simon Russell Beale (inexplicably loveable despite the hint of benign malevolence) should play me on the stage – I said I'd be happy to play Sir Simon Russell Beale on the stage. Perhaps sometimes I do? Surreal, eh?

❧

It is always a shock to be reminded that full-of-fun Ian Hislop is of normal human size. Strawberry Blonde Karl, for example, is convinced he's a glove puppet worked by Paul Merton from under the desk. But then who works Paul Merton? (Real name: Doris Klunt.)

৯৹

The worst book launch party I ever went to was for Clement Freud. It took place on a cordoned-off platform in Marylebone Railway Station – quite why nobody knew. The celebrity turnout was P. D. James, registered midget Ross Kemp, and me – and I was the one who refused to wear the conference-style identity badge. Richard Curtis and Emma Freud turned up later, pushing pushchairs. The way our little compound was cordoned off, it was like a police crime incident scene – apt for Phyllis James's Commander Dalgliesh of the Yard, now I think of it. A train, what I believe was called a Sprinter, was parked next to us, the carriages filled with small flower arrangements and photographs of Clement Freud, placed there by Clement Freud. We were herded aboard and had to listen to a speech by the publisher, to which Clement Freud was gracious enough to make a reply. 'I am so pleased with my book,' he said, 'I'd like to read it out to you.' And bugger me, he looked as if he would.

There was a table with drinks at the far end of the platform – so far away it could have been in Chalfont St Peter. Very pretty girls and boys patrolled with trays of drinks and canapés, but as it was about eleven-thirty in the morning it made an odd sight. 'I've been going backwards and forwards to Aylesbury for twenty years and they've never given me a glass of champagne,' said an indignant commuter. P. D. James, however, seemed to be waiting for the Orient Express to materialise. 'Do you suppose we'll be going aboard for a sit-down meal? Clement can organise anything!' she said, expecting a miracle.

She'll have been disappointed by the coupons we were given by the waiters and waitresses, which were to be exchanged for sausage rolls at the station buffet. 'No literary festivals today then, Phyllis?' I remarked in a jocular way, by way of making conversation. I then fled to the Groucho.

છ

As bad as things get with me, it has never come close to the late Barry Took. He left his wife, moved in with a much younger girlfriend, who soon left him, and then he had a stroke. He couldn't talk properly or remember vocabulary. 'Cabbages, green stuff, cabbages . . .' – this was eventually deciphered (by Francis Wheen) as meaning 'grass'. He sounded like a drunk, slurred and slow, searching agonisingly for the right word.

છ

A newspaper wanted me to write about what I thought was *Ypres Love*. I was picturing some romance involving a soldier during the First World War and his lost beloved. But no. Turns out they meant the Julia Roberts vehicle *Eat Pray Love*. That's not seeing it written down plus the commissioning editor's posh voice for you. Not my cup of tea so I 'passed' as they say – full-of-themselves rich bints of a certain age moving to Bali or Mali in their high heels is not something to be encouraged.

છ

A Leominster man has died after falling in his garden. 'He made light of it' at the time, but croaked later. He only had a small graze on his hand and his wife put a plaster on it. Come teatime, 'After one mouthful he said he couldn't eat any more and felt a bit sick. He rose from the table and was unsteady and fell back in his chair.'

Well, if this was St Mary Mead and I was Miss Marple, I wouldn't let it end there.

છ

Tony Curtis and Norman Wisdom have died, so who is to be the next winner of the Death Raffle? Max Bygraves? *Me*? It's Claire Rayner! I never liked the look of her – hard eyes. She was the sort of woman who created scenes in Harrow Library if the books she'd ordered were late. 'Don't you know who I am?' She'd throw stuff on the floor. It's ironic that an Agony Aunt with an OBE was the one who needed a bit of homely advice, but then architects never get around to finishing building their own loft extensions.

Of the Agony Aunts the only one I like is Mavis Nicholson, because she keeps her comments down to a minimum: *I'm the same, love. See a qualified doctor at once. Call the police. Don't you think it's pathetic at his age? I tried it once but I scraped my knees on the lino and Geoff's yachting cap blew off.* These cover most eventualities.

❧

I have had a letter from the Albanian Ambassador, asking me to visit his country – am I to be the new Norman Wisdom?

❧

When Tony Curtis was in London, to oversee an exhibition in Harrods of his dreadful paintings, he was a prisoner in his hotel for three days. 'I can't go out because my hair hasn't arrived,' he wailed. The one-time heart-throb was as bald as an egg, and his preposterous pompadour fooled nobody.

❧

I thought I was a goner. Crimson stools. Yes indeed. So to an appointment with Dr Twelvetrees – and don't I feel a fool? Not colon cancer at all, but the pickled beetroot I've been forking down from the Country Market.

❧

These miners in Chile that are being brought to the surface – it must be like leaving The Big Brother House, with the President of Chile playing Davina. Or it is like the last day of term, when you could bring your toys in. I bet it'll be a tourist attraction, being able to whizz up and down that mine shaft in the pod they made.

❧

Billings is back from two weeks in Ibiza. His hotel was packed with lesbians from Dusseldorf, according to him. 'I can say this for them, though. They didn't speak German when I was around. Not once.'

If you were on a narrow path up an Alpine ravine, with room only for one person, and a girl hiker was coming straight towards you, would you block her passage or toss yourself off? For asking that question, Max Miller was banned from the BBC for life.

⧽

I've been accusing everyone of sneezing and not clearing up the snot. But it turns out that I have been invaded by slugs. They have been leaving their glisten not only across the Turkey carpets but up the walls, across the bookshelves, and even amid my precious pile of VHS Ninja movies – *Surf Ninjas*, *Three Ninjas*, *Beverly Hills Ninja*, *Teenage Mutant Ninja Turtles I –VIII* etc.

Most infuriately, the slugs have been munching away at my Ludwig Bemelmans inscribed first editions. They seem to have a taste for the glue in the cloth bindings. The little shags must have returned night after night to feast on *Dirty Eddie*, *My War with the United States*, *Hansi*, *Sunshine* and *The Donkey Inside*. Most people will know Bemelmans for the Madeline series. I don't like those – too cute. But the drawings in his books about hotel life, about growing up in Austria (Gmunden – near Bad Ischl), travelling in Mexico and Ecuador: these I admire and (funds permitting) collect. His quick and confident sketches with dabs of gouache have a Matisse or Dufy quality.

His interests were my interests – cultivated Old World restaurants; unspoilt parts of Europe; Gramercy Park in Manhattan before they wrecked it by modernising it. He also liked his food. Among his output is *Luchow's German Cookbook*, a celebration of the eatery on East 14th Street. From the illustrations it was exactly my sort of place – mahogany, etched glass, gasoliers, antlers, a palm court orchestra playing operetta, ancient waiters presided over by a Herr Ober. It closed in 1982 and burned to the ground a decade later. The building was demolished and the site bought by New York University for a (functional) hall of residence. Now and again, doors and mantelpieces turn up for sale in reclamation depots across America.

Even when they still cling on, places like Luchow's have a melancholy about them, because they imply loss. I used to stay regularly (suite 412) at the Gramercy Park Hotel – I was there just before they ripped out the atmosphere and quintupled the prices. There were Bakelite phones with bells, not electronic peeps, and the doormen had whistles to call cabs. The Plaza has gone. The Algonquin was ruined twenty years ago. Is the Wyndham Hotel at 42 West 58th Street still intact? One of the (painful) delights of watching *Breakfast at Tiffany's* is seeing in the background a New York that's not there now – New York when it was at its loveliest. I don't think I can visit the place again, not only because I am thoroughly penniless.

Perhaps another reason why Old World New York has gone is that the German/Austrian/Hungarian immigrants have long been absorbed into the New World's warp and woof. There is no nostalgia for any homeland – Viennese orchestras, Bavarian beers, Blutwurst, Bratwurst, Leberwurst and Bockwurst. People don't feel any urgent need to recreate or preserve any of it, through the architecture or cuisine.

❧

Why do I hate *The Pride of Britain Awards*? Because these genuine, brave achievements – the factual truth of them – are sentimentalised. Everything is described and set up to induce weeping in the viewers. It is indistinguishable from *The British Soap Awards*, and not only because it is the same Botoxed people in the studio audience and the same Botoxed people making the presentations.

Why do celebrities think they are doing real people a favour if they allow them to share or at least witness their glitter? When Ant and Dec pretended to be their own wax models at Madame Tussauds, in order to surprise a lass who'd saved toddlers from a fire, I wanted the lass to throw Ant and Dec on a fire. It is all immensely condescending.

How the holy hell do these soap stars and television presenters think they have the right to confer honours or approval on (as it might be) soldiers from an Afghan bomb disposal unit? These soldiers should have shoved the plastic trophy up Jamie Oliver's arse/the *Little Britain* wallies' arse/Jonathan Ross's arse. Whichever one of them it was. J. K. Rowling's arse. These celebrities don't know the meaning of bravery or selflessness. The whole point of the official Honours system is that when the Queen pins on the medals and the awards are handed out in her name, it is impartial – there is nothing in it for *her*. She's not writhing around to advertise the fact that *I care*.

It is so patronising. What must it be like to have survived the Battle of Britain only to have to go up on the stage and be grinned at by Esther Rantzen? Not only that, the woman wants to shake your hand? You might start wishing Reichsmarschall Hermann Goering had won. 'You were shot down twice,' said Carole Vorderman, a woman who was awarded the MBE for being able to count. 'Oh no, once was enough,' said the air-ace.

There was a tinsel curtain, through which prize-winning cancer moppets and have-a-go pensioners came and went relentlessly.

Vegetarian restaurants used to be quirky, cranky. Now it is getting hard to find anywhere unabashedly serving meat. I hate this of course. I need fur. I need feathers. I have heard people – girls usually – say they won't eat anything 'that has a face'. Well I've seen plenty of root vegetables that seemed to be smiling, frowning and grimacing. Your average Maris Piper potato looks like David Cameron. Indeed a well-scrubbed potato could stand in for the Prime Minister at the more boring public functions. He could then have the night off to be with fragrant wife Samantha and children Arthur Elwen, Nancy Gwen and Florence

Rose Endellion. Anyway, I was taken by Anna to the smug and insipid Cafe Tantric in Worcester. I made a private protest by ostentatiously holding open Ernest Hemingway's *The Dangerous Summer* over my pallid mushroom omelette and insisting that we talked about bullfights. Childish, I know, but *you can't let them win*.

❧

Is it any wonder that I am known the length and breadth of the Herefordshire Balkans (the district where I hang my hat) as Screaming Lord Bile Duct?

Just as I was fearing that *one more cookery programme* and I'll finally flip permanently, there's one more cookery programme on – *The Great British Bake Off*. Sue Perkins is either Alan Carr's twin or they go to the same optician. Does anyone warm to the woman?

If that wasn't severe provocation enough, just as I was then thinking that *one more DIY programme* and the men in white coats will definitely be chasing me along the street with a butterfly net, there's a new DIY programme announced – *Help! My House Is Falling Down*, in which over-mortgaged people in deepest Essex cope with raw sewage, green mould, rats and subsidence. My verdict: folk in Brentwood are fools only to themselves.

I was talked down from the ledge, as it were, by my two dream girls, Princess Anne and Jo Brand.

The Royal Family is so marginal these days, *The Princess Royal at 60* was part of the sports slot. We can thus fully expect the Queen's Diamond Jubilee in 2012 to be covered by CBeebies. John Inverdale, however, failed to ask the questions I personally wanted answering.

Yes, I am aware that Princess Anne, born in 1950 on the same day as Jim Dale, and weighing 6 lb, is Patron of 200 charities and performs 600 engagements a year, but was it true that she was the only female competitor at the Montreal Olympics in 1976 not to be given a sex test?

Was her personal car number plate (1420 H) really obtained from a United Dairies milk float in Ealing? As a child, did she keep a ferret in a toolbox at Sandringham, which escaped and bit a corgi, giving it a septic ear?

My friend and colleague Colonel Craig Brown swears that he saw Princess Anne dancing on stage at the end of *Hair*, 'fully clothed in a purple trouser suit'. This requires further investigation, but all Inverdale went on about were HRH's cracked vertebra and concussion from riding mishaps.

Nevertheless, Princess Anne came over as enthusiastic, beadily intelligent, and she spoke in an oddly old-fashioned clipped Cockney voice that reminded me of the late character actress Irene Handl. Princess Anne is also evidently a brilliant mother – Peter and Zara Phillips spoke about her with pride and fondness. Leaving aside commoner Catherine Middleton, Duchess of Cambridge, Zara is the sexiest royal since Catherine Deneuve in *Mayerling*.

Which brings me to Jo Brand. If I were a woman I'd like to be Jo Brand. She is calm, confident, wildly funny and observant. She also evidently loves her crisps. You can appreciate how she'd have been a brilliant psychiatric nurse – a field in which she is fully qualified – and her professional knowledge and experience underpin *Getting On*, a three-part medical series of near-genius, which she wrote and stars in.

I was thinking *Getting On* was as good as *The Thick Of It*, when Joanna Scanlan, who plays dumpy Terri the secretary in that, appeared as Den Flixter, the pushy and horrible ward sister. Then Peter Capaldi materialised, not only in a cameo as a flirty doctor but in the credits as the director.

Capaldi began his career a quarter-of-a-century ago as the nice, gauche, bumbling lad in *Local Hero*. By the time of *The Thick Of It* and the character of Malcolm Tucker, he'd become capable of purple-faced, vein-popping sociopathic fury. Readers, I have made that same journey myself.

Jo Brand, as Nurse Kim, doesn't shove herself forward in *Getting On*, but she is solidly there, exuding a sort of kindly wonderment. As busy-body Sister Den and careworn Dr Pippa Moore (Vicki Pepperdine) fretted about mislaid stool samples and raffle ticket money, and expressed much more concern for politically correct bureaucratic procedures than they ever do over showing some common sense – common humanity – the slow burn of Brand's compassionate glances towards the defenceless patients spoke volumes.

People in the medical world have been assuring me that *Getting On* is painfully accurate, with everyone in hospitals these days being threatened with disciplinary action over nothing, with the elderly being sedated to shut them up, with panics, cover-ups and meaningless regulations and surveys about 'patient satisfaction'.

It was no comical exaggeration in *Getting On* when the ward sister tries to get a harassed doctor to sign a death certificate before a patient has actually died, to fudge the statistics about available beds.

The programme is shot in desaturated colours – dark ice-blue and blood reds – and is black, bleak, brilliant, and wholly to my warped taste. I can't wait for Series Two.

So lucky old me. Here it is. I was up until four in the morning watching every episode of Series Two of *Getting On*, as sent to me on a preview DVD by my old Rules luncheon companion, the producer Geoff Atkinson.

Bleak doesn't *begin* to describe this series about life in a modern NHS hospital. Again, it is lit and shot in such a way, the colours have been drained from the palette. Everything is an uncomfortable wan or Prussian blue. Occasionally, as in Series One, there is a flash of angry red – lipstick or a tulip. Flowers, of course, are quickly disposed of from the hospital ward for 'health and safety' reasons.

Apart from Jo Brand's Nurse Kim, the characters are all such complete monsters. As with *Oz*, I can't decide who is the most thoroughly loathsome, Sister Den or gayer Matron Loftus or Dr Pippa Moore? Lizardy Peter Capaldi, who directed it, appears as a senior consultant who gets the less senior consultants to reapply for their own jobs.

It really is a terrifying tale of how form-filling, statistics and protocols have eradicated sanity and decency. Auschwitz must have been run along these lines. Any jot of spontaneous human feeling – including cracking a joke – is liable to be misconstrued as 'inappropriate'. Patients are in pain and dropping dead in the corridors – but what matters is that the doctors, nurses, consultants and lawyers attend a lengthy tribunal about whether or not an off-the-cuff remark was homophobic.

There's a running gag about a woman travelling up and down from Edinburgh to see her dying mum, but unfortunately visiting times always seem to be over and the staff are inflexible. The series is harrowing and I laughed throughout. It is perfectly observed.

Jo Brand would be good at playing me in the biopic. Like Sarah Bernhardt playing Hamlet – though with a slight streak of panto, like when Barry is Edna. Jo and I look alike for a start. She is sometimes seen in Hereford.

❧

Yay! Ya! Onward to glory! OH YES!!!! Yay! What can that possibly mean or portend? Sadomasochistic Max Mosley in a homemade video clip? The yelp of a badger with its knackers in a trap? A St Trinian's pupil on the touchline during a lacrosse quarter-final? No – simply the way on-the-move Gyles Brandreth typically begins a letter to me, congratulating me about something or commiserating with me about something. India Knight once said 'Yay!' in my hearing, so I had to make an immediate about-turn, hurl myself into the traffic to flag down a taxi, and get a train back to Great Malvern.

You see, Doctor Lewis – he has standards. If ever I see a cocktail referred to as *lethal*, knickers as *frilly* or incompetence prefaced by the word *utter*, I have to close my curtains and take to my bed. I'm on pills. Should I know the writer or journalist concerned, the association is at an end.

Anna said that in a day nursery in Great Malvern she counted seven members of staff standing around observing the children and making notes in silence – nobody was actually *playing* with them, *interacting* with them, behaving *normally*. This is how it is all going: no connection, no kindness.

All these rules and regulations that are there and have come in to insist upon everyone caring and being concerned have in fact filled everyone with mutual suspicion and antagonism, driven them asunder. The best you get is a sugary smile. The mood is that of wary, righteous fury. Tempers are frayed to breaking point by paranoia.

People only relax when they talk to their computers, iPods, iPads, iPhones, Blackberries, Facebook and Twitter devices – where this is a sad illusion of congress.

These Kindle iPad gadgets for books – e-books; books with batteries: it's like on *Tomorrow's World* when boffins used to get excited that food would soon become these little pills. There'd be no need for cookery or meals, they gleefully predicted. I hated that notion. Meals are more than meals. Why do you think Jesus organised such a lot of his activities and philosophy around Kartoffelknodel, Wienerschnitzel, and Pfannkuchen with Preisselbeeren? Well, he would've if it had been on the Nazareth menu. He knew his breads and his wines, did Our Lord. Similarly, I love paper, binding, typefaces, inks, cover designs. Books as *books*. Because books are more than books. They are a way of life.

I suggested to madcap Rachel Johnson that a good marketing wheeze for *The Lady* would be to include handy cut-out-and-keep discount coupons for the Dignitas Clinic. My mother has taken out a subscription for *The Lady*, but that is by-the-by.

✎

Madcap Rachel Johnson told me that she has a farmhouse on Exmoor with only one lavatory. Guests find that they prefer to wait until they get back home before taking a crap, even if they have been staying for a fortnight. You could billet me there six months and I still wouldn't go. My parents had a caravan once and I *wouldn't go* until I got back home.

✎

The world is going mad. It's as bad as Sigmund's Freud's casebook. I've been reading about a child who thinks she's a cat. She mews and licks the carpet. Another pre-school tearaway keeps phoning up the fire brigade, who are duty-bound to turn up, bells clanging, hoses at the ready. Another child, in a documentary I saw, has such an imagination, he is convinced he is married and has a baby called Rocky, 'but I don't change the nappies'. The invented world is complete in every detail. The patient is eight years old. Mind you – I always used to think it weird, like something out of a Peter Cushing movie: dolls that *pissed*.

✎

Sister Wendy Beckett – one of my pin-up girls along with Primrose Shipman, Mrs Mills the piano-player, Bunty James from *How!*, Wincey Willis and spiritualist Doris Stokes – has upgraded from a caravan to a prefab. Give her time, she'll be taking out a lease on the Brighton Royal Pavilion.

✎

I found a note on my desk: 'Betty Marsden' – that's all it said. Had I been talking to my chum Clair Woo, the only other person in Britain who'd know who Betty Marsden was?* I tried calling her but as ever her phone rings for ages and then you finally get the answer machine. I think Woo keeps it on vibrate mode.

৯০

I've never heard stronger South African accents than the ones spoken by the proprietors of The Dewdrop Inn, Lower Broadheath, the Worcestershire village that was Elgar's birthplace – but even so, 'we used to be in Bournemouth' they assured me.

৯০

Nancy Havard Lewis, born in 1902. Apparently she turned a complete blind eye to the adulterous and suicidal shenanigans going on right under her nose in Swansea. She was so tranquil and serene she was almost totally dotty. She did nothing. I never saw

* Betty Marsden (1919–88) was a versatile radio stalwart – in *Round the Horne* she gave voice to 'funny' characters such as Buttercup Gruntfuttock and Celia Molestrangler, etc. She is Terry Scott's irritating and irrepressible wife in *Carry On Camping*. I do like Terry Scott.

Betty died with a glass of gin in her hand while talking to cronies at the Actors' Charitable Trust Home, in Northwood, a London suburb. God, her cronies must have been boring to have had that effect on anybody.

her read a newspaper or open a book. What she did was smoke. She'd puff away watching the smoke and the sunlight make lovely mauve shapes.

She'd sit there, when she came to visit us in Bedwas, not at all bored or blank, and if you sit there long enough doing fuck all, eventually cups of tea, hot food, cigarettes, all life's staples, will be brought to you, literally on a plate. She was like a member of the Royal Family, convinced she'd be taken care of – or like Dame Iris Murdoch, who thought that if you waited on a train platform patiently, a train would come. You didn't need to fret about timetables. Nancy had absolutely mastered this gift of being waited on hand and foot and chauffeured about. The only thing that annoyed my grandmother – who did much of the fetching and the carrying – was that she smoked in bed.

I liked her enormously, because there was a faint glint of mischief in her eye. She knew what game she was playing, but it was played without malice. She said to Anna, 'If he [meaning me] annoys you, polish the top of the stairs by the landing like hell.' She meant so that I'd slip and fatally injure myself. So you see – she'd contemplated murder after all.

A packed day for Great Auntie Nancy was going to see Emily my donkey in her paddock. She appreciated 'the way she comes to you when you call her'. Well, they tend to do that, donkeys and ponies. Nancy had a spaniel face and like a spaniel her eyes were moist and dark at the corners. She was always chuckling softly to herself. I inherited her blue porcelain coffee set, one of her and Den's wedding presents, which in all her days she'd never got around to unwrapping. It was still in the original brown tissue paper.

❧

Crime Wave Corner. More heavy-handed policing. A woman who dropped her cigarette butt in the street has appeared in the Magistrates Court. She has been handed a fixed penalty fine of £80 for 'littering' plus £50 costs. I am tempted to take up smoking so that I can deliberately scatter my cigarette butts in protest at this sheer tyranny.

'Don't know why I get so nervy in church,' one character says to another character in *The Sun Also Rises*. You do feel this in Spain, where the religious tradition is alive and bloody – there's a dark pagan sense – but not, I'm afraid, in the dear old C of E, which is manned by old ladies selling sponge cakes, where what matters most is the cleaning rota, the flower arranging rota, and the Mothers Union needlework exhibitions. The appeal of the C of E is that it is not particularly religious.

I like Hemingway's repetitive rhythms – the deceptive simplicity and clumsiness, like a person struggling to express himself, the newness of the vision. He could be Frankenstein's Creature.

The Groucho Club – it's not the real celebrities that you see (your Clints, your Dustins, your Marlons and your Patrick Mowers); it's the fact that it'll be James Nesbitt or at a pinch Hugh Laurie; and you don't want to go over and say hello in case you are rebuffed and snubbed – as I was by *fucking Howard Jacobson!* – because that would ruin watching television ever again, because when they come on you'd be reminded.

Dawn French and Jennifer Saunders have a dedicated lesbian following. I was surprised to hear this, but I do suppose that in their work men only make appearances when they can be cast as ninnies. Though I am not a lesbian (though I look like a lesbian – I look like my mother; though what she looks like is a little bloke: confusing, isn't it?) I did go and see them in St David's Hall, Cardiff. It was rubbish. I was half a mile away, so Dawn and Jen, who nevertheless are big girls, were dots in the distance. They didn't have a clue how to handle hecklers. It was lazily done

— an over-reliance on catchphrases. You knew they'd be speeding from the building in a limo when you were still in the queue for your coat. The souvenir programmes were ludicrously expensive. To cap it all, afterwards I was taken to a Harvester and frankly I'd rather be in China eating boiled baby.

♋

I wonder if I am related to Jerry Lewis? Or to Shari Lewis? Anyone remember her? Shari had a sock on her hand that she said was a puppet called Lamb Chop. I know I am related to Wyndham Lewis, because he was my father. Another Wyndham Lewis was my great-grandfather. My son Oscar's middle name is Wyndham. He's not Oscar Wyndham Lewis because that would be OWL. So we shoved a Nicholas in there. ONWL.

Whether my great-grandfather was the Vorticist poet and painter Wyndham Lewis is something that, when interviewed by the press, I have allowed to remain a mystery — but of course though in reality my great-grandfather was a butcher in industrial South Wales and had never heard of Ezra Pound or Edith Sitwell, or any of the poet and painter Wyndham Lewis's brainy chums, why in that case was there a signed and numbered subscription copy of *The Apes of God* on the bookshelf? I have it now. Copy number 747, which cost three pounds and three shillings.

So there are two copies in my house. Sir Francis Wheen gave a signed first edition (number 696) to his godson, ONWL, at his Christening. 'Sell it to your father when you want to go travelling.' Since he was six years old, Oscar has wanted me to cash in that damn pledge. Three guineas = three pounds fifteen pee. I can manage that.

I mention all this because I have been watching my cousin Jerry in *The King of Comedy*. He gives a great performance — a clown in repose. Jerry is silent and glum for much of the film — sullen. He's a revelation. Vastly better than the baby prattle of his famous films with Dean Martin. There is immense suppressed anger coming

301

off his character – it's as if this has built up during a lifetime of being laughed at. He lives in an empty glass house. Not much in the way of furnishings. The table is set for one person.

All this signifies his bleakness. In public Jerry has a hard surface niceness and considerable vanity, and yet his walk when he believes himself to be unobserved is really odd and uncoordinated – a jaunty tilt, as if torso and legs have only recently been introduced, or as if he has been untied and has pins-and-needles. What you realise is that here is a man used only to limousines. In the eighteenth century, grandees who moved from place to place by sedan-chair may have been like this.

࿎

My favourite comedies (and comedians) are the ones that aren't funny. Where Jack Nicholson's Joker was high camp and playful – pausing to admire a Francis Bacon portrait in the Gotham Art Gallery (everything else his goons are instructed to destroy); praising and envying Batman's toys (his flying-suits and souped-up cars) – what's funny about Heath Ledger's Joker? Heath Ledger's Joker is disturbingly psychopathic and delirious. Schizoid. Criminally insane. Fucking nuts. Dagenham. Everything about him is twisted, contorted, smeared and giddy – his body, his white clown make-up, his mind and morals. He is a Lord of Misrule. He has a need for chaos. When comedy is like this it is truly subversive – an agent of the devil. Dressed in pink and purple, Jack, meanwhile, was nearer to Caesar Romero.

Heath Ledger – his films have a different meaning now. It is impossible to look at his performances and not think of his death. James Dean, River Phoenix, Marilyn: their work too seems to be a foretelling, and to watch them gives you a sudden ache inside.

࿎

I had an interesting conversation with Martyn Goff, the man who ran the Booker Prize, about Anthony Burgess. Martyn said he once wrote a novel himself, called *Red at the Door*, and Burgess gave it a scathing review. They met at a dinner party soon afterwards – as is always the way. 'Oh, I only read the first thirty pages,' Burgess confessed. 'I'm writing a novel about Russia myself – and I was furious that someone had got in first.' Naturally they became friends. Goff went to Burgess's house and the great man was nursing his arm – his wife Lynne had pushed him down the stairs. Lynne was Welsh – from Bedwellty.

Goff and I agreed that in all the history of the Booker Prize, the biggest injustice was when Burgess failed to win for *Earthly Powers*. Golding's *Rites of Passage* was not only inferior, it was part of a trilogy. Burgess had said, 'Martyn, I'll only attend the ceremony if I've won. I'll be staying at the Savoy. Call me either way by six-thirty. I'm not going to the trouble and expense of hiring a dinner jacket if I've not won.'

Martyn Goff must've so enjoyed talking to me about Anthony Burgess, and been so impressed – *dazzled* – by my biography of Anthony Burgess, that to this day he hasn't regained enough composure or coherence to be able to tell his minions and successors to set about asking me to become a Booker Prize judge. I remain about the only person in the British Isles who has never been approached.

୨୦

Not only have I never judged the Booker, I haven't been on the radio for years, my debut on Sky was cancelled at the last minute because of the tiramisu in Japan, and I have never been invited to contribute jokes to *Have I Got News For You*, even though Ian Hislop was at Magdalen at the same time as I was.

୨୦

Evelyn Waugh, invited to stay by the Betjemans, declined as 'I don't think I like your children.' This is commendably honest. Nobody would dare say that to a parent today, or give that as an excuse for remaining at home. Anna told me that she has to spend a lot of time telling her patients that, when Mummy and Daddy split up, they mustn't blame themselves. It is not their fault. That they are innocent. But perhaps sometimes it is their fault and they are not innocent? Children can be such tiny swine. Adolescents are worse – for years and years I was driven to distraction by our lot, by their ingratitude and manipulation, and dreamt of running away and joining a circus, though that's what Tristan did. I think children give you cancer, with all the rage that gets bottled up. When one day I come home with my prostate bubbling in a jar I'll tell the boys, 'Look! You did that!'

The twisted muscle pain under the ribcage has got worse – as if by means of voodoo or auto-suggestion my enemies are having fun twisting a knife. I yelp out loud with the discomfort. The Deep Heat and the ibuprofen being ineffective, I got Doctor Twelvetrees to prescribe some proper anti-inflammatory pills – diclofenac: a miracle cure. He wanted me to give a sample of piss – but (a) I could only find a pickle jar and (b) I can't piss on demand. So we passed on the piss.

Whenever I got comfortable lying down, the phone would go or somebody would knock on the front door – for instance an old bag selling poppies. Talking of old bags, the doctor's waiting room, when I went for a follow-up appointment, was full of elderly ladies in rain capes and polythene rain-hoods. Harold Shipman would have passed out with joy. Doctor Twelvetrees being in Bechuanaland where it was raining frogs, the stand-in leech, when I was finally summoned, looked about seventeen, impossibly young and thin. There I was, fat and scant of breath and covered with lurid skin sores, like the Emperor Tiberius.

A beautiful autumn day – with a deep orange gorgeousness to the leaves and pumpkins; real pumpkins are in Gilbert's, the fruit and vegetable shop, and pumpkin-shaped candles are in Hawthorn Designs, the gift shop. Pumpkins have only recently started making an appearance here – an American innovation. In Wales at Halloween we made do with wrinkled swedes.

I went to a Bromyard & District Local History Society (founded 1966) coffee morning in the Oak Room at The Falcon. I've never been there before – John and Sylvia's hotel is a warren of ballrooms, parlours, lounge-rooms, three-ale bars and snugs. It was like the panelled chamber where Henchard, Hardy's Casterbridge mayor, would meet his fellow merchants to exchange corn.

I bought cake, marmalade and a strip of raffle tickets, numbers 356–365. I was phoned later to say I'd won a prize – and I never win prizes. I sent Sébastien round to collect the prize hamper, which contained crystallised ginger, pickled beetroot, a bag of seven potatoes, three cooking apples (windfalls), damson jam, marmalade (again), homemade walnut bread, a cake (again), horseradish sauce, a jar of spiced prunes in sherry (subsequently blamed for giving me the shits), and a framed picture made from a collage of coloured grains. There was also a fruit or vegetable that none of us recognised. A mango or yam or spherical courgette or green pumpkin (do they exist?). It baffled science. I hope to God it wasn't one of the Committee's sex aids that had dropped into the hamper by mistake. The Pocket Pleaser? The Rampant Rabbit?

The actual hamper was only for display purposes, Sébastien was told, and they wanted it back. So he put all the bits and pieces in a pink cardboard box that had contained Tropical Fruit Squash. 'Mrs Turner 1 bag in chiller' was written on it – code?

I'd picked up a leaflet earlier on forthcoming attractions – highlights were to include a visit to Webb's Chemical Manure Factory and a gripping talk on 'The Timber-Frame Buildings of North Herefordshire'. If any of my readers are interested in attending, call the Treasurer, Miss Polly Rubbery (01885 483318). I may go to 'Herefordshire Folk Customs and Morris Dancing' purely to heckle and hurl spherical courgettes and green pumpkins.

Back in Cornwall to carry on clearing up from the party, we chanced upon St-Just-in-Roseland, built next to a tidal creek. Morning Eucharist was about to start. There were no more than eleven of us making up the congregation – the last stand of Old England, reciting from the BCP – with nevertheless the combined age of over a thousand.

We could have been suspects in an Agatha Christie mystery, the retired major loudly saying 'Amen', the vicar's wife dashing up the aisle during the final hymn to switch the urn on, the former cathedral organist from Truro pounding away. There was a lady with the Alzheimer's who was worried that she'd lost her coat, which she had on. Outside, knocking at the windows, were giant ferns. The fuchsias and hydrangeas in the crammed graveyard – the slate tombstones teeter on ledges and terraces – have almost a Caribbean richness.

It is already thirty-six years since Norman Wisdom drank a cup of tea with Mrs Phyllis Bullock in her bed-and-breakfast establishment, 'Dolwen', in Kings Acre Road, Hereford. Norman had been appearing in cabaret at the Crystal Rooms. 'He was just Norman all the time. Everything he did was so innocent,' said Mrs Bullock.

Now let's imagine we are Professor Sir A. J. Ayer or Ludwig Wittgenstein and examine that statement for a moment, giving particular consideration to the language, the truth and the logic of it. Were one to say, e.g. 'He was just Hitler all the time. Everything he did was so innocent', would the same meaning pertain? Answer me that.

November

What am I still doing here? It could be worse. This week to the *flohmarkt* in Bad Ischl — which easily translates as the flea market in Bad Ischl. There were racks and racks of mouldy fur coats and old clothes and little leather suitcases in neat stacks. Yes, I was thinking the same. Like a storeroom in a Concentration Camp. As beautiful as Bad Ischl is, there was an overflow facility from Dachau in the neighbourhood. I expected to chance across bundles of hair and gold teeth. Still, none of this is the *place's* fault.

One of life's small pleasures is taking luncheon with elfin Michael Whitehall, the stand-up comedian Jack Whitehall's father or grandfather. Michael is a theatrical agent.*

Unless you are fortunate enough to be in the peer group equivalent of Sir Larry, Sir Ralph or Sir John G. — i.e. a big star for whom lucrative work is always going to be on offer, so all your agent need do is bank his percentage — actors evidently irritate their agents no end. Actors are so needy, so neurotic, so nutty. To keep sane everyone has to preserve a sensible distance from the dopey sods. 'How could anyone possibly want to see Peter Bowles on a *Sunday*?' Michael shrieked rhetorically. Mrs Bowles, possibly?

James Fox once loomed up to Michael in the Gents and wanted to know, 'Will I get top billing?' Anton Rogers materialised in

---

* I urge everyone to read Michael Whitehall's hilarious *Shark Infested Waters: Tales of an Actors' Agent*, Timewell Press, 2007.

Whitehall's honeymoon-suite to lament that, 'To be honest, I need a job. I thought this was going to be a really good year but it's turning out to be a disaster.' Would-be thespian Jeffrey Archer came running in (into the same honeymoon-suite? Surely not . . .) yelping, 'I want to play James Bond and you can get it for me.' David Tomlinson, out of work since *Mary Poppins*, was so exasperated that his calls were not being returned, he hired a room opposite his agent's office in Hanover Street and waved at him frantically through the window.

Michael doesn't think very highly of his calling, either. Agents are 'ill-bred, barely literate low-lifers'. I think that's what gets called *self-deprecation* nowadays, and Michael likes to pretend he's often not on the ball. He didn't want to join Cameron Mackintosh as a co-producer because Cameron 'had the look of a loser about him'. Michael thought he was being really inspired when he sent along Peter Sallis to audition for the role of a twenty-five-year-old French waiter.

I outrank Michael here, I think. My own colossal misjudgement: telling Lee Hall that his idea to write a film script about a boy ballet dancer in County Durham during the Miners' Strike had the stamp of a real non-starter.

He's been a one with the ladies, too, has Michael. He looked after former leading lady Dorothy Lamour, until he decided she'd be 'more comfortable on a zimmer frame than in a sarong'. My older readers will remember the Crosby/Hope *Road* pictures. And though Michael tried to fend off Ingrid Pitt by getting the conversation round to a passion-killer like 'Hitler's seizure of Danzig and the Polish Corridor in 1939', unfortunately Ingrid would have none of it. 'The only corridor she was interested in was the one leading to the bedroom.' Michael also banged the dinner gong with Lynne Frederick, *before* she married Peter Sellers or even David Frost. She was both a nymphomaniac and *incredibly boring*. That's a tough one.

Asked for a few typical tales of actors and their merry ways, Michael will describe seeing Stratford Johns pee in a bush on Wimbledon High Street. We had a good laugh about Leslie Grantham playing to half-empty houses because the audience had confused him with Leslie Crowther, who'd been dead for ten years. On location in Greece, apparently, Hugh Grant 'had a penchant for dirty girls', and Elizabeth Hurley, it transpired, couldn't walk and deliver dialogue at the same time. 'John Hurt doesn't advertise gravy,' Michael told me – a statement worth translating into Swahili as a class exercise in *Learn and Speak Swahili in Forty Days* by K. K. Virmani. He also said that John Le Mesurier was once mistaken for Daphne du Maurier, though I haven't got him to say by whom. Peter Bowles carries a handbag containing his cologne, which is why they won't let him into the Turf Club.

One of the few people Michael is not agreeably waspish about is the *Reach for the Sky* actor Kenneth More. 'Keep Kenny off the sauce,' was the order-of-the-day, which came too late as More, dressed in full costume as Chesterton's Father Brown for a Lew Grade television series, had already blabbed to journalists about his 'controversial new treatment' to activate his bodily fluids in an attempt to impregnate Angela Douglas. He was being required to dunk his knackers in a bowl of ice-cold water 'to try and razz them up. It all sounds unlikely but I'm giving it a try.'

Kenneth More was a generous fellow who'd think nothing of footing the bill for a cast and crew outing to a Berlin brothel. On the whole, however, actors are cheap. Derek Nimmo would charge his laundry to other people's hotel rooms under sundries. Elaine Stritch sub-let her Rolls at weekends (even if this meant she was marooned in Bedfordshire with Bob Monkhouse), and each night when in London would phone every restaurant until she got a complimentary table. At Christmas she gift-wrapped purloined Savoy Hotel towels. When she was filming *Two's Company* with

Sir Sinden, Michael Grade, then the Controller of Programmes for LWT, asked Elaine to return £5,000 worth of clothes to the costume department. The costume department is still waiting.

A particularly sly rumour is about Leslie Phillips, though you've got to give a lot of leeway to a man whose wives keep committing suicide. He turned down a part, sacked his agent, and then accepted the same part, thus avoiding payment of commission. Michael was philosophical, as he'd only have had to 'sit through the bloody first night and buy Leslie dinner afterwards. A blessing in disguise.'

But there's no ill feeling between them. Only the other day Michael and Leslie had lunch, during which, said Michael, 'Leslie talked about himself for two hours and I picked up the bill.' I felt a pang of guilt here. I always talk about myself for four hours, and Michael picks up the bill.

Food is a theme of our chat. Edward Fox is a frighteningly frugal host ('Damn, no wine') and the fruity Harry Andrews would wheel in the breakfast trolley as a pretext for a fumble under the bedclothes ('Good morning! A little surprise for you!').

One time, the gods decided to let useful character actor Moray Watson starve. Moray got lost on his way to a picnic lunch and having sought directions from the village idiot missed the meal. The shops were closed and when he came back to the house empty-handed tea had been cleared away and the butler was laying up for dinner – which turned out to be a diet-conscious sprig of broccoli and 'a tiny jelly with a dab of cream on it'. On his way whimpering to bed, the host warned Moray not to leave his room because of the security alarms – which, unless he felt like tackling a hundredweight of Old Bill, put paid to his secret plan to raid the kitchen for chocolate cake.

As for Michael's own background – you can see where Jack Whitehall is getting the comedy inspiration from. Michael's pipe-smoking grandfather was a transvestite who'd stroll in the garden 'in a large feathered felt hat, a floral print dress and high heels'. Another relative died of a 'floating kidney' – probably not funny, but it sounds funny. Yet another had been in Burma during the war and wouldn't let anything Japanese in the house, 'which put him at a considerable disadvantage when it came to electrical goods'. An uncle was a retired general, who as a functionary at Court had to have a pair of highly polished leather boots made to go with his ceremonial uniform. 'So what are you up to at the moment, love? Panto?' asked the cobbler innocently.

✺

A strange buzzing and squeaking noise at The Thorn. So Barman Adam dismantled the fire alarms and the smoke alarms. Tattoo Dan searched the loft. It was Shag Harris's spare hearing aid, which he'd lost when it fell in a pint pot earlier in the week.

How did Shag Harris get his name? This might have been a classic Rudyard Kipling *Just So* fable. The innocent explanation could be that he was a tobacconist, but I don't think so. When everyone said in stage whispers, 'It's Shag Harris. Shag Harris is in . . .' I turned around and there was this huge hairy heavy groaning party staggering to the three-ale bar. He then staggered and groaned his way back to a settle. He probably then lit a clay pipe, patted his pug. Shag Harris, or anyway his ancestors, were drawn by Hogarth.

✺

Firemen went to tackle a chimney fire at Didley and another in Kington, but both were out.

✺

I was bidden to St Albans Abbey to be anointed a Doctor of Letters (Hon DLitt*). This is getting to be a regular gig. Last year I was bidden to St Albans Abbey to be anointed a Doctor of Philosophy (PhD) – though I had to earn that one by writing a

---

* See Appendix: The Last Man of Letters.

thesis called 'The Art and Science of Biography'. But it was a swift upgrade nevertheless. Perhaps next year I'll be back in St Albans Abbey for my Coronation and I can hobble about in a crown like Larry Olivier as Richard III and then start executing my enemies – King Roger the Bad.

The afternoon was a bit like what the Royal Family must experience every hour of their lives – chauffeur-driven cars, equerries, one's path smoothed. There was no waiting around with plebs. Tea was served with the Faculty and St Albans worthies in the Town Hall. Then I was taken to a vestry for my robes. There was a lot of courtesy and nice fuss. Anna, Sébastien and Anna's parents had their own suite and train. Tristan couldn't come because of the circus, Oscar was in Falmouth, and my mother was on a minibus trip to Switzerland. She sent me a card saying 'Your father would be very proud.'

It was a *Star Wars* moment when I trooped down the aisle with the fanfares and organ going full blast. I expected Princess Leia to be there with Obi Kenobi ready to hand me and my droids a medal for having saved the Federation. What an array of multicoloured academic gowns. I was in Episcopal purple and resembled a gay New Hampshire bishop. One of the deans next to me was a DSc from Manchester Metropolitan. His gown was designed by Danny la Rue – I mean it had to be. There were pink feathers and bits of fur with sequins.

Having done my part – I had to address the assembly and my message basically was: everything you have been taught up until now you can forget – I sat there in my costume while hundreds of youngsters came across the dais to shake the hand of the Vice Chancellor and collect their scroll. I'm sure some of them came up twice. They look so alike, young people. Now and again there was a paraplegic in a motorised wheelchair, who'd get extra applause for his manoeuvring skills. Imagine that – if I finally met my death by being mown down by a paraplegic in a motorised wheelchair on the day of my Coronation. There were deaf graduates who did the *Vision On* stuff with an interpreter. Rastafarians. The blind. The cool. The cocky. My favourites were the fat girls who giggled and trotted on stage sideways, as if that made them invisible.

❧

Our hotel, St. Michael's Manor, Fishpool Street, St. Albans, was like a setting for a ghost story. A summer house next to a lake. Mist and complete stillness.

❧

Ann Widdecombe takes Size 2 shoes. That's not feet – that's trotters.

❧

Fat Balls. As God is my judge there is a sign outside the pet shop saying Fat Balls. I bought any number because seeing the sign always makes me laugh. I've dangled them about the garden, waiting for the robins to return from migration, if that is where they've been.

❧

When things started kicking off at The Princess Anne – recently refurbished by an old chap with long blond hair – Zany Antony went out and shut the gate of The Thorn and stood guard. I think he thought he was Sir Stanley Baker ready to repel the invading Zulu at Rorke's Drift. The effect was more Charles Hawtrey as Private Widdle on sentry duty up the Khyber Pass.

❧

Anna was told by Bob the Vicar that there is only one person in the whole of the Bromyard township who has taken exception to a little book I wrote called *Seasonal Suicide Notes*, full as it is with off-colour language and general exaggerated silliness. But who is this blue-nosed wowzer? *Who* is it? Who can it *possibly be*? Who is the total arsehole with no sense of humour that now merits dog shit through the letterbox? I gaze at everyone with suspicion – I find I can't trust or like anyone any more, in case they are *the one*. I am paranoid. If I were King Roger the Bad I would have to have the entire population of the Bromyard township killed immediately in ingenious medieval ways.

✃

What are we to make of *Angels in America*? I liked the American parts — the soap-operatic segments dealing with death and personal relationship disasters; the theme of bereavement or incipient bereavement; how it is when people leave one another. And in theory I ought to love the hallucinatory elements, the dream sequences and theatricality. But Dame Emma Thompson's angel was so declamatory — crashing through the ceiling and sounding off — that I wasn't moved. In fact I was bored.

Al Pacino was as ever a furious little troll, like the character he plays in *Dick Tracy*. Spiteful and snarling and foaming at the mouth in scene after scene after scene. He could teach even Brian Blessed a thing or two.

It's a homosexual *Wizard of Oz* (if that's not too tautologous) — *Oz* for the Aids generation.

✃

Though my family were butchers, they had a small domestic staff — maids-of-all-work, a wet nurse. Dolly the wet nurse lingered on into my childhood. She lived in a lean-to next to the slaughterhouse. It was so damp, the wallpaper was kept on the wall with drawing pins. The floor glistened and moved with glossy black beetles, like inlaid marbles. I was there a lot. Dolly's husband Mike sat in the corner, by the window. Outside the window was a heap of coal, which came up to the sill. There was also an iron mangle, into which I used to feed worms to give them a good squash. Mike was the kind of man who wore his hat indoors and he used to kill litters of kittens. I saw him once crouched over a bucket, knocking kittens on the head with his stick and plunging them into the water. He was completely absorbed. It was done so tenderly.

314

What a good thing he did this – Dolly's hovel was overrun with cats. They were on the table, under the table, in the beds. There was also an obese sausage dog called Johnny. Dolly only had an outside toilet. When she was installed taking a crap, I used to throw stones at the door. Her reaction was to start humming, then singing. As the stones rained down it was as if a coloratura soprano from La Scala Milan was locked in there, Montserrat Caballé or Birgit Nilsson, shrieking and complaining. She died during my first term at St Andrews and home for the Christmas holidays I went to her funeral. Thirty years on, I feel sad for her for the first time.

She was buried with Mike – and when they opened up the grave in St Barrwg's churchyard, two coffins were discovered. Everyone had forgotten that Mike had been married once before. It was said that on her own wedding night, Dolly was so petrified about what was meant to ensue, she sat rigid in the kitchen chair and refused point blank to go to bed. There weren't any children. She idolised my Great Auntie Nora, her particular charge or ward, who'd emigrated to New Zealand.* She'd parcel up old newspapers and post them off to Wellington. On Mondays I'd take round our *Observer* and *Sunday Times*, which were already a bit clipped and shredded because my parents loved collecting the coupons for discount sherry wine and Terence Conran salad bowls.

* Nora never took the trouble to be pleasant, indeed the opposite. When the modern Petronius, Duncan Fallowell, was at large in New Zealand, researching his masterpiece about the benighted place that in an early draft I joked was surely called *Me and Maoris' Cocks*, but which was eventually published as *Going As Far As I Can*, he asked old Nora if he could pay her a visit. 'I'd rather you didn't,' she said, slamming the phone down. Perhaps she was fully clued up on Duncan Fallowell? *The Devil travels fast*, as they say in Transylvania. This is probably unlikely – as when Meem, i.e. Little Auntie Mary from Usk, called in on Nora once, unannounced, she didn't even get offered a glass of water from the tap – and Usk to New Zealand is some distance.

The irony here is that Nora Evelyn, born in 1913, my grandfather's youngest sister – she was the youngest of *thirteen* – was a nasty little spoilt ratbag, with a mouth permanently turned down in disapproval. My grandfather said she strongly resembled Micky Dolenz from The Monkees, the only reference to popular culture he ever made in my hearing. Nora made State Visits to Bedwas now and then. Her husband, Uncle Jack, was a tractor salesman who'd had his knackers messed about with in a Japanese POW camp, presumably by the Japanese. I saw him once examining my grandmother's silver, with a magnifying glass and a little booklet of hallmarks. I wonder if any of the spoons, coffee pots, sugar bowls and rose bowls went missing afterwards, eh? It was a cheeky thing for him to be caught doing. Among The Lewis Papers is Nora's School Certificate from 1926, attesting that at Maesycwmmer Secondary School she 'gained successes' in Hygiene, Elementary Physics, and Needlework. Just the thing if you wanted to polish a Van De Graaf Generator and sew a little cosy for it. Perhaps there were openings in that line in New Zealand.

I never knew Dolly to get in a car, go on a bus, or ever leave her grace-and-favour lean-to. She hobbled about on sticks and looked like a kindly witch in a fairy story. You don't get proper little old women like this any longer, bent double wearing shawls and with hastily combed unstyled straight white hair. Today they all have their hips done, their cataracts done, they go to Jazzacise Class and Pilates. They wear pink-glitter lip gloss. They make sponsored jumps from helicopters in aid of Help For Heroes. They put on a helmet for the charity bike rides. They have the benefit of disabled toilets, wheelchair access and hearing loops. They don't any longer even go in for hairy warts.

Dolly had a sister in Scotland, whom I called Big Auntie Mary because I already had a Little Auntie Mary, known as Meem, who had a withered arm and lived in Usk selling grass seed to rugby clubs. We thought Big Auntie Mary's Scottish accent highly comical.

At some point Ada the Milk came to live with old Dolly – after Mike's death I surmise. Ada the Milk was the warden of the OAP Hall in St Mary Street, where the jumble sales were held. The lean-to was the dropping-off point for jumble, so the place was piled high with discarded woollens and bric-a-brac. Mike's job, I now remember, was to light the boiler in the slaughterhouse every Monday, when they boiled the pigs to scrape the bristles off. He'd been a quarryman at Trehir in his prime, at the far end of Pandy Road, nearly in Llanbradach. He was as hard as iron. I never heard him speak a word, or even grunt. It was not a peaceable silence. Gaunt and sinister, Mike emanated pure dark anger.

৯

Nannies in literature and films: *Agnes Gray*, *Jane Eyre*, *The Turn of the Screw*, others. They are generally ill-treated. Lonely and impoverished girls in isolated haunted houses – with an undercurrent of sexual tension in their plight (the master always has his eye on them); she's looking after these children yet she's not their mother (invariably she's younger than their mother) . . . The Sherlock Holmes story, 'The Copper Beeches', is particularly sinister. The shuttered room; the mysterious prisoner; the house guarded by wild dogs. Miss Hunter has to have her hair cut off and wears an electric-blue dress – she has to impersonate somebody. Why? 'Oh, Mr Holmes, I've never been so frightened!' On the other hand, there's the nanny-as-murderess theme. The very person to whom you entrust your children sets about their deliberate destruction. Bette Davis, my auntie, with her dangerous power, was cast in such a role innumerable times. *The Hand That Rocks The Cradle* . . .

❧

A car collided with an electricity pole on the B4349 at Clehonger. 'There were no reports of any injuries.'

❧

A man hit by a lorry in Edgar Street on Tuesday 'made a full recovery'.

❧

We are meant to find Cook and Moore's *The Hound of the Baskervilles* objectionably bad, but I can't help deriving pleasure from it. The cast – the art direction – the crumbling Baskerville Hall, where the bedrooms are awash with brown water, such is the damp . . . Kenneth Williams in his wig and straw boater, Irene Handl and Max Wall as the housekeepers . . . Milligan appears briefly as a comic policeman. What more could one want?

Terry-Thomas, in a sleek top hat and a black frock coat, enunciates beautifully as Doctor Mortimer. He looks good in those clothes, does Terry-Thomas. He had the Parkinson's, but there's no sign of dribbling or trembling. Hugh Griffith snarls and is goggle-eyed – a drunken lunatic, which is what he was in real life. He used to light his matches on the arse of his Oscar statuette. Peter Cook is poor, as always. He couldn't act for toffee. But Dudley's Welsh Mrs Watson makes me laugh. There's a particularly silly scene with Roy Kinnear, out on the moors

318

and flashing signals with his torch. It is a music hall of a movie, as if made in the Old Bedford, Camden Town, shortly before demolition.

Absolutely everyone who was in the film is dead.

❧

'I have been to Wales. It is a dreary country – even worse than England,' said Quentin Crisp. As only Welsh people like me are allowed to be anti-Welsh, I'd have knocked his block off if I'd met him, the grisly old nancy.

❧

I wish I could like Chaplin more. I *admire* him, but I don't like him much. Perhaps it works if you think of him as a ballet dancer, which was W. C. Fields's interpretation. The way he handles the flower given to him by the blind girl; the scenes of farewell – these are done as a stylised dance. Then of course there are the obviously choreographed set-pieces of the boxing ring scene – where the Tramp lashes out (he is not timid, not a coward).

I do wonder who or what The Tramp was *before*? His background – or (dread word!) his back-story? Tristan was in that walking stick and umbrella shop in High Holborn recently, and bendy canes such as the one Chaplin was always twirling and doing the comical business with don't come cheap. (I was delighted to know they are still on sale.)

For clearly he is a gent who has fallen on hard times – who is familiar with life's graces, like Newman Noggs in *Nicholas Nickleby*. There's that touching bit in *Nicholas Nickleby* when Newman recommends an inn to Nicholas in some distant town and he says, 'You may refer to me as *Mr* Noggs there.' Another person the Tramp may have been – Sir Andrew Aguecheek, with his heartbreaking line, 'I was adored once, too.'

He's fastidious and girlish is Chaplin. Sharp little teeth. Dapper, a dandy. I've seen old newsreel footage of him arriving at the Franz-Josef Hauptbahnhof in Vienna. He is mobbed by the crowds – really quite a frightening flood of people, who move like an immense shoal of fish or flock of birds. The police try to beat a path to his car. The next time the locals reacted like that when a visitor turned up it was Adolf Hitler. Perhaps they thought it was Chaplin again? History could have turned out so differently.

If there's one thing that went out of fashion and has not come back it is sentimentality. Flared trousers and white vinyl boots have come back. Mary Quant mascara has come back. The Bay City Rollers may one day come back. But sentimentality, never. Chaplin suffers because of this. *City Lights* comes over as repugnant, mawkish, manipulative.

I still don't understand the end. Does the blind flower girl – who is now the ex-blind flower girl – look pleased to see the Tramp or does she reject him? I can't decide whether Chaplin's face is crumpled with joy or with horror. As I understood it, they shot the scene over and over for several years to get it perfect. So why am I in a pickle? Thick or which?

❧

It is not the fact that they are *silent* that makes old silent movies seem as if they belong to another world – a world that is very much not ours – and actually the silence is beautiful and resonant. They are other-worldly because of the quality of the black-and-white photography, the pearly monochrome, the silver shimmer.

❧

Brendan Fraser has always been cast as the caveman, the Mountie, the jungle boy, the dufus – innocent and sweet. Untouched. Unfingermarked. So he is ideal as the equivalent of the Creature in *Gods and Monsters*. James Whale was a fascinating figure – who'd have thought he grew up in Kidderminster?* What with Kidderminster and his memory of the trenches of the First World War, no wonder his gothic horror visions were awakened. But

* Nobody will think that, because he didn't. Whale was born in 1889 at 41 Brewery Street, Dudley.

what's good about his horror movies and also about this movie is that really they are essays on loneliness and the search for friendship. I saw a photograph of Brendan Fraser recently. Fat and bald. A tragedy.

✺

Who'd you rather do, Shami Chakrabarti or Camila Batmanghelidjh? Crazy names! Crazy costumes! Camila Batmanghelidjh wears her brightly coloured knickers on her head. She's always full-on. I'm trying to work out why I feel such antipathy towards Shami Chakrabarti. Is it the *earnestness*? Despite the marshmallow face, like that of an angel child, there's a lack of self-doubt that is very off-putting. Never pauses when she's in full flow, to see or gauge what her interlocutor might be thinking or meaning. Her eyes are hard. I need a bit of endearing brittleness from people.

✺

My spell-check tried to change Hermione, as in Hermione Lee, to Hormones. You've got to laugh. She's another paid-up drear.*

✺

W. C. Fields and Mae West had one thing in common – a yearning to be delinquent. W. C. had a love of drink and Mae had a love of sex. Of course the Hays Code or the Breen Code or the Catholic League of Decency and which-what squashed any of *that* out of their movies, but Fields lived on in Les Dawson and Johnny Vegas and Mae West may yet pop out in Ruth Jones, unless Ruth goes soft.

In *My Little Chickadee*, the two great comics are in dreamy realms of their own. Mae is half in an erotic trance and Fields gets into bed with a goat. Though he slurs and seems to throw away or swallow his lines, he was powerfully attentive to language, with a unique rueful quality. I thought Maureen Lipman was putting in an appearance, but then I thought that's impossible. The Widow Rosenthal isn't that old. It was Margaret Hamilton.

* There goes Doctor Lewis's Honorary Fellowship at Wolfson, where Hermione Lee CBE, FBA, FRSL (*of course*) is President.

321

The Man on the Flying Trapeze has nothing to do with trapezes or with the circus. What Fields means to refer to is a man who is coping, who is just about at the end of his tether – who has to balance his life and existence alongside or amid a monster of a wife, a shiftless brother-in-law, a gorgon of a mother-in-law, a nasty boss, and so forth. He is bullied and harried by the police, by *everybody*.

In this film, where Fields plays it straight (he is not the Great McGonigle huckster figure but an ordinary man), the everyday monotony, the grinding routine and endless sense of responsibility he has to endure, very slowly slides out of control. For example, he has car problems and receives a sheaf of police dockets. Burglars get drunk in his cellar, so he joins in. There is a funeral sequence with mismatched wreaths. I watched this film with my jaw dropping at the recognition. Like Flaubert said of Madame Bovary, W. C Fields, *c'est moi*.

❧

I know less than fuck fuck-all about birds. I saw a robin (*Erithacus rubecula*) in the back garden. Do they go somewhere else during the summer? Somewhere nice, like Eastbourne? Fiji? Cromer? I'm only aware of them when it turns colder. Or perhaps it's that robins get left behind, and all the other birds fly south for the winter, so that's why they start to stand out? A *child* would know these things. I hang out my fat balls for them anyway.

This is noble of me, because I don't like birds. They have nasty reptilian eyes. You feel they could turn on us, if they felt like it. This is the subject of Hitchcock's *The Birds*, but Daphne du Maurier's original story is far more terrifying – the hawks and buzzards chewing at the farmhouse door, the gulls so thick on the foreshore that the sea looks white. Someone ought to re-make *The Birds* and set it in Cornwall, where it is meant to take place.

And if some go-ahead producer does re-make *The Birds* and gives it a happy ending, I will find out where they live and pay a little visit with my bedpan. ('Oh la, la, *la*, Monsieur le Docteur de Gallois, il a vraiment frappé le metteur en scene avec son bassin!')

ക

My current bedside book, *Learn and Speak Swahili in Forty Days* by K. K. Virmani (1989), is well worth a dip, as it tells you how to translate such absolute essentials as:

The king's wisdom has become weak.

The snake will pass the veranda.

The search for new shoes is over.

That house has not yet fallen down.

The doctor was late, the child had already died.

They will be drinking tea when we will enter the room with the dog.

The man whom we met yesterday has left taking away my cap.

John Hurt does not advertise gravy.

If you came out with that little lot, one sentence after another, the locals would think you were reciting poetry, perhaps something by Marianne Moore or Michael Horovitz, though not Geoffrey Hill because it makes sense. There's a lot in the book to do with ordering the servants about, growing things, legal disputes, the formalities of hello and goodbye. Hunting, gathering, cooking, constructing.

Without too much effort, however, K. K. Virmani could enterprisingly edit his text – getting rid of the Swahili part – and re-publish it as *Learn To Be A Ventriloquist in Forty Days*. I for one would laugh like hell to hear all those startling and surreal statements, about caps and kings, snakes and dead kiddies, issuing forth from a spooky little dummy. Such an act would go down an absolute storm at the Edinburgh Festival.

◊

I never warmed to Harold Pinter, with whom I once shared the lift at the National Theatre. Though in the end not even he could frighten away oesophagus cancer, which also killed John Thaw and my cousin John Walford Lewis. All that growling menace was meant to be in aid of trendy leftie liberalism and enlightenment, yet he was never less than dictatorial and sinister, in person and on the page. He was wholly convincing at being a torturer or despot.

I've been looking at his adaptation of Elizabeth Bowen's *Heat of the Day*. The spy, played by Michael Gambon, is watchful, taciturn, threatening, powerful, dark – a perfect Pinter character. If you'd given Pinter Dougie Byng's ballads to adapt, or Odd Ode man Cyril Fletcher's book on patios, he'd have injected menace.

In interviews I always thought Pinter inarticulate, as he paused and searched for words – and then he'd come out with utter banalities about American oppression and totalitarianism. His defenders argue that his stop-start guttural style had to do with a desire to be absolutely precise – but the effect (on me) was of portentousness and woolliness.

◊

Crime Wave Corner. Hereford Crown Court had to hear about how Paul Oseman had concealed drugs 'between his buttocks'. Judge Plunkett urged the defendant to kick the heroin habit and 'stay clean'. Well, yes, who wants to examine someone's sweaty arse, for drugs or indeed anything else? It's not what all those years in law school and doing the Latin and working your way up to becoming a judge was *for*, I agree. Definitely.

◊

My Anthony Burgess book, the very best thing I ever did, where I devised a form that represented its content – bombastic, grandiose, fol-de-rol – was a total disaster, critically and commercially. It was my Tati's *Playtime*, my Welles's *Touch of Evil*. It has its passionate admirers (God bless you, Kieran G., Duncan F., Jeremy L., Francis W., Sir Peregrine W., Lynn B. and Christopher S.!), but for the majority of (twatty) reviewers, who expect a biography to be unimaginatively representational and chronologically conventional, Doctor Lewis had given birth to a Mongol baby, which he should have hidden in an attic in Trethomas. Furthermore, he would be well advised *not to fuck again*. I knew how Nigel Hawthorne felt when his Lear was hammered and he vowed never to act again. Nor did he.

The proof copy was only in existence a day or so when I received a letter from someone calling himself Vladimir Dixon (a hoax surely as Vladimir Dixon is one of the spoof names in Samuel Beckett's volume about Joyce*), who said to quote Burgess as saying that his translator 'was in the Hitler Youth' was libellous. Well, maybe it was – but that's what Burgess had told me. In fact, Georges Belmont (d. 2008) was in Vichy – so he was a collaborator at least. Next, an old bag whom I said wasn't Burgess's mistress complained that she wasn't Burgess's mistress – which was my point surely? But she didn't like being mentioned in the same passage that mentioned the word 'mistresses'. Particularly irritating was that the bag in question – let's call her Lady Catbrain – was getting her daughter to write the silly letters and inflame the non-issue. Then the KGB/ Kafka-esque-sounding BBC Litigation & Branding Department (again a spoof outfit surely to Christ) said that they'd been informed (by whom?) that I'd quoted three or four words from

* Vladimir Dixon, who purported to be a minor poet of Russian verse, wrote the 'Letter of Protest' in Beckett's book, *Our Exagmination Round His Factification for Incamination of Work in Progress* (1929). There's a catchy title. Dixon is generally assumed to have been James Joyce himself, writing under a pseudonym.

Burgess's letters in 1961 to a producer of *Woman's Hour*. Did I have copyright clearance?

As all this happened at once – *during the same morning!* – I am convinced that one of my enemies was behind it, the same one no doubt who was sending those voodoo messages to my innards, creating the gastritis. Nothing was heard further, in fact. It was malice disguised as a mad practical joke. Such is my reputation, my publishers even wanted to believe I was behind it myself. I did not disabuse them of this possibility, but it may be yet another reason why Faber barred me from their parties.

My theory of biography – or anyway, the way I crafted my biographies: I came across a passage the other day by chance that describes perfectly what I have always tried to do. It's from Michael Crichton's *Jurassic Park*, of all odd or unlikely texts:

> . . . straight linearity, which we have come to take for granted in everything from physics to fiction, simply does not exist. Linearity is an artificial way of viewing the world. Real life isn't a series of interconnected events occurring one after another like beads strung on a necklace. Life is actually a series of encounters in which one event may change those that follow in a wholly unpredictable, even devastating way . . . That's a deep truth about the structure of our universe. But, for some reason, we insist on behaving as if it were not true.

We were in the cafeteria of B & Q in Kidderminster. A large greasy bluebottle crawled out of the spout of the milk flask. Horrible as this was in itself, it caught me at an off moment – and though I'm not squeamish as a rule (I was brought up in a slaughterhouse), it symbolised the horror of life, all of the evils of life.

Ten years ago. Dog shit and dead leaves. The damp darkness lasted all day. Tristan got the Midland Red to Worcester. He was the only passenger. A forlorn sight, this empty bus pulling past the house in the oily rain. The phone rang. My mother said they were coming home from France early as 'your father's rough'. It was hard to get any details out of her – she obviously didn't want to be overheard. 'I've never seen your father so ill' – 'What's the matter?' – 'His bottom end . . .' The bum cancer had begun. It transpired that for months he'd been shitting bloody mucus, had chronic diarrhoea, and this had got worse and worse until he was in continuous pain and permanently on the bog. The picture worsened. Weight loss, dehydration, diabetes, general enfeeblement. My parents went through a period of hoping it was all only irritable bowel syndrome or ulcerative colitis, or something similarly disagreeable but not life-threatening. Polyp was a word we heard a lot. But it was a tumour that had already begun to spread, beyond the bowel wall and into the liver. My father knew the truth, but didn't want to face it – and who can blame him. He had little over a year left.

It is already a whole year since former TV-am weather presenter Wincey Willis was spotted among the volunteers wrapping 'shoe boxes packed with goodies', which were then sent to children in the Ukraine. 'I did it for the first time last year and just got hooked completely,' said Wincey, who had quite possibly changed the subject and was being unnecessary.

December

What am I still doing here? It's a (please enunciate the next-but-one word with the rising pitch of Kenneth Williams at his most strident) complete *disgrace*. The party's over. Everyone has gone. The glasses are dirty. It's like staring into the abyss – though the abyss can be quite nice. I don't mind an abyss. I went to Argos for a bathroom light fitting. Talk about an abyss. Tattoo Dan said he saw me, though I didn't see him – this was a talking point at The Thorn. People sent Tweets and Twits and Twats about it.

We live such uneventful lives here in the Herefordshire Balkans, it is not difficult to stand out, even to become famous. Because Mary Kustle received her BA degree scroll from Princess Anne in person, she was asked to switch on the Bromyard Christmas Lights. The Bromyard and District Local History Society printed a special pamphlet when Mrs Docklow from Acton Beauchamp said she'd occupied the next toilet cubicle to Ursula Vaughan Williams at the Proms.

&

I suppose at this time of year public figures are meant to wish for World Peace or an End to Poverty. Not me. If I were a public figure I'd still prefer a large box of crystallised fruit.

Christmas comes around so quickly, I'd like it to take place only once every five or ten years. Because the novelty has quite worn off. Here in Bromyard, once they've taken the Christmas lights down, five minutes later – or so it seems to me – they are putting the Christmas lights up again. I'm always being scared to death by some chap with a screwdriver sailing past my window on a crane. Between him and the window cleaner I am convinced I am being persecuted.

Saying that, I love Christmas Dinner, so much so that in July when I cooked a turkey we got out the crackers, found some Christmas serviettes, and put on a CD of Christmas carols. Tristan came home for the weekend, so it was an appropriate topsy-turvy meal for a clown.

∾

I remember seeing Sam Prescott, the father of Fatty Prescott, in the cancer ward. I loved old Sam, the Worshipful Master at his Masonic Lodge and Mine Host of the Fwrrwm Ishta, where I first learned to drink. I came top of *that* class. Sam had gone in for a duodenal ulcer and the scan revealed a tumour on his kidney. He went into a diabetic coma and died. The hospital ward was an eye-opener – and I'm getting to the stage in life where soon they'll be moving up to make room for me.

They were neither geriatrics nor urgent surgical cases, the old men on Sam's ward. Just old men from the Rhymney Valley going bad inside. There was a chap called Trev who kept wandering off to fetch (he said) his keys. He had to get back to his new bungalow. Bonkers. The curtains were pulled around a bed for another man to do a shit – a commode-cum-wheelchair was brought by the nurse. A doctor was taking a blood sample from someone's neck. There wasn't much chatter – there weren't many visitors. What I took to be amusing cardboard sculptures of snails were receptacles to pee into. The only colour in the place came from the bottles of orange squash. A nurse rang a school playground bell and out we went – those of us who didn't have to stay behind. For ever.

Sam didn't last the week. For the funeral, there we all were in the bible-black suits. Because Sam had served in the Hitler War, the British Legion standard was paraded up the aisle behind the coffin by a chap in full paramilitary gear (gauntlets, a beret, a thick belt); he actually goose-stepped. The Reverend Warren's lugubrious manner was perfect for a funeral; it didn't matter if he made people depressed and tearful – it's at weddings and christenings where you had to keep a watch on him. He used to correspond with Gyles Brandreth about Scrabble.

The congregation was full of what Kingsley Amis would call the Old Devils. Doug Thomas, who'd taught me to spell, Teifion Thomas, who was the Deputy Head when I was a Mixed Infant. Teifion used to pound away at the piano when we had a school play, and nobody knew whether it was the National Anthem or 'Send in the Clowns'.

At Thornhill Crematorium, I was told about another old teacher of ours, from Bassaleg Comprehensive, Erwyn Spurling, who'd left the profession to go into the dry-cleaning business – and who ended up the defendant in a VAT fraud trial. Apparently, when he was in the dock he shit himself. 'Excuse me, my lord,' said Spurling's brief, keeping calm and certainly earning his fee on this occasion, 'but my client has shit himself. May I ask for a fifteen-minute recess?'

My father, who survived Sam by eleven years, has now been dead himself for seven years. I've been back to Wales hardly at all. It is too much of a surreal experience. The effects of age are speeded up, like a cartoon. Robust farmers were hobbling and wizened and will now be dead. People's mothers are hairy old ladies. Or dead. Spotty youths who went on to become handsome young men are now paunchy and bald and boring. The lissom little girls are harassed mothers with stretch marks. The wealthy go bankrupt – one is on the run in Portugal. Smallholders are millionaires, having sold their land to the M4 motorway developers.

When we did go back, we made a detour to Porthcawl, a place neither for the quick nor the dead. Peter Sellers stayed here with Kenneth

Griffith, when they were shooting *Only Two Can Play*. I wonder which hotel? The guest houses are gruesome now – chips with everything. What a rip-off, the Sunday lunch trade. You have to buy your drinks separately in the bar and fetch them yourself. We even had to locate and clean up the highchair. You can tell by that how long ago this was, my lot being (physically) grown up long since.

The Coney Beach funfair is so forlorn, I almost loved it. The adjacent steelworks, oil refinery and chemical factories ensure that an acid rain steadily falls. The beach was covered with tarmac and the sea a greyish scum. There was no salty sea smell – no birds. The seagulls have migrated inland, to find ploughed fields or to dive on toddlers or discarded burgers in shopping centres. Here the shops were selling clompy brown shoes, shapeless suits for old men or science teachers, fawn pullovers, Fair Isle-effect cardigans, and no doubt, if you asked, incontinence pads. There was an after-the-end-of-the-world look about the brownish-yellow stringy grass. Roads everywhere. Roads, roads, roads.

❧

We drove to an inn at the end of the world – beyond Ebbw Vale, beyond Tredegar. The warehouses, factories, broken viaducts and abandoned railway lines soon thinned out. We went over cattle-grids and past rocks that looked like tusks, which pushed through the bracken and the bogs. You expect there to be wolves – werewolves.

The road gave out and it was a gravel track. There was a disused quarry and a sheer drop. Though gored and scooped, the quarry looked like nature now, a black hill under a monochrome sky. Suddenly, along the skyline, kicking up dust, came a few dozen wild ponies. They were being rounded up for sale in Brecon – where they'd be sold off for dog meat as no one wants them for pets. They raced past, accompanied by two riders wearing caps, not helmets. Then we found a little pub, spick and span like a front-room. A piano. A green sofa.

Years later, when I was in Newbridge making a horror film with Faye Dunaway, I found my way to this place again. I even found my name in the guest-book. But it still seemed like an hallucination. If I told you what the spot is called and how to get there the magic will be obliterated.

✑

From my parents' house you could see Flat Holm, the island out in the Bristol Channel. It is where cholera victims were isolated. Not even Ingmar Bergman, the proud owner of a private island in the Baltic, could have dreamt up a bleaker place.

✑

The first person on Santa's knee at a Children's Magic Show at the Northholme Community Centre in Hereford was Beryl Brown, aged thirty-eight. You probably can't sit on Santa's knee if you are any younger than thirty-eight, because of the child protection laws. Every single adult in the British Isles is a suspected paedophile these days – so well done those ladies (average age, seventy-five) on the flower-arranging rota at Gloucester Cathedral, who refused to undergo Criminal Records Bureau Checks, as insisted upon by the ridiculous Dean and Chapter, because the flower-arrangers 'shared a lavatory with choirboys'.

As a highly indignant Mrs Corley told the press, 'What makes this all the more absurd is that the choirboys are at school when we are working in the cathedral arranging the flowers, so even if we did pose a threat we would never see them.'

Not only that, a Health and Safety Assessment was insisted upon, and the good ladies were told they had to use special gloves when handling the secateurs. 'Have you ever tried to arrange flowers while wearing gloves?' asked doughty mother of four and grandmother of eleven, Mrs Hayter. I've an idea – why don't these splendid ladies chase the Dean and his ridiculous Chapter up and down the aisle with pairs of secateurs, snipping at their bollocks, if they've got any? *That'll learn 'em.*

I can promise you one thing – the Health and Safety authorities would have put a stop to the Crucifixion. All those nasty *thorns*.

❧

We've had a bit of similar nonsense closer to home. Anna's parents take old folks from the congregation of their church back and forth to hospital, whether they want to go or not. No, that's a joke. They really do provide a free taxi service for people with appointments – though in truth, the old folk they go out of their way to assist are far younger than Anna's parents are themselves, who have already had a telegram from the Queen for their Diamond Wedding Anniversary.

Anyway, the church authorities have stepped in and said not only must my in-laws now have CRB checks, they also have to attend a compulsory course on 'How to Treat the Elderly Without Traumatising Them'.

Jumping out from behind a bush and shouting 'Boo!' will be an obvious one that's not to be on the menu, but what else? Letting go of the wheelchairs on the escalators at Merry Hill? Telling them that the consultant has given them the all-clear when in fact they are about to croak? That *would* be cruel.

There's no end of ways you could traumatise the elderly by tampering with their gadgets – tarantulas in the zip-up tartan bootees, loosening the nuts on their lightweight foldable walking sticks, increasing the voltage on magnetic knee straps, and inventing hairnets-of-death.

It would be a real challenge, murdering old folks in cosy ways.

❧

Crime Wave Corner. Christmas got off to a bad start in Leominster. Thieves stole the Christmas lights. The authorities say they are 'baffled'. The project manager said, 'We've arranged lights in big cities such as Swansea and Cardiff, but we've never had this before. It's such a shame. I really don't understand the type of people who would do this.' Maybe not people, however. Maybe the squirrel syndicate.

Every year I watch *Tinker Tailor Soldier Spy* and *Smiley's People* and every year I understand them less and less. They are getting to be impenetrable. The house on the canal where the mole gets flushed – is it the same house as the safe house? Surely the Circus would have known about it? Don't they keep anywhere under surveillance? What happened to the dog Bobchik? Why is he lying dead at the foot of the fire escape? Does Smiley report the death of Vladek Sheybal's character – who has been tortured on a boat – to the German police authorities? It'll look pretty fishy if he hasn't.

I'd seen the series only seven or eight times before I'd worked out that it *was* the Vladek Sheybal character who is dead on the boat. I hadn't recognised him in that glimpse we get of the tied-up naked body. That everyone has loads of aliases doesn't help. Bill Haydon is also Gerald.

Furthermore, surely Smiley's address in Bywater Street will be well known to Karla, so why hasn't Karla bumped him off long since? And the biggest mystery of all: Bernard Hepton's ridiculous wig. He has the marcelled wave of a Clarence House florist.

Does Alec Guinness drive those little Rover cars or is there a double? He also wears an array of coats and scarves – similar but not identical. A large wardrobe or continuity errors? The more I study Smiley's hats and shoes, the more confusing the chronology gets – unless he nips home to Bywater Street for a new outfit halfway through the day, except often he is in Switzerland or Czechoslovakia so it can't be that. It always makes me laugh when Scotland is used as the obvious location for a damp and slushy hellhole behind the Iron Curtain.

What a lot of smoking they do. I suppose people did then, in the Sixties and Seventies. They also drink in the office and all through the day, too. How puritanical we have become. But mostly I watch the programmes year after year not to make these sorts of notes but for Alec Guinness – all the mysteriousness of acting is in that great performance he gives.

He is immensely stylised, almost camp (though less camp that Ian Richardson's Bill Haydon – I can't really believe that women would keep falling for him); and in one or two shots I noticed his white make-up, the pale lipstick and the wig join. His large spectacles removed, Guinness has a Stan Laurel face. There's also something of the Peter Sellers of *Being There* in those old-fashioned heavy suits.

I noticed that Smiley never answers a single question – he looks blank and withdrawn, as if he hasn't heard. He never gives anything away about himself. This of course is the trained spy. But more than that, the silences reflect his guarded temperament. It is Smiley's nature to be enigmatic – as it was Guinness's, who was likewise secretive and sequestered.

What the series is now about for me is the power and resource of an old person. Smiley has been pulled out of retirement and he is immensely brave as he scurries about Hamburg, Leipzig and Thun. The landscape is wintry – everything is wintry. I also note his pseudonyms. He's variously Max, Mr Standfast and Mr Barraclough – Mr Barraclough is also Brian Wilde in *Porridge*, the somewhat vague warder, who is in the clouds in the same way that Smiley (and Guinness) pretends to be.

It is a world without women – unless they can be eccentric (Beryl Reid as Connie Sachs) or adulteresses (Sian Phillips – a sort of Mary Magdalen figure as Smiley's estranged wife). So a few hearty cheers for the chaps: Ian Bannen, whom Mark Rylance is getting to be like; Anthony Bate, as a comical and bumbling Cabinet Office big cheese; Alexander Knox, craggy and mournful as Control; Barry Foster, all too convincing as a shit of a senior civil servant – I've met people like that. The phoney joshing and matiness and crafty watchfulness. Bill Paterson is Foster's character's minion – his sycophantic laugh is spot on.

Two cars collided in Whittern Way, Hereford. 'There were no reports of any injuries.' Honestly, it is beyond a joke.

※

Nanoo tells me her long-term plan is to go to prison. Why spend £1,000 a week to be in an old folks' home, where the food is mush and the staff beat you up, when you can go to prison and be looked after for free, including first-rate medical care? This makes total sense. Why haven't more middle-class people thought of it? The only thing that put me off becoming a mass murderer was the prospect of visits from Lord Longford, but that danger has passed.

So – any day now my mother-in-law will be committing a crime, though she hasn't specified what. 'It won't cost me a penny cent and I'll attend every Craft Class,' said Nanoo, who has got it all worked out.

※

To the Groucho with Zany Antony, who proposed marriage to three Estonian waitresses and Lisa Marie. That's right. Elvis's daughter was in. He also bought a half-bottle of Manzanilla for another bird he chatted up who when she stood up was a dwarf.

※

While Zany Antony cracked on with his love life, I went to Pimlico to find Barbara Windsor. Now she is officially as beloved by the nation as the late Queen Mother, it is hard to believe that two decades ago Barbara Windsor and her career were in the doldrums. Ronnie Knight, her first husband, was in and out of jail and on the run in connection with arson attacks and a murder charge. Babs stood by him for years, but eventually got fed up with the constabulary pounding up her stairs in a dawn raid and saw through him as 'flash and arrogant'.

Then a disappointing pub venture in Amersham with her second husband, Stephen Hollings, left Babs with a personal financial liability of £922,000. But worse than the threat of bankruptcy – when Babs found employment in a provincial pantomime, she was given lowly fourth billing, beneath even Gyles Brandreth. *That* must have hurt. Her humiliation was complete.

Then the call came to play Peggy Mitchell in *EastEnders*. Babs shook off her blonde bombshell *Carry On* persona and for sixteen years played a grim old boot to perfection. As Peggy, landlady of the Vic, Babs dealt with abductions, cancer scares, shootings and bald, unshaven alcoholic offspring. Peggy was fractious and bitchy, crammed with extravagant emotions, and well able to throw a right-hook. 'Get out of my pub!' became her catchphrase.

She was television's premier strong matriarch, hardworking, loyal, and oddly highly attractive. There is a fair bit of the real Barbara Windsor in that description, as I've been finding out when I spent time watching *Dick Whittington* rehearsals this past month. Babs has a regal allure (Iris Murdoch was convinced she was related to Royalty) and is wholly at home leading a company of actors. With no children of her own, they become her surrogate family.

Though she left *EastEnders* in September 2010 and, at seventy-three, might well have been expected to retire and grow lupins, the thought of loafing about would be anathema to our Babs. Babs likes being useful, needed – and if she gets on exceptionally well with the younger members of the cast it is because, though indisputably the troupe's mother bantam hen, at moments Babs did remind me of a little girl, for whom all this acting malarkey is literally play.

Before the move down to Bristol, the *Dick Whittington* cast began putting the show together in a church hall in South London filled with folding chairs, none of which could bear my weight. Small and sprightly, and wearing a tight orange jersey, Babs distracted me from my discomfort by immediately making me think of Benny Hill's hymn of praise when he first clocked her half a century ago: 'You've got to see these tits – they're fantastic!'

Tearing my eyes away, I was introduced to man-mountain Eric Potts, who was not only playing the dame, he also wrote the script, with its gorgeously corny jokes about rattling your maracas. I met Andy Ford, the cherubic West Country Idle Jack, and I cowered from Granville Saxton, who looks like King Rat, the archetypal pantomime villain, even before he gets into costume and make-up. Elsewhere in the room were the director, the choreographer, and loads of scrumptious chorus girls and chorus boys – all slightly in awe of living legend Barbara Windsor MBE. 'Charlie Hawtrey would have made a nuisance of himself with those lads, the randy bugger! Oh he was naughty! Well, no, he wasn't actually. He was my favourite actor in the *Carry On* films. His career went back to the Will Hay films, though no one will remember those today. He ended up in Deal, drinking himself to death.'

No such unprofessionalism from Babs, who had had a particularly hard day the previous week, auditioning all these Dick Whittingtons. 'I spent all day looking at Dicks,' she said. 'I bet they came in all shapes and sizes,' I replied – suddenly plunged into a Bermuda Triangle of Talbot Rothwell oo-err missus *Carry On* film knob repartee. The lucky boy chosen was Owain Williams, an impossibly fresh-faced Welshman, who among other accomplishments is a qualified lawyer. 'If they mess you about, you'll know how to sue them,' I suggested. They love a ruck, the Taffs.

Like Peggy from *EastEnders*, Babs speaks her mind, and she unobtrusively got some dance steps changed – a Cockney knees-up that looked such fun I was on my hind legs and joining in eventually. There's a lot to remember – the drill, the tongue-twisting dialogue, the singing. I was that glad of a bag of doughnuts afterwards, offered by Owain.

On Boxing Day, Babs was to be celebrating sixty years in

showbusiness. In far-off 1950, she made her professional debut (at £3 a week) in pantomime at the Golders Green Hippodrome. Though she'd sat her Eleven-Plus exam a year early and had achieved the highest marks in Middlesex, Babs was less happy at Our Lady's Convent, Stamford Hill, than she was at Madame Behanna's Tap Dancing Academy, in Tottenham.

She won a talent contest at Stoke Newington Town Hall and by her mid-teens was touring the country as a soubrette, performing in musicals and singing in clubs – the sort of West End clubs that attracted both millionaire Hollywood stars and gangsters with names like Limehouse Willy and Big Scotch Pat, who'd turn up in their Ford Zephyrs.

There was an element of mad pantomime about Babs's turbulent early life – something she happily concedes ('I'm too old for all that now, darling!'). She dated Bing Crosby's son, George Best and sundry Krays, who were 'gentle, giggly and happy-go-lucky', though of course not always. When she married convicted hoodlum Ronnie Knight, the bride and groom were accompanied on honeymoon by Kenneth Williams. 'Anyone want to see my lovely bum?' asked Kenny, who also invited his mother, Louie, and his sister, Pat, to be part of the strange entourage.

In addition to appearing in nine *Carry On* films, Babs had roles in films that Diana Dors had turned down, worked with experimental theatre director Joan Littlewood ('she could be a right cow!'), and when Bernie Winters's dog Schnorbitz fell in Terry Scott's swimming pool, Babs dived in and pulled him out – a story that for me is the very Platonic Ideal of a showbiz anecdote.

Babs made Sid James so crazed with love and lust he dropped dead of a heart attack on stage in mid-performance, and she did a pantomime season with Gareth Hunt, whose piles exploded. 'He had to be taken to Plymouth General Hospital for an operation.'

Bernard Bresslaw, another colleague from the *Carry On* era, also died on stage, at the Regent's Park Open Air Theatre, but Babs had fallen out with him by then. They were in a summer show in Blackpool and Bernie made a silly fuss about taking the final curtain call – he pulled rank in a sad way.

Talking of curtain calls, after watching the lovely young dancers wiggle and jiggle and flash parts of their anatomy that are normally reserved for the men or women they marry, the *Dick Whittington* cast practised in front of me the bit at the end where they come on and take their bows. Babs refused to come on last – as might be her due. She wanted Dick and his girl Alice (Carly Day – bang tidy) to sweep to the footlights because, 'the show is about them'.

They rehearsed the sequence half a dozen times, with me as the audience clapping like mad. They then did the climactic Sultan of Morocco scene, with lots of sword fights, dancing, tumbling, and Fairy Babs's confrontation with King Rat. 'Get out of my pantomime!' she shrieked. You expected the *EastEnders* theme-tune drum beats to kick in.

No longer is pantomime the graveyard it once was. Kenneth Williams always boycotted them, telling Babs, 'Ooooh, no. I wouldn't go and see that crap, would I?' I myself remember being taken as a child to see tired old shows, with has-beens such as Ted Rogers or Freddy 'Parrot Face' Davies wearily going through the routines. Charles Hawtrey, in the dying days of his career, would spend the panto season in places like Telford or Cheadle, totally blotto.

In 2005, however, a new company called First Family Entertainment decided to revamp the genre. Now, so the associate producer, Laura Taylor, told me, they have a dozen new productions opening in the country's most prestigious venues, including Glasgow, Manchester, Liverpool and Richmond. American stars such as Henry Winkler, Patrick Duffy, Mickey Rooney and David Hasselhoff have been encouraged to make their first forays into pantoland – and it is as if the public is seeking out entertainment that is real, real flesh and blood performers, real acrobats and live dare-devilry. Houses are full and it is a reaction at last against too much soulless computerised gimmickry in films and games.

The traditional British pantomime has vitality, a unique exuberance, and *Dick Whittington* is costing over £1 million, with huge glittery sets and spanking new costumes. When we all shifted along the M4 to Bristol for the technical and dress rehearsals, Granville Saxton probably wished he could chop off his rat's tail, however. He kept tripping over the damn thing, as he made his entrance in puffs of green smoke. Babs, meanwhile, was in a huge pink crinoline and floating above the stage on a chrome hoop. I'd have been paralysed with vertigo, but she adored dangling on the wires, waving her wand.

It's always better for things to go wrong during a final dress rehearsal than in performance, so things went wrong. The lights went out, leaving the dancers to dance on in the pitch darkness. The backdrops flew in and out of their own accord. The chorus missed their cues because they'd got lost trying to find their dressing rooms after a costume change.

So there was a fair amount of tension. 'It's not as bad as *Twang!*, though, is it, Babs?' I said consolingly. In 1965, Barbara Windsor was a participant in one of the world's great theatrical disasters, Lionel Bart's Robin Hood musical, the would-be follow-up to *Oliver!* She played Delphina, 'a Cockney nymphomaniac'. They opened in Manchester and, as Babs told me, still incredulous after forty-five years, 'We had a full orchestra in Act One. In Act Two, a trio. Joan Littlewood gave up and told us to improvise. Ronnie Corbett went for a wee and his lines were cut. He said if he'd gone for a shit and had been away any longer, his role would have gone in its entirety. Lionel Bart was off his head on cocaine. At the end the audience stood up in total silence and walked out.

I suppose, if you are going to have a flop, make sure it's a big one.'

There was no chance of history repeating itself with *Dick Whittington*, which anyway was always going to be more my cup of tea than Derek Jacobi in *King Lear*. Though there was barely any time to have a breather between the end of the dress rehearsal and the curtain going up on the first public performance, everything seemed to fall into place. The set behaved itself. Andy Ford, as Idle Jack, had a kitchen scene involving inflatable phallic sausages that creased me. A break-dancing dwarf in a Cyrano de Bergerac plumed hat was a veritable sight to be seen. And then there was Eric Potts as Sarah the Cook.

Eric is the best pantomime dame since Les Dawson. It is wonderful to have a straight pantomime dame – he's all the funnier for not being camp. In reality Eric is shy and quiet, almost bashful. But my God he comes out of himself once he has climbed into these rococo outfits – vast petticoats with a seashell brassiere, sailor-suits that turn him into an elephantine Shirley Temple, a harem frock complete with nipple-tassels.

Eric and Babs re-enacted the classic keep-fit sequence from *Carry On Camping* where the bikini flies off ('Oooh, Matron! Take them away!'), and as Babs rightly said to me, 'The *Carry Ons* were pantomimes, weren't they? The Ugly Sisters, the Principal Boy, Baron Hardup – all the archetypal characters – and particularly the double entendres, the gaudiness, the way everything was exaggerated.'

Pantomime is the very opposite of English understatement, yet it works – it is needed. The topsy-turvy customs and vulgarity are an outlet for misrule. There is also something cosy and comforting about the familiar gags and situations. There's also something cosy and comforting about Babs herself, who has been a household name for my entire life. When she made her first entrance in Bristol there was a massive cheer and ovation. Yet beforehand, in her dressing room, with her wig on backwards, she was a nervous wreck, literally shaking with fear.

She'd not been on a stage for sixteen years and feared that she was now too small-scale, too used to television close-ups and out of practice when it came to reaching the distant gallery and rear stalls.

'When I started on *EastEnders* I thought I was too loud, too theatrical. I'd been doing my one-woman show about Marie Lloyd' – the Victorian music-hall artiste. 'I'd toured in these plays, bedroom farces and musicals. I did Joe Orton. I did Shakespeare. I've been on the end of the pier with Bernie Bresslaw. I'm tiny. I'm four-foot-ten. I've got tiny feet. So I'd been blowing myself up. Putting it across, you know what I mean? Now I had to cut it all right back. No more giggling and pouting. I got to be very muted for the cameras and the close-ups. I've had sixteen years of mumbling and whispering and being realistic. Second nature. Now I've got to go out there and knock 'em dead as Fairy Bowbells. I've got to be *larger than life* again, darling.'

She needn't have worried. The goodwill flowing between her and her audience was limitless, almost tangible – and she can still sing and dance.

The performance didn't end when the curtain came down. Like Vivien Leigh, Barbara Windsor gives another demonstration of star power at the Stage Door. The street was packed with well-wishers and autograph-hunters, including a coach-load of the disabled in their wheelchairs. Babs spent half an hour posing for photographs and signing souvenir programmes. Who knows, perhaps some of those little handicapped children threw away their crutches, permitted to walk again after the laying on of hands.

Though her hotel is only around the corner, Babs can't stroll back. She gets mobbed by office parties, who drag her in and insist on being hospitable. As she will never let her public down, and is always careful to keep the cheeky *Carry On* persona intact, this would mean she never gets a moment's privacy. Also, in these days of malicious Tweets and Twitterings, any momentary frown or admission of exhaustion would be transmitted around cyberspace instantly.

So instead little Scott, her adoring third husband, drives her the 100 yards back to the Marriott at top speed. A secret lift in the subterranean car park whisks her directly to her suite, which is in a turret. I was left there on my own once for some reason, a week or so earlier. I think I was leaving a pair of hand-blown glass balls for her Christmas tree. But I can boast to my grandchildren as yet unborn that I used Barbara Windsor's toilet. I saw her foot spa – I thought it was an MFI tool grinder, with these whirring wheels and brushes and lock-off button for easier gripping. I noted her jumbo packs of salt and vinegar crisps, her secret addiction. She has a huge four-poster bed with so many cushions and pillows, Scott must spend most of the night trying to find out under which one she's lurking.

Before Babs emerged from the Stage Door in a cloud of glory, I'd made my own less glamorous exit. The crowd looked at me expectantly. 'I wasn't in it,' I wailed. 'I really wasn't in it!' As if on cue they all said, 'Oh yes you were!' Fair play to them – but I think they assumed I was Eric Potts, out from under his magnificent and covetable frocks. I can honestly say that the last time I saw him, Eric was still flaked out in his dressing room, lying there in his bodysuit like a porpoise – a porpoise with mascara and mauve lip gloss. As Eric was eccentric baker Diggory Compton, Molly's father in *Coronation Street*, he was busy fending off thousands of urgent texts and emails regarding her demise under the tram.

But it did get me thinking. Eric is in his element as Sarah the Cook. I think I could be too. Spending all this time with the *Dick Whittington* company, my own inner pantomime dame is starting to be revealed. Oh yes it is . . .

ഗ

In his classic essay 'The Decline of the English Murder,' first published in 1946, George Orwell complained that, 'You never seem to get a good murder nowadays.' Well, he'd have perked up had he heard about the strangulation of 'landscape architect' little Jo Yeates in Bristol on the night of 17 December, which filled the papers for weeks.

Everyone had a lurid theory. A right *Inspector Morse* or *Lewis* plot, wasn't it, with creepy suspects galore? Where was Lynda La Plante? Somebody with her clout was needed to explore the powerful potential motives of sex or money or fear of scandal. Ruth Rendell and Phyllis James were surely itching to explain the despair and madness that had broken out in a classic detective-story setting of leafy suburban gentility. The case presented such psychological interest – a world in which respectability and stability had suddenly gone astray.

Here is my alibi (always 'cast iron') – I was in Barbara Windsor's dressing room at the Hippodrome, along with Eric Potts. Eric and I will be missing our way if we don't do the Ugly Sisters together next year. Also in the photograph: Oscar and his beloved, Hannah. Her father is a carpenter – just like Our Lord!

Yes, I know. Dame Barbara Windsor looks like a cardboard cut-out or photo-shopped in at Jessops. A strange crepe hat she put on top of her wig. God He Alone Will Knoweth what Dame Barbara Windsor looks like with the hairpiece off, the make-up off, the corset and the stays off, though little Scott will have an inkling. She probably has to unscrew a wooden leg and pop out a glass eye into the bargain. Plus remove her porcelain choppers. There'd be nothing left. Being a gentleman, I shall not speculate about her *mons veneris*, though possibly that baffles science as well.

Little Scott took this picture, so it is out of focus. Anna's cardigan gives her what I call The Squashed Strawberry Look.

ҩ

The Jo Yeates baroque murder plot, set in those gothic villas of Clifton. The ghastly Keith Floyd had his original restaurant in Clifton. Leonard Rossiter used to go. Leonard Rossiter wrote the preface for Keith Floyd's first cookery book. Leonard Rossiter found fame as a seedy, sexually frustrated landlord, Rigsby in *Rising Damp*. It all seemed to fit. 'Ah my leetle groy zells, Heestings!'

But it wasn't at all funny for poor Christopher Jefferies, whom the press, surely with police connivance, considered as good as guilty. Shameful. It had *nothing* to do with the man, yet he was persecuted in the papers – for his eccentric hair, his fondness for the poetry of Christina Rossetti, his long-legged walk, his fur-trimmed parka, his drainpipe trousers, his friendship with a man who had a comical name – Irving Steggles. Most condemning of all, he was seen on the news carrying a Waterstone's bag. What an oddball! He reads books! From the start he excited my pity. Should there be a crime in the Bromyard township going on these or similar lines I'd be lynched within hours. As a member of The

Prayer Book Society and the Neighbourhood Watch scheme, I wouldn't have a chance.

Mr Jefferies will have hated being called 'Chris' as much as Philip Larkin was never to be addressed as 'Phil'. He could win big bikkies in out-of-court settlements on this basis alone.

❧

It has been snowing in the Herefordshire Balkans. Usually if half a snowflake has fallen and the temperature drops slightly there is of course is *total travel chaos*. So imagine what it's like here now. Pathetic. We are marooned. Kirsty the bandy-legged practice nurse has been sledging – using a body bag from the stockroom. Body bags make brilliant toboggans. Apparently when there's a cold snap, the GPs' surgery orders in extra body bags, because the old folk start dropping off the twig like billy-o.

❧

I met a Scotsman in the Groucho who wanted to hit a chap who'd sat on my coat. I said that was a bit extreme. I then mesmerised him (the Scotsman, not the chap sitting on my coat) by demonstrating my Sherlock Holmes powers of deduction. 'Apart from the fact that you are a rugby fanatic, that you have been divorced and taken to the cleaners, that you now have a much younger new wife, that you have three children, two of whom don't speak to you, that as a youngster you had singing lessons, or were perhaps in the choir, and that you have an Airedale called Mrs Swainshill, I know nothing about you . . .' It's a great way of getting people to shit themselves even if you are only a little bit right.

My secret on this occasion – I'd got the information from the Scotsman's colleague, another Scotsman. Also the printed invitation for Andy Ripley's Memorial Service was on the bar. The chap was still trim – you only do that aged fifty-plus if you are a queer or if you've a younger woman on the go. Then he got Rod Melvin to accompany him on the piano in a few folk songs. There were dog hairs on his trousers. That the dog was an Airedale called

347

Mrs Swainshill was a chance in a billion, I concede. As Nigel Bruce would always harrumph, 'Oh I see. Nothing to it, Holmes!'

જી

Ex-teacher Mrs Daphne Henke had a front-page story in *The Hereford Times* demanding the urgent return of corporal punishment, and for the police to go into schools 'to administer the cane once a week for bad marks'. It all started to go wrong with 'the flower-power' generation, apparently.

I really don't think we should stop there. The cane should be used without stint on daft eighty-six-year-old women who come out with these extraordinarily offensive remarks. It should be against the law to be so completely silly and reactionary in public, even in the Herefordshire Balkans. 'Distrust all those in whom the urge to punish is strong,' said Goethe.

This fell flat when I told Francis Wheen, because he is convinced that Mrs Daphne Henke is one of my satirical pseudonyms, Edna Welthorpe-style. 'Or is she Paul Bailey?' asked Francis bewilderingly.

જી

Pathetic – the animal rights arseholes have stopped Hamley's toyshop in Regent Street from having a tank of real cavorting penguins.

Also, other equally pathetic news of note: Brian Blessed got into a scrap and stormed out of a dinner for the Federation of Wholesale Distributors, at the Savoy, because somebody said *Flash Gordon* was a bit ropey. 'Crap' was the word used. Blessed had to repay his £6,500 appearance fee. In my view, the excellent Blessed should have had his appearance fee doubled.

The Federation of Wholesale Distributors 'were left with no choice' but to move straight on to the charity raffle. Had one of the lots been by chance a video of *Flash Gordon*, starring Brian Blessed, I'd be prepared to start believing that after all there is a God.

If like me you are often to be found pottering around the Leopold Gallery, the Belvedere, Albertina, or the Historisches Museum de Stadt, in Vienna, you'll have had your fill of Egon Schiele paintings. What strange figures he depicted – the goblin children, changelings and pregnant women, everybody green and orange. His girls flashing their minge tunnels. The spidery genitalia. No pleasure principles – only an itch, disease, pain. His favourite colour was a jaundice yellow.

His people are indistinguishable from his trees and skeleton flowers, his wooden chairs or wooden boats. Everything is composed of thin black lines, like wires. The way Schiele swirls his shiny paint and varnish – the effect is of knotted wood, out of which troll faces and wood demons loom.

Illness and death stalk his pictures – and Schiele and Mrs Schiele were to die in the Spanish flu pandemic in 1918 – and his eroticism (if that's what it is) isn't inviting and sensuous but feverish, clutching, ravaging. Clothes are always being pulled up or pulled down, as for a medical examination.

I've been through that myself. When at St Thomas's they wanted to record the extent of my *Mycosis Fungoides* lesions, I had to go into a photographer's studio, strip completely and show off my lurid red patches, cock, balls, the lot. The only way to cope was to forget one's embarrassment and flaunt. 'Okay, Cecil Beaton, how do you want me?' I said to the photographer – who must have the worst job in London. He's probably in therapy now, after my visit. It's not a portfolio I ever want to look at, by the way. It needs to be filed under medical pornography.

Anyway, back to Egon. His figures are pleated, as if sewn – the joints and folds stitched and knotted, like dolls. This is the Austrian puppetry tradition. Also – when Schiele outlines his characters in a band of white paint or chalk, it is exactly like the winter trees here (I write this in Bad Ischl in a flowerless month), the black and leafless boughs and the inch or two of snow.

If Freud's views on the Viennese psyche are anything to go by, perhaps Schiele was representing his men and women accurately, without distortion? He painted and drew life as he saw it. Cold life.

ॐ

Austria: the Habsburg formality and ritual – the protocol and uniforms and hierarchy; the social stratifications. And then underneath all this, the bottled-up frustrations of their geniuses – Mahler, Bruckner, Wittgenstein, Klimt, Oskar Kokoschka, and of course Schiele and Freud – who were full of suffering and torment. The gorgeous fin-de-siècle cafés, and the cracking up. The obsession with death and sex, with dreams and suicide, which came together at the Mayerling hunting lodge, when Crown Prince Rudolf and his mistress, Baroness Mary Vetsera, blew each other's brains out. So now why do I feel so at home here, do you suppose? Well, it's a wine-drinking country and I like the promise of snow.

ॐ

My chum Kevin Whelan knew someone whose room-mate at St Andrews University was Maximilian Von Habsburg, so they are still about, the Archdukes – awaiting the call. They'll have the medals, sashes, ceremonial swords and uniforms with lots of gold frogging in the wardrobe. Otto Von Habsburg is I think still alive, aged about a hundred and fifty*, the grandson of Emperor Franz-Josef, whose mobilisation against Serbia when his heir was assassinated at Sarajevo kicked it all off back in the day.

My spell-check just tried to change Sarajevo to Sacramento. Oh to re-write history like that, at a touch of the button.

Anyway, not only that, Kevin, or maybe Max, had a girlfriend called Freya Von Groote. And if it's funny names you want, there's a Dennis Crapnell in Romford and a journalist in Ireland called Fiona Looney. Our funeral director here in the Herefordshire

---

* Archduke Otto Von Habsburg died on 4 July 2011 at the age of ninety-eight.

Balkans is Peter Gaunt. Anna's mum knows an Edna Cockin. The vicar of St Paul's in Blackheath (Birmingham) is the Revd. Sermon. The chinky takeaway in Bromyard is the Shun Fat. Their rival in Tenbury Wells is the Tam Pon (as God is my judge). I had a dermatologist once called Doctor Spittle. There's a firm of solicitors in Sligo called Argue & Phibbs. In Galway you will find many a Parrott, Otter, Rabitte, Mullet, Codd, Haddock, Fish and Salmon. The dentists in Burford, when we lived thereabouts, were Eager & Sharpley. An anagram of my chum Kevin Whelan's name is Even I Wank. Fair play to the man, he told me that himself.

❧

Mrs Toze has started knitting mobile phone cosies. She's branched out.

❧

My Christmas Cactus has burst into life. Dozens of reddish pink blooms, like prawns.

❧

I have had a card from Judi Bowker. The goddess speaks! 'I hope you are in good health at the moment,' she writes in an italic hand. What has she been hearing about me? Yet as Benedick says in *Much Ado About Nothing*, there's a double meaning in that.

❧

My origins are under the teeming sea. Back when dinosaurs ruled the earth and Raquel Welch wore a fur brassiere, the place where I was born and raised was a swampy lagoon. As the land subsided and the oceans moved, the primeval forests were flooded, covered with sand and gravel, with grits and shales, and in time the carboniferous rocks and fossilised coal measures were created. Forest after forest flourished, and was drowned.

Now, millennia later, just as the giant leaves and ferns were once pressed and pressed by the interminable things that came after them, the formation of the limestone, the faults and folds, so the decomposing bodies, the crushed bones and ashes in St

Barrwg's Churchyard, and in all the churchyards in South Wales, will mix with the black oily soil, and one day will form a new thin stratum of coal, or maybe only another layer of bitter dust.

When, between three and four in the afternoon ten years ago, I last saw the family grave in Bedwas, where all these people are buried, whether in their coffins or as ashes in their urns, a bony tree had taken root and sprung up through the middle of the plot, shattering and splintering the stones. It is black weed-choked rubble now.

'In time we shall pass on forever and be forgotten,' said Chekhov. 'Our faces will be forgotten and our voices, and most piercingly of all, no one will even know how many of us there were.'

Curtain

352

Epilogue:
Situation Normal – All Fucked Up!

The Super Moon, and I missed it. There were clouds. But I understand that the gravitational pull stranded ships in the Solent. Is the Super Moon also responsible for the hurricanes and the volcanoes, for the ash that fills the air from Iceland? Is the Super Moon what's making us go mad? Stock markets are collapsing; oil prices are rising; the Euro is proving a dud currency; Knut the polar bear cub has died in Berlin Zoo; there are earthquakes across the world and in Japan they had both an earthquake and what my mother calls a tiramisu – a great wave of coffee cake – that caused a meltdown at the nuclear power station in Fukushima.

The authorities think the way to deal with the massive conflagration and Chernobyl-calibre radiation leaks is to throw one or two buckets of water from a helicopter. The Tokyo water supply became contaminated. Radioactive particles of caesium, strontium, uranium, plutonium, cobalt-60 'and many others' have floated above the country and were detected by the Health Protection Agency as far away as Glasgow and Seattle. Radioactive iodine 3,355 times the maximum permitted by law has been detected in the sea. Everybody will now get thyroid cancer.

The next Super Moon is on 14 November 2016. The one after that, on 2 January 2018. I'll miss those, too, because the bumhole cancer or the prostate cancer will have begun with me long since. I'll be under the sod. Any minute now I'm also expecting the *Mycosis Fungoides* to remember that it was meant to have killed me three years ago, that I am already on Injury Time.

For the record, if you are about – if *anybody* is about – Super Moons will then shine down on 21 January 2023, 25 November 2034, and 13 January 2036.

❧

Gotterdammerung! The twilight of the gods! The damned! I do get this distinct end-of-the-world feeling, don't you? That we are on the brink of oblivion. That the devil has broken loose. Apocalypse now, or anyway quite soon. If our civilisation came to an end tomorrow, what would archaeologists centuries or millennia hence have to say about the way we live now, if they were basing their evidence and suppositions on what my mother accumulated in her decorative bowls: a large plastic bottle top, a surgical syringe, a broken Art Deco cigarette lighter, two golf balls, half of a broken biro, a brass hinge, a magnet, a mostly used 160 mg tube of eye ointment, rubber rings for castrating lambs, latch keys, light bulbs for a torch long lost, and lots of shirt buttons? Not exactly the Valley of the Kings, Knossos and Minoan Crete, or Schliemann's Troy, is it?

It must have been like this in the Edwardian era, with the world of steam yachts and parasols coming to an end with the First World War. Any surviving Victorian or Edwardian architecture these days is left to get dusty and damp. The innermost parts of inner cities are shopping concourses, with lots of glass and (as God is my judge) cocktail pianists. Glass roofs, glass elevators. But it is not sparkling and bright. These aren't crystal palaces. The places are smudgy and give me a headache.

You also get the same shops everywhere. Everywhere is the same as everywhere else. I only knew when I was in Bristol because a woman said 'Gurt lush!' I'm now rather pleased to see the anarchists handing out the *Socialist Worker* or anti-vivisectionist demonstrators with their poster displays of smoking beagles and wired-up cats. At least it adds a bit of interest. I get my own back by filling charity tins with forints and dinars.

I started getting particularly worried when Camilla and the

354

Prince of Wales were poked with sticks – there was an element of the French Revolution in the way the royal couple were singled out as symbols of unconscionable privilege.

Ragged and forlorn, the younger generation are protesting in London, as the costs of higher education get prohibitive – not that they'll get much of an education in any case: art courses don't teach art; theatre courses teach only street theatre and improvisation; ignorance is sanctioned – indeed knowledge and a feeling for the past are taboo: just about the worst and most immoral things anyone is allowed to aspire to be are middle class, socially competent and civilised. Anyway, acquiring knowledge takes effort – at best it has to be kept at a distance or stamped out – and anyone showing the slightest originality or intellectual spark is drugged on Ritalin from birth.

Computer technology intensifies (or symbolises) the problem, because information flickers past at such a lick. The senses have to be gratified briskly. There is no time for shades and subtleties to accumulate. Hence, with relationships also, people get quickly dissatisfied and irritated. Everywhere there are abandoned babies, broken homes, single mothers, because old-fashioned virtues such as commitment and duty are seen as vices. Nobody has sit-down dinners. It's all snacks and fucking *tapas*.

Marriage is virtually over, it is impossible to recall the time when divorce was scandalous, and with the courts giving super-injunctions to rich footballers, actors, columnists and television presenters, so they can keep their squalid affairs secret, adultery is tacitly condoned.

Not that there'll be any jobs for today's graduates even if they do knuckle down, stump up the rip-off fees and open a book. Everything is closing down, retrenching, except for the criminal fraternity and banks. Nor is there anywhere for anyone to live, not unless there is a wholesale destruction of the countryside for cement slums, as in Soviet Russia. The government's relaxation of the planning laws will abet this. With no fields left, no corn or cattle, agriculture is finished. With no farmers, no more farmers' wives employed in handicraft, e.g. Mrs Toze and her egg cosies and mobile phone cosies.

Bees are dropping like flies, so to speak. Hives are dying – the result of insecticides, herbicides, pesticides, all the poison that has been splashed about the land for decades, decimating the clover, the poppies, the knapweed, daisies and red campion. With no bees – no pollination. Plants will stop growing. We will starve.

Old people are refusing to die and release any inheritance. They are mopping up NHS resources, with their fucking hips and their fucking cataracts and their fucking dementia. I've given this mature thought and we must soon stop giving medical treatment to the old – they should be exterminated at (say) eighty-five or whenever they are past child bearing age, whichever is sooner.

People must learn that life is leasehold; they must have fewer babies, unless we can boil them and eat them. We'll be short of nutriment. There is literally no room left. These schemes of mine can easily be imposed by laws and penalties.

༄

As I write, there are revolutions across North Africa and in the Middle East, which will do nothing except provide fertile beds for extremist Islam. In Tunisia, President Zine El Abidine Ben Ali has been forced to resign and curfews imposed. King Mohammed VI of Morocco is besieged with corruption allegations. Egypt's President Mubarak has been deposed, and the ex-secret police are shredding documents. King Abdullah of Jordan and President Abdelaziz Bouteflika of Algeria are nervous. Bashar al-Assad of Syria is observing political unrest, demonstrations, lootings and burnings. His police opened fire in Damascus. Water supplies, electricity and telephone lines have been cut off by his security forces in the city of Deraa.

There is escalating unrest in Bahrain – King Hamed bin Isa

Al-Khalifa has declared martial law. Troops crossed the causeway from Saudi Arabia. There is vicious sectarian conflict between the Sunnis and the Shias. Pro-democracy activists have been arrested, hospital workers intimidated, children raped. One mother was shown her daughter's hairclip by a soldier. 'Take a look at this,' he said. 'It is the last of your daughter you will ever see.' The dialogue could be by Harold Pinter.

There is now Civil War in Yemen. Ali Abdullah Saleh declared a State of Emergency, so snipers fired on unarmed protesters, tribesmen stormed the government buildings, members of the Cabinet resigned or were sacked, and tanks drew up outside the Presidential Palace. Islamic militants – i.e. al-Qaeda – have seized a weapons factory.

In Libya, Colonel Gaddafi bombed his own populace. The only way to deal with the threat of rebellion – as Macbeth knew – is by murderous repression, arbitrary executions and bombardments. British planes and submarines have been fighting back on behalf of what are called the rebels, launching cruise missiles at Tripoli, which when you think about it is only across the water from Sicily. It is not remote. Europe will be inundated with refugees, who'll bring the germs and seeds of their backward desert cultures with them. It's going to be like the beginning of that film *Bram Stoker's Dracula*, with Gary Oldman hacking away at the Turks and Constantinople falling.

But who are these rebels? Who are these people that the West is gaily arming, their make-up and intentions? Shouldn't we be very worried indeed that al-Qaeda members and affiliates are present in the east of Libya, many of them veterans of the battles in Iraq? Today's plucky rebels usually become tomorrow's wicked insurgents. Parenthetically, it costs £271,296 for each and every eight-hour sortie from RAF Marnham, in Norfolk, to Tripoli and back.

☙

357

There is a nice little two-bedroom flat available for rent above Nikki B. Nails, the Bromyard manicurist's parlour. I have sent the details to Colonel Gaddafi. I do hope Colonel Gaddafi comes to live in the Herefordshire Balkans, along with Mubarak and the rest of them. In no time at all they'll be on the Parochial Council, drinking in The Thorn, and helping Sylvia from the Falcon Hotel run the Masonical fork suppers.

∾

The North Ship, rigged for a long journey from which no traveller returns; the postmen and the doctors going from house to house distributing bad news; time's rolling smithy smoke; the unplayed sheet music in the piano stool; the evening coming in across the fields, that lights no lamps, because fast falls the eventide: Larkin had such plangent images for what W. C. Fields called the fellow in the bright night gown, what Raymond Chandler called the big sleep, and what John Le Mesurier, in the announcement in *The Times*, called conking out. It amounts to the same thing.

∾

As Charles Darwin once said, 'We will now discuss in a little more detail the struggle for existence.' Did you know, for example, that above the heads of dinosaurs flew the Mesozoic birds? Scientists are still pondering the first eighty-five million years of avian development, studying the fossil records left by feathers and footprints. Did feathers become reptilian scales, or was it the lizards who took to the sky? Where do fish fit in? Evolution, with its principles of violent pain and ecstasy, its rewards and punishments, hasn't stopped, of course – we may ourselves be in the early stages of one day becoming angels. Or demons.

With the lips of Scarlett Johansson and the mouth of Jonathan Rhys Meyers; with the grin of Peter Duncan and the smile of Judi Bowker – humankind has already reached a peak of evolutionary perfection. So the next step, I surmise, is that we will metamorphose into cybernauts. Computers can already repair

358

themselves, scan every word ever printed, answer telephones, make predictions, fight wars. It won't be long before microchips will be implanted in our heads and eyes. We'll think things and suddenly know things, feel things – like having visions.

Flesh will melt, out of inertia*. Antibiotics and modern medicine mean more people live, but those that live on are weak, bloodless, impaired. Those that survive are not the fittest, they are the most compliant, the most susceptible. It will be the end of organic life. With these changes in our physical constitution, we are heading for an era of pure bodilessness – as bodiless as watercolour.

With the end of human meat, the end of human desire. A couple in Canada are already determined to raise what they call a genderless child. Even a spokesperson from the American Psychological Association's Lesbian, Gay and Bisexual Concerns Office (as God is my judge) was non-plussed by that one. Regarding potential harms or benefits, 'In the short term, in the long term, there's really just no basis for saying. This is not an area of research that exists, to my knowledge.'

No, but the area of common sense exists – long out of fashion though it may be. Yet today gender is suddenly abhorrent.† Differences are abhorrent. It is a puritanical coercion. Sex has

* People already can't be relied upon to sit down on a chair unsupervised. At the BBC's new £877 million headquarters in Salford Quays, a place that is unforgivably called MediaCityUK, 'All employees must attend a session in which they are taught how to use a chair to ensure that they are following health and safety procedures. Chair adjustment is part of the induction process.' The cost of relocating 1,500 staff in Manchester – and teaching them what chairs look like – has reached £86.5 million.

† Gender Studies are a sign of the times, unfortunately. You just know that underlying the course will be this air of polemical complaint, endemic *disappointment*. More silly still is that at Exeter University there is a Chair in 'French Discourses of Sexuality.' Yes, there is a *professor* of *that*. Papers on 'Catherine Deneuve's Lesbian Transformations' and so forth, I very much fancy.

always been associated with shame, with what D.H. Lawrence called 'a dread of the procreative body' – so already relationships are conducted between people who are hidden behind a screen in their lonely bedrooms. Social networking sites exist to keep people apart – their relationships are exclusively virtual, illusionary, pretend, false. I find the prospect devastating.

The risk is being removed from encounters, brief or protracted. When Philip Larkin at the end of 'An Arundel Tomb' said (sentimentally – I don't think he fully believed it) 'what will survive of us is love,' this is proving not to be the case. We are getting rid of the unreliable rudiments, in favour of what is thought to be purity and control and efficiency. Yet by eradicating our crazy side we eradicate our interesting side. We are going to be nothing but floating shadows. I fight against this like hell, to remain in my (pagan) cosmos.

൭

The skies are filled with poisonous steam, poisonous rain, and the poison is in the wound.

൭

There were cottages in the woods, down on the farm my family owned. Did I see an old couple in a half-ruined kitchen once, or did I imagine that? Did I imagine the firelight, the ghostly horses in abandoned stables, the gooseberries growing in abandoned gardens, where nettles flourished and ivy twisted around the walls? There were thistles and tufted grass. A dead pear tree. Reddening apples.

I know that at Cefn Porth, as the farm was called, there was a rude pavilion made of black corrugated iron, where my grandfather and his brothers and sisters spent the summer, when home from school. Dolly the wet nurse did the cooking. It must have been lovely once, the fields and the woods. But of course the woods were cut down, the hedges uprooted, the bogs drained, the wildlife exterminated and the fields enlarged – the fields sprayed with chemicals and presently as dead-looking as the moon. I remember the bulldozers about their work. I wish it had been left as it was, but no one had any notion of conserving anything. The word 'ecosystem' hadn't entered the language. I even think my father received generous grants from the European Union under the Common Agricultural Policy to help with the destruction.

Later there was a mad scheme called Set-Aside, where farmers would be paid by Brussels for not growing things or doing things. I used to say – can I please have a few million from the Set-Aside Fund so as not to bother *writing my fucking books* ? If farmers had an 'entitlement' to the money, when they removed their acres from agricultural production, then why not me, for removing myself from literary production?

I wonder if a lot may be explained about my temperament when you remember that I am from Monmouthshire? Monmouthshire was not properly England nor fully Wales, as we had absolutely no tradition of speaking the Welsh language – indeed the reverse. My great-great-grandparents spoke Welsh to each other, but deliberately didn't teach it to their children. They thought that would be a backward step.

It annoys me when sensible people (my beloved Jan Morris for example – who calls me 'The Mad Maestro' as if I'm a car) says that English is 'the language of the conquerors', as though the Welsh were Red Indians decimated by the White Man. That is pure sentimentality. I have no separatist feelings, no time for that Welsh Assembly lark, presided over by Arch Druids. Even a century and a half ago, smart Welsh people could see that English was the language of the future, of business and education. So on that basis – we'd best all learn Chinese. Chop chop.

My last visit to Bedwas. Houses have been built on every patch and corner. All the old houses and cottages displayed ghastly white plastic windows. Even Troedyrhiw has white plastic window frames, which are completely out of keeping. The garden and paddock had been built over, the trees sawn down.

The graves are overgrown, untended. My Grandma Lewis didn't want her ashes brought back to Bedwas to be interred with Grandpa Lewis – she was left behind at Croesyceiliog Crematorium, as was her wish. Very firm that she wanted this, and she wasn't the sort of person to put her foot down often.

The butcher's shop has been demolished, as has the slaughterhouse. There's a convenience store there now. The marble slabs were sent to a Newport salvage yard. It has all gone. All that work and struggle, weighing, chopping and serving meat for over a hundred years. The long hours. 'Everything alters, and one by one we drop away,' said Yeats.

We went in the evening to a restaurant called The Ingle-Nook, where old crone Rowlanda Hirst had lived long ago. There was a clatter, a yelp or two, some tumbling, unidentifiable flapping noises, a lengthy groan, the tinkle of broken glass, and there the proprietress was suddenly, in a heap next to the stone stairs, which curved behind the chimney-piece. She'd succeeded in falling down her own ingle-nook. She got up without too much embarrassment, came over to us and asked, 'Well, how was the fucking duck?'

Anyway – Monmouthshire. It is the point of entry into Wales, where one place becomes another place. It is peripheral. And so am I. On the coast the sea-walls need repairing and the sandy edge is wearing out. Like me.

If granted a wish by the fairies, I'd settle for being a minor version of – a footnote to – the great rococo unclassifiables: Coleridge, Pound, Ruskin, Welles, the people in whom I am steeped. But owing to a mixture of nature and nurture and Dame Fortune – who is a fickle gypsy, always blind and often tipsy – I am, I quite realise, a sensitive anarchist, too journalistic and eclectic to remain at Oxford; too donnish and literary to make a living in Fleet Street and Grub Street; too ironical and satirical to take anything totally seriously; too serious to be a lightweight pundit; too prickly to be part of any team or mob; too *Welsh* . . . 'His comfortable temper has forsook him, he's much out of health, and keeps his chamber.'

༄

Behind my work – even at its most comic or absurd – is nevertheless a highly informed intellectual (or pseudo-intellectual) mind. I am perhaps a surrealist figure. I put incompatibilities together – because I refuse to recognise the incompatibility – to create new chemical reactions, zany hits of colour.

༄

'You know, I'd quite like to have composed a philosophical work which consisted entirely of jokes,' said Ludwig Wittgenstein.

༄

Love me or loathe me, you cannot leave me or lose me. I am the imp in the bottle, the gargoyle that winks, the mad spirit found in fairgrounds, circuses, canal boats, taxidermy cabinets, tattooists' parlours, waxwork museums, ornately iced cakes.

༄

Beauty is *edible*.

༄

Objects, bric-a-brac, lend enchantment somehow – as if the people who are dead and who have left their things behind have only popped out for a moment. When they come back I will be joining them.

༄

When the Devil in the desert provided Jesus with a vision of the world it would have been like this – a list of discontents great and small: bald children in a cancer ward; fat asthmatic uncles fondling whiskerless quims; an aborted deformed foetus still palpitating in a grey cardboard dish; people falling from high windows and not being killed at once; an abandoned bird's nest with drowsy chicks; the mould on strawberries; dead cats sliding into the river; the basilisk smiling softly in its cave; the lung fluke and the tapeworm; the broken greenhouse; the actress who has lost her looks; the squirming of an eel's severed head; Francis Bacon imagery: what had once been the faces of apes, popes, gangsters; prisoners in a reinforced steel cage awaiting execution; a man sobbing, his hand over his face, and on the iron bedstead, the body of his slain mistress (as in a Sickert painting); a Mock-Tudor home in Hornchurch with electric gates; dogs and cats talking as you go down the street (as in a Gogol short story); the sinister fluttering of the roosting pigeons outside the lavatory window in Room 207 of the Royal Gatehouse Hotel, Tenby, which has since burned down, the frosted pane smeared with gritty white shit and feathers; the corpse with ingrown toenails; the child with a leg brace; the smoke rising from the Crematorium on a busy day; the envy and bitter rage of a man I knew from Sydenham Hill; the smell of burning tar and wet raincoats; the dog barking at a cornered squirrel; the dog that bit Oscar for no reason in the street in Vienna; the man who quit drinking and smoking and became a sanctimonious bore; the waterproof Elastoplast left on the side of the bath; grapeless grape stalks like birds' claws; a monkey's paw.

∽

Against the evils to come, I am closing the shutters, extinguishing the lights. I'm not being wholly metaphorical. I have been diagnosed with retinopathy – a side-effect of the diabetes that causes blindness.

∽

Up above what we called the Arch Field in Bedwas was the Brecon–Merthyr Railway Line. Or there was until it was torn up by Beeching. But a big bumper was put on the track when the passenger services ceased. Did the track end there, or begin?

Appendix:
The Last Man of Letters

Edited by Professor Johann Lampenschirm, M.D., D.Psych.

The following Citation was delivered by Professor Graham Holderness in St Albans Abbey on 10 November 2010, when the Honorary Doctorate of Letters was conferred upon the author by Professor Sir Tim Wilson, the Vice-Chancellor of the University of Hertfordshire.

Around this time of year it has become the vogue for people to write round-robins to enclose with their Christmas greetings. As an antidote to these relentlessly cheery communications,* the writer Roger Lewis began sending his friends letters about his life. They encouraged him to publish these funny but poignant observations.

The book, called *Seasonal Suicide Notes*, appeared in the autumn of 2009. It was billed as 'one man's heroic daily battles against indignity, untidiness and rush, and his fruitless search for order, peace and solvency'. Not only was it the perfect Christmas

---

* Still they come! The ever-boastful genre flourishes. Here are extracts from some *utter shockers* received by Doctor Lewis in 2010:

'Not having been able to get to Montserrat last January made our visit in November all the more special.'

'Sworn to secrecy as we were, Electric Airways' most high profile challenge was to prepare Nick Clegg for his pre-election TV debates.'

'When work allows, Fred and Lucy make good use of their free time. They've just returned from their first American road adventure – driving down the west coast in a Cadillac. They even made time, when in San Francisco, to visit the flat where I lived as a budding flower child in the Sixties. I don't remember enjoying this DINKY (double income no kids) lifestyle, do you?'

'I've added a sloe and apple jelly to my health repertoire.'

present, but it also attracted rave reviews, peppered with phrases like 'cult classic' and 'comic genius'.

Of course, as a writer, journalist and biographer, Roger Lewis has been informing and entertaining his readers for nearly thirty years. He is perhaps best known for his books on Peter Sellers, Laurence Olivier, Anthony Burgess and the *Carry On* actor Charles Hawtrey. But he is also a literary critic, and a regular contributor on art and culture to publications ranging from the *Spectator* to *GQ Magazine*.

His latest work provides glimpses of his upbringing in South Wales in the 1960s. As a child, he enjoyed movies, art and the theatre, but his cultural interests were completely at odds with the everyday reality of living with his family above his father's butcher's shop. He recalls feeling like Oscar Wilde in a mining village, and thinking it was a huge cosmic mistake that he had been born in the wrong place.

A few years later, though, he began to fulfil his literary ambitions. After gaining a First Class Honours degree in English Language and Literature from St Andrews University, he proceeded to Oxford. In his first term at Magdalen he quickly made his mark, winning The Charles Oldham Shakespeare Prize; The Matthew Arnold Memorial Prize; and the Chancellor's English Essay Prize. Then, as a Junior Research Fellow at Wolfson College, he published *Stage People*. It is this collection of profile essays about British actors and actresses that set him on his current career path.

By his early twenties, Roger Lewis was married to Anna Dickens, an educational psychologist, and soon had three young sons to support. Turning his back on academia, he began to make his living as a literary journalist, first writing book reviews and then biographies.

He has worked constantly ever since, writing regularly for the *Daily Mail*, *Mail on Sunday*, *Sunday Express*, *Daily Telegraph* and *The Times*. In our celebrity-obsessed age, he worries that writing about culture and literature is becoming an unwanted skill, and in a recent interview calls it 'an antiquated trade, as much use as knowing about thatching a house or sailing a sailing ship or ploughing a field with a horse'.

In 1994, Roger Lewis published *The Life and Death of Peter Sellers*, which was widely acclaimed. The *New Statesman* went as far as saying the book represented perhaps the most searching life of a non-classical actor ever written. It was later made into a multi-award-winning film, starring Geoffrey Rush and Charlize Theron, and earned Roger Lewis a special citation from the American Academy of Television Arts and Sciences. Other books on Laurence Olivier and Charles Hawtrey were similarly well received. However, critics were less impressed with his 2002 biography of Anthony Burgess. He defended it with characteristic robustness, arguing that, as in his previous work, he had deliberately chosen a structure to reflect the personality of his subject.*

* It should be noted for the record that even when first published, Doctor Lewis's *Anthony Burgess* was chosen as a Book of the Year by Lynn Barber, Jan Morris, Graham Ball (Literary Editor of the *Sunday Express*), Stephen Bayley, Francis King, Peregrine Worsthorne and Christopher Silvester, among others.

Duncan Fallowell wrote in *The Times*: 'Lewis is up to necromancy . . . He is determined to shake Burgess alive – and he succeeds magnificently. The book abounds with such sublime moments of resurrection, on the wings of Lewis' mordant humour. The two of them wrestle for every page, and so do the main text and extensive footnotes that open like trapdoors into unexpected worlds. Is this fission or fusion? Either way, the energy release is enormous . . . Burgess is made more mysterious by Lewis' passionate engagement.'

Boyd Tonkin, likewise, was particularly perceptive in *The Independent*: 'Lewis' *Anthony Burgess* ought to be read as a hugely entertaining comic fiction that explores all the agonies of authorship, and the toxic connection between the biographer and subject – a delirious mixture of William Boyd and Vladimir Nabokov . . . A grotesque, off-the-wall book-biz satire . . . a scabrous Christmas treat.'

When the paperback was published a year later, Christopher Hirst, also in *The Independent*, said: 'Every line crackles with electricity and animus . . . As much satire as biography, this is a splenetic masterpiece.'

Roger Lewis now lives in Herefordshire – a timeless part of England that he cherishes – where he shares a home with his wife and some 20,000 books. He is an avid watcher of old films, as well as being a bibliophile.

A Fellow of the Royal Society of Arts; the Royal Geographical Society; and the Royal Asiatic Society,* Roger has also been a Visiting Professor at Birmingham City University. This year he was officially nominated for the Oxford Chair of Poetry and ruffled some literary feathers, as a non-poet campaigning against pompousness.

In his writing, Roger Lewis offers forthright opinions and arresting insights into literature and life. His observations are often humorous but always eloquent, original and thought-provoking.

Some years ago he gained a PhD at this university.† We are now pleased to recognise his widely acclaimed published work with a further award. Vice-Chancellor, I would ask you to confer an Honorary Doctor of Letters on Roger Lewis.

Despite such positive coverage, the last words seem to have been Anthony Thwaite's, who called Lewis's book 'silly and posturing'. In retaliation, Doctor Lewis has insisted that on the Cholmondley/Chumleigh or Bottomley/Bumleigh principle, *Thwaite* should be pronounced *Twat*.

* Though not the Royal Society of Literature – a total scandal. Yet quite why Doctor Lewis is so desperate to mingle with those wallies and get up close to the dandruff is a mystery.

† His thesis, *The Art and Science of Biography*, was Shandyistic in the extreme, but will the *verrückten kleinen Dichter* ever get around to preparing it for commercial publication? The man is his own worst enemy.